Pure

Sun 5/16/21

Slavery

B & N

555 5th Ave
(46th St.)
NYC

SLAVERY

INTERPRETING AMERICAN HISTORY

Edited by

AARON ASTOR AND

THOMAS C. BUCHANAN

The Kent State University Press

Kent, Ohio

© 2021 by The Kent State University Press, Kent, Ohio 44242
ALL RIGHTS RESERVED
Library of Congress Catalog Number 2021005744
ISBN 978-1-60635-422-3
Manufactured in the United States of America

Library of Congress Cataloging-in-Publication Data
Names: Astor, Aaron, 1973- editor. | Buchanan, Thomas C., 1967- editor.
Title: Slavery : interpreting American history / edited by Aaron Astor and
    Thomas C. Buchanan.
Other titles: Interpreting American history series.
Description: Kent, Ohio : The Kent State University Press, 2021. | Series:
    Interpreting American history | Includes bibliographical references and
    index.
Identifiers: LCCN 2021005744 | ISBN 9781606354223 (paperback) | ISBN
    9781631014499 (epub) | ISBN 9781631014505 (pdf)
Subjects: LCSH: Slavery--United States--Historiography. | Slavery--United
    States--History. | African Americans--Social conditions.
Classification: LCC E441 .S6355 2021 | DDC 306.3/620973--dc23
LC record available at https://lccn.loc.gov/2021005744

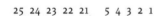

25 24 23 22 21   5 4 3 2 1

Contents

Foreword

Interpreting American History Series

Of all the history courses taught on college campuses, historiography is one of the most challenging. The historiographic essays most often available are frequently too specialized for broad teaching and sometimes too obtuse for the average undergraduate student. Every day, frustrated scholars and students search for writings that offer both breadth and depth in their approach to the historiography of different eras and movements. As young scholars grow more intellectually mature, they remain wedded to the lessons taught within the pages of historiographic studies. As graduate students prepare for seminar presentations, comprehensive examinations, and dissertation work, they often wonder why that void has remained. Then, when they complete the studies and enter the profession, they find themselves less intellectually connected to those ideas of which they once showed a mastery, and they again ask about the lack of meaningful and succinct studies of historiography . . . and the circle continues.

Within the pages of this series, innovative young scholars discuss the different interpretations of the important eras and events of history, not only focusing on the intellectual shifts that have taken place, but on the various catalysts that drove these shifts. It is the hope of the series editors that these volumes fill those aforementioned intellectual voids and speak to the young scholars in a way that will supplement their other learning; that the same pages that speak to undergraduate students will also remind the established scholar of his or her historiographic roots; that a difficult subject is made more accessible to curious minds; that ideas are not lost among the details offered within the classroom.

BRIAN D. MCKNIGHT, the University of Virginia's College at Wise
JAMES S. HUMPHREYS, Murray State University

Introduction

In the 1979 preface to the second edition of *The Slave Community: Plantation Life in the Antebellum South,* historian John Blassingame confessed his puzzlement over a source's portrayal of a Giles County, Tennessee, slave preacher named George Bentley. The *African Repository* in 1859 described Bentley as a "regular Southern pro-slavery person" and "preacher in charge" of a congregation of local slaveholders.[1] Blassingame had read about Bentley before but assumed that this account was a hoax or otherwise unreliable. The *Repository's* depiction of Bentley as "unwilling to be sold out of his master's family" certainly did not reflect the autonomous communities of resistance that Blassingame had emphasized in his original 1972 publication of *Slave Community.*[2] Where could a man like Bentley fit within Blassingame's narrative of collective struggle and defiance?

To understand a figure like George Bentley meant coming to grips with the "intriguing, complex, opaque" institution of slavery as a whole. "The more the student of the peculiar institution reads," Blassingame wrote in the second edition, "the more the conviction grows that antebellum Southerners persisted in deviating from the beliefs and behavioral patterns historians have ascribed to them."[3] In fact, Blassingame's original thesis had been critiqued from the beginning. In the years following the first edition's publication, scholars like Herbert Gutman, Leslie Howard Owens, George Rawick, Eugene Genovese, Albert Raboteau, Stanley Engerman, and Earl Thorpe challenged Blassingame's depiction of singular and unrelenting community resistance. Responding to these critics, Blassingame examined newer primary sources on African American religion and folk life to better understand and contextualize a figure like George Bentley, who had negotiated his own position within the slave system. Blassingame also began to look more critically at white antebellum religious institutions to better assess relationships like Bentley's with the white community of Lynn Creek, Tennessee. Over the course of the 1970s, one of the giants in the study of slavery found himself confronting a field that was changing rapidly in response to newer methodologies, newer sources, and newer contemporary political realities.

The study of any field's historiography can be daunting, in that it requires a thorough understanding of the underlying history, methodological developments over time, and contemporary politics and culture of historians' own times. This is especially the case with the historiography of slavery, which reflects, among other things, changes in the legal and political status of African Americans in the twentieth and twenty-first centuries. Americans have vigorously debated and interpreted the role of slavery in American life since enslaved people first landed on North American shores and long since after. Contemporaries and later writers and scholars up to the present day have explored the meaning of slavery as a system of labor, an ideological paradox in an ostensibly *free* political and social order, a violent mode of racial exploitation, and a global system of human commodification and trafficking.

Although the depth of Americans' historiographical engagement with slavery is not surprising given the turbulent history of race in America, the range and sheer volume of the writing on the subject, spanning over two centuries, can be overwhelming to someone encountering the field for the first time. *Slavery: Interpreting American History* introduces key themes of this historiography at a level suitable for advanced undergraduate and graduate students, professional historians new to the field, and other readers interested in the study of American slavery. Whereas not every historian of American slavery is included in the pages that follow, contributors have worked to highlight the key debates and conceptual shifts that have defined the field. Aaron Astor begins with an overview of the historiography of slavery, highlighting the key interpretive developments over time. Calvin Schermerhorn then addresses historians' assessments of the economics of American slavery, and especially its role within global capitalism. Ryan Quintana's chapter considers how historians have interpreted the politics of slavery from the American Revolution to the Civil War. Katherine Chilton examines the use of gender as a category of historical analysis of slavery, an approach that did not emerge in full until the 1980s. Sean Condon explores the especially contested historiography of slavery and the family, with many of its debates directly affected by contemporary politics of the Black family. Walter Rucker's chapter reviews the literature on slave resistance, taking into account the work of scholars like Blassingame as well as those who draw explicit comparisons with other areas of the Black diaspora. Likewise, Colleen Vasconcellos incorporates Atlantic world scholarship as she takes the measure of the historiography of the Atlantic slave trade. Kelly Birch and Thomas Buchanan assess the literature on free African Americans and their complex relationship to slave society. Finally, Aaron Astor surveys the historiography of emancipation during the American Civil War, and especially the debates over the roles enslaved people played in their own liberation.

These chapters certainly do not encompass all themes of slavery studies. For example, there are no specific chapters dedicated to varieties of labor, constructions of race, or the development of an internal slave trade; these and other key themes are incorporated into the chapters as appropriate. Note also that this volume is dedicated to the study of slavery in the United States (and its precursor territory). Contributors have certainly highlighted the transnational, comparative, and Atlantic world scholarship that has informed the field, but the emphasis has been on slavery within the boundaries of the current United States.

Each of the chapters in this book follows a roughly similar chronological framework, divided into five historical periods corresponding to significant shifts in the research agenda. First, there are eighteenth- and nineteenth-century participants and observers of slavery and their allied postwar partisans who either decried its immorality or defended the institution. These voices run the gamut from narratives of enslaved men and women who resisted and escaped bondage to polemical defenses of slavery in the decades before the Civil War to antislavery activists writing as early as the 1750s. These contemporary accounts established the terms in which later professional historians have interrogated the institution of slavery.

Second are the early professional historians in the late nineteenth and early twentieth century, who trained under the German university model and were committed to an *objective* depiction of history *as it was*.[4] These scholars rejected the anecdotal testimony of the partisans and generated a white supremacist scholarly consensus that slavery was largely benign. The most influential among them was Georgia-born Ulrich B. Phillips, a professor at Yale and the University of Michigan. Phillips described slavery as an unprofitable *way of life* more than an economic system.[5] These early professional historians accepted some of the antebellum antislavery critiques, especially those that portrayed slavery as backward and an impediment to national progress, but they generally praised slavery as a mode of racial control. As George Fredrickson and Christopher Lasch would later write, "By compiling instances of kindness and benevolence of masters, Phillips proved to his own satisfaction that slavery was a mild and permissive institution, the primary function of which was not so much to produce a marketable surplus as to ease the accommodation of the lower race into the culture of the higher."[6] Not all early professional historians fit within this white supremacist canon, however. African American scholars like W. E. B. Du Bois, Carter G. Woodson, and the contributors to the *Journal of Negro History* generated a powerful counternarrative taken up more fully by *mainstream* historians later in the twentieth century.

A third interpretative era came with mid-twentieth-century scholars, working from the late 1930s through the late 1950s, who rejected the racist portrayal of African Americans dominant in the early professional years. Chief among them was Kenneth Stampp, whose *The Peculiar Institution* in 1956 emphasized the physically and psychologically oppressive nature of slavery, thus directly challenging Phillips's work.[7] Going even further was Stanley Elkins, whose 1959 study compared slave plantations to Nazi concentration camps.[8] Other historians of the era, particularly post-World War II Black scholars like John Hope Franklin, and Marxist scholars like Eric Williams and Herbert Aptheker, emphasized Black resistance more than did Elkins, though their work was still largely ignored among mainstream academics.[9] That would change in the 1960s.

The fourth—and arguably most robust—period of slavery historiography incorporates those writing within what has come to be called the *long Civil Rights tradition,* an extended period that stretched from the early 1960s to the turn of the twenty-first century. These scholars thought that their midcentury counterparts did not go far enough to counter racist portrayals like Phillips's, and they sought to provide a much more fine-grained understanding of slave life, culture, gender, and identity.[10] But it was the disagreements among such scholars—exemplified by Blassingame and his critics in the 1970s—that made this era so intellectually rich. Methodological innovations also defined this period, as historians mined quantitative data and slave narratives collected by the Works Progress Administration (WPA) Federal Writers' Project to tell a social history of slavery from the bottom up.[11] Scholars in the late twentieth century revisited earlier interpretations of slave labor, resistance, and cultural life while incorporating gender as a central category of analysis. In the 1990s, historians widened the temporal and geographic scope of study by taking in the new Atlantic world scholarship and by reckoning with the fundamental changes to the slave system between the seventeenth and nineteenth centuries.

Scholars writing in today's post-Civil Rights era—the fifth historiographical period—from the early 2000s onward have reconceptualized and challenged some of the Civil Rights-era scholarship, especially with regard to democracy, capitalism, memory, and American national identity.[12] A mixture of hope and frustration, with African Americans' economic status and the persistence of police violence and yet the increasingly multicultural makeup of society and the academy, has encouraged scholars to reassess the relationship between slavery and capitalism, and the vexing and persistent contradiction of democracy and white supremacy in American political history. Three sociopolitical events have accentuated this recent turn in the literature: the Great Recession of 2007-2009, the election of a Black president, and a reinvigorated violent white nationalist movement, epitomized by the murder of nine worshippers at the Emanuel African Methodist Episcopal Church in Charleston, South Carolina. In addition to these moments, the four hundredth anniversary of the Dutch ship carrying "20 and odd negroes" to Virginia has stimulated widespread popular and academic interest and reappraisal, including especially the *New York Times*'s "1619 Project," which earned the Pulitzer Prize for Commentary·in 2020.[13] Widespread protests in response to the murder of George Floyd by Minneapolis police in May 2020 have intensified attention on the legacies of slavery and ongoing patterns of institutional racism.

This newer literature emphasizes continuities between slavery and postemancipation, while paying closer attention to chronological changes within the slave system. Methodological developments in the early twenty-first century have also been immense. Newer scholarship on memory has engaged the field of public history, bridging past and present. Interdisciplinary approaches that interrogate the complex intersections of power have also enriched this newer literature. At the same time, newer compilations of sources online, including creative mapping technologies, have allowed historians to mine the evidentiary record more thoroughly and make their findings available to a wider audience.

In each chapter, contributors address why certain contemporary events and methodological innovations shifted the interpretative landscape. This includes the appearance of marginalized outside voices—from early African American historians, radical theorists, and Caribbean scholars in particular—whose voices were not always heard by mainstream historians in their own time. In fact, major historiographical shifts often involve the *dis-*

covery or *revival* of long-ignored scholarship, especially in light of newer political realities. At the same time—and at the risk of repetitiveness—some of the leading figures in the field, like Phillips, Stampp, Blassingame, and Genovese, appear multiple times throughout this volume because their work addresses so many different themes.

The book that this volume seeks most clearly to emulate (but update) is Peter J. Parish's *Slavery: History and Historians* (1989).[14] Parish's historiography remains the best single volume addressing key thematic approaches to the field. But in the three decades since its publication, new themes have emerged—most notably, gender and family life—that this volume explores in great depth. In addition, the topics that Parish covers in chapter-length detail, such as the "Business of Slavery," have witnessed extensive changes over the last thirty years. Thus, there is a clear need for a single volume that updates Parish and that pulls together the different strands of the historiography for a general academic audience.

Our hope is that students and scholars of American history will find much in *Slavery: Interpreting American History* to guide their own research. Readers can trace how leading historians writing in varying circumstances have continually reinterpreted this changing field. The literature of slavery studies is as robust today as ever before. What emerges in this volume is a testament to one of the most distinguished historiographies in American life—one whose innovations and insights reach far behind the study of slavery itself. It is hoped that emerging scholars reading these pages will be inspired to ask new questions and contribute new voices to this troubling but intellectually rich scholarly tradition.

Notes

1. "Negro Acting as Pastor for White People," *African Repository* 35, 255-56.
2. "Negro Acting as Pastor for White People," *African Repository* 35, 256.
3. Blassingame, *Slave Community,* rev. ed. (1979), vii–viii.
4. For a sound analysis of the early historical profession, the German university model, and the search for objectivity, see Novick, *That Noble Dream.*
5. U. Phillips, *American Negro Slavery.*
6. Fredrickson and Lasch, "Resistance to Slavery," 315.
7. Stampp, *Peculiar Institution.*
8. Elkins, *Slavery.*
9. J. Franklin, *Slavery to Freedom;* E. Williams, *Capitalism and Slavery;* Aptheker, *American Negro Slave Revolts.*
10. See J. Hall, "Long Civil Rights Movement."
11. Congress created the Works Progress Administration (WPA) in 1935 as part of President Franklin Roosevelt's New Deal to relieve the economic hardship of the Great Depression. According to the Library of Congress, this national works program (renamed the Work Projects Administration in 1939) employed more than 8.5 million workers—both skilled and unskilled—on 1.4 million work projects before it was disbanded in 1943. The WPA's Federal Writers' Project, created to provide employment for historians, teachers, writers, librarians, and other white-collar workers, produced a massive compilation of former slaves' narratives between 1936 and 1938; the total collection represents more than two thousand interviews and is publicly available through the Library of Congress. Rawick, *American Slave;* Federal Writers' Project, *Slave Narratives,* https://www.loc.gov/collections/slave-narratives-from-the-federal-writers-project-1936-to-1938/about-this-collection (accessed Nov. 9, 2020).
12. The framework adopted here is indebted to chapter 4 in Meier and Rudwick, *Black History and the Historical Profession,* "The Historiography of Slavery"; and to Towers, "Partisans, New History, and Modernization."
13. Hannah-Jones, "The 1619 Project"; for the Pulitzer citation, see Barrus, "Nikole Hannah-Jones Wins Pulitzer Prize for 1619 Project."
14. Parish, *Slavery: History and Historians.*

CHAPTER ONE

Slavery Historiography

Overview of Contemporaries and Historians

AARON ASTOR

"I can speak of Slavery only so far as it came under my own observation," Solomon Northup wrote in his 1853 narrative, *Twelve Years a Slave*, "only so far as I have known and experienced it in my own person."[1] His gripping account of kidnap, enslavement, torture, and return to freedom provided antebellum readers a truthful account often read alongside slave narratives from Frederick Douglass and Harriet Jacobs, and fictional works like Harriet Beecher Stowe's *Uncle Tom's Cabin,* released just a year earlier.[2] But Northup testified to the ages and to the historians to follow, offering "a candid and truthful statement of facts" that could be considered "without exaggeration, leaving it for others to determine, whether even the pages of fiction present a picture of more cruel wrong or a severer bondage."[3] Historians—the "others to determine"—would indeed assess the words and experiences of the enslaved for the next 165 years.

Interpretations of enslavement during the antebellum years have not always been analyzed in historiographical essays. But it is important to consider them as the original interpretation that set the terms of discussion for later amateur and professional historians alike. Americans debated slavery's place in North America during the first decades of British colonization in the seventeenth century, especially as indentured servitude and American Indian bondage gave way to large-scale African slavery after the 1670s. By the mid-eighteenth century, slavery existed in all thirteen British colonies (and in the French and Spanish colonies later to become part of the United States), albeit to varying degrees. The Chesapeake and Carolina colonies employed the institution most vigorously, although some places within the mid-Atlantic and New England depended heavily on slavery as a social and economic force. Few whites protested the growing system in the first half of the eighteenth century, but enslaved Africans and their descendants resisted most vehemently through a series of revolts in New York in 1712 and 1741, and along the Stono River in South Carolina in 1739.[4]

The first organizational opposition to slavery among whites came from the Quakers, who voiced opposition to the slave trade as early as the 1690s and mobilized against slavery in the late 1750s. John Woolman and Anthony Benezet founded antislavery organizations in Philadelphia that drew support from other dissenters—religious and secular—who joined in protest against an institution that they argued ran contrary to basic English principles of human liberty. Woolman's pamphlet, *Some Considerations on the Keeping of Negroes,* published by the Philadelphia Yearly Meeting in 1754, represented one of the earliest religious critiques of slaveholding.[5] At the same time, the Meeting issued an official *Epistle of Caution and Advice concerning the Buying and Keeping of Slaves,* which noted, "to live in Ease and Plenty by the Toil of those whom Violence and Cruelty have put in our power, is neither consistent with Christianity, nor common Justice."[6] Continuing with language to be repeated by religious abolitionists up through the Civil War, the epistle admonished, "and we have good reason to believe, draws down the Displeasure of Heaven, it being a melancholy but true Reflection, That, where Slave keeping prevails, pure Religion and Sobriety decline, as it evidently tends to harden the Heart, and render the Soul less susceptible of that holy Spirit of Love, Meekness and Charity."[7]

Although the Quaker antislavery movement was the first to attack slavery on moral and religious grounds, it was not the first attempt to limit slavery in North America. James Oglethorpe founded the Georgia colony as an experiment in prison reform for indebted

Englishmen. The Oglethorpe Plan for Savannah and the Georgia Colony promoted a doctrine of self-help, social equality, and modesty, which he believed would be undermined by the presence of African slavery. The Georgia Colony prohibited the importation of enslaved Africans because "the White man, by having a Negro Slave, would be less disposed to Labour himself.[8] At the colony trustees' request, Britain's Parliament officially outlawed slavery in Georgia in 1735—partly to prevent Spanish Florida from raiding the colony and using enslaved people to undermine the British colonies—though it would revoke this edict in 1751. In many ways, Oglethorpe's antislavery foreshadowed the *free soil* movement that developed in the mid-nineteenth century in the Northern states, which argued against slavery on economic and ideological grounds rather than on moral or religious principles.[9]

By the 1770s, an international antislavery movement had emerged, with the English abolitionist Granville Sharp corresponding with like-minded Americans in seeking an end to the Atlantic slave trade and to slavery generally. This transatlantic partnership was further enriched by the work of Thomas Clarkson and William Wilberforce of the next generation. Drawing from Sharp's advocacy, Lord Mansfield, chief justice of the British King's Bench, decided in *Somerset v. Stewart* (1772) that slavery was illegal on English soil.[10] Both sides of the Atlantic felt the ruling's electrifying effect, with Massachusetts's Supreme Judicial Court awarding Elizabeth Freeman, or Mum Bet (1781), and Quock Walker (1783) their freedom under the 1780 Massachusetts state constitution in cases resembling the *Somerset* case.[11]

The American Revolution, with its call for "inalienable rights to life, liberty and the pursuit of happiness," stimulated a serious reappraisal of slavery in the newly emerging nation. The self-designated independent state of Vermont abolished slavery in 1777. Pennsylvania, with its strong Quaker tradition, passed "An Act for the Gradual Abolition of Slavery" in 1780, which acknowledged the deliverance of the American colonies from Britain and sought to "extend a portion of that freedom to others."[12] Other New England states would follow Pennsylvania's example and pass their own gradual abolition laws, also citing the spirit of the American Revolution. New York (in 1799) and New Jersey (in 1804) similarly abolished slavery through gradual laws. Meanwhile, the Northwest Ordinance of 1787, passed on the eve of the new Constitution, banned slavery from the territory north of the Ohio River. States in the upper South also debated the future of slavery; the Presbyterian minister and Kentucky Constitutional Convention member David Rice hoped to ban slavery in that state's inaugural 1792 constitution.[13] Capturing a growing national sentiment, Benjamin Franklin—then the president of the Pennsylvania Society for Promoting the Abolition of Slavery—appealed to the new US Congress in 1790 to "devise means for removing the Inconsistency from the Character of the American People."[14] Later antislavery activists pointed to this sentiment in the late eighteenth century to argue that the framers of the Constitution had envisioned the United States to be emerging as a nonslaveholding country, despite the proslavery compromises. In 1852, the abolitionist Massachusetts senator Charles Sumner would declare, "according to the true spirit of the Constitution and the sentiments of the fathers, [slavery] can find no place under our National Government."[15]

Yet a more poignant protest against slavery came from those held in bondage. Enslaved Africans in America and the Caribbean began to write against slavery in the late eighteenth century, and in 1791 organized the first successful revolt in Saint-Domingue on the island of Hispaniola. Publication of the first slave narratives by Olaudah Equiano and Phyllis Wheatley added weight to the antislavery cause in the late eighteenth century. *The Interesting Narrative of the Life of Olaudah Equiano* (1789) had a more immediate effect on the debate over the British slave trade. But the narrative's criticism of slavery's impact on both slaves and slaveholders influenced the larger transatlantic debate, which resulted in the abolition of the British slave trade in 1807.[16] Wheatley's poems appeared earlier, in 1773. Though her poems rarely addressed slavery directly, the phenomenon of an enslaved woman writing for an international audience that included the court of King George III and George Washington served as a powerful critique against the dehumanization wrought by slavery.[17] In Philadelphia, the Reverend Richard Allen's creation of the African Methodist Episcopal Church in 1787 linked free and enslaved African Americans and gave a permanent structure to Black voices for emancipation within a major American city. The Haitian Revolution of the 1790s added force and words to the call for emancipation, with the Haitian general Toussaint L'Ouverture issuing his call for emancipation in the language of Enlightenment and the French Revolution. "I want Liberty and Equality to reign in St Domingue. I am working to make that happen. Unite yourselves to us, brothers and fight with us for the same cause," L'Ouverture proclaimed in 1793.[18] The effect in North America was immediate: Black exiles carried stories of revolution and liberation—prompting slave revolt plots in Richmond in 1800 and in Louisiana in 1811—while whites warned of terror and race war. The legacy of the Haitian Revolution would profoundly affect the American slavery debate for the next sixty years.

Nonetheless, slavery's defenders dug in during and after the Revolution. Many slaveholders joined the Patriot side when, in late 1775, the British colonial governor of Virginia Lord Dunmore promised freedom to enslaved men who fought for the British. South Carolina's political leaders vigorously opposed any interference with slavery; the British general Henry Clinton's plan to emancipate enslaved South Carolinians joining the British army encouraged many South Carolina slaveholders to support the Revolutionary cause just as Dunmore had done in Virginia. By the time the Constitution was drafted in 1787, the framers understood that the Carolinas and Georgia would not support the new framework of government unless some protections for slavery were secured. These would include a series of compromises regarding representation in Congress, fugitive slaves, and the Atlantic slave trade.

The text of the Declaration of Independence was ambivalent about slavery as it blasted the King for having "excited domestic insurrections amongst us" while proclaiming "natural rights" to "life, liberty and the pursuit of happiness." Thomas Jefferson, considered the document's primary author, would exhibit his own conflicted opinions on slavery in his *Notes on the State of Virginia* (1832) and his refusal to manumit his enslaved men, women, and children while calling for restrictions against the expansion of slavery into the Northwest Territory. The contradictions within Jefferson's own life and mind would manifest in a contested politics of colonization, fugitive slave policy, and westward expansion for the next several decades, especially among those living in the United States' upper South and lower North.

However, a series of events around the turn of the nineteenth century buttressed the institution of slavery and lent it more political weight in the fast-growing republic. The cotton gin made short-staple cotton profitable so long as planters could obtain land and enslaved laborers to work the rich soil of the old Southwest. Territorial expansion via war, treaty, and forcible removal of American Indians from the Southeast accelerated the expansion of slavery. By 1820, when Kentuckians settling in mid-Missouri in the 1810s applied for admission to the union as a slave state, it was clear that slavery was not, in fact, dying out on its own, as many of the Founding Fathers had seemed to think it would.

The Missouri Compromise debate was the first of many political crises brought about by the controversy over the extension of slavery. Intense debate following New York senator James Tallmadge's amendment to forbid slavery from Missouri caused an aging Thomas Jefferson to remark, "this momentous question, like a fire bell in the night, awakened and filled me with terror. I considered it at once as the death knell of the Union."[19] Ten years later, another series of events would force the debate over slavery to the center of American politics. Publication of David Walker's *Appeal to the Coloured Citizens of the World* in 1829, Nat Turner's revolt in Virginia in 1831, Virginia's 1831-32 debates on emancipation, the South Carolina Nullification Crisis of 1832, and the creation of the American Anti-Slavery Society in 1833 together ignited the debate over slavery and gave it greater salience in American politics than ever before. Slave narratives written by activists like Solomon Northup, Harriet Jacobs, Frederick Douglass, and Sojourner Truth circulated over the next few decades among a growing network of Black and white abolitionists and helped press the case for emancipation throughout the Union (and abroad).[20] Compelling legal cases and public confrontations over fugitive slaves and territorial slave law from the 1830s through the 1850s concentrated Northern public opinion even more on the immorality of slavery, while at the same time polarizing and radicalizing Southern opinion in slavery's defense.[21]

With the battle lines drawn after 1830, Southerners' "necessary evil" slavery defense, articulated by the likes of Thomas Jefferson, gave way to a more vigorous "positive good" defense of the institution. This shift provided Southern partisans with ideological cover for a social system that brought untold riches to planters in the expanding cotton belt. Following the 1832 debate over slavery in the Virginia legislature, Thomas R. Dew defended slavery as ordained by the Bible and essential to civilization, despite religious abolitionists' protests and the recent uprising led by Nat Turner.[22] In 1837, South Carolina senator John C. Calhoun proclaimed slavery a "positive good," a system in which the "Central African race had never existed in so comfortable, so respectable, or so civilized a condition as that which it now enjoyed in the Southern states."[23]

The controversies surrounding the Texas annexation (1845), the Mexican cession (1848-50), and the Kansas-Nebraska Act (1854) further exacerbated political conflict over the future of slavery in America and encouraged proslavery voices to grow louder in the 1850s. Scientific racists like Drs. Samuel A. Cartwright and Josiah C. Nott argued that Blacks suffered from mental diseases that made them unsuited for freedom.[24] Other influential Southerners such as William J. Grayson and George Fitzhugh concluded that the enslaved were protected from the ravages of Northern wage labor, and that the protections of slavery marked the Southern system as superior.[25] Proslavery ministers like Charles Colcock Jones defended slavery as a form of racial paternalism sanctioned by the Bible.[26] The Southern publisher J. D. B. DeBow envisioned a slave-based empire based out of New Orleans, fueled by filibusterers like William Walker.[27] The former senator James Henry Hammond argued that slavery provided the basis for whites' political freedom, a kind of *herrenvolk democracy* where the lowest white man in society was promised a higher social position than African Americans toiling in the "mudsill."[28] Both Northerners and Southerners joined in fear of emancipation, citing crime and general debauchery as likely consequences. Blackface minstrel shows mocked Black freedom for Northern white, working-class audiences, reminding them of their exalted—though precarious— status in American society.[29] Constitutional arguments, backed by the Supreme Court's *Dred Scott* decision in 1857, claimed that slave property was no different than any other species of property and must be acknowledged and protected in the federal territories of the West.[30] American proslavery voices were as confident as ever in the moral and economic value of slavery in 1860 on the eve of the American Civil War—as long as slaveholders maintained effective control over all three branches of the federal government.

Some antislavery moderates explicitly emphasized the damage slavery inflicted on white Northerners. In the midst of the Industrial Revolution, Northerners prized wage labor—what they called *free labor*—as a bedrock of democratic republicanism. These moderate opponents of slavery cited the institution's stifling of the dignity and efficiency of free labor; the violation of free soil in the West by avaricious slaveholding aristocrats; the formation of a powerful slaveholder political conspiracy (called the *Slave Power*); and slavery's general backwardness in a modern democratic civilization. The Pennsylvania congressman David Wilmot would emerge as an influential voice for free soil. His famous Wilmot Proviso in 1846 would ban the extension of slavery to lands ceded by Mexico. Wilmot proclaimed, "I plead the cause and the rights of white freemen. . . . I would preserve to free white labor a fair country, a rich inheritance, where the sons of toil, of my own race and own color, can live without the disgrace which association with negro slavery brings upon free labor."[31] Some white Southerners echoed Wilmot's free soil argument. In 1858, a white North Carolinian named Hinton Rowan Helper wrote *The Impending Crisis of the South,* which castigated slavery and slaveholders for delaying the economic progress of ordinary white Southerners.[32] Helper,

Wilmot, and the Free Soilers were not utopian social reformers like James Oglethorpe, but their critique of slavery for its deleterious effect on white society echoed that of the Georgia Colony's founder. These critics also set the terms of debate for future historians regarding the economic costs of slavery for nonslaveholding white Southerners.[33] These antislavery moderates acknowledged the constitutionality of slavery in the Southern states, but hoped to put it "on the road to ultimate extinction," in Abraham Lincoln's words, by preventing slavery's extension into the western territories.[34] As this debate intensified in the 1850s, Lincoln and William Seward of the new antislavery Republican Party argued that slavery and freedom marked two different civilizations—a "house divided"—producing an inevitable "irrepressible conflict" between them.[35] In 1860, Lincoln's presidential victory altered the political calculus of slavery for good, as the South and its slaveholding Northern allies no longer controlled national politics. The "irrepressible conflict" would come with South Carolina's secession in December 1860 and the Civil War in 1861.

The combined actions of the Union army, Congress, President Lincoln, and the enslaved themselves during the Civil War destroyed the *peculiar institution,* a process discussed in greater detail later in this volume.[36] Partisan amateur historians who followed the Civil War generally extended and elaborated the critiques of slavery made during the late antebellum period. Northern white partisans stressed the role of the arrogant Slave Power in causing the war.[37] A new debate emerged over how slavery ended during the war, with African American historians like George Washington Williams arguing that enslaved people played a key role in their own freedom—a view that would receive much more attention in the late twentieth century.[38] The tumult of Reconstruction encouraged African Americans and their Radical Republican allies in the North to highlight the centrality of slavery in bringing about the war, as that would justify more thoroughgoing reforms of Southern life. Interestingly, Southern partisans such as Alexander Stephens and Jefferson Davis countered at first, not by reprising the proslavery arguments they made before 1861, but simply by downplaying the significance of slavery in Southern life and, especially, in the Confederate cause. After the violent overthrow of Reconstruction, however, Southern partisans repeated their old claims that slavery was a benign institution, with the political purpose of demonstrating that African Americans were ill-equipped for freedom. This view of a *benign slavery* gradually became dominant in white circles across the nation as white Northerners and Southerners achieved national reconciliation on a mutual embrace of segregation and racism.[39]

By the early twentieth century, a new generation of professional historians trained under the German-influenced university model calibrated and refined these Southern-sympathizing *reconciliationist* accounts. Though popular historians continued to publish in these years, and followed nineteenth-century trends, the new scholars were united by an interest in archival evidence, social science methods, and claims of objective argumentation. The scholars who joined the new professional cause wrote with much greater unity of interpretation than did their nineteenth-century counterparts, making the underlying racism of late nineteenth-century accounts the basis for a new consensus.

Most scholars of the American South in the early professional era from the 1890s to the 1920s focused on the failure of Reconstruction, but Ulrich B. Phillips applied the emerging consensus of professionalism and racism to slavery in his archetypal *American Negro Slavery,* published in 1918, and in *Life and Labor in the Old South,* published in 1929.[40] Phillips was a white Southerner, but one who spent his formative years being trained and then working in Northern universities, and was part of the New South school of historical study that was led by Columbia University's William A. Dunning and included prominent Southern historians Philip A. Bruce and Holland Thompson. These scholars were interested in modernization, industrialization, and efficient labor systems. Unlike scholars of the day focused on the post-Civil War period, Phillips extended the "modern" South backward, portraying Southern antebellum planters as modern businessmen who were shackled to a system of slavery, one brought to the region by

Yankee traders but that ultimately (by 1860) proved unprofitable. The great genius of planters, for Phillips, was not only their ability to create efficient divisions of labor but also their ability to create a paternalistic relationship with their enslaved labor force. This relationship seemed to smooth over problems between labor and capital that were everywhere to be seen in the early twentieth century.[41] In the end for Phillips, the unprofitability of slavery made it less a business than a life for planters. For Phillips, the *benign* master/slave relationship nurtured strong, Christian African American families centered on marriage, delegitimized slave resistance (described by Phillips as *slave crime*), and provided humanitarian care for a race unprepared for freedom. Other historians, like James Ford Rhodes, concurred with Phillips, claiming that enslaved people "remained patiently submissive and faithful to their owners" during the Civil War right up to the last days of the Confederacy.[42]

The first critics of this interpretation were African American scholars—most prominently W. E. B. Du Bois, the first African American PhD from Harvard and an early scholar of African American history. Du Bois explicitly critiqued the assumptions that African Americans were not part of the mainstream of American history. In his 1935 Marxian interpretation *Black Reconstruction in America,* he depicted emancipation and Reconstruction as a class-based workers' revolt.[43] Although he focused on emancipation and its aftermath, he also contributed an early analysis of the end of the African slave trade. Du Bois interpreted the end of the slave trade not as a result of humanitarian forces, but as a product of the fear that the Haitian Revolution would be duplicated on America's shores should the trade continue. He castigated America's "moral cowardice" for its failure to suppress illegal importations after the ban took effect in 1808. He also contributed a study that engaged the enslaved Black family.[44] Du Bois argued that slavery hindered the ability of the enslaved to participate in normal family life, thus directly challenging Phillips.[45]

Another key source of criticism of the Phillips school emerged when Carter G. Woodson established the *Journal of Negro History* (now the *Journal of African American History*) in 1916. Woodson and the historians he collaborated with at his journal did not produce an interpretation of slavery as sweeping as Phillips's, but rather focused their efforts on combating the prevailing view that African Americans were not suited for freedom. The first issues of the *Journal of Negro History* delved into the spectrum of Black experience before the Civil War, including articles on slavery in Appalachia and free African Americans in Cincinnati, as well as traveler accounts of slave life in the eighteenth century.[46] The overarching theme was persistence and progress in the face of discrimination and oppression. The *Journal of Negro History*'s historians shared the establishment professionals' interest in modern research techniques but disagreed vigorously with their conclusions. They countered the white supremacist narrative of the Phillips school as they fought the realities of Jim Crow in their own time. Most African American historians, however, remained outsiders to the dominant interpretations and were ignored by the leading white scholars.

The first shift among white, professional historians away from the Phillips school came in the 1930s with the Progressive historians, who emphasized economic divisions between agrarian and industrial factions. Much of this literature focused on the Civil War's causation and less on slavery as a social system per se. These historians viewed the antebellum North and South less as two contrasting civilizations than as one larger capitalist nation whose leaders exploited sectional arguments over slavery in order to advance the power of economic elites. Shortsighted politicians bungled the nation into war by exaggerating the difference between slavery and freedom.[47] Historians in this transitional period rarely challenged the Phillips school's racist assumptions or its characterization of master/slave relations. That change would come during and after World War II, and once again would be driven by African American historians.

As fascist regimes drew the world into World War II and sentiment against segregation grew at home, historians decisively turned against the early professional consensus that slavery was a benign institution. From the late 1930s until the late 1950s, new interpretations emerged that emphasized the slavery regime's oppressive nature and attempted to take the full measure of its exploitive force. African American scholars such as E. Franklin Frazier, John Hope Franklin, Luther Porter Jackson, and Lorenzo Greene—no longer outsiders despite continued discrimination within the academy—joined leading white scholars such as Richard Hofstadter, Kenneth M. Stampp, and Stanley M. Elkins in revising the history of slavery. While these scholars launched new, overarching interpretations of the lives of the enslaved, the shift also affected scholars studying the slaveholders' world. Stampp's *The Peculiar Institution: Slavery in the Antebellum South,* published in 1956, was particularly influential and is discussed extensively in this volume.[48] A member of the Socialist Party in his graduate school days in the 1940s, Stampp emphasized the cruel exploitation of enslaved people, especially the poverty and physical coercion that were central to the institution. This examination led to a reassessment of the relative power of enslaved people. The historian Earl Lewis has written that Stampp sought a middle ground between Phillips and Woodson, as enslaved men and women came to be seen "as neither the childlike creatures manufactured by Phillips nor as the complete designers of their own fate."[49]

Stanley M. Elkins followed Stampp's analysis but put his ideas into an interdisciplinary and comparative context. His 1959 work, *Slavery: A Problem in American Institutional and Intellectual Life,* compared slave plantations to Nazi concentration camps.[50] Slavery was a total institution and one that had debilitating effects on slave personalities, who often took on the servile *Sambo* persona in response to the overwhelming power of the master class. In this respect, Elkins subscribed to Phillips's *moonlight and magnolias* myth, though only because enslaved people were forced to conform to submissive roles in the face of the slaveholders' overwhelming power.[51]

Marxist historians in the mid-twentieth century vigorously rejected this depiction of enslaved laborers as purely passive victims. These scholars, such as Herbert Aptheker, found much more resistance among enslaved people than did other scholars, and were much more aware of slavery's large-scale and transnational role in capitalist development than were mainstream scholars. Echoing Du Bois's *Black Reconstruction,* Aptheker's 1943 *American Negro Slave Revolts* posited enslaved workers as a working class prone to revolt against slaveholders and their control over the means of production.[52] His analysis found over 250 American slave revolts. Although subsequent scholars have criticized his methods and totals, Aptheker offered a powerful challenge to the Phillips thesis. Elkins and other contemporary mainstream scholars largely ignored his conclusions, but Caribbean historians like Eric Williams and C. L. R. James concurred with Aptheker, in both his Marxian assessment of slavery as a global form of class oppression and the importance of slave rebellion in the Western Hemisphere.[53] Along with Melville Herskovits, the American anthropologist of African cultural "survivals," these scholars pioneered Atlantic and Pan-African approaches that would be reengaged later in the twentieth century.[54]

Changes within the emancipation and Civil War literature evince the shifting scholarly mood of the midcentury period. Scholars such as Benjamin Quarles, Dudley Taylor Cornish, and John Hope Franklin emphasized the role of African American Union soldiers and thereby challenged the early professional descriptions of passive African Americans during the Civil War. These historians put enslaved people at the center of the story of emancipation as agents of their own liberation. This narrative of active resistance would help trigger the next phase of slavery studies, drawing strength and inspiration from the modern Civil Rights movement.

As the Civil Rights, Black Power, and New Left movements of the 1960s demonstrated the power of ordinary people to challenge and change the societal structures around them, so too did scholars seek to document the world of slaves' thoughts and actions as they confronted the world created by the master class. No longer content with portraying enslaved people as Stampp did—as "white men in black men's skins, nothing more, nothing less"—scholars looked to African and Afro-diasporic cultural roots of slave resistance. August Meier and Elliott Rudwick, who conducted extensive interviews with key participants in this shift, found that it was not led by a few seminal scholars, but rather was the result of "individual historians, coming out of varied theoretical origins and theoretical assumptions," responding to the social and political climate of their generation.[55]

Meier and Rudwick wrote on Civil Rights-era scholars in 1986, but what is interesting is how long their basic operating assumptions held sway. Whereas the Civil Rights movement stalled in the 1970s, historians continued to write within the long Civil Rights tradition until the end of the century. As more Black scholars entered the historical profession and universities created Black studies departments, the study of slavery expanded.[56] Black and white scholars continued to expand the field with an outpouring of research that dwarfed all that had preceded it. Slavery studies rose to the top of the American history agenda and remained there even after other fashionable fields of these years (such as labor history) began to wane in status by the late 1990s.

One of the significant early elements of the Civil Rights-era research agenda was a new, penetrating analysis of American racism. These scholars excavated the white supremacist ideas used to justify enslavement, at the very time that American society was challenging persistent racial discrimination. This move began in the 1960s with books such as Leon Litwack's *North of Slavery* (1961), which examined free Blacks' experiences with Northern racism.[57] The two towering achievements in this vein were Winthrop Jordan's *White over Black* (1968) and George M. Fredrickson's *The Black Image in the White Mind* (1971), both of them sweeping and deeply researched accounts of the development of racism from the earliest contacts between whites and Blacks along the shores of Africa in the fifteenth century through the early twentieth century.[58] When Edmund S. Morgan's *American Slavery, American Freedom* countered in 1975 that racism emerged in Virginia *after* the codification of slavery in the late seventeenth century, a major debate among scholars ensued.[59] Later books, such as Stephen Innes and T. H. Breen's *"Myne Owne Ground": Race and Freedom on Virginia's Eastern Shore* (1980), supported Morgan and made clear that racism had a complicated history and was not as unchanging and uniformly coercive as

Fredrickson suggested.[60] This provided a hopeful history for a 1970s society struggling against persistent structural racism.

The slave community school of thought of the late 1960s and 1970s was at the center of the shift toward a Civil Rights interpretation. The slave community school shifted the emphasis decisively by seeking to understand slavery not through the eyes of slaveholders, but from the perspective of the enslaved. No longer content to view enslaved men as Sambos or powerless pawns in coercive systems, these scholars focused on culture as a place where creative resistance seemed most evident. Drawing on the work of Aptheker, Herskovits, and other scholars of Afro-Atlantic societies, a new generation of historians viewed cultural production as inherently political. Elliott Rudwick, Vincent Harding, John W. Blassingame, Eugene Genovese, Sterling Stuckey, Albert J. Raboteau, Herbert G. Gutman, Lawrence W. Levine, and Leslie Howard Owens viewed enslaved people's culture as an autonomous creation, a world that was beyond master class control. The strength of these scholars' combined work was in their interpretation of slave religion, oral tradition, foodways, aesthetics, musical traditions, and the limits of resistance.

Perhaps no element of slave culture came in for more profound reassessment than the slave family. Elkins had argued that the slave family was not a "meaningful unit," a notion that newer scholars found unconvincing. But when the assistant US secretary of labor (and later US senator) Daniel Patrick Moynihan published a report in 1965 portraying Black family life in urban America as pathological, suggesting causes stemming back to slavery, it added public imprimatur to a policy approach that denied the vitality of African American culture. The stage was set for a wholesale historiographical revision of the Black family.[61] Gutman led the effort. Using naming patterns to show extended kin networks among enslaved women, men, and children, he argued for a stable slave family structure.[62] Blassingame and Levine showed how families were used to transmit alternative cultural values, while Genovese saw the slave family as a recognized institution around which slaves and masters bargained for control.[63] Following from the focus on slave empowerment, scholars generally argued that enslaved people were able to form families that were stable, meaningful, and of enduring importance in African American communities.

To make such arguments, these scholars relied on sources that had been dismissed by earlier historians, including slave narratives and interviews with formerly enslaved people, published serially in the 1970s by George Rawick and others as *The American Slave: A Composite Autobiography.*[64] Lawrence Levine pioneered the scholarly use of folktales and spirituals that endured in African American life. Ira Berlin, Leslie Rowland, and several other scholars at the University of Maryland mined the extensive Freedmen's Bureau (officially the Bureau of Refugees, Freedmen, and Abandoned Lands) and wartime records of the National Archives for evidence of self-emancipation during the Civil War. Later scholars would turn to the voluminous court records of the American South to reveal new forms of slave resistance.[65] This search for new sources, which penetrated daily life and allowed for readings from enslaved people's perspective, would be a continuing theme of the long Civil Rights-era scholarly agenda. By the end of the century, the plantation records Ulrich Phillips used were considered a fairly limited way to research enslavement.

Another trend during the 1960s and 1970s, developing at the same time as the slave community school, was the shift toward quantitative or *cliometric* histories of slavery. These scholars picked up on the democratic spirit of the time and the desire to write ordinary people into history but sought to add methodological rigor to a historiography that was often reliant on textual analysis. The trend was first evident in the historiography of the slave trade. Philip Curtin's *The Atlantic Slave Trade: A Census,* published in 1969, added greater specificity to midcentury accounts, which tended to focus on individual atrocities during the trade.[66] Curtin analyzed slave trade records, providing new information on how the volume of the trade changed over time, as well as national carriers and where exactly the trade focused in West Africa and the Americas. His estimate that 9,566,100 enslaved Africans came across the Atlantic began a *numbers game* controversy that would engage scholars into the next century.

The most famous publication of the quantitative vogue, however, was Robert Fogel and Stanley L. Engerman's *Time on the Cross,* published in 1974, which created a firestorm of controversy as it applied the techniques of neoclassical economics—with its rational choice actors and utility-maximizing subjects—to slavery.[67] Extending Stampp's midcentury arguments, the authors argued that slavery was profitable, efficient, and expanding. They also argued that enslaved workers enjoyed better material conditions than free white workers, and that the domestic slave trade did not destroy slave families to the degree that many scholars of the long Civil Rights movement era maintained. Slaves, Fogel and Engerman further claimed, adopted the bourgeois Protestant work ethic with opportunities for advancement and sought to bargain with masters for rewards. Slave community scholars responded with vigor, criticizing the weakness of the evidence and the general tone, which downplayed enslaved people's exploitation far more than other Civil Rights-era scholars. Among their criticisms was Fogel and Engerman's claim that whippings were rare on plantations, despite providing limited evidence, and that they failed to consider how such public events could terrorize enslaved families in the quarters. Although Herbert Gutman's book-length critique effectively obviated *Time on the Cross* to many historians, the authors' emphasis on profitability and capitalism would bear mentioning in later books by Gavin Wright, Claudia Golden, and other scholars of the new economic history.[68] Robert Fogel's own reinterpretation of Southern economic history in *Without Consent or Contract,* published in 1989, received more favorable reviews.[69]

Not all historians of the economic and social system of slavery relied on econometric methods. Perhaps no scholar reoriented the field of slavery studies in the 1970s more than Eugene Genovese, a Marxist historian who defined the slaveholders as precapitalist seigneurial paternalists. Genovese emphasized that "capitalism" was not simply the presence of markets; rather, it was a relationship of production based around wage labor and appearing at a particular historical moment. Genovese's 1965 work, *The Political Economy of Slavery,* resurrected a key element of the Phillips school, describing slavery as a way of life and not as a mode of profit maximization.[70] After a series of invigorating exchanges with members of the slave community school, Genovese published the epochal *Roll, Jordan, Roll* in 1974.[71] Seeking to expunge the racism at the heart of Phillips's work while maintaining fealty to Phillips's model of slavery as a precapitalist social system, *Roll, Jordan, Roll* assessed the various elements of slave life as a balance of accommodation and resistance. Drawing from the Italian theorist Antonio Gramsci, Genovese described the master/slave relationship as a system of hegemony.[72] The planters' real power in such a system was that of individuation, which allowed for individual slave acts of resistance so long as they never posed a collective threat to the institution. This interpretation rejected Fogel and Engelman's profit-maximizing school and Elkins's "closed system" of total domination, while also tempering the revolutionary implications of the slave community school. Some scholars, including James Oakes, soon challenged Genovese's interpretation of slavery as precapitalist, but most direct challenges to Genovese would not come until the new century.[73]

Historians influenced by Genovese's model of slavery as "*in* but not *of*" capitalism began to refine and expand the slave community school's findings in the last two decades of the twentieth century. The most important addition to the early slave community studies was the inclusion of women into enslavement analyses. Scholars in the late 1960s and 1970s were very much invested in countering the Moynihan report, which portrayed matriarchal African American families and emasculated African American men. The slave community school took issue with the presumed pathology of enslaved men and thus emphasized the active role of men in enslaved families and in slave resistance. But the result was a field that privileged male experiences. Directly addressing these flawed assumptions, Deborah Gray White's *Ar'n't I a Woman? Female Slaves in the Plantation South,* published in 1985, traced women's lives though the life cycle, portraying enslavement through the experiences of enslaved

women. White discovered a range of female institutions on plantations that suggested neither matriarchy nor patriarchy within the
enslaved family, but a relative equality, born from the reality of family separations, but nurtured through the creative force of women's
actions.[74] Elizabeth Fox-Genovese added to the revision with her
analysis of both white and Black women in the plantation household. Her analysis showed the limited possibilities for solidarity between white and Black women in plantation settings, where the paternal master's power divided women, each dependent in different
ways on his rule.[75] Suzanne Lebsock's analysis of free Black women
emphasized the relative equality in free Black families versus white
families, with rates of property ownership that were more evenly
divided between the sexes compared with white households. But
she also emphasized the various racist processes that made this relative independence possible.[76] Together, these 1980s scholars made
tremendous strides in including African American women in historical accounts of slavery.

But the biggest shift in the 1980s and 1990s occurred with the
incorporation of gender as a category of analysis. Drawing on what
Judith Surkis called the "linguistic turn" in the historical field, this
new cultural history drew from literary theory and anthropology to emphasize the signs, symbols, and expressions—referred
to broadly as the discourse—of slave society.[77] Feminist historians employed gender theory to explain how enslaved women and
men and slaveholders made sense of their lives, and established,
defended, and challenged gendered archetypes. Drawing on the
work of White and Fox-Genovese, Kathleen M. Brown's *Good
Wives, Nasty Wenches, and Anxious Patriarchs,* published in 1996, argued that the shift to legalized slavery in the late seventeenth and
eighteenth centuries was linked with attempts to shore up patriarchal authority in a colonial setting and to distinguish the legal
relationship between "good wives" and "patriarchs" from their servants and slaves.[78] Jennifer L. Morgan added to the emerging reinterpretation of slavery's origins with an analysis of women and the
slave trade that argued that white impressions of African women
as uniquely able to "suckle over their shoulder" while working

made them excellent candidates for field work. Slaveholders in the Americas valued enslaved women both for their productive and reproductive capacities, while elite women were removed from productive labor.[79]

Other gender scholars challenged the historiography of accommodation and resistance, which inevitably portrayed enslaved women as more accommodating than enslaved men. Stephanie M. H. Camp's *Closer to Freedom,* published in 2004, argued quite powerfully that women's resistance was simply different than men's, conditioned as it was to their commitments to raising children. Camp illustrated distinct patterns among female runaways, for instance, who would often desert plantations temporarily, not willing to completely abandon family members. She also uncovered examples of enslaved women turning their meager dwellings into political centers where abolitionist ideas could be nurtured.[80] Enslaved people also turned to aesthetics as a mode of resistance. Shane White and Graham White's *Stylin': Afro-American Expressive Culture from Its Beginnings to the Zoot Suit* (1998) revealed how hair styles and clothes were part of the politics of everyday life in the slave quarters.[81] The two Australian scholars later published a book on slave song, *Sounds of Slavery* (2005), further examining the culture of the enslaved.[82] Regarding the slaveholders' worldview, Stephanie McCurry's *Masters of Small Worlds* (1995) identified the planter-paternalist model as a gendered form of household organization in the South Carolina Low Country that smaller slaveholders sought to emulate.[83] By the 1990s, scholars increasingly embraced gender analysis as an essential component in analyzing slavery.

At the turn of the twenty-first century, historians of slavery began to refine, expand, and challenge some of the key insights drawn from scholars during the long Civil Rights movement. In an era of stagnant wages, police violence, and mass incarceration of people of color, and the persistence of human trafficking, the optimism of a nation moving toward ever-greater freedom no longer fit with the immediate experience of many Americans. Political debates (and occasionally violence) over reparations and public memory of the Confederacy and the Old South have launched newer reconsiderations of slavery's centrality in America's history. An invigorated white nationalist movement has lent immediacy to this new scholarship, as has the proliferation of Black Lives Matter protests against police violence specifically and institutional racism generally. The Great Recession of 2007-2009 encouraged scholars to reconsider capitalism's relationship to slavery. At the same time, the election of President Barack Obama, who wrapped his candidacy in the mantle of Lincoln (including launching it in Springfield, Illinois), concentrated public attention on the historical import of that moment. Newer social studies standards, public museums, and monuments to slavery along with the reality of a multicultural twenty-first-century America have engaged ordinary Americans with the newer directions in the study of slavery.

In this fifth period of slavery historiography, historians are expanding their work into culture and gender, exploring transnational contexts of slavery and emancipation, reconsidering the power and politics of the enslaved, and reexamining the economic foundations of American capitalism. Perhaps most importantly, scholars have followed Ira Berlin's lead and historicized slavery, viewing it not as a stable sociological system in the antebellum Deep South but as an institution in constant flux.[84] This approach is not entirely new. Peter Wood's influential *Black Majority: Negroes in Colonial South Carolina from 1670 to the Stono Rebellion* (1973) did much to expand scholarly interest into the early decades of American slavery.[85] But with the Atlantic world's emergence as a historical analysis zone in the 1990s, scholars became much more attuned to the specificities and variations in patterns of slave importation, and began to stress the interplay between various African and European cultural influences, particularly in the colonial period.[86] Berlin coined the term *Atlantic creole* to describe the mixed cultural background of the earliest African migrants to America. Other scholars, emphasizing times and places of direct and continued slave importation, noted much more ethnic continuity between Africa and America than had previously been understood. Early historians writing of this continuity, such as Daniel C. Littlefield, Judith A. Carney, Margaret Creel Washington, and Gwendolyn

Midlo Hall, showed the persistence of African ethnicity in colonial South Carolina's Low Country and in colonial Louisiana. These scholars demonstrated that earlier Atlantic comparisons emphasizing greater creolization in North America compared with other slave trade destinations were too generalized.[87] For example, John Thornton's work on Kongolese in the Atlantic world emphasized the specific cultural heritages of enslaved people from particular regions of Africa, and the processes through which Afro-Atlantic identities developed.[88] Michael A. Gomez's *Exchanging Our Country Marks* (1998), using newly available slave trade data on the online database *Slave Voyages,* stressed that specific cultural traits from specific African ethnic groups persisted to a greater degree in various locations throughout America than previous studies had shown.[89] Walter C. Rucker added to the field by showing how these African ethnic transferences helped create the bedrock for slave resistance and slave revolt plots.[90] Dylan C. Penningroth extended this transnational framework to discuss the relationship of kinship to property, tracing the views of property among the enslaved to West Africa.[91] Newer works have also explored other forms of forced labor in early America and their relationship to African slavery. Christina Snyder, for example, has shown that colonial Indian slavery was far more significant in early British expansion than was previously thought.[92]

Historians have also refined the chronology of slavery by locating political continuities between slavery and freedom. Steven Hahn's *A Nation under Our Feet* (2005) deployed an expansive definition of politics, identifying a politics among the enslaved that emphasized collective struggle over the terms of freedom more than a liberal struggle for individual rights—efforts that manifested during Reconstruction and beyond. Justin Behrend, in *Reconstructing Democracy: Grassroots Black Politics in the Deep South after the Civil War* (2015), focused on the construction of democracy among the enslaved as they encountered and shaped a world of uncertain freedom in the Natchez district in present-day Mississippi and Louisiana.[93] Thavolia Glymph, in *Out of the House of Bondage* (2008), assessed the transformed political relationship between plantation mistresses and enslaved women before, during, and after emancipation.[94] Tera Hunter's 2019 analysis of mixed marriages between enslaved and free African Americans, titled *Bound in Wedlock*, addressed the complications surrounding "validation" of such marriages after emancipation.[95] All of these scholars interrogated the politics of the enslaved, both within and outside the household, and revealed the ways in which those political understandings developed in slavery shaped the lives of freed people.

Whereas some scholars have located the politics of freed people in the context of prior enslavement, others have noted continuing oppression despite slavery's formal end. Building off Dale Tomich's concept of a "Second Slavery" (1988) that extended far beyond formal emancipation, these historians have emphasized the psychological, economic, and cultural legacies of enslavement.[96] For example, Saidiya V. Hartman's *Scenes of Subjection* (1997) demonstrated slaveholders' power in the realms of "pleasure, paternalism, and property" in ways that made fresh the horror of slavery for a generation used to viewing violence as spectacle.[97] Hartman's target was American liberalism itself, which in the words of one reviewer "perpetuate[s] the repressive legacies of slavery" out of a desire "to uphold the liberal values of middle-class social control."[98] Nell Irvin Painter's *Southern History across the Color Line* (2002) stressed the enduring psychological damage of enslavement and the torture of Black bodies.[99] Daina Ramey Berry's *The Price for Their Pound of Flesh* (2017) viewed the commodification of Black bodies in the slave trade as a process of dehumanization that continued long after emancipation in the form of "spectacles of black death."[100] Douglas Blackmon's *Slavery by Another Name* (2008) directly linked the system of slavery to mass incarceration in the late nineteenth century—a topic of enduring relevance in the twenty-first century.[101] Ibram Kendi's *Stamped from the Beginning* (2016) emphasized the persistence of racism in a nation supposedly defined by the liberal values of equality, freedom, and justice.[102] Jim Downs's *Sick from Freedom* (2012) addressed the immediate epidemiological consequences of slavery and emancipation.[103] And in a 2007 essay taking much of the slave community school to task, Walter Johnson, author of *The Chattel Principle* (2005), a book on the internal slave trade (among others), criticized the notion of "agency" as a concept that obscured the lived experiences and cultural realities of the enslaved.[104] These works broadly reject the slave community school's triumphal narrative of resistance and emancipation and instead emphasize the continuing legacy of slavery and oppression.

Twenty-first-century scholars have reconsidered Eugene Genovese's conception of slavery as a form of precapitalist seigneurialism and paternalism, instead describing it as embedded in capitalism and the nation's definitions of political freedom. In some ways, the field is moving in the direction of Morgan's *American Slavery, American Freedom,* a long Civil Rights-era classic that first argued that American republican ideas emerged out of enslavement.[105] Sven Beckert's *Empire of Cotton* (2014) identified slavery and the cotton economy as central to the growth of industrial capitalism worldwide.[106] Adam Rothman's acclaimed *Slave Country* (2005) picked up where Morgan ends in the Revolutionary era, showing how capitalism expanded slavery in Jefferson's "empire of liberty."[107] Edward E. Baptist connected capitalism's "busts" (namely, the financial panics of 1819, 1837, and 1857) to the lives of the enslaved, revealing how speculation could lead to the breakup of enslaved families.[108] Looking at the internal accounting of slavery as a business, Caitlin Rosenthal's *Accounting for Slavery* (2018) addressed the "scientific management" of and "human capital" on plantations.[109] Seth Rockman's *Scraping By* (2009) revealed how slavery was an integral part of capitalism in early national Baltimore—how elites made use of the enslaved alongside "free" workers, weighing the benefits of each while ensnaring all in poverty and myths of dependence and laziness—framing slavery as part of a larger story of class conflict and capitalism's emergence.[110] Joshua Rothman's *Flush Times and Fever Dreams* (2012) addressed slavery's expansion to the old Southwest during the Jacksonian era, reiterating slavery's centrality to the nation's growth.[111] Calvin Schermerhorn's *The Business of Slavery and the Rise of American Capitalism* (2015) considered the business of the interstate slave trade and its link to transatlantic credit networks.[112] Most recently, Stephanie E. Jones-Rogers, in *They Were Her Property* (2019), reexamined the role of white women as economic actors in the slave trade.[113] This new willingness to link slavery with larger economic transformations and to connect enslaved chattel's experiences with other workers has led others to expand our very notions of what *slaves* are and who they were in American economic history.[114] Two edited collections—*Slavery's Capitalism: A New History of American Economic Development* (2016), edited by Beckert and Rockman, and *New Directions in Slavery Studies* (2015), edited by Jeff Forret and Christine Sears—each highlight the connection between commodification of enslaved African Americans and the growth of global capitalism.[115]

In the wake of the Civil War sesquicentennial in 2011, and with modern partisan rivalries hardening, historians have reassessed the politics of slavery and sectionalism in the years before the Civil War. Matthew Karp and Carl Paulus have explored slaveholders' control of foreign policy and fear of insurrection.[116] R. J. M. Blackett has reassessed the Fugitive Slave Act of 1850. Stanley Harrold has located the Civil War's origins in the contests over slavery—many of them having to do with fugitive slaves—in the slave/free borderland.[117] Graham Peck and Dana Weiner have reconsidered antislavery politics in the key Northern state of Illinois. Michael Landis and Christopher Childers have examined the *doughfaces,* or proslavery Northern Democrats, and tensions of popular sovereignty in the western territories.[118] Kimberly Welch, Kelly Kennington, Lea VanderVelde, and Anne Twitty have all looked at *Dred Scott v. Sanford* and enslaved people's access to the law.[119] With intensified public debate over citizenship and immigration, Martha Jones has demonstrated the importance of birthright citizenship in Black legal thought leading up to the Fourteenth Amendment.[120] And historians have not restricted their reassessments of the politics of slavery to the immediate antebellum era. Matthew Mason, Jonathan Earle, and John Craig Hammond have each reconsidered the politics of slavery in the early republic and the Jacksonian era.[121] David Waldstreicher and Sean Wilentz have reevaluated slavery at the time of the Constitution's drafting and ratification.[122] In a moment of new synthesis, Manisha Sinha, Patrick Rael, Seymour Drescher, David Brion Davis, and David Blight have all pulled the lens back on abolitionism broadly in the early nineteenth century, including Blight's fresh biography of Frederick Douglass. Each of these scholars has placed both enslaved and free African Americans at the heart of the abolitionist movement.[123]

Newer scholarship on specific regions like the border states, Appalachia, the Texas borderlands, the Louisiana sugar parishes, and the North has added nuance to political debates over slavery. These studies have helped reshape historians' understanding of the geographic and legal boundaries of slavery as well as the contested nature of freedom outside the plantation belt of the Deep South. These regional works have done more than fill in geographic gaps in the literature; they have also highlighted the demographic mix and the varieties of social stratification in different areas of enslavement.[124] All of this scholarship underscores the different chronologies of slavery and emancipation between the American Revolution and the end of 1865. If anything, the regional studies showcase the contingent nature of slavery's rise and fall across the vast American landscape.

The new field of memory studies has also garnered scholarly attention. Much of this work emerged out of the Civil War memory field, especially the work of David Blight.[125] The massacre at Emanuel AME Church in Charleston in 2015 concentrated new attention on the memory of slavery and emancipation, as evidenced in Ethan Kytle and Blain Roberts's *Denmark Vesey's Garden,* which examined the contested memory of slavery in that city.[126] Micki McElya exposed the powerful myth of the *faithful mammy* in the twentieth century and its hold on the white Southern imagination.[127] Anne Bailey followed the descendants of those sold in the massive Butler plantation slave auction in 1859, thus linking the late antebellum internal slave trade to African American genealogy and memory.[128] The public history and museum studies field has engaged the challenges facing the interpretation of slavery at historic sites, notably in an extensive study conducted by Jennifer Eichstedt and Stephen Small.[129] Highlighting the more unusual forms of slavery tourism,

Tiya Miles examined the popularity of so-called haunted tours, where "specters"—often in the form of enslaved former residents—guide modern tourgoers through historic plantation homes.[130] Interest in the slave labor that produced modern institutions has fueled research into the use of enslaved laborers at universities like Georgetown, Alabama, and Virginia.

In some ways, the current field is fragmented, making difficult any broader interpretations of American slavery in the twenty-first century. Transnational approaches, memory studies, public history, digital scholarship, medical history, regional histories, new histories of capitalism, carceral history, and many other themes make for a lively but fractured discipline. If anything defines the scholarship of the twenty-first century, it is a renewed emphasis on chronological change—viewing slavery as a dynamic system—as opposed to the sociological and anthropological snapshots that characterized much of the antebellum-focused literature through the 1970s. As twenty-first-century scholars ponder the enduring consequences of the Civil Rights movement, historians have looked back and reconsidered just how much the institution of slavery changed before 1865—and how much did not change for emancipated people and their descendants after 1865. The increased public interest in slavery's legacies, especially in the wake of the Great Recession, the election of Barack Obama (and then Donald Trump) to the presidency, and the persistence of police violence and protest, has encouraged broader reformulations from both academic and nonacademic historians, especially those who connect the legacy of America's *peculiar institution* to modern struggles over racial justice.

NOTES

1. Northup, *Twelve Years a Slave*, 18.
2. Douglass, *Narrative*; Jacobs, *Incidents in the Life*; Stowe, *Uncle Tom's Cabin*.
3. Northup, *Twelve Years a Slave*, 18.
4. On the New York slave revolts, see Berlin and Harris, *Slavery in New York*. On the Stono Rebellion and its causes, see P. Wood, *Black Majority*.
5. Woolman, *Some Considerations*.

6. *Epistle of Caution,* 2.

7. *Epistle of Caution,* 2-3.

8. Martyn, *Account,* 8. Martyn was the secretary for the Georgia Colony trustees.

9. The Republican Party of the 1850s advanced the slogan "Free Soil, Free Labor, Free Men, which meant preventing slavery's expansion into the western territories.

10. *Somerset v. Stewart* (1772).

11. *Brom and Bett v. Ashley* (1781); *Commonwealth v. Jennison* (1783).

12. "An Act for the Gradual Abolition of Slavery," Mar. 1, 1780.

13. Opie, "Melancholy Career."

14. B. Franklin, "Petition."

15. Sumner, *Freedom National,* 8.

16. Equiano, *Interesting Narrative.*

17. Wheatley, *Poems on Various Subjects.*

18. Tyson, *Toussaint L'Ouverture,* 28.

19. Thomas Jefferson to John Holmes, Apr. 22, 1820, Thomas Jefferson Papers, Library of Congress, https://www.loc.gov/item/mtjbib023795.

20. Sinha, *Slave's Cause.*

21. Blackett, *Captive's Quest.*

22. T. R. Dew, *Review of the Debate.*

23. 13 Reg. Deb. 718 (1837).

24. Nott and Gliddon, *Types of Mankind;* Cartwright, "Diseases and Peculiarities."

25. Grayson, *Hireling and the Slave;* Fitzhugh, *Cannibals All!*

26. C. Jones, *Religious Instruction.*

27. DeBow, "General Walker's Policy."

28. Cong. Globe, 35th Cong., 1st Sess. 962 (1858).

29. Roediger, *Wages of Whiteness.*

30. *Dred Scott v. Sandford* (1857).

31. Cong. Globe, 29th Cong., 2d. Sess. 317 (1847).

32. Helper, *Impending Crisis.*

33. Merritt, *Masterless Men,* emphasizes the slaveholders' class oppression of poor whites, directly confronting the work of Frank Owsley. See Owsley, *Plain Folk.* See also Forret, *Race Relations.*

34. Lincoln, "Speech in Chicago," in Basler, *Collected Works of Abraham Lincoln,* 2:491.

35. Lincoln, *Proceedings;* Seward, *Irrepressible Conflict.*

36. The last chapter of this volume explains the process through which slavery ended during the Civil War, and the debates over emancipation among historians.

37. Towers, "Partisans, New History, and Modernization," 241.

38. G. Williams, *History of the Negro Troops.* See also J. Wilson, *Black Phalanx.*

39. Blight, *Race and Reunion.*

40. U. Phillips, *American Negro Slavery;* U. Phillips, *Life and Labor.*

41. Singal, "Ulrich B. Phillips."

42. Rhodes, *History of the Civil War,* 381.

43. Du Bois, *Black Reconstruction.* John R. Lynch criticized Rhodes as early as 1917, but focused mostly on Rhodes's interpretation of Reconstruction. See Lynch, "Some Historical Errors."

44. Du Bois, *Negro American Family;* Du Bois, *Suppression of the African Slave Trade.*

45. E. Lewis, "To Turn as on a Pivot," 766; Du Bois, "Reconstruction and Its Benefits."

46. See the *Journal of Negro History,* vol. 1, nos. 1 and 2 (January and June 1916).

47. See for example Randall, "Blundering Generation."

48. Stampp, *Peculiar Institution.*

49. E. Lewis, "To Turn as on a Pivot," 770.

50. Elkins, *Slavery.*

51. The moonlights and magnolias myth refers to a romanticized portrayal of plantation slavery, especially in the 1939 film *Gone with the Wind.*

52. Aptheker, *American Negro Slave Revolts.*

53. James, *History of Negro Revolt;* James, *Black Jacobins;* E. Williams, *Capitalism and Slavery.*

54. Herskovits, *Myth of the Negro Past.*

55. Meier and Rudwick, *Black History,* 276.

56. Deborah Gray White's personal reflection discusses the continuation of racism in the academy. See D. White, "'Matter out of Place.'"

57. Litwack, *North of Slavery.*

58. W. D. Jordan, *White over Black;* Fredrickson, *Black Image in the White Mind.*

59. E. Morgan, *American Slavery.*

60. Breen and Innes, *"Myne Owne Ground."* Other scholars would eventually support Fredrickson's position. See for example J. H. Sweet, "Iberian Roots of American Racist Thought."

61. Moynihan, *Negro Family.*

62. Gutman, *Black Family.*

63. Blassingame, *Slave Community;* L. Levine, *Black Culture.*

64. Rawick, *American Slave.* Forty-one volumes were published in total, of which vols. 2-17 consist of narrative transcriptions prepared by the Works Progress Administration (WPA) Federal Writers' Project as part of the New Deal from 1936 to 1938.

65. Berlin et al., *Freedom: A Documentary History of Emancipation.* Six main documentary volumes have been published, plus four other companion volumes.

66. Curtin, *Atlantic Slave Trade.*

67. Fogel and Engerman, *Time on the Cross.*

68. Gutman, *Slavery and the Numbers Game.* See also Goldin, *Urban Slavery;* and G. Wright, *Political Economy.* For a more recent overview, see G. Wright, *Slavery and American Economic Development.*

69. Fogel, *Without Consent or Contract.*

70. Genovese, *Political Economy of Slavery.*

71. Genovese, *Roll, Jordan, Roll.*

72. Gramsci, *Selections from the Prison Notebooks.*

73. Oakes, *Ruling Race.*

74. D. White, *Ar'n't I a Woman?*

75. Fox-Genovese, *Within the Plantation Household.*

76. Lebsock, *Free Women.*

77. See Surkis, "When Was the Linguistic Turn?"

78. K. Brown, *Good Wives.*

79. J. Morgan, *Laboring Women.*

80. Camp, *Closer to Freedom.*

81. S. White and G. White, *Stylin'.* See also S. White, *Stories of Freedom.*

82. S. White and G. White, *Sounds of Slavery.*

83. McCurry, *Masters of Small Worlds.*

84. Berlin, *Generations of Captivity.*

85. P. Wood, *Black Majority.*

86. Mintz and Price, *Birth of African-American Culture;* Berlin, *Many Thousand Gone;* P. Morgan, *Slave Counterpoint;* Sparks, *Two Princes.*

87. Littlefield, *Rice and Slaves;* Carney, *Black Rice;* Creel, *"Peculiar People";* G. Hall, *Africans in Colonial Louisiana.*

88. J. K. Thornton, *Africa and Africans;* Haywood and Thornton, *Central Africans, Atlantic Creoles.* For a more thorough history of the Atlantic world, see J. K. Thornton, *Cultural History.*

89. Gomez, *Exchanging Our Country Marks.* For the slave trade database, see Eltis et al., *Trans-Atlantic Slave Trade: A Database on CD-ROM;* or the *Slave Voyages: The Trans-Atlantic Slave Trade Database* website, https://www.slave voyages.org.

90. Rucker, *River Flows On.*

91. Penningroth, *Claims of Kinfolk.*

92. Snyder, *Slavery in Indian Country.* Many books have described the continuation of slavery in the modern world economy. The classic text is Bales, *Disposable People.* See also Rushforth, *Bonds of Alliance;* and Miles, *Ties that Bind.*

93. Behrend, *Reconstructing Democracy.*

94. Glymph, *Out of the House of Bondage.*

95. Hunter, *Bound in Wedlock.*

96. Tomich, "'Second Slavery.'" See also Kaye, "Second Slavery"; and Mathisen, "Second Slavery."

97. Hartman, *Scenes of Subjection*, 4.

98. Morton, "Review: *Scenes of Subjection*."

99. Painter, *Southern History across the Color Line*.

100. Berry, *Price for Their Pound of Flesh*, xiii.

101. Blackmon, *Slavery by Another Name*.

102. Kendi, *Stamped from the Beginning*.

103. J. Downs, *Sick from Freedom*.

104. W. Johnson, "Slavery, Reparations, and the Mythic March of Freedom"; W. Johnson, "On Agency." See also W. Johnson, *Soul by Soul*; and W. Johnson, *River of Dark Dreams*.

105. E. Morgan, *American Slavery, American Freedom*.

106. Beckert, *Empire of Cotton*.

107. A. Rothman, *Slave Country*.

108. Baptist, "Toxic Debt."

109. Rosenthal, *Accounting for Slavery*.

110. Rockman, *Scraping By*.

111. J. Rothman, *Flush Times*.

112. Schermerhorn, *Business of Slavery*.

113. Jones-Rogers, *They Were Her Property*.

114. *Chattel slavery* is the term for the ownership of human beings as movable property, able to be bought, sold, given, and inherited. Children of slaves were born enslaved. Slaves in this context were legally dehumanized into chattel, with no personal freedom or agency to decide the direction of their own lives.

115. Beckert and Rockman, *Slavery's Capitalism*; Forret and Sears, *New Directions*. See also Forret, *Slave against Slave*.

116. Karp, *Vast Southern Empire*; Paulus, *Slaveholding Crisis*.

117. Blackett, *Captive's Quest for Freedom*; Harrold, *Border War*.

118. Peck, *Making an Antislavery Nation*; D. Weiner, *Race and Rights*; Landis, *Northern Men with Southern Loyalties*; Childers, *Failure of Popular Sovereignty*.

119. Welch, *Black Litigants*; Kennington, *In the Shadow*; VanderVelde, *Redemption Songs*; Twitty, *Before Dred Scott*.

120. M. Jones, *Birthright Citizens*.

121. Mason, *Slavery and Politics*; Earle, *Jacksonian Antislavery*; J. C. Hammond, *Slavery, Freedom, and Expansion*.

122. Waldstreicher, *Slavery's Constitution*; Wilentz, *No Property in Man*.

123. Sinha, *Slave's Cause*; Rael, *Eighty-Eight Years*; Drescher, *Abolition*; D. Davis, *Problem of Slavery*; Blight, *Frederick Douglass*.

124. For regional studies outside the cotton, rice, and tobacco belts, see Mutti Burke, *On Slavery's Border*; Astor, *Rebels on the Border*; Salafia, *Slavery's Borderland*; C. Phillips, *Rivers Ran Backward*; Dunaway, *Slavery in the American Mountain South*; Torget, *Seeds of Empire*; Rodrigue, *Reconstruction in the Cane Fields*; Diemer, *Politics of Black Citizenship*; Grivno, *Gleanings of Freedom*;

D. Smith, *On the Edge of Freedom;* Epps, *Slavery on the Periphery;* Warren, *New England Bound;* Miles, *Dawn of Detroit;* Kiser, *Borderlands of Slavery;* and Brooks, *Captives and Cousins.*

125. Blight, *Race and Reunion.*

126. Kytle and Roberts, *Denmark Vesey's Garden.*

127. McElya, *Clinging to Mammy.*

128. A. Bailey, *Weeping Time.*

129. Eichstedt and Small, *Representations of Slavery.* This challenge has been addressed in popular media as well. See M. Cohen, "Slavery in America."

130. Miles, *Tales from the Haunted South.*

CHAPTER TWO

American Slavery and the Economy

CALVIN SCHERMERHORN

Slavery in the nineteenth-century American republic supported substantial economic growth and development, led to immense prosperity for slaveowners, and made slaveholding commercial agriculturalists—those who called themselves planters—the wealthiest class of Americans. Banking, shipping, and other collateral industries thrived on slavery, and cities like New York became clearinghouses for slave-grown products. In general, the bound workforce situated on slave labor camps in the American South generated reliable and even substantial returns on investments. Slaveowners used the capital embodied in enslaved people to raise money to expand productivity and boost technological development.[1] Yet contemporary and scholarly debates of the nineteenth and much of the twentieth century drew a veil over slavery's centrality to American economic growth and capitalist development, framing slavery instead in terms of political interests, social institutions, and moral choices.

This chapter details the historiography of economic interpretations of slavery—in particular, how economic analyses of an institution founded on the promise of financial gain evaded historians for generations. Before the field professionalized, nineteenth-century historians and political economists generally agreed that slave-based agriculture was an inefficient vestige of a colonial past, and that a Southern economy reliant on a handful of staple crops,

principally cotton, was less advanced and less viable than industrial, free, and diversified alternatives. As the field professionalized
in the late nineteenth and early twentieth centuries, scholars endorsed those contentions with evidence.

During the first half of the twentieth century, a handful of
economic historians contended that slavery paid returns on investments, and by the mid-1950s, the prevailing view of slavery's
economic backwardness was under siege. By that decade's end,
economists measuring inputs and outputs confirmed that slave-
based agriculture repaid investments and generated profits. That
insight came in the context of great methodological change. In
the 1960s, econometric historians published a wealth of studies
concerning plantation slavery and enslaved people. The 1970s and
1980s were the heyday of econometric slavery studies pointing to
plantation slavery as being a viable, robust, and sustainable system. By the 1990s, the economics of American slavery took on renewed importance, as slaveholders were seen increasingly as economic actors who defended a vastly profitable enterprise through
political manipulation and ultimately a self-destructive civil war.
Comparisons and connections with other areas of the Atlantic ba-
sin challenged the seeming peculiarity of United States slavery.

In the twenty-first century, viewing African American slavery
in North America in larger contexts led to studies of slavery's
capitalism and of proslavery imperialism. Pessimism about global
capitalism in the wake of the Great Recession encouraged scholars
to look more critically on slavery's role in fostering capitalism's
growth. Nineteenth-century American slaveowners who were
once thought to be backward-gazing paternalists now seemed
to have been forward-looking capitalists. Parochial Southerners
turned into cosmopolitan imperialists. The peculiar institution became less peculiar as the South was suddenly situated right next to
the rest of the world and increasingly integrated into it. Enslaved
people once viewed as inflicting damage on owners' property to
preserve community and family relationships (such as through arson or sabotage) appeared as savvy market actors developing strategies within far-flung networks.

Historians in the early nineteenth century developed a robust nationalist narrative that painted the United States as exceptional and racial slavery as a regrettable artifact of a colonial past. William Grimshaw and George Bancroft were among a school of popular historians who submerged slavery in a triumphalist narrative that endorsed American expansion, including manifest destiny. African Americans were problematic outsiders in the American historical narrative, and slavery was at the periphery of a divinely ordained republic.[2] Like historians, political economists paid little attention to slavery, treating it as problematic when they did. American political economists like Henry Charles Carey and Francis Wayland contended that the abundance of North American land seemed to solve problems of population growth and rents, and that expansion was emancipatory. But not all spoke with one accord. Thomas Cooper endorsed chattel slavery and free trade, but he premised his proslavery argument on a racialized understanding of disease. "Nothing will justify slave labour in point of economy," he argued in 1826, "but the nature of the soil and climate which incapacitates a white man from laboring in the summer time; as on the rich lands in [Low Country] Carolina and Georgia." Although Cooper registered his doubts about the morality of slave trading, the president of South Carolina College fell in line with the sensitive sectional issue of slavery.[3]

Southern scholars tended to endorse slavery as a social system, but they also held that it was noncapitalist and inefficient. University of Virginia professor and political economist George Tucker concurred with Grimshaw and Bancroft that American slavery was a marginal institution subject to laws of population growth and labor pressures. In an analysis of the 1840 census, Tucker discovered that slaves' forced migration from the upper South to the lower South caused "extraordinary mortality" in the short term as a result of the abrupt transition to a hostile climate, disease environment, and workplace.[4] Profits provided the motivation for such forced migration. But Tucker clung to the contention that slavery as an institution would die of natural causes. He shied away from economic analyses of slavery in his four-volume opus, *The History of the United States* (1856-58), which ratified the prevailing view that foreign empires fastened slavery on Southern colonists. The seeds of disunion—which Tucker warned against in his final volume— were planted with the arrival of the first African-descended slaves. In *Political Economy for the People* (1859), Tucker contended that expansion *eroded* slavery. Labor mobility onto slaveholding lands would cause a decline in slave prices.[5] Such was a political bromide at a time when the republic was on the verge of dissolving over the politics of slavery's extension.

College of William and Mary professor Thomas Roderick Dew noticed a peculiar economy of slavery in his native Virginia. "Virginians can raise [slaves] cheaper than they can buy; in fact it is one of their greatest sources of profit."[6] Dew advocated Ricardian free trade, and his economic analysis of slavery turned on viewing enslaved people as property whose interests aligned with their owners rather than as the subjects of owners' expropriations. "The happiness, rights, &c. of the slave, are in this case supposed to be merged completely in those of the master," he argued. Dew's "economical point of view" was to view enslaved people "in the light of property alone, like horses and cattle, and not like men."[7] That *chattel principle* was the cornerstone of abolitionists' economic critiques of slavery.

Antislavery activists and especially abolitionists unfolded the best-developed economic analysis of slavery in contemporary America. Like Tucker, Henry Stanton understood that the domestic slave trade was vital to the sectors of the economy that relied on slave labor. In 1839, Stanton argued that "the internal slave trade is the great jugular vein of slavery; and if Congress will take the same weapon with which they cut off the foreign trade, and cut this vein, slavery would die of starvation in the southern, and of apoplexy in the northern slave states."[8] Cotton was a global commodity, a fact understood by the African American abolitionist Charles Lenox Remond and the British abolitionist George Thompson. Both urged Britain to abolish slavery in British India and to encourage free labor cotton cultivation there in order to undermine American slavery.[9] The American abolitionist Wendell Phillips articulated a concise economic analysis of American slavery, charging in 1853 that slavery was upheld by "a money power of two thousand millions of dollars," invested in slaves, exporting cotton, and hogging political power unfairly.[10] In short, slavery and money were tied to corruption and antidemocratic politics.

Proslavery apologists like the polemicist George Fitzhugh disagreed. He took a prevailing view of capitalism as a system of labor exploitation and contrasted it with an idealized version of Virginia slavery ripped from proslavery fiction. "A Southern farm is the beau ideal of Communism," he contended in 1850. "It is a joint concern, in which the slave consumes more than the master, of the coarse products, and is far happier, because although the concern may fail, he is always sure of a support; he is only transferred to another master to participate in the profits of another concern." Instead of theorizing Southern cotton production as Ricardian comparative advantage or endorsing free trade, as other Southerners did, Fitzhugh updated and inverted critiques of capitalism by Thomas Carlyle and Karl Marx, contending not only that the class struggle born of moneyed interests was absent in the slave South but also that slavery was a bulwark against the pernicious modernization that poisoned social relations under capitalism.[11]

After the Civil War, pro-Confederate apologists like Edward A. Pollard revived the script of slavery as a benign organic social institution, viewing the prewar past through a mnemonic fog. Pollard contended that slavery was a blessing for the South and the nation, which "bestowed on the world's commerce in a half-century a single product whose annual value was two hundred millions of dollars." Enslaved people had been released from slavery's supposedly beneficial social relations too early, Pollard claimed, and his elegy to the moribund slave society was a synthesis of Southern political economists like Dew, polemicists like Fitzhugh, and authors like William Gilmore Simms.[12]

Emancipationists like William Wells Brown and George Washington Williams vigorously disputed that economic analysis and the recrudescent racism it sanctioned. But Brown updated rather than challenged the economic consensus formed by prewar historians like Bancroft. In *The Negro in the American Rebellion* (1867),

Brown contended that "the vast wealth realized by the slave-holder had made [Confederates] feel that the South was independent of the rest of the world," and that "prosperity had made him giddy" and arrogant. Brown's vindication of the Union cause underscored the moral rightness of fighting against slavery, arguing that Confederates "dreamed of perpetuating slavery, though all history shows the decline of the system as industry, commerce, and knowledge advance."[13] Williams argued against racism and for an emancipationist script yet agreed that plantation agriculture was morally corrosive. "Cotton and cupidity led captive the reason of the South," he argued, "and, once more joined to their idols, the slave-holders no longer heard the voice of prudence or justice in the slave marts of their 'section.'"[14]

The centrality of the Civil War and its fiercely contested memory obscured slavery's economics. For instance, American historians refused to articulate responses to the contentions of European political economists such as Marx, who argued that slaveholders were capitalists. "The price paid for a slave is nothing but the anticipated and capitalized surplus-value or profit, which is to be ground out of him," Marx argued in volume three of *Capital* (1894). It would take half a century for historians to argue that an enslaved person was as much a part of a capitalist system as a power loom or a cotton bill of exchange.[15]

Economics as a discipline began to coalesce in the 1890s, and historians began to use quantitative analyses to supplement traditional manuscript sources. By the close of the nineteenth century, the Harvard-trained W. E. B. Du Bois framed American slavery in terms of transatlantic markets and economic processes. But his conclusions regarding the economics of American slavery did not differ substantially from those of his predecessors. A student of prominent German economists including Gustav von Schmoller and Adolph Wagner, Du Bois's dissertation and book *Suppression of the African Slave-Trade to the United States of America* (1896) argued that the rise of the nineteenth-century cotton South was related to the rise of industrial England. "The development of Southern slavery has heretofore been viewed so exclusively from the ethical and social standpoint," Du Bois contended, "that we are apt to forget its close and indissoluble connection with the world's cotton market." But the development of that linkage was fatal. The "whole South began to extend its cotton culture, and more and more to throw its whole energy into this one staple." That arrested "economic development along proper industrial lines" and the resulting backward system was toppled solely by civil war.[16] Du Bois influenced scholars outside of the United States, including C. L. R. James, whose *The Black Jacobins: Toussaint L'Ouverture and the San Domingo Revolution* (1938) was a Marxian class analysis of the Haitian Revolution. But as an African American intellectual and critic of the Jim Crow South, Du Bois stood outside the mainstream of the American academy.

Professional historians of the early twentieth century continued to argue that slavery was a cultural rather than an economic institution. Ulrich B. Phillips's scholarship shaped the field for a generation. He argued in *American Negro Slavery* (1918) and elsewhere that slavery was an unprofitable schoolhouse of bondage in which whites instructed as they enslaved inferior African-descended people.[17] Phillips was deeply interested in questions of economy, and his *Life and Labor in the Old South* (1929) analyzed such things as slave prices over geographic space and time, comparing them to cotton prices. But Phillips's lasting contribution was a narrative of slavery as fundamentally benign and the South as a backward economy.

In economic terms, Phillips contended that Southern plantations were inefficient by the standards of free labor enterprises and that financial panics inevitably burdened planters with bad debt. "The slaveholding regime kept money scarce, population sparse and land values accordingly low," he contended. "It restricted the opportunities of many men of both races." That interpretation aligned with nineteenth-century political economists and reflected the view that cities and factories were artifacts of capitalism and modern economic development. "Plantation slavery had in strictly business aspects at least as many drawbacks as it had attractions," Phillips explained. "But in the large it was less a business than a life; it made fewer fortunes than it made men."[18] He argued that "the plantation system . . . was less dependent upon slavery than slavery was upon it," which was the lynchpin of the argument that slaveholders chose an inefficient economic regime for social reasons.[19] His interpretations of plantation life influenced a number of contemporary historians, including Charles S. Davis, Edwin Adams Davis, Ralph B. Flanders, and Weymouth T. Jordan.[20]

Phillips's New South school, led by led by William A. Dunning, had its contemporary critics, such as African American scholars like the Harvard-trained Carter G. Woodson. Woodson castigated slavery but agreed with Phillips's economic analysis. In *The Negro in Our History* (1922), Woodson contended that slavery was "the undoing of the South": "It prevented the growth of towns and cities and shut out manufacturing, leaving the South dependent on the North or European nations." Slavery promoted "unwise investments, and overstocking the markets with southern staple crops . . . caused a scarcity of money, cheapened land, and confined the South to one-crop farming at the expense of its undeveloped resources."[21] Like Du Bois, Woodson's main focus was on rewriting American history to include African American people and their contributions.

The Phillips school's economic analysis did not go unchallenged. North Carolina native William E. Dodd, a University of Chicago professor who also served as US ambassador to Germany (1933-37), termed the cotton South a "new economic El Dorado" that repaid investments in lands and slaves handsomely.[22] Lewis Cecil Gray's two-volume *History of Agriculture in the Southern United States to 1860* (1933) used statistics and economic analyses to argue that slave-based commercial agriculture was viable and that slavery benefited the South's agriculture rather than injured it.[23] But the popularity of Phillips's work and its narrative effectiveness dulled the influence of Dodd and Gray's work. When University of Kentucky professor Clement Eaton published his first edition of *A History of the Old South* in 1949, he relied on Gray's economic contentions, but he reverted to Phillips's findings in a revision published in 1966.[24] Gray's conclusions and methods influenced scholars like Joseph C. Robert, Robert R. Russel, and Thomas P. Govan.[25]

Another Phillips critic used a business history approach. Frederic Bancroft argued in *Slave-Trading in the Old South* (1931) that slavery was dependent on an interstate slave trade that splintered families and made slave traders lots of money, and that their wealth conferred prestige and social acceptance that Phillips had denied they had achieved.[26] As the historian John David Smith pointed out in a 1981 review of Phillips's scholarly legacy, Bancroft accused Phillips of "failing to recognize in his own evidence proof of large-scale slave breeding from which the planters earned immense profits."[27] Like Phillips, Bancroft was trained at Columbia University. He contended that slave traders were fundamentally businessmen, and he cataloged their great variety and scope of operations. Bancroft focused on the economic culture of slave trading rather than the economics of slavery or why the trade was so profitable and appealing to so many businessmen.

While Americanists churned over the Phillips thesis, scholars outside the United States developed an influential economic analysis of New World slavery. Few American historians of slavery initially responded. Oxford-trained Eric E. Williams argued in *Capitalism and Slavery* (1944) that an emerging class of free-trade capitalists brought the terrible drama of Atlantic world slavery to an end, and that American slavery and abolition were best explained in terms of economics rather than race. Instead of British moral fiber, English manufacturing interests that had once supported the slave trade (some of which sourced their cotton from the American South) prevailed over an entrenched West Indian mercantile sugar interest that had held sway in the eighteenth century. C. L. R. James and Lowell Joseph Ragatz influenced Williams. He used Phillips's interpretation of United States slavery without challenging it directly, although he rejected the paternalist argument. A Trinidadian, Williams taught at Howard University in Washington, DC, and eventually became Trinidad and Tobago's prime minister. His legacy included spurring a debate concerning the economics of slavery and the transatlantic slave trade. But despite comparative studies like Frank Tannenbaum's *Slave and Citizen* (1946), that debate did not mature among American historians until the 1970s.[28]

In the 1950s, midcentury historians stormed the Phillips school. Kenneth M. Stampp led a revision with *The Peculiar In-*

stitution (1956), which argued that plantations were profit-making enterprises that relied on credit and exchange. "The expectation of profits from staple production, not the limitations of slavery, led to specialization rather than diversification," Stampp argued. Nor was slavery inherently inefficient as a labor system. "Slavery's economic critics," he charged, "overlooked the fact that physical coercion, or the threat of it, proved to be a rather effective incentive" to work, as did small rewards or incentives.[29]

Economists endorsed Stampp's contentions with new and substantial statistical methods. Yet the cliometricians—history's economists—initially favored elegance, which confined historical questions to measurable data limited to the nineteenth-century American South. In an influential 1958 article that was subsequently enlarged and published as *The Economics of Slavery and Other Studies in Econometric History* (1964), Harvard-trained economists Alfred H. Conrad and John R. Meyer used econometric calculations to argue that the South's staple crop economy was a profitable use of its resources, especially in the 1850s. Conrad and Meyer used neoclassical economic models and included prices of slaves and cotton, worker productivity, enslaved people's life expectancy and reproduction rates, and the costs of slave ownership. They contended that the allocation of slave labor from less labor-intensive regions of the South to sites of intensive staple crop production complemented the efficient staple crop regimes of the lower South. Along with Douglas C. North and Donald Gordon, they pioneered cliometrics. Economic historians like North investigated the cotton economy's growth, arguing that the "enormous comparative advantage of cotton" shaped Southern development.[30]

Cliometrics promised a way to objectively measure historical data and weigh competing contentions. Economic historians confirmed through quantitative analyses that prices for slaves rose along with populations, and that high profits from cotton justified specialization rather than pointing to a disadvantage from a lack of diversification. But econometrics did not sweep away disagreement. John E. Moes contended in 1960 that Southern investment patterns sucked up the South's limited internal financing capabilities.

Douglas F. Dowd, Robert Fogel, Edward Saraydar, Richard Sutch, Harold Woodman, and Yasukichi Yasuba extended, tested, and critiqued Conrad and Meyer's cliometric studies of slavery. Their work expanded interest in American economic history while it invited controversy.[31]

In the 1960s, as the era of the long Civil Rights movement was taking shape, analyses of the economics of American slavery clashed with arguments concerning its culture. Methodological disagreements deepened between cultural historians, who retrieved a past that seemed deeply relevant to the Civil Rights movement, and cliometricians, whose methods held the allure of scientific accuracy. The conflict occurred at precisely the moment when the United States was undergoing one of the most profound social changes in a century. The stakes were high: if slave labor camps had been profitable, then enslaved workers ostensibly complied; if on the other hand planters failed to turn a profit, slave resistance could be seen as the reason. Rising historians like Eugene Genovese explored slaveholding culture and concluded that it was an impediment to capitalist development.[32]

A confluence of developments within the historical profession shaped that conversation. Economists branching into history had a kinship with the new social history and new labor history of the 1960s, which investigated broad processes and deep structures. Those movements were influenced by the Annales school, which broadened the range of human activity suitable for historical study, and by British historians like E. P. Thompson. Charles Dew suggested an alternative to the emerging debate by investigating nonagricultural slavery. New Left and new labor historians like Robert Starobin examined enslaved people in factory settings, arguing that slavery was perfectly compatible with recognizably capitalist processes in the United States, including industrial development. Scholars such as Barrington Moore contended that slave ownership obstructed democracy rather than capitalism, slaveholders being dependent on the Industrial Revolution for their markets.[33]

A fault line quickly emerged between cultural and econometric analyses of the economy of slavery in the Old South. The new social history endorsed econometric analyses, but when it came to the sensitive issue of American slavery, cliometricians' preference for theoretical elegance and measurable functions ran afoul of a robust historiography detailing African American culture and enslaved people's strategies. Robert Fogel and Stanley Engerman's *Time on the Cross: The Economics of Negro Slavery* (1974) was at the center of much of that disagreement. They argued that slaveholders understood economic incentives and drove workers to be more productive than free laborers. Consequently, the plantation complex paid substantially higher returns than free labor farms, and enslaved Americans were taller and lived longer than their Caribbean counterparts.[34] The book received popular attention and then sharp criticism, including a book by fellow econometrists Paul A. David, Herbert G. Gutman, Richard Sutch, Peter Temin, and Gavin Wright, which pointed out errors. The new labor historian Gutman countered in particular that violence was slavery's great economizer: sticks accomplished what carrots could not.[35]

Amid that debate, Eugene Genovese argued in *Roll, Jordan, Roll: The World the Slaves Made* (1974) that sociology explained slaveholders' apparent economic shortcomings. He used Antonio Gramsci's theory of cultural hegemony to explain American slavery, arguing that its essence was the ephemeral contests between masters and slaves. He endorsed Ulrich B. Phillips's view of slavery as fundamentally unprofitable and paternalistic but rejected the Phillips school's racism. Genovese contended that large slaveholders were at best backward-looking or prebourgeois capitalists; they desired money, but the plantation regime of accommodation and resistance prevented it. He further claimed that enslaved people were largely responsible for arresting capitalist progress. Genovese's thesis also vindicated much of the prevailing Civil War historiography while giving enslaved Americans the kind of agency that labor historians saw in industrial workers. *Roll, Jordan, Roll*'s success indicated that cliometricians could ignore culture at their peril. Perhaps a measure of how slavery had risen in importance in American historical studies, both *Time on the Cross* and *Roll, Jordan, Roll* shared Columbia University's Bancroft Prize for 1975.[36]

Economic historians took up Genovese's challenge by accounting for nineteenth-century American culture. Claudia Goldin and Gavin Wright used econometric analyses to challenge long-held views concerning the elasticity and profitability of slave labor, but they did so by scrupulously accounting for historical contexts. Goldin trained under Fogel, and her *Urban Slavery in the American South, 1820–1860: A Quantitative History* (1976) argued that urban slavery and industrial slavery competed successfully with free labor, that cities were not the enemies of slaveholders, and that factory work was compatible with slave labor. Wright's *The Political Economy of the Cotton South: Households, Markets, and Wealth in the Nineteenth Century* (1978) contended that slave-based cotton agriculture was profitable but not optimal, and that slave-based agriculture thrived on economies of scale. Wright investigated different regions over time and concluded that slavery was sustainable and would not have ended except for an external force such as the Civil War. His focus on the postwar South broadened in *Old South, New South: Revolutions in the Southern Economy since the Civil War* (1996), in which he echoed Roger L. Ransom and Richard Sutch's concern, expressed eighteen years earlier in *One Kind of Freedom: The Economic Consequences of Emancipation*, over the economic lives of ex-slaves. Other economic historians pursuing similar lines of inquiry included Ralph V. Anderson, Fred Bateman, Heywood Fleisig, Robert E. Gallman, Laurence J. Kotlikoff, Robert A. Margo, Donald Schaefer, Mark D. Schmitz, Richard H. Steckel, and Thomas Weiss. Yet cliometricians never did form a consensus regarding slavery's economics. Bateman and Weiss, for instance, argued in *Deplorable Scarcity* (1981) that investments in slaves and lands, along with a lack of diversification, hamstrung modern development in the Old South. Herbert Gutman argued that African American families were particularly resilient even during a prolonged demographic catastrophe. Stanley Engerman crossed geographic borders and situated American slavery in a comparative context.[37]

By the late 1970s, historians could no longer ignore Eric Williams's work even if they disagreed, and the economics of American slavery became part of a wider conversation concerning the scope of New World slavery since the fifteenth century. Philip D. Curtin's *The Atlantic Slave Trade: A Census* (1969) inaugurated a debate over the numbers of captives shipped from African shores to the Americas and beyond, a debate joined by Roger Anstey, William Darity Jr., Seymour Drescher, Stanley Engerman, J. E. Inikori, Paul E. Lovejoy, and James A. Rawley, among others. As the *numbers game* developed, it deepened into slaving's effects on African societies, enslavers' political and economic strategies, and the African diaspora—topics that Africanists had explored previously but that received renewed interest from scholars like Walter Rodney. Scholarship on the economics of Caribbean slavery flourished, exemplified by Bancroft Prize-winning *Slave Population and Economy in Jamaica,* by Barry W. Higman (1977). In the process, Williams's *Capitalism and Slavery* received renewed attention as scholars debated slavery in relation to capitalism. Rather than the parent of freedom, capitalism suddenly seemed connected to the development of Atlantic world slavery.[38]

Within the subfield of US slavery, that contention seemed controversial. By the 1980s, the Civil Rights era had ebbed and a pro-business conservatism was ascending in the United States. The economics of American slavery became a counternarrative to the tenets of modern conservatism, which held that deregulation boosted entrepreneurship and that growth would benefit all. Against that view, nineteenth-century slaveholders became object lessons in capitalist excess and greed and a cautionary tale when it came to privatizing returns and socializing risks. James Oakes's *The Ruling Race: A History of American Slaveholders* (1982) argued that middling, migrating slaveholders were petty capitalists. Eugene Genovese and Elizabeth Fox-Genovese countered with *Fruits of Merchant Capital: Slavery and Bourgeois Property in the Rise and Expansion of Capitalism* (1983), arguing that like prerevolutionary France, the nineteenth-century slave South was "a bastard child of merchant capital and developed as a noncapitalist society increasingly antagonistic to, but inseparable from, the bourgeois world that sired it." The Genoveses used an international approach to support the thesis that slaveholders' commitments to slavery arrested modern economic growth, and their interpretation influenced scholars of the early American republic and Civil War such as John Ashworth.[39]

Scholars investigating the economics of slavery outside the United States context were less interested in that debate than in how systems of slavery and slaving ramified through the early modern world. Sidney Mintz's *Sweetness and Power: The Place of Sugar in Modern History* (1985) and Joseph C. Miller's magisterial *Way of Death: Merchant Capitalism and the Angolan Slave Trade* (1988) detailed the rise of slavery's capitalism in its global configurations on modern trajectories. World slavery scholar Igor Kopytoff theorized slavery's commodification, and Dale Tomich argued that modern technology ushered in a "second slavery." Critiquing a divide between Americanists and others, David Brion Davis urged Americanists to look at "the big picture" and away from a nationalist historiography with the Civil War as its center of gravity.[40] Robin Blackburn's *The Making of New World Slavery: From the Baroque to the Modern* (1996) credited commercial strategies rather that imperial dictates with the rise of a slave labor complex in the Americas, which generated ideas of race as part of the modern world. Blackburn explained the development of slave societies in the Americas as a primitive accumulation of capital necessary for the Industrial Revolution in England. Her rich synthesis drew the British colonies and early United States into that epochal historical drama.[41] Meanwhile, scholars like David Eltis and David Richardson reached the culmination of the *numbers game* in a database called *Slave Voyages: The Trans-Atlantic Slave Trade,* published on CD-ROM in 1999 and since digitized, expanded, and made available to the public online.[42] In that broad frame, the United States was far from being exceptional. Eltis contended that "any differences, between U.S. and non-U.S. regions" in the booming Atlantic complex of the nineteenth century, "will be matters of emphasis rather than substance."[43] In other words, the United States was part of a broader process of modern development.

Historians of colonial North America reached similar conclusions. Allan Kulikoff's *Tobacco and Slaves: The Development of Southern Cultures in the Chesapeake* (1986) linked culture to quantitative analyses, owing much to Goldin and Wright's econometrics and the wide angle of transatlantic slave trade scholarship. A flourishing of scholarship on slavery or touching the colonial Chesapeake included some of the most influential historians of early America—Blackburn, Davis, T. H. Breen, Lois Green Carr, Jack P. Greene, Philip D. Morgan, and Lorena S. Walsh, among others.[44] Comparative studies also shed light on US slavery from outside the national frame. Peter Kolchin's *Unfree Labor: American Slavery and Russian Serfdom* (1987) and Shearer Davis Bowman's *Masters and Lords: Mid-Nineteenth-Century U.S. Planters and Prussian Junkers* (1993) each delved into the structure of two slave societies.[45]

In the late 1980s, historians of North America began to detail enslaved people's forced migration and not merely slaveholder migration. Michael Tadman's *Speculators and Slaves: Masters, Traders, and Slaves in the Old South* (1989) quantified the domestic slave trade and analyzed the slave market using quantitative methods akin to Kotlikoff, Peter Passell, and Wright. In the 1990s, scholars such as Jonathan Pritchett used econometric analyses to detail the demographics of captives transported in the interstate slave trade.[46] As work on the domestic slave trade flourished, econometric studies of other areas of African American slavery challenged earlier economic contentions and paid close attention to anthropometrics. Robert Fogel updated the thesis of *Time on the Cross* in *Without Consent or Contract: The Rise and Fall of American Slavery* (1989), restating the contention that slavery was efficient, profitable, and capitalistic, but tempering *Time on the Cross*'s arguments and adding a new section on abolitionism. Fogel and fellow cliometrician Douglass C. North won the 1993 Nobel Prize in Economic Sciences for their achievements in economic history.[47]

Looking beyond plantation economics, Walter Johnson contended that the market economy had a Southern flavor. *Soul by Soul: Life Inside the Antebellum Slave Market* (1999) argued that the domestic slave trade was at the center of Southern life rather than on its peripheries. Enslaved people exercised some sway in the auction theater shaping their sales, but slaveholders constructed ideas of race and honor out of how they bought and sold and consumed slaves. Edward E. Baptist, Steven Deyle, Robert Gudmestad, David Lightner, and Daina Ramey Berry, among others, deepened an analysis of slave trading that illustrated its connections to the broader process of slavery's market development.[48] That flourishing scholarship on enslaved people's mobility complemented one of the crowning achievements of the long Civil Rights-era slavery studies: a historicization of stages of slavery's development with migration at the center, exemplified by Ira Berlin's Bancroft Prize-winning *Many Thousands Gone: The First Two Centuries of Slavery in North America* (1998). It situated Southern slavery in a much larger and more geographically expansive process. At the same time, scholars like Ronald Bailey followed chains of supply out of the South.[49]

In the 1990s, economic historians of North American slavery such as Peter Coclanis, James L. Huston, and John Majewski probed new problems that persisted within a national frame, such as why the slave South seemed to grow less robustly than other parts of the United States east of the Mississippi River between 1815 and 1860, which could also explain the causes of the American Civil War.[50] Responding to Fogel, econometric studies revised slavery's anthropometrics, including estimates of nutrition and height of enslaved people, and rethought the seeming burden of slave ownership compared with the costs of turnover.[51] Economic histories seemed to confirm that slaveholders were modernizers who kept democracy rather than capitalism at bay. But that system also seemed to be dividing against itself—a major cause of the Civil War.[52]

In the post-Civil Rights era, the economic history of American slavery increasingly became allied with the study of capitalism, modern development, and globalization. By the first decade of the twenty-first century, historians were less worried about a strict definition of capitalism than the vibrancy of exchange systems that flourished in the modern world. Slavery and slaving were at the center rather than the outskirts.[53] Scholars of capitalism since Fernand Braudel, including Ian Baucom, Marcus Rediker, and Immanuel Wallerstein, explained capitalism as a broad and indeterminate historical process of commercialization.[54] Debates that turned on Marxian or other definitions of capitalism receded in importance as Americanists like Anthony E. Kaye, Seth Rockman, Joshua Rothman, Amy Dru Stanley, and Stephanie Smallwood contended that American capitalism was not only consistent with unfree labor, that it depended on it.[55] Econometric analyses of American slavery by scholars including Shawn Cole, Bradley T. Ewing, Bonnie Martin, Mark Thornton, and Mark A. Yanochik looked in places historians had heretofore largely ignored, like railroad development and mortgaging.[56] Scholars such as Nelson Lichtenstein recovered a usable past from such history, comparing eighteenth-century merchant capitalism to twenty-first-century globalized supply chains that hide unfree labor.[57]

In the 2010s, the economics of American slavery lurched out of the national frame, as historians of slavery's capitalism made robust claims as to slavery's importance in the growth of capitalism, finance, and imperialism. Joseph C. Miller contended that antebellum United States slavery was novel in world history because of the peculiarities of its history: most enslaved people were English-speaking and native born. Slaveholders were full-fledged participants in a vibrant democratic culture, even if beholden to far-off lenders and customers of far-off factories. Most slaveries had no equivalent concept of race, and most enslavers were not the political insiders that American slaveholders were. Such insights came in the context of the Great Recession of the early twenty-first century, which stemmed optimism in unregulated economic growth and further eroded American exceptionalism.

The field was reshaped by scholars of a new history of capitalism whose work revised earlier understandings of the economics of slavery. Walter Johnson's *River of Dark Dreams: Slavery and Empire in the Cotton Kingdom* (2013) detailed a voracious class of slaveholders eager to expand into Latin America and the Caribbean even as they created a slave security state on a landscape of sexual violence.[58] Slave-based agriculture was central to a global web of finance, and slaveholders had hemispheric ambitions. Edward E. Baptist's *The Half Has Never Been Told: Slavery and the Making of American Capitalism* (2014) argued that slavery's capitalism was the robust center of American economic growth and innovation, and that "the commodification and suffering of forced labor of African

Americans is what made the United States powerful and rich."[59] Such claims echoed nineteenth-century abolitionists' understandings of the reasons and motivations of slaveholders. But historians explained the nuts and bolts of a process scarcely comprehended at the time, including chains of finance and trajectories of people. The hidden engine of modern economic growth was the African-descended family and the Black bodies working in the field or abstracted in debt instruments that coursed through the arteries of transatlantic trade.[60]

Sven Beckert's *Empire of Cotton: A Global History* (2014) connected the Southern cotton plantation system to the early modern European state's transformation toward global capitalism. Focusing on commodity chains, Beckert advanced a coherent narrative of slavery as a vital element in capitalism's expansion from the sixteenth to the nineteenth centuries.[61] A collection of essays on *Slavery's Capitalism,* edited by Beckert and Rockman in 2016, solidified the new consensus that global capitalism depended on commodity chains underwritten by enslaved Africans.[62] Studies like Caitlin Rosenthal's *Accounting for Slavery: Masters and Management* (2018) showed roots of supposedly modern industrial management in eighteenth- and nineteenth-century plantation management. Meanwhile, Alexandra J. Finley's *An Intimate Economy: Enslaved Women, Work, and America's Domestic Slave Trade* (2020) and Justene Hill Edwards's *Unfree Markets: The Slaves' Economy and the Rise of Capitalism in South Carolina* (2021) revealed slavery's capitalism from the ground up, in enslaved capitalists and female participants in slavery's capitalism, creating a more robust framework for understanding what capitalism means as much as earlier work explained capitalism's relationship to slavery.[63] And controversy over the *New York Times*'s "1619 Project," which included the leading contentions regarding slavery made by scholars of the history of capitalism, showed that this is a live public debate.[64]

The German physicist Max Planck wryly observed that science proceeds funeral by funeral, and the historiography of American slavery is no different. Interpretations have changed according to social contexts and institutional imperatives. But all that change is incremental. In the 2000s, scholars continued to publish provocative assessments of slavery's economy within a regional or national frame with the Civil War at the center.[65] The consensus that emerged in the 2010s has extended that revision to take in slavery's connection to the growth of global capitalism. Nineteenth-century North American slaveholders seem to have been capitalists, democrats, entrepreneurs, and innovators, and their prime commodities were cotton lint and the bodies of African-descended Americans compelled to produce it. Chains of cotton and credit extended far from the punishing fields and canebrakes where enslaved people toiled. Slavery's capitalism had global ramifications. Enslaved people paid the price of slaveholders' heartless business calculations with shortened lives, shattered families, and miserable living conditions, driven to toil endlessly and suffer physical privations, displacements, and the social, sexual, and personal violence of a culture of exploitation and intergenerational theft. They responded with resiliency and creativity, exercising considerable ingenuity under severe constraints.

NOTES

1. W. Johnson, *River of Dark Dreams;* Baptist, *Half Has Never Been Told;* J. Rothman, *Flush Times;* Rockman, *Scraping By.* The author thanks Christopher F. Jones and W. Caleb McDaniel for the insights they shared with me and the late Joseph C. Miller for publishing *Slavery and Slaving in World History: A Bibliography,* without which this essay would be much poorer.

2. Grimshaw, *History of the United States;* G. Bancroft, *History of the United States.*

3. T. Cooper, *Lectures on the Elements of Political Economy,* 95; Barber, *Economists and Higher Learning;* O'Connor, *Origins of Academic Economics.*

4. Tucker, *Progress of the United States,* 94–95.

5. Tucker, *History of the United States;* Tucker, *Political Economy.*

6. T. Dew, *Review of the Debate,* 55.

7. T. Dew, *Lectures on the Restrictive System,* 10.

8. Stanton cited in Lightner, *Slavery and the Commerce Power,* 102 (third quotation).

9. E. Gray, "'Whisper to him the word 'India.'"

10. W. Phillips, *Speech of Wendell Phillips,* 36.

11. Fitzhugh, *Sociology for the South*, 245-46; Fitzhugh, *Cannibals All!*

12. Pollard, *Lost Cause*, 48-49.

13. W. Brown, *Negro in the American Rebellion*, 51-53.

14. Williams, *History of the Negro Race*, 36.

15. Marx, *Capital*, 3:940.

16. Du Bois, *Suppression of the African Slave-Trade*, 152.

17. U. Phillips, *Slave Economy of the Old South*.

18. U. Phillips, *American Negro Slavery*, 401.

19. U. Phillips, "Decadence of the Plantation System," 37.

20. P. Newman, "Ulrich Bonnell Phillips"; C. Davis, *Cotton Kingdom in Alabama*; E. Davis, *Plantation Life in the Florida Parishes*; Flanders, *Plantation Slavery in Georgia*; W. T. Jordan, *Hugh Davis and His Alabama Plantation*; Sydnor, *Slavery in Mississippi*. See also Elkins, *Slavery*, chapter 1; and J. Smith, "Historiographic Rise, Fall, and Resurrection of Ulrich Bonnell Phillips."

21. Woodson, *Negro in Our History*, 117-18.

22. Dodd, *Cotton Kingdom*, 8.

23. L. Gray, *History of Agriculture*.

24. Eaton, *History of the Old South*.

25. Robert, *Tobacco Kingdom*; Russel, "General Effects of Slavery"; Russel, "Effects of Slavery"; Govan, "Was Plantation Slavery Profitable?"; J. Moore, "Review of Lewis C. Gray's *History of Agriculture*."

26. F. Bancroft, *Slave Trading*.

27. J. Smith, "Historiographic Rise, Fall, and Resurrection," 143.

28. E. Williams, *Capitalism and Slavery*; R. Smith, "Was Slavery Unprofitable?"

29. Stampp, *Peculiar Institution*, 394, 400.

30. North, *Economic Growth of the United States*, 123; Conrad and Meyer, *Economics of Slavery*; Conrad and Meyer, "Economics of Slavery."

31. Moes, "Absorption of Capital in Slave Labor"; Sutch, "Profitability of Ante-Bellum Slavery"; Rothstein, "Cotton Frontier"; Goldin, "Cliometrics and the Nobel."

32. Genovese, *Political Economy of Slavery*.

33. C. Dew, *Ironmaker to the Confederacy*; Starobin, *Industrial Slavery in the Old South*; B. Moore, *Social Origins of Dictatorship and Democracy*; Aitken, *Did Slavery Pay?*

34. Fogel and Engerman, *Time on the Cross*.

35. David et al., *Reckoning with Slavery*; Gutman, *Slavery and the Numbers Game*.

36. Genovese, *Roll, Jordan, Roll*; Gramsci, *Selections from the Prison Notebooks*; Lears, "Concept of Cultural Hegemony."

37. Ransom and Sutch, *One Kind of Freedom*; Kotlikoff, "Structure of Slave Prices in New Orleans"; Bateman and Weiss, *Deplorable Scarcity*; Anderson and Gallman, "Slaves as Fixed Capital"; Schaefer and Schmitz, "Relative Ef-

ficiency of Slave Agriculture"; Schmitz and Schaefer, "Paradox Lost"; *Fleisig,* "*Slavery, the Supply of Agricultural Labor, and* the Industrialization of the South"; Gutman, *Black Family in Slavery and Freedom;* Margo and Steckel, "Heights of American Slaves"; Engerman, "Quantitative and Economic Analyses"; Goldin, *Urban Slavery;* G. Wright, *Old South, New South;* Wright, *Political Economy.*

38. Curtin, *Atlantic Slave Trade;* Thomas and Bean, "Fishers of Men"; Rodney, *How Europe Underdeveloped Africa;* Anstey, *Atlantic Slave Trade;* Inikori, *Forced Migration;* Inikori, "Measuring the Atlantic Slave Trade"; Drescher, *Econocide,* 197-223; Temperley, "Capitalism, Slavery, and Ideology"; Rawley, *Transatlantic Slave Trade;* Lovejoy, "Volume of the Atlantic Slave Trade"; Darity, "Numbers Game"; D. Davis, *Problem of Slavery;* Solow and Engerman, *British Capitalism;* J. Miller, "Numbers, Origins, and Destinations of Slaves," 381; Higman, *Slave Population and Economy.*

39. Oakes, *Ruling Race;* Genovese and Fox-Genovese, *Fruits of Merchant Capital,* 5; Genovese and Fox-Genovese, "Slavery, Economic Development, and the Law"; Ashworth, *Slavery, Capitalism, and Politics,* vol. 1.

40. Mintz, *Sweetness and Power;* J. Miller, *Way of Death;* Kopytoff, "Cultural Biography of Things"; Tomich, "'Second Slavery'"; Kolchin, "Big Picture," 467.

41. Blackburn, *Making of New World Slavery.*

42. Eltis, "Volume and Structure"; Inikori, *Africans and the Industrial Revolution;* Eltis et al., *Trans-Atlantic Slave Trade: A Database on CD-ROM.*

43. Eltis, *Economic Growth,* 186-87.

44. Kulikoff, *Tobacco and Slaves;* Galenson, "Labor Market Behavior"; Sweig, "Importation of African Slaves"; Bailyn, "Slavery and Population Growth"; T. H. Breen, *Tobacco Culture;* McCusker and Menard, *Economy of British America;* Menard, Carr, and Walsh, "Small Planter's Profits"; Walsh, "Plantation Management"; D. Davis, *Slavery in the Colonial Chesapeake;* Blackburn, *Overthrow of Colonial Slavery;* J. Greene, *Pursuits of Happiness;* Carr, Morgan, and Russo, *Colonial Chesapeake Society.*

45. Kolchin, *Unfree Labor;* Bowman, *Masters and Lords.*

46. Tadman, *Speculators and Slaves;* Kotlikoff and Pinera, "Old South's Stake"; Freudenberger and Pritchett, "Domestic United States Slave Trade"; Pritchett and Freudenberger, "Peculiar Sample."

47. Coelho and McGuire, "Diets Versus Diseases."

48. Baptist, "'Cuffy,' 'Fancy Maids,' and 'One-Eyed Men'"; Deyle, *Carry Me Back;* Gudmestad, *Troublesome Commerce;* Berry, *Price for Their Pound of Flesh;* Lightner, *Slavery and the Commerce Power;* Bergad, "American Slave Markets."

49. Berlin, *Many Thousands Gone;* Berlin, *Generations of Captivity;* R. Bailey, "'Those Valuable People'"; Kennedy, "Hidden Economy of Slavery."

50. Coclanis, "Tracking the Economic Divergence"; Majewski, "Who Fi-

nanced the Transportation Revolution?"; Majewski, *House Dividing;* Huston, *Calculating the Value;* Anderson and Gallman, "Slaves as Fixed Capital"; Gallman, "Slavery and Southern Economic Growth."

51. Komlos and Alecke, "Economics of Antebellum Slave Heights"; Hanes, "Turnover Cost."

52. Egerton, "Markets without a Market Revolution"; Coclanis, "How the Low Country was Taken to Task"; Andrews and Christy, "Profitability of Slavery"; Dunaway, *First American Frontier;* Kulikoff, *Agrarian Origins.*

53. Rockman, "Unfree Origins"; Rockman, "What Makes the History of Capitalism Newsworthy?"

54. Braudel, *Capitalism and Material Life;* Wallerstein, *Capitalist Agriculture;* Rediker, *Slave Ship;* Tomich, "Wealth of Empire"; Baucom, *Specters of the Atlantic;* Wallerstein, *Modern World-System IV;* J. Miller, *Problem of Slavery as History;* Kaye, "Second Slavery."

55. Dattel, *Cotton and Race;* Deyle, "Rethinking the Slave Trade"; Egerton, "Slaves to the Marketplace"; Follett, *Sugar Masters;* Rockman, *Scraping By;* Rothman, *Flush Times;* Schermerhorn, "Capitalism's Captives"; Lynd and Waldstreicher, "Free Trade, Sovereignty, and Slavery"; Stanley, "Wages, Sin, and Slavery"; Smallwood, *Saltwater Slavery;* Guterl, *American Mediterranean.*

56. Yanochik, Thornton, and Ewing, "Railroad Construction and Antebellum Slave Prices"; S. Cole, "Capitalism and Freedom"; Dari-Mattiacci, "Slavery and Information"; Acemoglu and Wolitzky, "Economics of Labor Coercion"; B. Martin, "Slavery's Invisible Engine."

57. Lichtenstein, "Return of Merchant Capitalism."

58. W. Johnson, *River of Dark Dreams.*

59. Baptist, *Half Has Never Been Told,* xxi.

60. J. Miller, *Problem of Slavery as History;* Schermerhorn, *Business of Slavery;* Rothman, *Flush Times;* Baptist, *Half Has Never Been Told;* Boodry, *Slavery's Capitalism;* Rockman, "Slavery and Abolition along the Blackstone."

61. Beckert, *Empire of Cotton.*

62. Beckert and Rockman, *Slavery's Capitalism.*

63. Rosenthal, *Accounting for Slavery;* Finley, *Intimate Economy;* J. Edwards, *Unfree Markets.*

64. Serwer, "Fight Over the 1619 Project."

65. Ashworth, *Slavery, Capitalism, and Politics,* vol. 2; Scarborough, *Allstons of Chicora Wood.*

CHAPTER THREE

American Slavery and Politics

RYAN A. QUINTANA

Slavery has long been central to the broader history of the nation's political past. From the nation's founding through post-Civil War reconstruction, slavery and slaves lay at the heart of American politics. Partisan identity and conflict, foreign relations, economic policy, the warp and woof of political participation, and the contours of citizenship itself were all animated, to varying degrees, by the peculiar institution. Most significantly, historians have struggled for generations to understand the convulsive events that led the nation to Civil War. They gazed upon the battlefields of times past and saw the tragedy of hundreds of thousands of men killed in the ferocious fighting that consumed the nation, the glory and joy of millions of African American men and women fighting for and experiencing freedom for the first time, and the humiliation of an entire region's worldview and economic standing shattered. Historians strove to understand why and how such tumultuousness came to pass.

The sublimity of such an event exerted a type of gravitational pull on the historiography of American politics and slavery, defining and directing scholarship for over a century. To understand this historiography, one must confront the vast and often-bitter scholarship on Civil War causation, for it was there that historians located the politics of slavery, and it is in the face of such scholarship that a new generation of historians has reassessed slavery's political history.

Because so much of the historiography of American politics and slavery revolves around the sectional conflict and the coming of the Civil War, many of the debates' central issues were formulated not with the professionalization of the field, but rather took shape in the midst of the tension that consumed the nation in the decades preceding the war. Would-be Republicans, abolitionists—both moderate and radical—and future Confederates all made wide-reaching claims about the political history and trajectory of the still-young nation in the antebellum period. These assertions reflected the varied perspectives that individuals held regarding the institution of slavery, but more importantly, they represented decisive articulations of the political, ideological, social, and economic reasoning for civil war, and would thus come to shape the immediate memorialization of the conflict and much of the historical work that followed.

Loudest among these voices were the radical abolitionists. Angered not simply by the actions of slaveholders but also by what they perceived as the federal government's unflinching support of slavery and slaveholders, they came to believe that the Constitution was a proslavery document forged as a compromise between freedom's ideological champions and slavery's entrenched defenders. This conciliation, they believed, had permanently sullied the nation's founding document, and in fact had immediately undermined the American liberal experiment. Subsequently, radical abolitionists like William Lloyd Garrison, Frederick Douglass, and Wendell Phillips questioned the propriety of participating in a government that they believed was designed to protect the institution of slavery. More importantly, abolitionists crafted a national narrative within which they found themselves—one in which the institution of slavery seemed not to wither but to thrive.[1]

In defense of this position, Wendell Phillips penned what might be considered one of the first historical interpretations of the Constitutional Convention that placed slavery at the center of the document's creation, *The Constitution, a Proslavery Compact* (1844). Writing in the midst of the radical antislavery movement's rise, Phillips argued not with slavery's advocates but rather with his more moderate antislavery peers who believed that the Constitution only seemed to tolerate slavery but did not protect it. Examining Madison's papers and the Constitution itself, Phillips argued that "with deliberate purpose, our fathers bartered honesty for gain, and became partners with tyrants, that they might share in the profits of their tyranny." In other words, radical abolitionists argued that the protection of slavery was not the result of the powerful influence of proslavery Southerners in Congress or in the White House, but was rather the outcome of a self-conscious compromise—a concession to slaveholders for the construction of union. In crafting such an argument, Phillips and the abolitionists not only played a key role in disrupting the peaceful union that many imagined existed in the mid-nineteenth century, but also importantly established significant precedents within the historiography of politics and slavery. The abolitionist critique of the Constitutional Convention removed the Founders, the document they produced, and the union they constructed from the pedestal on which they had theretofore rested, and subsequently disrupted the liberal ethos that rested at the center of the nation's history. By openly denying the Founders' commitment to liberty, radical abolitionists uprooted the Constitution from its central role in America's national narrative, and simultaneously denied that the arc of that narrative necessarily bent toward freedom.[2]

While radicals were busy defaming the entirety of the American experiment, others witnessed the conflict over the future of slavery occurring in their midst not as a failure of the nation, but rather as a struggle between two radically oppositional perspectives on the nation's future and the meaning of its political past. Throughout the 1840s and 1850s, erstwhile Whigs and Democrats, Free Soilers, and the leadership of the newly formed Republican Party in the North, along with proslavery ideologues, planters, and politicians in the South, increasingly came to argue that there existed in the United States "two radically different political systems; the one resting on the basis of servile or slave labor, the other on voluntary labor of freemen." At the heart of this paradigm lay a conceptualization of American political history that would dictate the historiography for nearly a century. Although it varied depending on one's sectional or partisan perspective, the argument established that political parties had long found compromisable positions on the issue of slavery (the Missouri Compromise was consistently held up as example), but that due to the influence of abolitionists, Radical Republicans in the North, or the Slave Power and the Democrats in the South, or simply because of the perceived incompatibility of two increasingly oppositional economic and social systems, the political system—and the future of the republic—was no longer sustainable. By the middle of the 1850s, though individual positions varied widely and individuals still sought compromise, virtually all agreed with William Seward that a violent conflict over the nation's future was inevitable.[3]

In his now-famous 1858 speech on the sectional divide, Seward called the struggle over slavery "an irrepressible conflict between opposing and enduring forces, and it means that the United States must and will, sooner or later, become either entirely a slaveholding nation, or entirely a free-labor nation." The inevitability of conflict between slavery's advocates and opponents would eventually come to be seen as prescient and would shape much of the early historiography, as future historians came to perceive the nineteenth-century politics of slavery as a prelude to war. In this viewing, the nuanced and complicated reality of political contests became compressed as individuals and groups sought to understand and justify their present dilemma. "The history of the Democratic party commits it to the policy of slavery," Seward argued, from its rise in the 1820s through the convulsive events of the 1850s. From Seward's perspective, it was Democrats and not the Founding Fathers who had maintained the institution of slavery. "It has been the Democratic party, and no other agency, which has carried that policy up to its present alarming culmination." To prove his point, Seward highlighted the central events in American political history whereupon Democrats had proven their fealty to the cause of slavery: the *gag rule,* which prevented antislavery petitions from being read in Congress; the annexation of Texas; the Mexican-American War and the question of slavery in the territories acquired in the ensuing peace; the fugitive slave law; and the battle over the Kansas-

Nebraska Act. Seward's analysis of the sectional conflict cast a long shadow over the history of American politics and slavery. Not only did he argue that conflict was irrepressible—an argument that historians would maintain until well into the twentieth century—but he and his Republican allies also made clear the moral urgency of their actions, and placed the conflict over slavery squarely within the realm of politics, fixing the gaze of future historians upon the specific crises that he highlighted in his speech.[4]

Of course, antislavery voices were not the only ones heard in the years leading up to the war. Just a few short months before Seward made the "irrepressible conflict" case to his gathered constituents in Rochester, New York, South Carolina's James Henry Hammond delivered his equally famous proslavery exposition to Congress. Responding to Kansas's admission under the Lecompton Constitution—but also more generally to the rhetoric of free labor and abolition that he and other Southerners saw as increasingly dangerous—Hammond presented a synthesis of what was by then a well-developed proslavery thesis, arguing that the institution of slavery and the plantation economy strengthened the republic, protected society, and provided the only guarantee of political freedom. For Hammond, the South's greatest strength arose "from the harmony of her political and social institutions." This harmony, he argued, "gives her a frame of society, the best in the world, and an extent of political freedom, combined with entire security, such as no other people ever enjoyed upon the face of the earth." Of course, this freedom and security was premised on the subjugation of enslaved African Americans—a truth that Hammond and other proslavery advocates rarely shied away from. In fact, it was this great truth that they believed was explicitly threatened by the rhetoric and actions of radical abolitionists and the Republican Party. As Hammond argued, "in all social systems there must be a class to do the menial duties, to perform the drudgery of life." And the South had "found a race adapted to that purpose to her hand." As Hammond unabashedly explained to his congressional audience, "we use them for our purpose, and call them slaves." More importantly given his congressional setting, Hammond affirmed, "our slaves do not vote. We give them no political power." Hammond compared this with the North, where he and other proslavery Southerners watched the steady stream of immigrants, the angry cries of abolitionists, and the reform movements that sinuously stretched toward the South and imagined not progress but instead the potential downfall of the American republic.[5]

Hammond, Seward, Phillips, and numerous other proslavery advocates, abolitionists, and politicians of every partisan and sectional stripe thus contributed significantly to the historiography of American politics and slavery by establishing the basic parameters through which generations of historians would approach the issues of Civil War causation, slavery, and American politics. They contributed not just the material for research but the lenses through which the conflict would be seen. For generations, historians roundly accepted the notion that the war was inevitable—an *irrepressible conflict.* They embraced the abolitionists' and Republicans' moral certitude and accepted their basic outline of a slave power pushing the nation past compromise and toward war. At the turn of the century, Progressive Era historians, though they altered their narrative to minimize slavery's centrality, continued to accept as truth sectional antagonisms and the notion that the nation was made up of oppositional forces that could not avoid conflict. And when the revisionists—so called because they radically confronted the long-accepted views of Civil War causation, forever altering our perception of antebellum-era politics—challenged these interpretations in the early twentieth century, they attempted to validate the arguments laid forth by former Confederates, arguing that the slavery system was not morally repugnant and that the war was caused not by Southerners but rather by a "blundering generation" of politicians who did nothing to avert a crisis caused by outspoken agitators.[6]

But to the victors went the spoils, and in the decades immediately following the Civil War, historians and partisans of the Union cause perpetuated the narrative of the nation offered by abolitionists and their more moderate Republican allies. As John William Burgess argued in his 1897 work on antebellum politics, *The Middle Period,* "this history must be written by an American and a Northerner, and from the Northern point of view . . . because the victorious party can and will be more liberal, generous, and sympathetic than the vanquished; and because the Northern view is, in the main, the correct view." Importantly, for these postwar historians, the narrative, unlike that crafted by radical abolitionists, was far less pessimistic. In their telling, slavery was essential to the nation's past, but only in its demise. Gone were the excoriations of compromising nineteenth-century politicians, replaced instead by a narrative of a nation bound for freedom, opposed only by the slaveholders' selfish interests. From this perspective, the nation stood on the summit of history: the historian's role was simply to narrate the secular eschatology of freedom. Historians thus thought it their duty to describe the moral rightness of the Union victory in defeating the Southern slave power and of the subsequent trajectory of the nation. To do so, they felt compelled to demonstrate "to the South its error"; to do otherwise would "fail in accomplishing one of the highest works of history, the reconciliation of men to the plans of Providence for their perfection." Importantly, in laying the guilt of slavery at the South's feet, this historical narrative also further distanced the nation and its underlying principles—set apart from the erroneous ways of the South—from any direct contact with unfreedom.[7]

Despite their narrow and slightly biased perspective, these early historians firmly established slavery's centrality within American political history and maintained the intimate connection between the politics of slavery and the onset of civil war. Although much of this work was done early on by memoirists and amateur historians like the Massachusetts senator and later US vice president Henry Wilson, by the end of the century, as the field transitioned to our second historiographical era, professional historians and scholars like Burgess, James Schouler, John Bach McMaster, Hermann Edward Von Holst, and James Ford Rhodes all embraced and reified much of the argument proffered by Seward and the abolitionists. As Rhodes argued, in the decades leading up to the Civil War, "the question of negro slavery engrossed the whole attention of the country. It then became the absorbing controversy in Congress and dominated all political contests." The future of slavery, Rhodes contended, consumed the entire nation, enveloping "every thinking citizen" and growing "to be the paramount political topic discussed in the city mart, the village store, and the artisan's workshop."[8] And yet, despite placing slavery at the center of American political history and the buildup to war, these same historians maintained the narrow geography of slavery, fixing the blame for the Civil War and the guilt of slavery squarely on Southern shoulders. In so doing, they reified the sectionalization of American history and continued to distance the nation from the darker travails of its slaveholding past.[9]

This trend continued with the work done by the Progressive school of historians at the turn of the century. As the field professionalized, leading historians embraced a scientific approach to their research and writing, seeking an *objective* understanding of the past—a method popularized in Germany's leading universities. This new approach to historical research and writing coincided with the rise of nationalism, as American historians, like their peers in Europe, sought to locate and define the unique ethos of the emergent nation-state. The nationalist project in the United States took on many forms, from the annual Los Angeles La Fiesta parade and the staged cultural events at the 1893 World's Columbian Exposition held in Chicago to the discourse of empire and civilization that gripped the nation as the United States crossed the Pacific to bring freedom to the Philippines. In each case—and many others—the nation became overtly associated with whiteness, which was explicitly set apart from racialized *others* and then solidified through cultural reproduction. Just as Columbian Exposition organizers conspicuously omitted African Americans from most of the fair's proceedings, so too the same generation of historians begin to relegate slaves and slavery outside of the nation's narrative. Wrapped in the garb of nationalism and its intrinsic racial presumptions, the emergent generation of Progressive historians offered an analysis of the nation's past that increasingly marginalized the role of slavery. When historians did engage the history of slavery—and many did, focusing primarily on the institution's social and economic history—they were led by historians like Ulrich B. Phillips and William Dunning, who largely echoed the early twentieth century's presumptions of white supremacy. Phillips provided scholars with a view of African Americans and slavery that made the institution seem benign, if outdated and economically backward, while Dunning and his students challenged long-held presumptions about Reconstruction and the post-Civil War South. At the heart of their work lay a tacit approval of white supremacy that decidedly shaped their analysis of the South. More importantly, their work effectively diluted the moral dilemma of slavery within American history, allowing their peers to seek alternative forces at work in the American past.[10]

And so they did. Frederick Jackson Turner, a onetime colleague of Phillips, argued that American exceptionalism emerged not out of the moral contest over slavery but rather through the uniquely American experience of the frontier. Turner made clear his opinion on the more traditionalist narratives of American politics in his oft-quoted critique of the German-born Hermann Von Holst: "in his [Von Holst's] attention to slavery he has lost sight of the fundamental, dominating fact in United States history, the expansion of the United States from the Alleghenies to the Pacific." Turner negated slavery and the experience of the enslaved in pursuit of a narrative that privileged westward movement, the sectionalization of the nation, and the evolutionary experience of the frontier. Turner certainly acknowledged that slavery was an "important incident" in American history, but believed that the institution was insignificant to the real forces that propelled the nation forward, and primarily located it as a force in the sectionalization of the nation. Like so many others, Turner confined slavery to the South and sought to dilute its meaningfulness to the broader scope of American history.[11]

Still, not everyone turned away from the complicated reality of a nation built on slavery. W. E. B. Du Bois offered forth his Harvard dissertation and first manuscript, *The Suppression of the African Slave-Trade* (1896), as a distinct counter to both the more celebratory narratives of the nation's past and those that increasingly marginalized slavery. Completing his work at the end of the nineteenth century, as racial violence crescendoed across the continent and as the Supreme Court validated Jim Crow segregation in *Plessy v. Ferguson*,[12] Du Bois eschewed the language of romanticization common among earlier generations of historians. Instead, his argument picked up where the radical abolitionists left off, subtly damning the nation for maintaining slavery. As the historian Saidiya Hartman has noted, Du Bois could not conceal his "great disappointment" in the events he witnessed all around him. Just as Turner, Phillips, and Dunning embraced the sentiments of their age, so too did Du Bois, only his work bore witness to the dark side of that intellectual and cultural milieu. Observing and mournfully lamenting the violent lynching of thousands of Black men, women, and children across the United States, Du Bois wrote not of the abolitionists' moral successes nor of the nation's progress, but rather of the continual legislative failures and political compromises that led to the ceaseless pillaging of African shores. As Hartman rightly noted, his was not a history of the nation's development and improvement (How could it be with all he continued to witness?) but rather one of disappointment. In Du Bois then, we hear aloud the radical abolitionist whose critical gaze turned on the nation as a whole, not simply the South.[13]

And Du Bois was not alone. Throughout the Progressive Era of American historiography, isolated historians continued to trumpet the centrality of slavery to America's political history, and to criticize those who sought to marginalize its role in the nation's past. Nevertheless, more prominent scholars within the field overshadowed their contributions. Charles Beard was chief among the Progressive historians who limited slavery's role in American politics. For Beard, the primary theme of the American past was the economic conflict between, as he saw it, the two great forces in American history—agrarianism and industrialism. Beard wrote during the economically tumultuous period following World War I, as class conflict, inequality, and a dramatic shift in the nature of work (from farms to factory) inspired Beard to turn a more critical gaze toward the nation's economic history than many of his older peers. He also shined a critical light on the Founding Fathers—condemning them for their self-interested compromises, highlighting the forces that stood to gain in the union's dissolution, and noting the Civil War's inevitability. Yet he was mostly uninterested in slavery's role in the great conflict that he saw at the center of American history. For Beard, plantation agriculture and its bondage-based labor system was but one aspect of agrarianism, and as such, he primarily considered it only in its opposition to industrialism and merchant capitalism. The same was true for Arthur C. Cole, whose closer treatment of the years immediately preceding the war in *The Irrepressible Conflict* (1934) went beyond Beard's narrow economic analysis, yet still argued that slavery was hardly "the crux of the sectional issue." The Progressives then continued to decenter slavery within American political history. They maintained that the nation and its politics was neatly divided into sections, but that these sections were distinguished by their respective commitments to an agrarian or industrial way of life, and not defined by the institution of slavery.[14]

Following in the Progressive's intellectual path, a group of historians led by a young generation of Southern scholars further challenged traditional narratives of antebellum political history, Civil War causation, and slavery's role in American history. Frank Owsley, a distinguished Southern historian, was one of the first to mount a sustained critique of the historiography of Civil War causation in his influential essay "The Irrepressible Conflict," published in 1930. Owsley's argument mirrored Beard's and Cole's, in that he too defined the conflict as one between an industrialized North and an agrarian South. However, he did serve as an important bridge between the Progressives and the emergent revisionist school by directly challenging the presumption of Southern responsibility in the events leading up to the war. Owsley argued that the "Southern historians of the Dunning school" had become "convinced that slavery as a moral issue" was too simple an explanation for the political and social conflict that led to war. Slavery, Owsley opined, only became a part of this conflict as Northern politicians, particularly Whigs, sought to check the South's expanding power. Importantly, he continued, slavery was not even an "essential part of the agrarian civilization of the South," which he argued was primarily made up of nonslaveholding whites—an idea he would expand on in his influential work, *Plain Folk of the Old South* (1949). Owsley's argument reflected the defensive posture prevalent among the new generation of Southern scholars. He argued not only that the South was "conquered by war and humiliated and impoverished by peace" but also that there was a second "conquest of the Southern mind." The efforts of politicians, educators, and historians had been "to remake every Southern opinion, to impose the Northern way of life and thought upon the South," and to "write 'error' across the pages of Southern history which were out of keeping with the Northern legend."[15]

Building off this argument, the revisionists offered an entirely new interpretation of the politics of slavery and Civil War causation. This new, interpretive approach to pre-Civil War politics was born out of the rejection—like Owsley's—of older scholarship that placed too much of the burden of war on Southern slaveholders. More importantly, the revisionists discarded the long-standing presumption that the Civil War was inevitable: revisionist historians began to question fundamentally the historic necessity and moral importance of war as they reeled from the aftermath of one world war while staring down the barrel of another. James G. Randall, Avery O. Craven, Charles Ramsdell, and even Owsley denied the inevitability argument, eschewing the war romanticization and moral sentimentalizing that they believed informed much of the earlier scholarship on Civil War causation. In its place, they argued that the war was in fact a "repressible conflict," brought on only by a "blundering generation" of politicians whose "egocentric sectionalism" and intense "partisanship" escalated tensions and led to a "needless war," which, they argued, was wholly preventable. They contended that irresponsible agitators—radical abolitionists and to a smaller degree fire-eating Southerners—had aroused sectional passions to the point of war, and that politicians had failed to find the compromise positions that had defined much of American political history up to that moment. The revisionists also moved beyond the Progressive argument that the nation was made up of two fundamentally oppositional forces that spiraled headlong into war. Instead, anticipating the move toward consensus within the field, they posited that there was little difference between North and South—that indeed "both northern and southern people in 1861 were alike profoundly attached to the principles of free government. . . . Their ideology was democratic and identical."[16] Rather than focus on broad cultural or economic influences leading to war, the revisionists turned instead to the individual actions (or inactions) of historical actors, and sought the contingency that led to what they claimed was an exceptional moment in American history.[17]

Although there is much to critique in the revisionist argument, it is important to note that these historians simply continued the trend prevalent in so much of the historiography—the minimization of slavery's role in the nation's past. But in forgiving the South for its sins and placing blame for the war largely on the abolitionists, the revisionists reached the historiography's nadir. The subsequent challenge to revisionists that emerged in the post-World War II era was as much a critique of the broad marginalization of slavery in all of American history—and of African Americans throughout the nation—as it was to a singular school of historical thought. The refutation of the revisionist argument, then, turned on its rejection of slavery as a moral cause of the Civil War. That denial that came under increased attack after the end of World War II, as ever more scholars became aware of and incensed by the gross injustice and hypocrisy of race relations in a nation ostensibly dedicated to the principles of freedom. A number of scholars—Arthur Schlesinger Jr. and Bernard DeVoto most notably—summed up the absolute need for historians to confront the evils of the past and not simply note their inevitable passing, as earlier generations had done. DeVoto noted that revisionist history refused to "put itself in the position of saying that any thesis may have been wrong, any cause evil, or any group of men heretical." Schlesinger avowed that "man generally is entangled in insoluble problems," and history "is consequently a tragedy in which we are all involved, whose keynote is anxiety and frustration, not progress and fulfillment." Because, Schlesinger continued, nothing "exists in history to assure us that the great moral dilemmas can be resolved without pain," historians and scholars cannot turn away from the "duty of moral judgment on issues so appalling and inescapable as those involved in human slavery."[18] Whereas DeVoto and Schlesinger passively critiqued revisionist scholarship, others more directly assailed it. Writing to his adviser in 1946, Kenneth Stampp angrily called out the revisionists: "James G. Randall is a damned Negro-hating, abolitionist-baiting doughface. . . . I'm sick of the Randalls, Cravens and other doughfaces who crucify the abolitionists for attacking slavery."[19]

The revisionists, then, were at the heart of a significant turn in the slavery historiography. Stampp would go on to publish his seminal work, *The Peculiar Institution,* in 1956, inspiring countless inquiries into the social and cultural history of slavery. Nevertheless, despite this dramatic shift in the field—a shift very evident in many of the essays in this book—very few of these newly inspired historians turned their attention directly toward the politics of slavery. For more than a decade, the only major work to be published on the topic was Allan Nevins's four-volume history of the 1850s, in which he reiterated the revisionist argument that the war was, in part, caused by politicians' ineptitude. However, Nevins did also argue that vast sectional differences, of which the ethical impasse of slavery was central, precluded any real compromise between the sections. Instead, historians interested in the moral question of slavery turned their attention to the institution of slavery itself and to the abolitionists, who had been caricatured as irresponsible agitators in revisionist scholarship. Still, although Dwight Dumond and Louis Filler provided much-needed surveys of the antislavery movement, their work largely looked past Civil War causation and the dominant political questions raised by revisionists, causing David Donald to note that by 1960, historians no longer seemed interested in the politics that led to war.[20]

And to a certain extent, Donald was correct. Historians interested in slavery, motivated by the broader dynamics of the long Civil Rights era, largely turned their attention away from politics—and the wealthy, white men who dominated such narratives—and began gravitating toward social and cultural history. Still, while historians increasingly looked away from political history, the questions asked and answered in the long Civil Rights era had a dramatic effect on the historiography of politics and slavery. The 1960s and 1970s saw several works published that profoundly altered the way historians perceived the nineteenth-century politics of slavery—not least of which was Donald's own two-volume biography of Charles Sumner. And, in a 1960 Harmsworth Lecture at Oxford University titled "An Excess of Democracy," Donald, inspired by the dramatic social change then being experienced in the United States and around the world, challenged the revisionist narrative: "If we must admit that propagandists and agitators, abolitionists and fire-eaters, whipped up sentiment in both sections, are we not required to ask further why that public could be thus aroused, and why on these specific issues?"[21]

Bookending the 1960s, Eugene Genovese and Eric Foner, in works that signaled the start of careers that would transform our understanding of the history of slavery, responded to Donald's question and reenvisioned the political worlds of slavery and antislavery, respectively. Each moved beyond both the arguments laid out by the revisionists and more traditional narratives of the sectional crisis by investigating more fully the worldview of slaveholders and the ideology of political antislavery. In so doing, both returned to the argument that the war was, to a certain degree, a foregone conclusion. However, both sought to do so in a way that would holistically reconcile the moral dilemma of slavery with the economic, social, and cultural concerns that they believed equally animated the era. As Foner would argue, "moral opposition was certainly one aspect of the Republican ideology, but by no means the only one, and to explain Republicans' actions on simple moral grounds is to miss the full richness of their ideology." Genovese also thought the question of moral values too narrow. Instead, he postulated that the ethical clash preceding the Civil War was one between oppositional worldviews. While his proposition seemed to echo the material determinism of Beard and the Progressives, Genovese's study of the plantation South sought to move past a comparison of the agrarian South and industrial North that denied the centrality of slavery. Instead, he argued that slavery lay at the heart of the Southern worldview as "the very foundation of a proper social order, and therefore as the essence of morality in human relationships." Importantly then, both Foner and Genovese answered Donald's question, and did so in a way that dramatically recentered slavery in the nineteenth-century political economy and moved past the long-held presumptions that the Civil War was solely the result of economic self-interest, political malfeasance, or moral outrage over slavery.[22]

Nevertheless, despite profoundly questioning many of the central arguments within the historiography, neither Genovese nor Foner questioned the temporal or spatial emphases that lay at the heart of nineteenth-century political history. Neither questioned the sectional nature of slavery's politics or the periodization of the conflict over slavery, leaving unchallenged the North/South divide that had long defined the field, as well as the emphasis on the two decades immediately preceding the war. Instead, these important shifts, which are now central to nineteenth-century political history, occurred piecemeal over the next few decades. First, building off Lee Benson's pioneering work in political behavioral analysis, Joel Silbey and the emergent school of political history dubbed the *new political history* began to argue against the emphasis on sectionalism and the Civil War within antebellum American politics. As Silbey argued, historians faced a danger in focusing on these issues too much: "in centering attention on the war and its causes we may ignore or play down other contemporary political influences and fail to weight adequately the importance of non-sectional forces in antebellum politics."[23] Though their focus often remained on the decades leading up to it, the *new political historians* sought to understand antebellum politics outside the context of the Civil War, instead highlighting the *ethnocultural* issues—religion, immigration and ethnicity, and economic concerns, all derived from scrutinizing voter rolls—that they argued equally affected nineteenth-century politics.[24]

The new political history went a long way toward disrupting the gravitational pull of the Civil War in nineteenth-century history, but in so doing, it was frequently dismissive of slavery's role in shaping nineteenth-century politics. Nevertheless, the new political history along with the social and cultural history of the 1970s and 1980s effectively redirected the efforts of a generation of nineteenth-century historians. In part, this shift was premised on the scholarship newly focused on the politics and ideology of slavery in the Revolutionary era. Just as Bernard Bailyn offered a fresh take on the ideology of the American Revolution, Duncan MacLeod, Robert McColley, Staughton Lynd, William Freehling, and, most significantly, David Brion Davis all similarly turned their attention to the Revolutionary and early national eras, questioning the role of slavery in the nation's founding.[25] Davis, importantly, did more than simply shift the chronological emphasis of the field; he also pulled the problem of slavery in American history outside of its narrow geographic confines, placing the conflict over bondage within the broader context of worldwide revolution and abolition.

Still, despite a new emphasis on slavery as a global phenomenon, much of American historiography persisted in placing the political history of slavery within the confines of the South. And yet the field continued to move in different directions as a new generation of Southern historians emerged, inspired by their rejection of the revisionists, the methods of the new political history, and the provocative arguments made by Genovese, Kenneth Stampp, as well as the new social and cultural histories of race, class, and gender that were then being written in the 1960s and 1970s. J. Mills Thornton, for example, challenged Genovese's argument by turning his critical gaze away from the planter class and toward the mass of poor, nonslaveholding whites that made up Alabama's electorate. In so doing, he complicated the picture of politics and the narrative of the South by highlighting the ethnic, cultural, and, most importantly, economic concerns that defined the power struggles within Alabama's white community. These, he argued, and not solely the self-aggrandizement of the planter class, lay at the center of antebellum Alabama politics.[26]

Whereas Thornton placed poor whites at the heart of his narrative, William W. Freehling instead highlighted the significant role that enslaved and free Blacks played in the radicalization of South Carolina politics. Perhaps anticipating his later call for the integration of political and social history, Freehling argued that it was not simply economic or political concerns that led to Andrew Jackson's "Nullification Proclamation" and the ensuing crisis of 1832-33; rather, he contended that South Carolina's radicalization was premised on the demographic reality of the nation's foremost slave society, where a significant Black majority continually applied direct and indirect pressure on white Carolinians, shaping and shifting their political decisions. In many ways, this mirrored earlier arguments that posited white fears of racial adjustment as central to Southern decision-making. But while Freehling noted the worries of white Carolinians, he moved well beyond the racial presumptions of earlier works, which assumed that these fears were premised on innate Black inferiority and white supremacy. In so doing, he introduced a significant question that would come to shape the field: in what way did enslaved people—as opposed to the institution of slavery—shape the nation's political history? In addition, by focusing on the decades following the War of 1812, Freehling moved the narrative of sectional conflict and Civil War causation away from the decades immediately preceding the war.[27]

All these developments profoundly altered the last few decades of scholarship. As historians in the post–Civil Rights era revealed the everyday lives of the enslaved and the social and cultural history of the South, they provided a depth to our understanding of slavery in American history that political historians have embraced in a variety of ways. The role of slavery in nineteenth-century American politics is no longer denied, nor is its role in the sectional crisis or the buildup to war. American historians take for granted that slavery was a foundational institution from the nation's inception through the Civil War. Having moved past these seemingly basic questions, historians have refocused their energies, seeking to better understand the nuances of American political history. Certainly, many are still drawn to the question of Civil War causation. However, many more have been moved by the pathbreaking work done by social and cultural historians, and have brought the weight of slavery—understood now in much more vivid detail— to bear in any number of historical debates. Focusing on class, race, and gender as categories of analysis, social historians have brought to the surface, in ways never previously understood, the complicated history of women, African Americans, poor whites, immigrants, and American Indians as nineteenth-century political actors. These historians demonstrated not simply how politics affected a wide range of people, but how those individuals, seemingly excluded from participatory roles in the American polity, directly shaped the political process. The result has been a complete reassessment of nineteenth-century politics—its loci, its practice, its cultural meaning, and its participants. Historians subsequently had to refigure slavery's role in broad historiographical debates, and historians like Steven Hahn, Dylan Penningroth, Stephanie McCurry, Stephen Kantrowitz, and William Link have made clear that slaves and freedmen must also be considered as central political actors in the nineteenth century.[28]

Likewise, the work of a new generation of historians has pushed the field to move beyond Civil War causation as the central theme in the historiography. Matthew Mason, Seth Rockman, David Waldstreicher, Adam Rothman, John Craig Hammond, and numerous others have turned the attention away from the decades immediately preceding the Civil War and forced historians to consider slavery's centrality to the political struggles and compromises of the early nation.[29] There they have not only located political antislavery's early rise but also complicated our understanding of slavery's role in the nation's development. This shift in the chronological focus of the politics of slavery has also shed new light on issues previously considered solely in a Civil War context. Numerous scholars have reassessed the work done on abolitionists, the free soil (and free labor) movement, and the downfall of the second party system.[30] Some of the best work, especially that of Manisha Sinha, Richard Blackett, and Andrew Delbanco, has recentered free African Americans, including fugitive slaves, as prime drivers of the abolitionist movement.[31]

Though scholars have turned more toward the politics of slavery in the early republic, the Civil War sesquicentennial has witnessed a reassessment of the politics of slavery in the 1850s. Focusing on politics in Washington, Rachel Shelden and Joanne Freeman have considered the intimate—and violent—politics of slavery debates after 1850.[32] Aiming for the broad middle of Northern political opinion, Adam I. P. Smith highlighted the challenge of the Northern conservative majority that opposed slavery and also the chaos of immediate emancipation, while Daniel Crofts analyzed the famous Corwin Amendment—"the original" Thirteenth Amendment—that would have protected slavery as a means to preserve the union.[33] At the same time, historians like Edward Ayers, Christopher Phillips, Nicole Etcheson, and John Inscoe have reassessed the regional politics of slavery, especially along the "Middle Border" (as Christopher Phillips termed the regions at the edges of the North and South) and in Appalachia.[34]

Finally, it seems that historians are now beginning to look beyond the political history of slavery as solely confined to the South. Seth Rockman, Edward Baptist, Sven Beckert, Walter Johnson, and a new generation of young scholars are fundamentally altering the way that historians perceive slavery's relationship to the nation's dynamic political economy.[35] Caleb McDaniel, Matthew Clavin, and Edward Rugemer have explored transnational networks of abolitionism and emancipation, while Alison Efford, Mischa Honeck, and Niels Eichhorn have focused on transatlantic antislavery ideology emerging from the 1848 revolutions, especially among German immigrants. Matthew Karp and Carl Paulus turned toward slaveholders' political control of American foreign policy on the eve of secession, highlighting both aspirations of a slaveholding empire and fears of a Haiti-style insurrection.[36] By demonstrating that slavery was not simply a lingering vestige of a premodern past, but rather central to the economic and political development of the nation and the rise of global industrial capitalism, these scholars are critically removing slavery from its confines within the South and placing it at the very heart of American and global history.

NOTES

1. A tremendous amount has been written on radical abolitionists, some of which is discussed below. Some of the more exciting work on abolitionists includes Delbanco, *Abolitionist Imagination;* Stauffer, *Black Hearts of Men;* and Laurie, *Beyond Garrison.*

2. W. Phillips, *Constitution, a Proslavery Compact.*

3. Seward, *Irrepressible Conflict.*

4. Seward, *Irrepressible Conflict.*

5. J. H. Hammond, *Selections,* 311-22. For more on Hammond and the politicization of the proslavery argument, see Faust, *James Henry Hammond,* 331-59.

6. Randall, "Blundering Generation."

7. Burgess, *Middle Period,* x-xi.

8. Schouler, *History of the United States;* McMaster, *History of the People;* Von Holst, *Constitution and Political History;* Rhodes, *History of the United States.*

9. For more on the nation-state and historical narrative, see Duara, *Rescuing History,* 1-50.

10. Much has been written on the culture of white supremacy and empire that prevailed at the turn of the century. See for example Rydell, *All the World's a Fair;* Raibmon, *Authentic Indians,* 34-73; Kaplan, *Anarchy of Empire;* and Domosh, "'Civilized' Commerce." On the La Fiesta parade in Los Angeles, see Deverell, *Whitewashed Adobe,* 49-90. Both Ulrich Phillips and William Archibald Dunning were prolific scholars, but their seminal texts are Phillips, *American Negro Slavery;* and Dunning, *Reconstruction, Political and Economic.*

11. F. Turner, "Problems in American History"; F. Turner, *Frontier in American History;* F. Turner, "Significance of the Section."

12. *Plessy v. Ferguson* (1896).

13. Du Bois, *Suppression of the African Slave-Trade.* See also, especially, the introductory essay by Saidiya Hartman in the 2007 Oxford edition of *Suppression of the African Slave-Trade.*

14. Beard, *Economic Interpretation of the Constitution;* Beard and Beard, *Rise of American Civilization;* A. Cole, *Irrepressible Conflict;* A. Cole, "Lincoln's Election an Immediate Menace to Slavery?" For an excellent analysis of the Progressive Era in American historiography, see Hofstadter, *Progressive Historians.*

15. Owsley, "Irrepressible Conflict"; Owsley, *Plain Folk.*

16. Craven, *Repressible Conflict;* Randall, *Lincoln the President;* Randall, "Blundering Generation"; Ramsdell, "Changing Interpretation"; Owsley, "Fundamental Cause of the Civil War."

17. For an excellent review of revisionist literature, see Bonner, "Civil War Historians."

18. Schlesinger, "Causes of the Civil War" (quote on 981); DeVoto, "Easy Chair."

19. Kenneth Stampp to William Hesseltine, Mar. 1, 1946, quoted in Novick, *Noble Dream*, 349.

20. D. Donald, "American Historians"; Nevins, *Emergence of Lincoln*. For key examples of the work on abolition that emerged in the postwar era, see Dumond, *Antislavery;* Duberman, *Antislavery Vanguard;* and Filler, *Crusade against Slavery.*

21. D. Donald, "Excess of Democracy," 25.

22. E. Foner, *Free Soil, Free Labor, Free Men;* Genovese, *Political Economy of Slavery.*

23. Silbey, "Civil War Synthesis," 131. For more on the new political history, see Bogue, "United States"; Fehrenbacher, "New Political History"; and E. Foner, *Politics and Ideology,* especially 1-33.

24. For an excellent example of the behavioral studies that inspired this new take on political history, see Benson, *Concept of Jacksonian Democracy.* For examples of the new political history that specifically challenged the centrality of sectionalism, see Silbey, *Shrine of Party;* Silbey, *Party over Section;* Formisano, *Birth of Mass Political Parties;* and M. Holt, *Forging a Majority.* Michael Holt moved beyond the emphasis on ethnocultural issues alone in a later groundbreaking work that continued to replace slavery with republicanism as the central issue in the political crisis of the 1850s. M. Holt, *Political Crisis of the 1850s.*

25. Bailyn, *Ideological Origins;* MacLeod, *Slavery, Race, and the American Revolution;* McColley, *Slavery and Jeffersonian Virginia;* Lynd, *Class Conflict, Slavery, and the Constitution;* Freehling, "Founding Fathers and Slavery"; D. Davis, *Problem of Slavery in the Age of Revolution;* D. Davis, *Problem of Slavery in Western Culture.*

26. J. M. Thornton, *Politics and Power.*

27. Freehling, *Prelude to Civil War.* Freehling called for the integration of social and political history in his aptly titled *The Reintegration of American History: Slavery and the Civil War* (1994). In addition, his two-volume work on the long politics of disunion in the South has become standard fare in the field. See Freehling, *Road to Disunion,* vols. 1 and 2. Drew Gilpin Faust's biography of James Henry Hammond must also be considered central to the new work being done on Southern political history. See Faust, *James Henry Hammond.*

28. For just a small sample of the work still being done on Civil War causation, see Varon, *Disunion!;* Fehrenbacher, *Slaveholding Republic;* and Ashworth, *Slavery, Capitalism and Politics* (two volumes). For an example of the intersection of the historiography of politics and slavery with broader historiographical debates, see the following works that directly engaged the questions related to republicanism and liberalism that consumed the profession in the 1980s and 1990s: M. Holt, *Political Crisis of the 1850s;* Oakes, *Slav-*

ery and Freedom; McCurry, *Masters of Small Worlds;* Ford, *Origins of Southern Radicalism;* and Morrison, *Slavery and the American West.* And the following list represents just a small sample of the expansive literature that is now reconsidering the historiography of politics and slavery; it is in no way exhaustive: Hahn, *Nation under Our Feet;* Penningroth, *Claims of Kinfolk;* McCurry, *Confederate Reckoning;* Kantrowitz, *More than Freedom;* Link, *Roots of Secession;* and Furstenberg, *In the Name of the Father.*

29. Mason, *Slavery and Politics;* Rockman, *Scraping By;* Waldstreicher, *Slavery's Constitution;* A. Rothman, *Slave Country;* J. C. Hammond, *Slavery, Freedom, and Expansion.* For an excellent introduction to the new work being done in the field of slavery and politics in the early nation, see Hammond and Mason, *Contesting Slavery.*

30. Melish, *Disowning Slavery;* Earle, *Jacksonian Antislavery;* Laurie, *Beyond Garrison.*

31. Sinha, *Slave's Cause;* Blackett, *Making Freedom;* Blackett, *Captive's Quest.* See also Delbanco, *War before the War.*

32. Shelden, *Washington Brotherhood;* Freeman, *Field of Blood.*

33. A. Smith, *Stormy Present;* Crofts, *Lincoln and the Politics of Slavery.*

34. Ayers, *In the Presence of Mine Enemies;* C. Phillips, *Rivers Ran Backward;* Etcheson, *Bleeding Kansas;* Inscoe, *Mountain Masters.*

35. Rockman, "Unfree Origins"; Baptist, "Toxic Debt"; W. Johnson, *Chattel Principle.*

36. McDaniel, *Problem of Democracy;* Clavin, *Toussaint Louverture;* Rugemer, *Problem of Emancipation;* Efford, *German Immigrants, Race, and Citizenship;* Honeck, *We Are the Revolutionists;* Eichhorn, *Liberty and Slavery;* Karp, *Vast Southern Empire;* Paulus, *Slaveholding Crisis.*

CHAPTER FOUR

American Slavery and Gender

KATHERINE CHILTON

Although many images of slavery show enslaved women working in the fields like men, their gender marked the lives of enslaved women in different and distinct ways. Most significantly, enslaved women continued to bear children, which, given the fragile nature of slave relationships and marriages, were often the defining moments of their lives. Drawing on kin and friendships in the female slave community, women raised children and taught them the strategies necessary to grow up in bondage. Enslaved women did labor in the fields, but they rarely performed the same labor as men. Enslaved men were more often assigned to the skilled work needed on Southern plantations and farms, and women to the manual labor of picking cotton or hoeing rice, yet within the fields women learned to wield great skill ginning cotton or building *mudworks* in the rice paddies. Women's work also took them inside, where, as domestic servants, they negotiated the lighter work but closer quarters of both the great houses and more modest farms of the South. Wherever they performed productive labor for their owners, at the end of the day, all enslaved women began the reproductive labor of caring for their families, cooking, cleaning their quarters, sewing clothes, and growing additional provisions in their small garden plots. Their family ties and responsibilities meant that women were less likely to resist slavery in overt ways like running away or rebelling. But through subtler forms of resistance like truancy, stealing time or provisions, or reclaiming their bodies for enjoyment rather than work, enslaved women challenged their owners' control and made space for their own priorities. In Southern cities, where enslaved women often outnumbered men, women took advantage of urban freedoms to fraternize with free people of color, slip away from owners, or work themselves toward freedom. Gender also marked the lives of white women, both the *plantation mistress* of lore and the wives of lesser yeoman and laborers who buttressed slave society. Ideas of womanhood and manhood defined by race were at the center of the Southern social structure that created and supported the institution of slavery.

Despite the centrality of both enslaved women and ideas of gender to Southern slavery, the experience and importance of women has only really been recognized in the slavery historiography since the 1980s. While the debates and dissensions outlined in the introduction and other chapters in this volume marked the transitions between the major periods of slavery historiography, from the nineteenth century to the long Civil Rights movement, for the most part, these debates paid little attention to the lives of women. Reflecting broader attitudes toward the place of women in society and the academy, much slave scholarship uncritically wrote about the experience of men as if it described all the enslaved. Although part of the long Civil Rights tradition, the new generation of female scholars that has challenged these long-held assumptions were more influenced by the women's liberation movement of the early 1970s.[1] Publishing their work during the 1980s, pioneering women's historians revealed the importance of the women in slavery by uncovering the life of the Southern plantation mistress and the enslaved women who labored in her household and in the fields. As gender analysis began to dominate the field of women's history in the 1990s, new studies used cultural history methodology to reexamine the development and maintenance of the system of racial slavery and demonstrate the centrality of constructions of gender, race, and class to the evolution, preservation, and wartime challenge to patriarchy in the South. Studies of enslaved women's experiences drew on concepts of gender to emphasize not only that enslaved women had differing experiences of slavery than men, but also that incorporating these variations into the history of slavery was critical to a full understanding of central concepts of slave life, such as family, labor, resistance, and culture. As Stephanie Camp has suggested, recent work on gender and slavery has demonstrated how "women's history does not merely add to what we know; it changes what we know and how we know it." Historians in this field have produced some of the most important studies within gender as well as slavery history, and have begun to deliver on gender's promised potential as a category of historical analysis.[2]

During the nineteenth century, some slavery participants and observers—particularly members of the abolitionist movement—evoked the experiences of enslaved women in their quest to sow contempt for slavery and sympathy for the enslaved. Popular slave narratives by Black women such as Sojourner Truth and Harriet Jacobs presented the female experience and gave readers a glimpse of the sexual exploitation that was often a daily feature of slavery for women. Yet, as Margaret Washington has argued, their accounts were closely controlled by abolitionist editors and presses to present the most socially acceptable or politically useful versions of their stories. The abolitionist Olive Gilbert sanitized or excluded instances of sexual exploitation in the narrative of Sojourner Truth.[3] Harriet Jacobs presented perhaps the most honest portrayal of women's lives in slavery, but she struggled to find a publisher until the abolitionist Lydia Maria Child wrote an introduction and encouraged Jacobs to change the names of the participants.[4] These accounts of women's lives were largely lost to scholars until they were authenticated and republished in the 1980s.[5] Black women's voices were rarely represented in the works of early professional historians, who instead relied on plantation records and other sources created by white men. Even in their dissension with the romantic vision of slavery presented by Ulrich B. Phillips and his students, Black scholars W. E. B. Du Bois and E. Franklin Frazier emphasized that slavery had impeded enslaved men's ability to head their families, giving women a significance in their families and the slave community that was presented as detrimental. Although there were a few pioneering Black women historians in the early professional era, few wrote about slavery and, perhaps unsurprisingly given their struggles as Black professional women in the academy, none focused on women's history.[6]

The midcentury historians, particularly Stanley Elkins, continued this interpretation of slavery as damaging to enslaved men's masculinity. Published in 1959, Elkins's *Slavery: A Problem in American Institutional and Intellectual Life* employed psychological analysis to argue that American slavery was a total institution, akin to a Nazi concentration camp, which dehumanized enslaved people and stripped them of their culture. Particularly, he argued that bondage denied enslaved men their manhood, as the slaveowner was always the ultimate source of authority on the plantation and even within enslaved people's own families. Scholars and policy makers looking for causes of the disproportionate number of female-headed households that had come to stigmatize African American family life in Northern inner cities by the 1960s seized on the implication that slavery was responsible for damaging Black masculinity and the Black family. When the assistant US labor secretary (and later US senator) Daniel Moynihan cited this research in a 1965 report to Congress, known as the Moynihan Report, historians began to challenge this presentation of slavery and the assumption that there could be a causal connection between slavery and contemporary social issues.[7]

Inspired by the whirlwind of change in society and the academy promised by the Civil Rights movement and the rise of African American and Black studies, the first scholars of the long Civil Rights movement produced a series of groundbreaking studies of Southern slavery and slave life. The work of scholars such as John Blassingame, Eugene Genovese, and Herbert Gutman emphasized the resilience of the slave family and community and the complex web of accommodation and resistance that characterized life on Southern plantations.[8] Putting enslaved people at the center of their analysis, these historians, like their contemporaries in labor history and other fields flourishing under the influence of social history methodologies, sought to uncover history *from below* and give a voice to the voiceless. Just as in these other fields, however, the view from below and the voices represented were often uncritically accepted to be male. These scholars generally neglected the differences between men and women in their treatment of slavery or made male experience the normative portrayal in their discussions, particularly those of community, culture, and resistance. To a certain extent, this generalization over gender was just part of a larger tendency within this scholarship to paint a broad picture of antebellum slavery. In their eagerness to utilize sources created by the enslaved themselves—particularly published slave narratives and the testimony of former slaves collected by the Works Progress Administration (WPA) during the 1930s—historians created an often-static picture of life on Southern antebellum plantations, flattening or disregarding distinctions in time period, region, crop, and plantation size. Their neglect of the different experiences caused by the gender of the enslaved was thus just one of the complexities that was often missing from these analyses.

When scholars of the slave community school of the late 1960s and 1970s did engage with gender, it was primarily to refute Frazier's and particularly the Moynihan Report's charge that slavery had been damaging to enslaved men. In their attempt to restore enslaved men's masculinity, the slave community school created a presentation of slavery that privileged male experience and downplayed the role of women in order to emphasize the natural masculine roles of enslaved men. This approach was perhaps most explicitly recognized in Herbert Gutman's *The Black Family in Slavery and Freedom* (1976), which was published specifically to counter the Moynihan Report. Based on an exhaustive search of plantation records from across the South and marriage registers of formerly enslaved men and women during the Civil War and Reconstruction, Gutman argued that the majority of enslaved people lived in stable, two-parent families, where fathers played an active role in raising their children. However, as Sean Condon explains in detail in the next chapter on the slave family, Gutman's emphasis on stable, two-parent families suggested that Black families exhibited paternalistic or patriarchal tendencies of their own, not influenced by the slave master.[9] Similarly, John Blassingame portrayed enslaved men as the unquestioned head of their monogamous family units, arguing that "the black male faced no obstacle (other than his mate) in exercising authority in his family." Beyond their families, Blassingame also emphasized the role of men as the chief architects of resistance and rebellion on the slave plantation, and the most likely to run away or foment trouble among the enslaved. In countering the brutalized *Sambo* stereotype proposed by Elkins, Blassingame put forward two additional enslaved characters, but both his dissembling *Jack* and violent *Nat* were obviously male, and no female alternatives were included.[10]

Similarly, when describing "the world the slaves made" in response to the paternalism of their masters, Eugene Genovese's model of the slave plantation built predominately on the experiences of enslaved men and paid little attention to the gender differences that shaped resistant behavior such as stealing, arson, shirking work, or running away. In his discussion of the slave family, Genovese also described the masculine honor of enslaved men, who sought to protect their wives and provided for their families by hunting and fishing. In keeping with his focus on the paternalistic relationship between masters and slaves, Genovese emphasized the role of the owner in encouraging such gender relations on the plantation, including the division of labor within the household so that men took care of the livestock while women washed, cleaned, and cared for the children. Instead of a "debilitating female supremacy," Genovese saw a more egalitarian relationship in the slave quarters created by the overarching power of the plantation master.[11]

Despite the achievements of the slave community school scholars in drawing attention to the slave family and community, their emphasis on slave masculinity and normalization of the male experience represented a significant interpretive absence. During the 1970s, just as the women's rights movement developed to challenge the sexism and patriarchy practiced in the Civil Rights and Black Power movements, a growing number of young women's historians sought to challenge the invisibility of women in the historical narrative. By 1982, the growth and development of the field of women's history led historian Catherine Clinton to question the dominant interpretation of slavery, asking "where were the women?" across the landscape of Southern history. Although Gerda Lerner, in her documentary history titled "Black Women in White America," had demonstrated in the early 1970s that the sources to study the experience and perspective of enslaved women could be found, the skepticism and even hostility continued toward female scholars who suggested women and slavery as an important topic. Indeed, the Library of Congress did not even have a subject entry in its card catalog for "women and slavery."[12] By the end of the decade, however, Clinton's own work, as well as new scholarship by Elizabeth Fox-Genovese, Jacqueline Jones, and particularly Deborah Gray White, had begun to address this silence and to demonstrate the importance of women's distinctive experiences as slaveowners and slaves. These scholars, although part of the long Civil Rights movement tradition, provided a critique of the male-focused scope of earlier scholarship, and particularly the assertion of male dominance in the Black family. Their studies of the slave South and the slave system showed how centering analysis on women challenged rather than simply added to the narrative of slavery. Reacting also to the invisibility of African American women in much of the new women's history scholarship and the growing field of African American studies, Jones and White sought to reveal the lives of Black women in slavery.[13]

The first of these studies to be published, Catherine Clinton's *The Plantation Mistress* in 1982, explored the real lives of the plantation mistresses who were revered in Southern literature and lore, revealing their unceasing work running the household, supervising enslaved workers, and ministering to the needs of the sick on their plantations. Most of all, Clinton argued that the plantation mistress was trapped in a dependent position by the slave system of the antebellum South, where "cotton was King, white men rule, and both white women and the enslaved served the same master." Angry at their position and at the responsibilities of slaveowning, many women deflected their guilt over slavery toward their husbands or more often the enslaved themselves, to free themselves from personal responsibility for the horrors of slavery that they witnessed on a daily basis.[14] This view of the "Big House" and the lives of white women during slavery was further expanded and in some respects challenged by Elizabeth Fox-Genovese's study of the experiences and interactions of slave mistresses and enslaved women *Within the Plantation Household*. Like her husband Eugene Genovese, Fox-Genovese emphasized the overarching role of the slave master, the paternalist power who dominated the lives and shaped the gender identities of white and Black women. Yet she argued that this shared domination did not bring white and Black women together, as plantation mistresses, although they could be sympathetic to the plight of their slaves, ultimately realized that their privileged position was based on the ownership of human property. White female Southern critics of the slave system, like the Grimké sisters, were thus the exception rather than the rule. Fox-Genovese pointed to the limitations of the 1970s scholarship that emphasized "normal" nuclear family relationships and paid respect to the equal strength of enslaved women and men, and instead sought to recognize the limitations on enslaved women's roles as mothers, wives, and daughters caused fundamentally by their bondage.[15]

Particularly singling out Gutman's work, Jones and White challenged the insistence on the male-dominated nuclear family as the dominant structure in slave life. In 1985, White contributed the first full-length study of enslaved women with *Ar'n't I a Woman? Female Slaves in the Plantation South*, which, like the famous quote by Sojourner Truth that titled the book, sought to draw attention to the distinct experiences of enslaved women. White argued that two different systems within the institution of racial slavery existed for men and for women: while slaveowners expected women to work in the fields, they also recognized women's reproductive potential. Although women performed similar field labor to men, within the home they performed valuable reproductive labor for their families—cooking, cleaning, and caring for children. White argued that the inability of enslaved men to protect or provide for their wives created equality within the family, not matriarchal or patriarchal relationships. Women's role as mothers shaped their life cycles differently from men, making the turning points in women's lives their entry into the community of women through childbirth. Given the reality of family separations, women's most enduring relationships often were with their children and other women in the slave community. In this analysis, the existence of matrifocal forms of family reflected a positive recognition of the strength of female institutions within the slave community. Yet White also recognized how women's responsibilities as mothers were a double-edged sword, severely limiting their ability and opportunity to resist slavery.[16] In the chapters of her study of Black women and their families from slavery to the present, *Labor of Love, Labor of Sorrow* (1985), Jones also asserted the more egalitarian relationship of the slave quarters in her discussion of the antebellum period. She argued that the division of family labor in the quarters along gender distinct lines was an act of resistance to the slaveholders' tendencies to ignore gender differences in allocating work in the fields.[17]

Despite the pioneering contributions of these women's historians, their significance to the historiography of slavery was to a great extent marginalized by other trends in the development of slavery studies during the 1980s. Reacting to the static picture of the antebellum South created by the scholarship of the previous decade, new work on the slave South led by Ira Berlin and other scholars emphasized in-depth, local, and specialized studies of different regions, topics, and periods of slave history. As Peter Parish commented in his 1989 historiography *Slavery: History and Historians,* the telescope of the slave community school had moved to the microscope. Historians who sought to bring women's experiences and perspective into the history of slavery were seen as part of this trend of drawing attention to the variety and distinctiveness within the slave system. Indeed, Parish devoted just eight lines to detailing the contributions of studies that demonstrated the differences between women's experience of slavery and the normative male experience posited by earlier scholars. Peter Kolchin, in his acclaimed synthesis of the field, *American Slavery* (1993), continued this presentation of women's experiences as a subspecialty in slave studies more similar to slave religion, resistance, or family rather than a central part of these topics. These assessments neglected the interpretive achievements of the new studies of women and slavery produced during the decade, which went beyond additive history to suggest the ways that women's experiences challenged accepted understandings of slavery and the slave South.[18]

Despite this overshadowing within the larger field, the questions raised by historians like Fox-Genovese and White surrounding gender and gender relations in many ways set the stage for the next wave of gender and slavery studies. Assessing the legacy of *Ar'n't I a Woman?* on the twentieth anniversary of its publication, Leslie Harris commented that although "a work of women's history, it provides a model for a gendered history of slavery."[19] While these women's history scholars had emphasized the experiences of women, in their dialogues with the dominant presentation of slave history as male history, they showed that the lives of slaveowning and enslaved men and women were not lived separately and would need to be addressed together in the future. As the broader field began to transition from women's history to gender history, a new generation of historians influenced by the presentation of gender as a category of analysis began to bring this tool to bear on slavery and the slave South.[20] Just as the scholars of the 1970s had been inspired by the burgeoning field of social history, young scholars emerging in the 1990s brought the insights and methodology of cultural history to bear on slavery studies, using techniques such as textual analysis to show the interrelation between ideas of race and gender and the creation and maintenance of racial slavery. Although commitments to the social ideals of the long Civil Rights movement continued to influence scholars, the movement's waning influence in society meant that this development largely came from influences within the academy.[21] Increasingly, scholars drew on postmodernist theories from their colleagues in literary criticism, critical studies, and other fields to argue that race, class, and gender were historical constructions that must be examined together.[22] In this effort, historians of gender and slavery created some of the most influential scholarship in the field of gender history, and began to demonstrate the radical potential of using gender alongside race and class to extend women's history beyond the traditional world of women to explore power relationships in society and the use of gender to legitimize social relations. In many ways, they demonstrated the potential proposed by feminist historians such as Joan Scott, who argued that gender would not only provide "new perspectives on old questions" but also "redefine the old questions in new terms."[23]

Kathleen Brown's work on colonial Virginia was one of the first studies to demonstrate the potential of gender to reconceptualize an "old question" when she revisited the debate over the origins of racial slavery in America. Historians, particularly Edmund Morgan and Winthrop Jordan, had argued over the nature and timing of the origins of racial slavery, trying to determine whether racism determined the creation of slavery or followed the development of legal enslavement for Africans alone.[24] Yet despite the focus of this debate on the development of slavery in colonial Virginia, it paid little attention to the role of gender in "constituting racial categories and legitimating political authority." Drawing on cultural analysis of seventeenth-century literature and the tracts intended to promote colonization of the New World, Brown demonstrated that even before the first settlers landed in Virginia, they were influenced by descriptions and images that contrasted the good wives and strong patriarchs of the Old World with the virgin lands and femininized native peoples of the colonies. Brown showed how from the beginning of European settlement, the culture of the new colony was set up to support male authority, by limiting women's choices to being either a "good wife" who stayed in the private world of her own household or a "nasty wench" who behaved in ways considered unbecoming to women, such as working in the fields or conducting sexual relationships outside of marriage.[25]

Treating men as well as women as "gendered historical subjects," Brown's analysis showed how the major legal bases that established racial slavery were intimately tied to developing ideas of gender as part of an attempt to distinguish the "good wives" of the colony from their servants and slaves. When colonial law defined enslaved women in the same taxation category of laborers as enslaved and white men, it suggested that Black women had an equal productive capacity to men. The extension of this distinction to include free women of color demonstrated how the privileges of freedom would henceforth apply only to white women, and the white men who benefited from their labor; free men of color had no claim to be the head of their households. When Virginia law in 1662 made slavery a hereditable condition through the mother, this solidified the connection between gender and racial slavery, as only enslaved African women could pass their condition on to their children.[26]

Jennifer Morgan built on this gendered framework in her analysis of enslaved women in colonial South Carolina and Barbados. She added an important contribution in her depiction of the foundation of European racial ideas and the legitimization of slavery in cultural constructions of Black women as "natural" laborers. Like Brown, Morgan analyzed the ideas and images of race and gender constructed by contemporary travel narratives of encounters between Europeans and native women in Africa. She argued that authors' comments on the natural strength and reproductive capacities of women who could seemingly "suckle over their shoulder" while working in the fields spurred the connection between forced labor and race in the English colonies. Arguing that "gender furnished one of the crucial axes around which the organization of enslavement and slave labor in the Americas took place," Morgan used statistical and textual analysis of wills and probate records to demonstrate that colonial slaveowners quickly began to value enslaved women not only for their laboring strength but for their reproductive capacity to produce "increase" that would continue to profit their estates.[27] Together, these studies have pushed historians and teachers to recognize the role of gender in the legal creation of slavery in the American colonies, and particularly in the resultant association of race and permanent enslavement.

As new studies began to employ a gendered analysis of slavery and the lives of enslaved women during the colonial and antebellum periods, they demonstrated that understanding women's experiences was important to nearly every field within the history of slavery. Particularly in the areas of slave labor and slave resistance, historians demonstrated that women's distinct experiences were fundamentally connected to their reproductive abilities, and defied simple dichotomies between accommodation and resistance or skilled and unskilled labor. In terms of slave labor, a number of studies began to point to the significance of women's dual "laboring" role as workers and potential mothers. As Jennifer Morgan identified, for enslaved women, "the effort of reproducing the labor force occurred alongside that of cultivating crops."[28] Yet despite the conflation of male and female slave labor in colonial law and custom, recent scholarship has drawn attention to the variety of work performed by enslaved women and the differences between male and female labor roles that developed as the South became a "slave society." Scholars seeking to assert the masculinity of enslaved men and women's historians critiquing this overemphasis had both focused on the division of work done within the slave community, seeing this as a reflection of the enslaved people's own ideas about labor roles for men and women.[29] Following Ira Berlin and Philip Morgan's influential appeal for more attention to the labor of the enslaved, historians have tried to provide equal focus to the field or house work that formed the majority of enslaved women's daily employment and the productive labor that women performed for their families, but that was no less work.[30] Although enslaved women did take on the majority of the tasks that provided food and nurture for their family, recent scholarship has attempted to temper the idea that this necessarily represented resistance to the tendency of owners to ignore gender conventions when assigning fieldwork. Slaveowners typically reflected white gender norms when they distributed food and clothing rations to the female head of the household, or possibly were influenced by the greater likelihood that mothers would care for their children after family separations.[31]

Countering the idea that slaveowners disregarded gender when assigning agricultural labor work or tasks, local studies of gender and slavery have revealed the wide variation in labor roles between men and women. In South Carolina, enslaved women during the colonial and antebellum periods were in fact more likely than men to be agricultural laborers, as the skilled work on the coastal rice plantations was reserved for men. Initially, enslaved African women brought their expertise in rice cultivation and harvesting to the Americas, and were forced to teach enslaved men the skills to grow and thresh the rice, dissolving the gender differences between men and women. By the antebellum period, however, as Leslie Schwalm has demonstrated, "field work was slave women's work," so field labor was central to women's experience of slavery. Enslaved women hoed the fields, prepared for the rice planting, and performed the difficult and dirty mudwork of repairing and maintaining the ditches that contained the water in the rice fields, as well as the delicate task of sowing the rice seed. In contrast, although men also were assigned to the heavy mudwork, men were more likely to be the drivers in the field or artisans on the plantation, including carpenters, blacksmiths, or coopers, creating opportunities for them to be hired to other plantations or sent to market or on other errands.[32]

However, as Daina Ramey Berry's work on slave labor in antebellum Georgia asserted, this is not to suggest that enslaved women were without skills. On the Low Country cotton and rice plantations of coastal Georgia where women did much of the agricultural work, many of the tasks assigned to women, particularly ginning cotton, required great skill and experience. Skilled labor therefore "crossed gender lines" as the agricultural labor regime involved skilled work, challenging the binary that defined male labor as trades and skilled and women's labor as agricultural and therefore unskilled.[33] Nevertheless, the definition of skill remained a "gendered and socially contingent attribute," as even though female nurses and midwives on Southern plantations were considered skilled workers by the slave community, their knowledge and experience was disregarded by plantation owners. Skills possessed by women did not necessarily give women access to the privileges and opportunities that gave skilled or artisan enslaved men more opportunities for mobility, resistance, and flight.[34]

This is not to say that enslaved women did not resist the conditions of their bondage through a variety of methods. Recent

scholarship has challenged the simple dichotomy of accommodation and resistance created by models based on normalizing slave
resistance with male behaviors. Historians of the 1970s generally
emphasized the methods of active resistance practiced by enslaved men as the most meaningful in challenging the system of
slavery in their attempt to prove the limited power of the institution of slavery to destroy the spirits of enslaved people.[35] Clearly,
the greater mobility of enslaved men, especially skilled artisans,
allowed them more opportunity to run away, and men were more
likely to be the leaders of slave revolts and plots. Enslaved women,
who were tied to the plantation through field labor and particularly through their children, had less ability to engage in those
methods of resistance that could result in freedom. One of the
major contributions of gender analysis has thus been to suggest
that instead of concluding that these differences meant that men
were more resistant, "women's experience . . . suggests that the
language of resistance and accommodation is always already insuf-
ficient."[36] As Jennifer Morgan suggested, many enslaved women
did not choose between resistant or accommodating behavior, but
often experienced these simultaneously as they gave birth to children who brought them joy and love, but whom they doomed to
a life of bondage enriching their owner's estate. If women chose
not to have children, they could celebrate their resistance to their
owners' domination but still mourn the loss of the family they sac-
rificed. Rather than adding women's experiences toward the accommodation side of the spectrum of resistance, gender analysis
has argued that this spectrum assumes too much about the meaning of behaviors under an oppressive regime.[37]

Drawing on James Scott's definition of everyday resistance, historians have begun to challenge the portrayal of female slave resistance as less effectual than more overt forms of action. Stephanie
Camp's *Closer to Freedom* (2004) has shown how recognizing the
"subtler forms" of resistance practiced by women not only adds to
our knowledge of women's experience of slavery, but also adds to
our understanding of slavery as a whole. While enslaved women

did not have as many opportunities as men to become permanent runaways from slavery, they often engaged in temporary truancy from the plantation to escape punishment, protest treatment, or avoid work. This did not make truancy a *female form* of resistance as men also engaged in this behavior, but it showed the significance of this more covert form of resistance, particularly during the antebellum period as paternalist slaveowners struggled to contain enslaved people geographically on the plantation and control time management as a sign of their mastery.[38]

In slavery, for women, the personal and private could also be political arenas of conflict and resistance—particularly the disputed terrain of their very bodies. Enslaved men and women who slipped off to the woods for illicit parties and so-called *frolics* reclaimed their bodies from the control of their owners, giving their activities significance beyond mere personal gratification and enjoyment. Dressing in their nicest clothes, curling their hair, and even appropriating their mistresses' clothing turned enjoyment of their bodies into a political act. Fiercely contested between slave and slaveowner, the terrain of the body demonstrated how personal and everyday *female* acts of resistance did not simply accommodate to slavery or act as a safety valve but defied planters' attempts to confine and control enslaved women.[39] Within the plantation household, female servants resisted the control of their mistresses by working slowly, stealing time to tend to their own family or personal needs, seeking their own pleasures, and defying attempts to confine them to the plantation household. As Thavolia Glymph asserted in *Out of the House of Bondage* (2008), however, many scholars have followed the interpretation of plantation mistresses, who cast these behaviors as personality or racial defects of their unwilling servants based on the gendered assumption that women's actions were the result of frustration rather than defiance. Recognizing these actions as part of the day-to-day acts of resistance that were the principal "weapons of the weak" available to many enslaved people—not just women—helps to rethink other confrontations between slaves and owners within and outside the household.[40]

Glymph's work focused on the plantation household, but enslaved women's domestic work also opened other avenues for resistance. In Southern cities, the demand for domestic servants to labor in white households resulted in the overrepresentation of enslaved women in the urban population of the South. Recent studies of free women of color have shown the deep connections between enslaved and free women of color in cities like Charleston and Baltimore, and suggested that enslaved women also benefited from the *freer* conditions of urban life to pursue permanent emancipation. Amrita Chakrabarti's 2011 study of free women of color in Charleston, South Carolina, argued that enslaved "women were as engaged in working to emancipate themselves and their families as they were in their daily resistance to enslavement." Like resistance to enslavement, women also faced different challenges and used different tools on their path to manumission than men. As enslaved women's domestic labor was less valued than men's work in various trades in the city, they were unlikely to be able to earn their way to freedom, but, particularly in the cities of the lower South, they were able to pursue relationships with white men, sexual or otherwise, that could result in their emancipation. Once free, Black women recognized the relationship between slavery and gender by working to manumit their daughters first and prevent another generation from being born into bondage.[41] In upper South cities like Baltimore and Washington, enslaved women were also limited to domestic labor, where they worked alongside free women of color and immigrant women, but they pursued opportunities like term slavery to find a path to freedom for themselves and their children.[42]

The model of paternalism that provided the foundation for racial slavery and the very way of life in the Old South is another *old question* recast by gender analysis. Beyond examining the complicity of the individual women who were a part of the slaveowning society, recent scholarship has shown the central role of constructions of gender alongside race and class in creating and maintaining the Southern racial system and supporting slavery. These analyses both draw on and challenge Eugene Genovese's model of a slave South dominated by the planter class, whose paternalistic control of their slaves supported the hegemonic domination of white society. Kathleen Brown's study of colonial Virginia emphasized the origins of racial slavery and the creation and solidification of a patriarchy based on white male elite dominance of their wives and children, the enslaved, and the polity. The creation of masculine gentility in the public world of politics, which allowed elite Virginians to claim the mantle of paternalism, depended on female withdrawal into the private world of the household.[43] Brown's scholarship on the foundations of slave society, as well as studies by Stephanie McCurry and others, have shown that issues of women and gender should not be separated into the private sphere and away from politics and political ideology. As McCurry argued in her study of yeoman households in South Carolina, Southern yeoman farmers' support for slavery and planter power was built on their ability to attain mastery of their own households and families. Whether or not they owned slaves, Southern yeomen continued to support slavery and secession as it underscored their position as "masters of small worlds."[44]

Although the patriarchal system of the slave South was built on planter dominance of their wives and families as well as the enslaved, historians have continued to debate whether this made white elite women victims of this hegemony. Against those arguing that their dependent position made plantation mistresses more sympathetic to their enslaved workers and even quiet abolitionists, Thavolia Glymph detailed the widespread violence perpetrated by slaveowning women.[45] Gendered assumptions about who could wield this control precluded many contemporary observers and scholars from seeing female violence as evidence of power. Glymph argued that, like their slaves, white women's agency has been obscured by stereotypes that presented female violence as "spontaneous outbursts of rage"—a defect of personality rather than a calculated action within the slave system's continuum of domination and resistance. Despite the supposed oppression of patriarchy, white women, unlike their enslaved property, were not without resources and because of their race could always turn to the courts and civil society for redress of abuse. Suffering patriarchy did not make Southern women into feminists any more than sympathy for their enslaved workers transformed them into abolitionists; ultimately they experienced a very different kind of vulnerability to male power than did the women they held in slavery. In fact, as Stephanie Jones-Rogers has argued, white women jealously and brutally guarded their economic influence over slave property and in slave markets.[46]

However, as recent studies have made clear, the challenge to patriarchy and the position of white women created by the Civil War did force many Southern women to question their commitment to slavery. Elite women, who had accepted their dependent position in the paternalistic world of the Old South in return for their husbands' protection and support and the status of their elite position as slaveowners, found this bargain called into question by the war and the inability of the Confederacy to continue this arrangement. With more and more men called away to fight, slaveowning women, finding themselves in charge of managing increasingly rebellious slaves and contending with marauding Union forces, no longer could claim their privileged position as dependents. As Drew Faust suggested, "white men's wartime failure to provide women with either physical safety or basic subsistence cast this world and its social assumptions into question." The wives of yeoman farmers and poor white Southerners also grew increasingly assertive during the war as they struggled to survive with their husbands called away to fight. In *Confederate Reckoning: Power and Politics in the Civil War South,* Stephanie McCurry built on her study of antebellum yeoman women to show how yeoman and poor white women challenged the Confederate vision of who would be included as citizens of the new slaveholding republic. Using their identity as soldiers' wives to form a new political constituency, they forced the Confederacy to recognize that women were not simply dependents but active participants in the war. Research by Faust, McCurry, Catherine Clinton, Nina Silber, Laura Edwards, and LeeAnn Whites has helped to demonstrate that the Civil War was not simply a conflict between warring men, but because Southern paternalism was built on a gendered foundation, the conflict created what Whites aptly termed a "crisis in gender." Indeed, as Faust and McCurry have provocatively suggested, the desertion of Southern women from the cause may have been one of the sources of Confederate failure.[47]

Studies of the experience of enslaved women have also made this connection between the behavior of enslaved people and their conduct during the Civil War and Reconstruction. Although much of the literature on the Civil War and Reconstruction separates the drama and chaos of the conflict from the antebellum period, recent work has drawn on the example of scholarship from other slave societies to connect slavery and emancipation more closely. Formerly enslaved women drew on their experience during slavery as they set their ambitions and priorities for freedom.[48] Particularly, enslaved men and women drew on the egalitarian basis of their relationships within the slave family and community as they sought to define their new role as free laborers. While angry land owners decried the "evil of female loaferism" when freedwomen decreased the number of hours they were willing to work in the fields, Leslie Schwalm argued that this behavior did not reflect women's refusal to work or an attempt to "play the lady." Rather, building on customs during slavery that allowed enslaved families in South Carolina to raise food crops and livestock for their own subsistence, many women—with their husbands' support—during and after the war sought to limit agricultural labor and their supervision by white employers in favor of reproductive labor for their families.[49]

Enslaved people who had worked as domestic servants also drew on the long tradition of contesting labor relations with their mistresses as they negotiated their new roles as free workers. Domestic servants who had stolen or borrowed their owners' clothes for their *frolics* in the woods during slavery became bolder during the war, audaciously using their mistresses' toiletries or donning their finery as they departed the plantation in search of freedom. Others refused to do tasks they had performed as slaves, insisting that they would only perform the kind of labor they were hired for. Like female field workers, formerly enslaved people also demonstrated their preference for domestic work that allowed them the greatest control of their labor and the least white supervision, particularly preferring laundry work or skilled work such as cooking to general domestic service. In these ambitions, the formerly enslaved mirrored the choices that free women of color had been making for decades to "survive and thrive" in the hostile environment and limited employment choices of the antebellum South. Thus, as Glymph argued, enslaved women's resistance during slavery, although the least acknowledged, clearly shaped the struggles of enslaved women after emancipation.[50]

In recent decades, women's and gender history have contributed significantly to our knowledge and understanding of slavery. Historians have demonstrated gender's role in shaping the experience of enslaved women, but also in creating and maintaining racial slavery in the South. These studies have helped to demonstrate the utility of gender analysis within the field of slave history and beyond. As scholars of the post-Civil Rights generation push beyond gender history that focuses mainly on the experiences of women, new insights are likely to be produced, both by adding men to the analysis and by using gender to analyze the male experience of slavery. Toward this end, Lydia Plath and Sergio Lassuna edited a series of essays on masculinity as a category of analysis in the antebellum South. Lassuna later explored the process through which enslaved men negotiated their masculinities through recreational pursuits and resistance. Moving on from the contentious debates over slave masculinity and matrifocality that characterized the long Civil Rights era has offered scholars an opportunity to make a fresh examination of enslaved gender roles and sexuality, both male and female.[51]

Moving beyond the national approach, scholars of slavery in the Atlantic world and of Western and non-Western systems of slavery have begun to suggest the ways that women's experiences of slavery were different to men's, and to explore how accounting for gender challenges our conceptions of slavery and the world slave system.[52] These approaches offer further evidence that, more than simply another subfield of slave history, gender and slavery studies should be an integral part of the post-Civil Rights agenda of connecting slavery to the transformations of society in the United States and beyond.

Notes

1. Many of the first women's liberation activists were radicalized by their own experiences in Civil Rights organizations and the New Left, where they found that patriarchal and even sexist attitudes toward women persisted despite the movements' revolutionary rhetoric. The Civil Rights movement's gains—particularly the passage of legislation that forbade employment discrimination based on race or sex—also opened up opportunities for women in the academy and the professions. See particularly Evans, *Personal Politics;* and MacLean, *Freedom Is Not Enough.*

2. Camp, *Closer to Freedom,* 3; J. W. Scott, *Gender and the Politics of History,* 28-50.

3. Truth, *Narrative of Sojourner Truth, A Bondswomen of Olden Time.*

4. Washington, "'From Motives of Delicacy'"; Truth, *Narrative of Sojourner Truth;* Jacobs, *Incidents in the Life of a Slave Girl.*

5. Historian Jean Fagan Yellin researched the life of Harriet Jacobs to prove that Jacobs, and not Lydia Maria Child, had written her narrative. See Jacobs, *Incidents in the Life of a Slave Girl;* and Yellin, *Harriet Jacobs.* Nell Irvin Painter's biography of Sojourner Truth drew new attention to Truth's life and her place as a symbol of antislavery and women's rights. See Truth, *Narrative;* Painter, *Sojourner Truth;* and Washington, *Sojourner Truth's America.*

6. Anna Julia Cooper received her PhD in 1925 from the Sorbonne in Paris with her dissertation on "The Attitude of France on the Question of Slavery between 1789 and 1848." See Dagbovie, "Black Women Historians."

7. Elkins, *Slavery;* Frazier, *Negro Family;* Moynihan, *Negro Family.*

8. Parish, *Slavery,* x.

9. Gutman, *Black Family.*

10. The creation of a slave community based on a normative male experience may also have been a function of Blassingame's methodology. Of the seventy-six slave and former slave autobiographies that he heavily used as evidence, only four were written by women. Blassingame, *Slave Community,* 92-93, 104-31, 133-35.

11. Genovese, *Roll, Jordan, Roll,* 482-94, 500, 597-98.

12. Lerner, *Black Women in White America;* D. White, "'Matter out of Place.'"

13. Hull, Scott, and Smith, *All the Women Are White.*

14. Clinton, *Plantation Mistress,* 35, 196.

15. Angelina and Sarah Grimké, who converted to Quakerism after being raised in a slaveholding family in Charleston, became noted abolitionist speakers and authors. See Lerner, *Grimké Sisters;* and Fox-Genovese, *Plantation Household,* 29, 35, 39, 47-48.

16. D. White, *Ar'n't I a Woman?*

17. Jones, *Labor of Love,* 11-79. See also the revised and expanded anniversary edition (2010).

18. Parish, *History and Historians*, x, 91-92; Kolchin, *American Slavery*. This approach to viewing gender as a subfield of slavery history has continued in later works on the historiography of slavery, including M. Smith, *Debating Slavery*. In her 2007 essay marking the twentieth anniversary of the publication of Deborah Gray White's *Ar'n't I A Woman?*, Leslie Harris argued that even in the twenty-first century, slavery studies remain fragmented, and many subfields and syntheses of slave history have failed to pay conscious attention to gender and the insights of gender scholarship. L. Harris, *"Ar'n't I a Woman?,"* 153. This essay, while presenting the historiography of gender and slavery as a discrete chapter in this volume, thus seeks to emphasize the contributions that historians of gender and slavery have made in moving studies of women and slavery beyond its own subfield to an integral part of discussions of slave labor, resistance, family, community, and culture.

19. L. Harris, *"Ar'n't I a Woman?,"* 153. Reflecting the pivotal nature of Deborah Gray White's work, two journals published special editions to mark the anniversary of *Ar'n't I a Woman?*'s publication. See the summer 2007 issue of the *Journal of Women's History* (specifically pages 138-69, the essays by Daina Ramey Berry, Stephanie Camp, Leslie Harris, Barbara Krauthamer, and Jessica Millward, and a response by Gray herself); and the winter 2007 issue of *Journal of African American History*, which featured a special issue on "Women, Slavery, and Historical Research," pages 1-95).

20. Collections of this work include Patricia Morton, *Discovering the Women in Slavery;* and Gaspar and Hine, *More than Chattel.*

21. In their essay on the historiography of slavery, August Meier and Elliott Rudwick suggested that new schools of historical interpretation are either the product of social factors acting on a generation of scholars or the result of the influence of "seminal works." They argued that the slave community school of the 1960s was the result of the social climate of the Civil Rights era, but that the "new paradigm" of cultural history popularized in the 1990s seems to have been more the result of interdisciplinary influences within the academy, particularly from anthropology and literary criticism. Meier and Rudwick, *Black History and the Historical Profession*. For a discussion of the rise of cultural history, see Burke, *What Is Cultural History?*

22. E. Higginbotham, "African-American Women's History."

23. J. W. Scott, *Gender and the Politics of History*, 50.

24. W. D. Jordan, *White Man's Burden;* E. Morgan, *American Slavery.*

25. K. Brown, *Good Wives*, 2, 41, 104.

26. K. Brown, *Good Wives*, 3, 107-36.

27. J. Morgan, *Laboring Women*, 12-49, 69.

28. J. Morgan, *Laboring Women*, 144-46.

29. See for example Blassingame, *Slave Community*, 92-93; and J. Jones, *Labor of Love*, 11-79.

30. Berlin and Morgan, *Cultivation and Culture*, 1-45.

31. Schwalm, *Hard Fight for We,* 47.
32. J. Morgan, *Laboring Women,* 162-63; Schwalm, *Hard Fight for We,* 19-23.
33. Berry, *Swing the Sickle,* 2, 13-34.
34. Fett, *Working Cures,* 111-13, 125. See also Schwartz, *Birthing a Slave,* 143-87.
35. See in particular Blassingame, *Slave Community,* 104-31; and Genovese, *Roll, Jordan, Roll,* 597-657.
36. J. Morgan, *Laboring Women,* 166-67.
37. Follett, "'Lives of Living Death.'"
38. J. C. Scott, *Domination and the Arts of Resistance;* J. C. Scott, *Weapons of the Weak;* Camp, *Closer to Freedom,* 2-3. 39.
39. Camp, *Closer to Freedom,* 61-67, 91. Camp's analysis also draws on Tera Hunter's conceptualization of pleasure as a form of everyday resistance for black female domestic workers in the postbellum period. Hunter, *To 'Joy My Freedom,* 168-86.
40. Glymph, *House of Bondage,* 70-71, 91-92; J. C. Scott, *Weapons of the Weak.*
41. Myers, *Forging Freedom,* 8, 39-77.
42. Building on Suzanne Lebsock's pioneering study of Petersburg, Virginia, new studies have emphasized the relationships between enslaved and free black women in the urban South. Lebsock, *Free Women of Petersburg.* See also Myers, *Forging Freedom;* Rockman, *Scraping By,* 100-32; and King, *Essence of Liberty.* For a Northern perspective on slave and free black urban women, see E. A. Dunbar, *Fragile Freedom;* and Adams and Pleck, *Love of Freedom.*
43. K. Brown, *Good Wives,* 319-66.
44. McCurry, *Masters of Small Worlds.*
45. Clinton, *Plantation Mistress;* and M. Weiner, *Mistresses and Slaves.*
46. Glymph, *House of Bondage,* 32-62; Jones-Rogers, *They Were Her Property.*
47. Faust, *Mothers of Invention,* 242; McCurry, *Confederate Reckoning;* Clinton and Silber, *Divided Houses;* Whites, *Crisis in Gender;* Whites, *Gender Matters;* L. Edwards, *Scarlett Doesn't Live Here Anymore.*
48. Anthologies that collect this emerging scholarship include Scully and Paton, *Gender and Slave Emancipation;* and Campbell, Miers, and Miller, *Women and Slavery.*
49. Schwalm, *Hard Fight for We,* 187-233.
50. Camp, *Closer to Freedom,* 120; Hunter, *To 'Joy My Freedom,* 4; Myers, *Forging Freedom,* 8; Glymph, *House of Bondage,* 95.
51. See for example Foster, "Sexual Abuse of Black Men"; Rahman, "Strangest Freaks of Despotism"; Harris and Berry, *Sexuality and Slavery;* Plath and Lassuna, *Black and White Masculinity;* Lassuna, *My Brother Slaves;* and Hilde, *Slavery, Fatherhood, and Paternal Duty.*
52. See particularly Campbell, Miers, and Miller, "Women in Western Systems of Slavery."

CHAPTER FIVE

American Slavery and Families

SEAN CONDON

Enslavement in the Atlantic world began when men, women, and children were stolen away from their homes and separated from their kin. If they survived the Middle Passage, enslaved people formed and attempted to maintain family ties whenever possible, but these ties were always subject to the whims of their owners, whose drive for mastery was wedded to their desire for profitable plantation enterprises.[1] Throughout the Americas, slave marriage was not recognized by law, and enslaved people had no legal recourse if they were targeted for sale by their owners. In addition, slaveowners always had the authority to discipline and punish slave parents and children and to sexually exploit slaves as well. Vulnerability was thus a defining characteristic of enslaved families.

The precarious nature of enslaved family life took place in a particular demographic context. Unlike most other places in the Americas, the enslaved population in North America started to experience natural increase (that is, more births than deaths) in the eighteenth century, a trend that accelerated in many parts of the United States after the Atlantic slave trade ended in 1808. As a result, by the early nineteenth century, the slave population in the United States was predominantly native-born, and the ratio of males to females was roughly equal. At the same time, while slavery eroded in Northern states in the decades following the American Revolution, it rapidly expanded beyond the Eastern Seaboard into the Southwest as migrating planters supervised the construction of plantations that produced short-staple cotton and sugar. Western expansion led to the formation of an interstate slave trade that forcibly moved more than one million enslaved people over the course of the nineteenth century. The particular demographic context for slaves in the United States provided both a greater likelihood for enslaved men and women to find marriage partners and have children (relative to the enslaved in other parts of the Americas), but at the same time, it constantly threatened such families with forced separation. Like slaves elsewhere in the Atlantic world, enslaved men and women in the antebellum United States responded by crafting families in which people related by blood and marriage often connected with extended family members or others not necessarily related by blood or marriage; such relationships could be every bit as close, meaningful, and vulnerable to the power of slaveowners as any other family form.

Profound and passionate disagreements regarding the nature of enslaved families can be traced back to the time of slavery itself.[2] In the antebellum period, as slavery was expanding demographically and geographically, two important cultural shifts underscored the importance of intimate ties within nuclear families. One change involved the relationship between husbands and wives, as romantic love and emotional intimacy between spouses became a more important ideal. The other change centered on the relationship between parents and children. For a variety of reasons, people began to believe that environment profoundly shaped children and that parents needed to be more than stern disciplinarians: children needed a nurturing environment and a great deal more guidance and support in order to become fully independent adults.[3] This shift occurred first among members of the emerging middle class, and the ideas spread through different kinds of literature that emphasized the crucial role that family relationships played in shaping individual lives. These changing cultural values were embraced by antislavery activists, who came to argue that slavery's pernicious effect on enslaved families was perhaps the most powerful argument against the peculiar institution. Abolitionists like William Lloyd Garrison, Harriet Beecher Stowe, and Frederick Douglass often emphasized the ways that slavery assaulted the family connections of the enslaved, highlighting the prevalence of slave sales separating husbands from wives and parents from children, documenting a Southern legal framework that refused to recognize the sanctity of slave marriages, and exposing the sexual exploitation of enslaved women at the mercy of predatory owners.[4] In response, some white Southerners argued that the problems identified by abolitionists were the result of isolated cases of abuse, neglect, or economic misfortune, and not evidence of systematic exploitation, while some proslavery ideologues argued that slaveowners were paternalists who protected their "family, white and black."[5]

In the several decades that followed the Civil War, most white Americans—both Northern and Southern—came to embrace a sentimental view of the Old South that borrowed liberally from the proslavery arguments that slaveowners were paternalistic and that the enslaved themselves were content with their place in life and loyal to their masters. Sentimental fiction often articulated these views, but they also appeared in memoirs and histories of the late antebellum and Civil War years. For example, Jefferson Davis's 1881 history of the Civil War period argued that enslaved people had been "trained in the gentle arts of peace and order and civilization; they increased from a few unprofitable savages to millions of efficient Christian laborers." These histories provided little insight into or concern for the slave family; they were typically more concerned with comparing a supposed golden age with the industrial age's increasingly contentious and violent labor relations.[6]

At the end of the nineteenth century—when the popular view of slavery was largely the slavery's apologists' memory, when segregation was being firmly planted in the South, and when scientific racism was widely accepted within higher education in the United States and Europe—the first generation of professional historians emerged. Ulrich Bonnell Phillips and his students shaped the dominant scholarly interpretation that emerged at this time. Phillips combined a fairly uncritical reading of the slaveowners' records and writings with a set of racial assumptions that was popular among whites in the Jim Crow era, and as a result he articulated a view of slavery not very different than the proslavery arguments of the antebellum period. His *American Negro Slavery,* first published in 1918, was over five hundred pages long but mentioned slave families only in passing. On one occasion, Phillips provided a lengthy quote from the Southern planter and proslavery ideologue James Henry Hammond, who stated that "[slave] marriage is to be encouraged . . . as it adds to the comfort, happiness and health of those who enter upon it, besides insuring a greater increase."[7] In another place, Phillips argued that slaveholders tended to provide instruction in Christian morality and "the customs of marriage and parental care." In referring to the slaveowners' impact, Phillips concluded that "their despotism . . . was benevolent in intent and on the whole beneficial in effect."[8]

While the accounts of Phillips and his followers became the standard narrative informing US history textbooks in the first half of the twentieth century, several dissenters critiqued their interpretation—most but not all of whom were Black scholars. For example, in 1909, W. E. B. Du Bois offered an account of slavery discounting the supposed generosity of the slaveowner and providing a sharper focus on the enslaved themselves. Relying heavily on published travelers' accounts from the antebellum period, Du Bois argued that there was a significant difference between the experience of enslaved field workers and those slaves who worked as domestic servants, with only the relatively small number of domestics having enough autonomy and free time with which to develop and maintain fairly strong family ties. For Du Bois, that left a majority of enslaved field workers who experienced a life of unremitting toil in which family relationships were not protected. As a result, these men and women often were unable to perform expected familial roles. For example, enslaved adult men were unable to exercise "authority . . . to govern or protect his family."[9]

Another critique of the mild view of slavery promulgated by Phillips and his followers was Frederic Bancroft's 1931 monograph on the interstate slave trade.[10] Many scholars of the 1920s and 1930s were shaped by progressive views that were critical of economic inequality and its effect on American democracy. These scholars tended to believe that economic self-interest was the most important factor motivating individual thought and action, and they directly critiqued previous historians who discounted or downplayed economic motives. Following Phillips's lead, most conventional work on the antebellum South emphasized whites' paternalism and their interest in maintaining racial control over enslaved people. Bancroft's study relied primarily on newspaper accounts, and he documented both the widespread nature of the slave trade across the South and its profitability. Phillips had argued that slave sales had been relatively infrequent, and that owners had taken slave family connections into account in most cases. Bancroft's considerable evidence showed that children were often sold apart from their parents, and that profits were the most important consideration for slaveowners and traders. Bancroft's work did not reach a large audience when published, but like Du Bois's, it was rediscovered by historians of the long Civil Rights era and inspired a great deal of work that has generally supported its conclusions.

Like Du Bois, E. Franklin Frazier—who first published *The Negro Family in the United States* in 1939—emphasized the ways in which the institution of slavery threatened the family life of enslaved men, women, and children. For Frazier, the separation of spouses made it difficult for two-parent nuclear families to be maintained, and as a result, enslaved men had difficulty establishing and maintaining authority within their families; the result was often a family dynamic in the slave quarters largely shaped by enslaved adult women.[11] Frazier argued that these family structures were the result of slavery itself, not the result of cultural attitudes brought from West Africa. Writing before World War II, Frazier and Du Bois did valuable work to call into question the romantic myths of the Phillips school and to document the challenges facing twentieth-century Black Americans, but both scholars seem to have had an idealized family type in mind—a family with two resident parents in which the husband had the role of breadwinner and primary decision maker, and the woman's role was that of nurturing wife and mother; Frazier and Du Bois both considered deviations from this ideal type problematic.

By the 1940s, the Phillips school's interpretation came under sustained attack as a growing number of scholars rejected the racialized assumptions at the heart of its arguments. As the introductory essay in this volume makes clear, most of these midcentury scholars were influenced and repulsed by the rise of fascism in Europe and elsewhere. An early bellwether of this change came from cultural anthropologists, who by the 1930s were rejecting hierarchical cultural models in favor of recognizing and attempting to understand the causes and consequences of cultural difference.[12] In 1941, the anthropologist Melville J. Herskovits argued that the differences in slave family structure that Frazier identified were not simply the result of American slavery's oppressive nature, but were also influenced by the nature of family and community organization in West Africa, including the existence of polygamy and the relatively small stigma attached to divorce.[13] Rather than interpreting these different social structures as a deviation from the supposed norm, Herskovits argued that they are better understood as an effort to adapt West African cultural practices to a new and difficult environment. Herskovits's views did not have much of an impact among most midcentury scholars of slave families, who tended to emphasize the oppressive nature of American slavery, but Herskovits's perspective would be rediscovered and amplified by historians of the long Civil Rights tradition, as well as by recent historians.

Scholarly interest in slavery began to increase after World War II for several reasons. Partly, it was shaped by the emergence of a new generation of Black scholars like John Hope Franklin, who built on the earlier antiracist work of Du Bois, Bancroft, and Frazier.[14] In addition, the rise and fall of fascist empires in Europe bred scholarly interest in understanding the nature and causes of American racism.[15] Like many white abolitionists of the antebellum period, many of these mid-twentieth-century white scholars wrote with the belief that enslaved people had little power to shape their own lives. For example, as Kenneth Stampp noted in his general study of slavery, published in 1956, slave marriages lacked any legal recognition and could be ended at the master's whim. Stampp argued that the slave family itself had "minor social and economic significance, and that fathers had a pretty minor role." Given these conditions, Stampp concluded, "it is hardly surprising to find that slave families were highly unstable."[16] Stanley M. Elkins amplified Stampp's arguments, arguing in 1959 that because slaveowners' power was complete, they were the only source of authority for the enslaved: "All lines of authority descended from the master, and alternative social bases that might have supported alternative standards were systematically suppressed."[17] Although he granted the existence of slave families, Elkins argued that the slave family was not a "meaningful unit," and that because of their total dependence on the master, enslaved men could never attain "all the true attributes of manhood," like being an independent provider and decision maker. The relationships that formed within slave families were therefore fundamentally different than relationships in free families. Elkins relied heavily on psychological theories and the extant secondary literature, and he examined very few primary sources beyond some planters' and travelers' accounts.

The scholarly arguments that slavery decimated Black family life gained considerable traction after the Moynihan Report was published in 1965. In a document prepared for US congressional hearings, the assistant labor secretary Daniel Patrick Moynihan argued that poverty and attending social disorder was fully entrenched in urban Black communities, that many Black families were "unstable" and "in many urban centers [were] approaching complete breakdown," and that the root cause was a "tangle of pathology" that began under slavery. Moynihan hoped that by illuminating a significant and long-standing problem, he could secure more funding for federal programs to alleviate poverty.[18]

The 1960s would see a dramatic increase in scholarly interest in slavery, much of it motivated by the Civil Rights movement and a broader interest in social history. Historians driven by the promise and challenge of civil rights and antiracism turned with new interest to slavery studies. Early Civil Rights movement victories highlighted the ability of people with little formal political power to bring about change. A rising generation of historians working from the mid-1960s into the 1980s targeted Elkins's emphasis on the passivity of the enslaved and their inability to effectively resist dehumanization—and Moynihan's popularization of that interpretation. These scholars dismantled Elkins's central contention that enslaved people were simply victims of a total institution. To do so, they examined sources that had largely been overlooked by previous historians of slavery. Some of these sources—like slave narratives written in the nineteenth century and interviews of elderly former slaves conducted under the auspices of the WPA in the 1930s—allowed careful readers much greater access to the perspectives of the enslaved themselves. By the late 1960s, the analytical power of computers allowed historians to examine other sources, like census records and plantation account books, much more systematically. Although these public records could not provide direct insight into the worldview and mentality of the enslaved, their aggregation could shed light on the structure of slave families across time and space. The historians of slave families of the 1960s and 1970s arrived at a variety of different interpretations, but they generally contended that while enslaved people lacked legal authority or much cultural power, they were subjects who labored to shape the world around them in subtle but significant ways, and were not simply objects who were acted upon. Most of these studies acknowledged the myriad challenges facing antebellum enslaved Americans, but they all tended to emphasize the autonomy and power of slave families and communities. Later scholars of the long Civil Rights tradition—mostly in the 1980s and 1990s—continued to grant slave agency but placed relatively more emphasis on the slaveowners' power to limit and contain that agency.

One of the most important long Civil Rights-era scholars was Herbert Gutman, who combined an interest in cultural identity with an ability to use the emerging quantitative methods of historical demography. Trained as a historian of labor and the working class, Gutman came of age at a time when British labor historians, particularly E. P. Thompson, were exploring the cultural differences between social groups in English history. Gutman's central accomplishment as a labor historian was to argue that the people who formed the backbone of the industrial workforce in nineteenth-century America developed their own distinct culture, one often at odds with the largely native-born, middle-class American culture that claimed to be universal and normative.[19] Gutman brought this concern with cultural difference to his work on slave families. In *The Black Family in Slavery and Freedom* (1976), Gutman argued that enslaved men and women emerged from slavery with a relatively stable and coherent structure, and with their own distinct familial mores and traditions. For example, his close examination of plantation registers allowed him to argue that enslaved naming patterns provided important "clues to the significance enslaved people attached to the enlarged kinship group."[20] Specifically, Gutman found that enslaved male children were often named for male relatives, including fathers, uncles, and grandfathers. Other analysis of plantation accounts led Gutman to find that while enslaved women would often become pregnant before marriage, they would tend to get married after the birth of that first child. He also found that unlike their white contemporaries, enslaved people of African descent appeared to have had fairly strong taboos against blood-cousin marriage. In addition to his focus on cultural questions, Gutman also offered a pioneering analysis of census records to help provide a more specific picture of the structure of African American families during slavery and in its aftermath. His analysis of mid-nineteenth-century census records and Reconstruction-era marriage registration records showed that a majority of African Americans during and immediately after the Civil War lived in two-parent families.

Gutman's study was the only book-length work to focus solely on the slave family, but practically all the major examinations of slavery in the 1960s and 1970s included some investigation of slave families. One set of works—most notably those by John Blassingame and Lawrence Levine—examined the culture and community of enslaved African Americans in the antebellum United States. Both scholars were interested in the ways that enslaved families helped to develop and transmit cultural values and attitudes. For Blassingame, one of the slave family's most important functions was to provide enslaved children with the ability to survive the psychological assaults of being enslaved: "Since slave parents were primarily responsible for training their children, they could cushion the shock of bondage for them, help them to understand their situation, teach them values different from those their masters tried to instill in them, and give them a referent for self-esteem other than their master."[21] Levine's comprehensive study of African American folklore and oral traditions also emphasized the way that enslaved adults (whether related kin or not) would pass on cultural values to the younger generation through the telling of folktales. For example, many slave tales "were utilized to inculcate a vision of the good and moral life by stressing the ideals of friendship, cooperation, meaningful activity and family love."[22] Although both scholars acknowledged the masters' power to disrupt the family lives of enslaved people, both also emphasized the independence of slave culture and the role that enslaved families played in buttressing that autonomy.

Whereas Blassingame and Levine probed the nature of slave cultures and communities as largely separate from the world of slaveowners, Eugene Genovese's work emphasized the dynamics of the master/slave relationship. According to Genovese, slaves and owners together created a web of relationships in which the enslaved largely accepted the "paternal" authority of owners but worked within that relationship to gain concessions from the owner. Genovese argued that most slaveowners were clearly aware of the nature of slave family relationships, and as self-styled "paternalists" they continuously involved themselves in their slaves' family lives because they believed they had both a right and a responsibility to do so. At the same time, enslaved people were often able to use planters' self-conceptions as benevolent paternalists to bargain or petition for themselves and their family members. Ultimately, like other scholars of the 1960s and 1970s, Genovese found that despite many obstacles, "slaves created impressive norms of family life, including as much of a nuclear family norm as conditions permitted, and that they entered the postwar social system with a remarkably stable base."[23]

Perhaps the most unique 1970s account of the slave family came from two historians who emphasized economic history, and who were the most enthusiastic proponents of what they called *cliometrics*. In *Time on the Cross* (1974), Robert Fogel and Stanley Engerman championed quantitative methods as ways to analyze historical records in a comprehensive way. Rather than relying on anecdote or story, they argued that massive analysis of blocks of census, tax, and probate records could completely undermine conventional wisdom. Overall, Fogel and Engerman critiqued a long-held stereotype that American slaveowners were antimodern and anticapitalistic. They argued that slaveowners were economically *rational* given the economic context and the legal framework that existed in the pre-Civil War United States.[24] Their interpretation of economic rationality had a host of implications, including ones that affected slave families. Because the Atlantic slave trade became illegal in 1808, and because enslaved people were considered such valuable property, Fogel and Engerman argued that "it was to the economic interest of the planters to encourage the stability of slave families and most of them did so."[25] They attempted to support this argument by marshalling evidence that young children were not usually sold away from their mothers, and that in some cases families were sold together.[26] In addition to being economically rational in attempting to maximize profits, antebellum American slaveholders were also shaped by "Victorian attitudes" regarding sex and marriage.[27] In other words, according to Fogel and Engerman, planters emphasized strong, stable families, as well as the limitation of sexual activity to married couples. They did not dispute that some white men failed to live by the dominant sexual morality of their day, but they argued that the sexual exploitation of enslaved women by white men was not frequent enough to have "undermined or destroyed the black family."[28] Because Fogel and Engerman's interpretations were so novel and contrarian, and because their tone seemed somewhat dismissive of what they called *nonquantitative* history, they were immediately barraged with criticism.[29] Although their overall argument that antebellum Southern planters were interested in profitability has been borne out by subsequent analysis, their contention that concerns over profitability led planters to protect slave families has been vigorously rebutted in much of the subsequent literature.

Scholars working within the Civil Rights tradition of the 1960s and 1970s fundamentally transformed the understanding of enslaved families by emphasizing the ability and agency of the enslaved to construct and attempt to maintain meaningful relationships within a system that continually assaulted their humanity. In his introduction to this volume, Aaron Astor rightly notes that this *long Civil Rights tradition* stretches from the 1960s to the end of the twentieth century, and in many ways, the literature on the slave family fits this periodization. Work on the slave family in the 1980s and 1990s continued to rely primarily on the methods of social history to produce a large number of finely grained studies that added detail and further refinement to the broad pictures Gutman and the other scholars painted of the slave community. However, in some ways, the 1980s and 1990s literature on the slave family marked a departure from the earlier work in ways that foreshadowed the literature of the twenty-first century. Most importantly, the work of the 1980s and 1990s began to call into question some of the more optimistic conclusions reached by scholars of the 1960s and 1970s, while at the same time attempting to redefine what scholars mean when they refer to "slave families."

In the 1980s and 1990s, scholars of slave families pursued three broad critiques of the work of the 1960s and 1970s. One critique, articulated by Ira Berlin in 1980, argued that despite the fact that African slavery in North America existed for two and a half centuries, most of the literature on slavery in the United States focused on the late antebellum period (at the expense of examining earlier periods), while at the same time obscuring regional differences that tended to make the slave South appear homogeneous.[30] Berlin called for more specialized studies that focused on variables like slave population, agriculture, economy, and politics; his work also synthesized studies that were already appearing in the late 1970s and 1980s. For example, historians of the colonial Chesapeake provided some of the most detailed studies that were sensitive to structural change over time and across space to deeply enrich the understanding of slave demography and family structure. Scholars like Russell Menard, Allan Kulikoff, Jean B. Lee, and Philip Morgan used probate inventories, tax lists, and other public records to delineate the emergence of a demographic base for family formation after the devastating period of discontinuity caused by the Atlantic slave trade. The spread of African slavery in the Americas meant widespread destruction of African families, as individuals were taken from families and communities and transported across the Atlantic to planters interested solely in their labor power. As many scholars have shown, the sex ratio of enslaved Africans brought to the Americas was consistently skewed in favor of males. As a result, immigrants from Africa rarely had the ability to form and enjoy lasting family relationships, and they were less likely to have children. Life expectancy for newly arrived Africans was very low, and it took constant imports of enslaved Africans from across the ocean to keep the slave population growing. However, by the first quarter of the eighteenth century in the Tidewater Chesapeake, an increasingly larger percentage of native-born slaves equalized the sex ratio, increased the birthrate, and allowed for the first time the demographic possibility of family life for a significant portion of the enslaved population. Furthermore, prior to the American Revolution, relatively few Chesapeake slaves were sold or otherwise forced to leave the region, although forced migration would become much more common following American independence from Great Britain. Chesapeake scholars have debated the extent to which the demographic conditions necessarily led to sustained kinship bonds—especially given the relatively small size of the median slaveholdings. This work highlighted the importance of understanding the demographic context for enslaved family formation.[31]

In 1989, Michael Tadman's emphasis on the demographic context for family formation returned to the issue of the interstate US slave trade in the nineteenth century. Tadman echoed Frederic Bancroft's earlier work, arguing that the forced migration of enslaved men, women, and children was not a peripheral aspect of antebellum slavery, but in fact central to the institution. Tadman targeted Genovese and Fogel and Engerman by emphasizing that the extensive nature of the interstate slave trade suggested that slaveowners were more motivated by short-term profit than they were paternalism. Tadman's exhaustive quantitative analysis of slave sales supported his view that the threat of a marriage being ended or a child sold from his or her mother was very real, especially in the upper South. Tadman estimated that one out of three enslaved children in the nineteenth-century upper South were sold out of state and therefore separated from their parents. If in-state sales are also considered, he estimated that roughly half of all enslaved children in the antebellum upper South were sold away from their parents.

While scholars focusing on the colonial Chesapeake and elsewhere in North America continued to bolster Berlin's critique by underscoring slavery's spatial and temporal complexity, another critique of the revisionist scholarship also emerged. Among the first to articulate this second critique was Peter Kolchin, who began to call into question the revisionists' emphasis on slave autonomy. In a work comparing slavery in the antebellum United States to serfdom in nineteenth-century Russia, Kolchin identified a number of factors suggesting that slaveowners in the United States had the means, motive, and opportunity to constantly interfere with their slaves' lives, both in the field and in the slave quarters.[32] In an effort to emphasize enslaved autonomy and agency, Kolchin argued, early Civil Rights–era scholars risked going too far in de-emphasizing the great limits and challenges to that agency, and therefore risked neglecting the constant threats to slave family life, community, and autonomy. Scholars focusing on particular regions and time periods further elaborated on Kolchin's critique.[33]

Another important facet of revisionism missing from earlier work was an interpretation that focused on the perspective and agency of enslaved women. From the work of Du Bois and Frazier up through Stamp and Elkins, scholars interpreted a lack of enslaved male power as a marker that slave families were not normative. Women's historians of the 1980s began to call this interpretation into question by critically examining the mythic ways that enslaved women had been described and understood by white

SEAN CONDON

Southerners, and by looking closely at both women's roles within slave families and their relationships with husbands and children. In 1985, Deborah Gray White published one of the central early works employing this perspective.[34] White argued that slave families were not patriarchal or matriarchal, but "unusually egalitarian."[35] Similarly, as Katherine Chilton describes in her essay on gender and slavery in this volume, Jacqueline Jones concurred by noting the resistance that such gender roles represented to the planters' family ideals.[36] In 1988, Elizabeth Fox-Genovese's monograph explored the relationships between white and Black women in the antebellum South. Whereas some scholars have suggested that Southern patriarchy had created a society in which Black and white women shared a lack of power and privilege, Fox-Genovese argued that white and Black women did not typically identify with each other, and instead identified with members of their own race. As a result, enslaved women did not usually have allies among female members of the slaveholding class, and their own family ties were always vulnerable to the whim and legal authority of their owners, both male and female.

The methodological and interpretive insights acquired during the long Civil Rights era culminated in the 1990s with a number of richly detailed local and regional studies of enslaved families. In particular, two very detailed books focusing on different regions of the nineteenth-century South helped to further deepen scholars' understanding of slave families by suggesting that the old dichotomy of two-parent versus single-parent family formation needed to be jettisoned, and replaced with a recognition that kinship connections could take a great variety of forms as enslaved individuals sought a sense of belonging in the face of constant threats. The first of these works was Ann Patton Malone's *Sweet Chariot: Slave Family and Household Structure in Nineteenth-Century Louisiana* (1992), which examined slave families in nineteenth-century Louisiana.[37] Malone's work focused on the household structure of slave communities through a quantitative analysis of plantation records, making arguments both about family structure and about the meaning and nature of slave families. To make the argument about slave

118

family structure, Malone examined the probate records of multiple parishes in Louisiana in order to show that the slave family "was far more diverse and adaptable than previously believed."[38] Malone found in her sample of over ten thousand enslaved people in more than three thousand household units that while two-parent households accounted for nearly half of all people in her sample, and single women with children about 15 percent of the sample, a variety of extended and multiple families—as well as solitary men and women—made up the rest of her sample. After detailing the varieties of enslaved family structures, Malone tried to explain how enslaved people understood and experienced family life. The title of her book, *Sweet Chariot,* is taken from the words of a slave spiritual, and just as religious faith could provide at least some relief and respite "for people living under a degrading, dehumanizing system of forced and permanent servitude," Malone argued that enslaved people strove to make family relationships serve that same purpose.[39] To make this argument, Malone combined the large-scale samples from probate and other public records, which provided snapshots of a family at a moment in time, with plantation records from a number of estates that kept exceptionally detailed records, which allowed her to trace the separations and reformulations of families over time. She argued that a familial ideal can be discerned among the enslaved: a "closely knit and interrelated collection of simple families, built around couples and their children, but which would also try to integrate singles into the community."[40] Malone concluded by arguing that enslaved people struggled mightily to form and maintain stable families and communities, since these kin connections were always threatened by separation by local and long-distance sale, planter migration, and estate division at the death of an owner. In the face of this constant threat of separation, Malone argued that there existed "a persistent urge within a fragmented slave community to reunite or rebuild despite the pain associated with such efforts and adjustments."[41]

In 1996, Brenda Stevenson published her study comparing family life among whites and Blacks in Loudon County, Virginia, titled *Life in Black and White: Family and Community in the Slave South.* Like

Malone, Stevenson argued both that enslaved families were under constant fear of separation, and that enslaved families existed in a great variety of forms. Stevenson contended that it was difficult for enslaved Virginians to form and maintain two-parent households in which both parents could live together with children because so many marriages were by necessity between people from two different plantations, given the relatively small size of most northern Virginia slaveholdings. Furthermore, Stevenson found "very little evidence which suggests that a nuclear family was the slave's sociocultural ideal."[42] Instead, she argued that while many enslaved people did live in families with monogamous marriages and co-residential nuclear families, many lived in a variety of other kinds of families, including ones with single-parent households, spouses who lived on different plantations (also known as *abroad* marriages), and a great variety of other arrangements.[43] What stands out from this great diversity, according to Stevenson, is that for the enslaved, the "most discernible ideal for their principal kinship organization was a malleable extended family that, when possible, provided its members with nurture, education, socialization, material support, and recreation in the face of the potential social chaos that the slaveholder imposed."[44] Despite examining very different kinds of social, economic, and physical environments at opposite ends of the interstate slave trade, both Malone and Stevenson reached very similar conclusions regarding both the flexible structure of enslaved families and the challenges facing those relationships.

Other regional or state studies in the 1990s reinforced their conclusions, including several works on South Carolina by Larry Hudson, Emily West, and Norrece T. Jones. Jones argued convincingly that planters' ability to break up slave marriages and sell children from parents was their most potent tool in compelling labor from the people they owned. The interpretation that emerged in the 1990s continued to inform scholarship on the slave family after the turn of the twentieth century. Emily West built on a number of articles completed in the 1990s to complete a book on slave marriage in South Carolina.[45] In an interpretation that combines

Berlin's and Kolchin's critiques, Wilma Dunaway argued in *The African American Family in Slavery and Emancipation* (2003) that historians have tended to underestimate both the importance of small slaveholdings as well as the power of slaveowners themselves. Dunaway, who has written extensively on life in nineteenth-century Appalachia, argued that in their efforts to be profitable, planters developed a variety of strategies that threatened the viability of enslaved family ties, and that "too many recent studies have the effect of whitewashing from slavery the worst structural constraints."[46]

At the end of the twentieth century, historians of the slave family began to turn away from long Civil Rights-era social historians' concerns by spending less time tracing family structures and more time trying to understand the meaning and significance of those family relationships—whatever form they took. In broad terms, this shift was influenced by the general historiographical turn from social to cultural history. In addition, as Aaron Astor notes in his introduction, historians of slavery have also recently spent more time trying to integrate slavery into broader historical themes, especially the history of capitalism and the emergence of democracy, as well as stressing the constraints facing slaves over their ability to respond and resist. Recent work on slave families has also been informed by two other broad historiographical trends. First, the emphasis on histories that transcend the nation-state as the unit of analysis has led a large number of scholars to embrace Atlantic history and focus renewed attention on the role that African cultures played in the formation of slave family practices and structures. Second, there has been a greater recognition that modern family life does not seem to fit the *traditional* mold, and scholars of family history more generally have emphasized the more fluid and complex nature of family structures over time.[47]

One important work that marked the shifting historiography was Walter Johnson's 1999 monograph *Soul by Soul: Life inside the Antebellum Slave Market*. Johnson built on Tadman's work to argue that the interstate slave trade was not marginal but rather central to the experience of enslaved people in the nineteenth-century US

South. Nearly all slaves faced the possibility of sale away from loved ones, and Johnson highlighted the cultural ramifications of such a world: enslaved men and women not only tried to prevent such sales, but also had to develop mechanisms in order to recreate family life if their own was ruptured. In a sustained critique of Eugene Genovese's concept of *paternalism,* Johnson argued that slavery was fully part of the expansion of capitalism, and that paternalism was little more than a mental world created by slaveholders to justify and ennoble their actions. To planters, enslaved people were first and foremost commodities that through their work and their market value provided planters with the potential to enjoy mastery.[48]

Dylan Penningroth's work presented another approach to understanding the meaning of family life. Penningroth shed valuable new light on the relationships among enslaved people by examining the property they owned in the decades prior to emancipation. By working on their own plots in the evenings and on Sundays, by taking advantage of opportunities to hire themselves out, and by calling on the labor of family members, a significant portion of antebellum slaves were able to accumulate productive property like horses, pigs, and cattle, as well as agricultural products, and even cash. Penningroth argued that enslaved people's property ownership sheds light on relationships in slave families and communities, because for the enslaved to accumulate property, they typically had to be able to rely on the labor of other enslaved people; as Penningroth put it, "in regions with a flourishing slaves' economy, being part of a family or community often meant having to work for other slaves."[49] Not only did slaves need kin to acquire this property, but this property was typically used to support and maintain kin in turn. Examining claims of property and the conflicts that could result offers a powerful reminder that kin and community connections were not created in the notations on planter's daybooks. Penningroth argued that students of slave families and communities needed to keep in mind "moments when slaves chose to reject kin or communal ties as well as those moments of embrace. Focusing on kinship's limits anchors it firmly back in historical contexts and reminds us that although it could be adaptable and expansive, black kinship was never universal or automatic."[50] On the other hand, relationships forged in the creation and use of property could resemble or replace missing or stolen family connections. In other words, Penningroth's work was a reminder that historians must go far beyond the demographic contexts of slave families to look for evidence of the nature and significance of slave ties. In order to focus on the importance of fictive kin relationships, Penningroth updated a venerable tradition in studies of American slavery—the comparative approach—by integrating the history of enslaved families in the United States more fully into the history of enslaved families in the broader Atlantic world.[51]

Whereas Penningroth relied on Reconstruction-era property claims records to get at the cultural meanings behind family structures, other recent historians have plumbed other sources to further delineate the meanings behind family structures. Marie Jenkins Schwartz explored the power relations between slaveowners and slaves in terms of slave pregnancy and childbirth.[52] Phillip Troutman examined the rare letters written between enslaved family members in the nineteenth-century South, illuminating the ways that enslaved men and women utilized the sentimental language that was so widespread in American culture as a whole in the first half of the nineteenth century.[53] Others, like Martha Hodes and Tiya Miles, investigated relationships that crossed the boundaries of both enslaved status and *race*. Hodes's *White Women, Black Men: Illicit Sex in the Nineteenth-Century South* (1997) delves into relationships between white women and Black men in the nineteenth century. Miles's work focused on a microhistory of one family that began when a Cherokee man developed a lifelong relationship with an enslaved woman he had purchased.[54] Recent work on slave families has continued to highlight both the importance and fragility of kinship networks among enslaved people. Emily West's 2012 study of free people of color who sold themselves back into slavery concluded that the most important factor in such a decision was the effort to maintain family ties. James H. Sweet's 2013 historiography of slave families emphasized the importance of flexible and inventive kinship traditions in West Africa that served as models throughout the Atlantic world.[55]

Emancipation posed its own legal and emotional challenges to Black families emerging from slavery. Heather Williams's *Help Me to Find My People* (2012) mined newspaper advertisements and private letters cataloging the wrenching process through which recently emancipated women and men reconstituted their families after decades of forced separation.[56] Tera Hunter's *Bound in Wedlock* (2019) interrogated the relationship between marriage contracts and slavery, and the ways in which emancipation imposed new, arbitrary strictures on Black family life.[57] Like much scholarship in recent years, Hunter emphasized the enduring legacies of enslavement on generations of Black Americans after emancipation. Given this vibrant and continuously evolving historiographical tradition, it is likely that questions about the enslaved—and recently emancipated—family will continue to provoke new examinations and produce rich new interpretations in the future.

NOTES

1. The Middle Passage is the term coined by eighteenth-century traders to describe the slave trade between Africa and the Americas. For a suggestive argument that enslaved men and women began forming close connections on the Middle Passage itself, see Mintz and Price, *Birth of African-American Culture*, 42-51.

2. For previous historiographies of the slave family, see Parish, *Slavery*; Kolchin, *American Slavery*; Jabour, "Perspectives on the Historiography"; D. Davis, "Review of the Conflicting Theories"; Pargas, "Boundaries and Opportunities"; and J. H. Sweet, "Defying Social Death."

3. For a classic overview of these changes, see Mintz and Kellogg, *Domestic Revolutions*. For a study that focused on the relationship between husbands and wives, see Jabour, *Marriage in the Early Republic*.

4. For a general statement on this, see Stewart, *Holy Warriors*, 43.

5. For example, see Faust, *Ideology of Slavery*.

6. J. Davis, *Rise and Fall*, quoted in Blight, *Race and Reunion*, 259.

7. U. Phillips, *American Negro Slavery*, 269.

8. U. Phillips, *American Negro Slavery*, 328.

9. Du Bois, *Negro American Family*, 49.

10. F. Bancroft, *Slave Trading.*

11. Frazier, *Negro Family.*

12. For a general description of this development, see Novick, *Noble Dream,* 143–45.

13. Herskovits, *Myth of the Negro Past,* 30.

14. J. Franklin, *Slavery to Freedom.*

15. Myrdal, *American Dilemma;* Tannenbaum, *Slave and Citizen.*

16. Stampp, *Peculiar Institution,* 344.

17. Elkins, *Slavery,* 128.

18. On the Moynihan report's impact, see J. Patterson, *Freedom Is Not Enough.*

19. Gutman, "Work, Culture, and Society."

20. Gutman, *Black Family,* xxiii. Several scholars have picked up on naming analysis to shed greater light on kin connections among the enslaved. See especially Cody, "Naming, Kinship"; and Cody, "There Was No 'Absalom.'" See also Inscoe, "Generation and Gender."

21. Blassingame, *Slave Community,* 79. More recent work has expanded on the dynamic of child-rearing, with several important works focusing on the experience of childhood itself. See King, *Stolen Childhood;* and Schwartz, *Born in Bondage.*

22. L. Levine, *Black Culture,* 97.

23. Genovese, *Roll, Jordan, Roll,* 451–52.

24. Fogel and Engerman, *Time on the Cross.*

25. Fogel and Engerman, *Time on the Cross,* 6.

26. Fogel and Engerman, *Time on the Cross,* 6.

27. Fogel and Engerman, *Time on the Cross,* 129.

28. Fogel and Engerman, *Time on the Cross,* 131.

29. For example, see David et al., *Reckoning with Slavery.* Also see Gutman, *Slavery and the Numbers Game.*

30. Berlin, "Time, Space, and the Evolution of Afro-American Society." Berlin later published two book-length works that fleshed out these regional and temporal patterns: *Many Thousands Gone* in 1998 and *Generations of Captivity* in 2003.

31. On the early slave experience, see Menard, "Maryland Slave Population." On the eighteenth century, see Kulikoff, "Origins of Afro-American Society"; and Kulikoff, *Tobacco and Slaves,* 317–80. Jean Butenhoff Lee questions Kulikoff's assumption that slaves could develop regular community and kinship relationships outside their owners' property, arguing that community formation did not occur as quickly as Kulikoff claims. See Lee, "Problem of Slave Community." See also Philip D. Morgan's culminating work, *Slave Counterpoint.*

32. Kolchin, "Reevaluating the Antebellum Slave Community"; see also Kolchin, *Unfree Labor.* Kolchin summarized these findings in *American Slavery, 1619–1877,* 138.

33. For example, see Dusinberre, *Them Dark Days.*

34. D. White, *Ar'n't I a Woman?*

35. White, *Ar'n't I a Woman?*, 158.

36. J. Jones, *Labor of Love*, 11-79.

37. Malone, *Sweet Chariot*.

38. Malone, *Sweet Chariot*, 5.

39. Malone, *Sweet Chariot*, 6.

40. Malone, *Sweet Chariot*, 5.

41. Malone, *Sweet Chariot*, 2-3.

42. Stevenson, *Life in Black and White*, 160. See also Stevenson, "Distress and Discord."

43. For other work on cross-plantation marriages, see West, "Surviving Separation"; West, "Debate on the Strength of Slave Families"; and West, *Chains of Love*.

44. Stevenson, *Life in Black and White*, 160.

45. N. Jones, *Born a Child of Freedom;* West, "Surviving Separation"; Hudson, *To Have and to Hold*.

46. Dunaway, *African American Family*, 4.

47. For one popular account, see Coontz, *Way We Never Were*.

48. W. Johnson, *Soul by Soul*. See also Deyle, *Carry Me Back*.

49. Penningroth, "My People," 168; Penningroth, *Claims of Kinfolk*.

50. Penningroth, "My People," 170.

51. For one prominent example, see J. Morgan, *Laboring Women*.

52. Schwartz, *Birthing a Slave*.

53. Troutman, "Correspondences in Black and White."

54. Hodes, *White Women, Black Men;* Miles, *Ties that Bind*.

55. West, *Family or Freedom;* J. H. Sweet, "Defying Social Death."

56. H. Williams, *Help Me to Find My People*.

57. Hunter, *Bound in Wedlock*.

CHAPTER SIX

American Slavery and Resistance

WALTER C. RUCKER

Robin, dying at the gallows in colonial New York City, reflected on the series of events that led him to his ultimate fate. In the process, he revealed insightful details about the nature and risks of slave resistance. Convicted on April 11, 1712, in the stabbing death of his owner Henrich Hooghlandt, Robin had knowledge of a plan crafted by several slaves to rebel against the whites of the city and to secure their freedom. For his involvement, the court magistrates sentenced Robin to a slow death by starvation while hung up in chains in public. For five days, he languished in the same posture, rendered delirious by extreme discomfort, hunger, and thirst while being tormented daily by the city's white residents. Through the painful fog, Robin was lucid enough to divulge details about the rebel plan to the Reverend John Sharpe—chaplain of the English garrison at New York.[1]

Robin's posttrial confession to Sharpe revealed that the insurgents were inspired by an African-born conjurer who provided them with a mystical powder said to render them invulnerable. After performing a blood oath to ensure their loyalty, about twenty men conspired to torch a wooden outhouse and to kill any whites who attended the fire. Just after midnight on April 6, the group set about its bloody work in the streets of New York City using edged weapons, clubs, and guns to kill nine and injure seven others. After forces from nearby Fort George dispersed the rebels into the northern forests of Manhattan Island, about thirty Black men in the vicinity were rounded up and charged with crimes ranging from conspiracy to murder. Some committed suicide to avoid capture, torture, and execution. At least one other managed to escape the dragnet and was never brought to trial. In all, New York courts executed twenty-one enslaved men allegedly involved in the revolt. Some were burned alive, others—like Robin—were *gibbeted,* or chained up in public, while a few suffered breaking on the wheel.[2] A slave revolt, with all of its attendant risks and few rewards, could only be an enterprise for the most intrepid and heroic among the enslaved. Indeed, one could contend that among the most courageous Americans in the colonial and antebellum periods were the few enslaved women and men who gave their lives for the chance to be free.

In many ways, the 1712 New York City slave revolt epitomized the varieties and range of slave resistance in North America. Despite the fact that most enslaved people never involved themselves in such risky ventures as mass rebellions or conspiracies, a sizable number engaged in everyday or individual acts of resistance, including work slowdowns, feigned illness or pregnancy, arson, and poisonings. Others attempted temporary or permanent escapes— becoming outliers living on the edges of slave societies or forming independent maroon enclaves. Between outliers and maroons were the thousands—mostly men—who left their owners and pretended to be free in cities or on merchant ships. For some enslaved women and men, such drastic measures as suicide or infanticide became the only effective way of striking back at an oppressive system. Finally, mass rebellions and plots—like the 1712 New York City revolt—captured the imagination of generations of enslaved people while shaping public policy throughout colonial and antebellum North America.

The history of concerted efforts by enslaved people to throw off the shackles of bondage has not always been found in the pages of US history books, nor has the possibility of slave resistance been embraced by a wider American public until recently.

To understand why, one must imagine a world in which interpretations about slavery were monopolized and generated by those most vested in this vile system of labor exploitation—slaveowners. In the world that slaveowners made or imagined, practically everything rested on a series of interconnected ideas: that Africans were unredeemable savages; that slavery was Africans' salvation, as it introduced them to civilization and Christianity; that slaveowners were generally kind and paternalistic toward their slaves, at worst treating them like their own children; and that enslaved people loved their owners, knew their place, and enjoyed their lives as slaves. As ridiculous as these rationales—developed first by slaveowners seeking to defend their peculiar system of human bondage—may sound, they were taught in US high school and college classrooms through the 1960s, and as a result conveyed damaging and lasting misperceptions about African Americans to generations of Americans. In this context, the very idea of slave resistance threatened the viability and continuation of these ideas. If enslaved people resisted, then they must be more human than many assumed. Likewise, expressions of sometimes violent opposition meant that they loved neither their masters nor slavery—a damning condemnation of a central feature in early US history. In addition, they could not perceive their masters, nor most whites, as kind and benevolent if they were rising against them. If the enslaved resisted, then it naturally follows that they fully understood the oppressive weight of labor exploitation, the systematic rape of thousands of girls and women, the mutilation, the high rates of morbidity, and the short life expectancies as circumstances that humans should never be forced to endure. So, the topic of slave resistance has been deeply connected to broader understandings of the nature of slavery.

As more participants, observers, and defenders than scholars, nineteenth-century slaveowners developed a range of ideas that professional historians would grapple with well into the 1900s. Among the concepts created by these antebellum participants was the myth of happy slaves and benevolent masters—known as the moonlight and magnolias interpretation of plantation life—which

functioned as an important psychological mechanism for slaveowners. Historian Eugene Genovese first employed the phrase *moonlight
and magnolias* to mean the nostalgic and romanticized view of the
antebellum South championed by many slavery apologists. Popularized in depictions of the antebellum South in the 1939 film *Gone
with the Wind,* the moonlight and magnolias interpretation emphasizes the genteel and paternalistic nature of plantation society while
ignoring or minimizing the daily horrors faced by the enslaved.[3]

In addition to romanticizing the slave plantation, slavery apologists developed through their literature and popular imagination
a character whom they thought best captured enslaved African
Americans collectively—*Sambo.* This happy-go-lucky, docile, and
lazy buffoon became the dominant stereotype of African American
men during the antebellum period.[4] From the vantage of hindsight,
it seems strange that most Americans would have accepted—at one
time in their collective history—a stereotype of African American
men as docile and harmless. This was indeed the case, and this
specific aspect of the moonlight and magnolias plantation myth
played an important psychological role for white Southern elites.
Understanding, as most slaveowners probably did, that slavery was
a brutal, inhumane, and evil system of exploitation, it would be
impossible for whites in the plantation South to rest easy in their
beds at night with thoughts that every slave potentially wanted
to wreak vengeful and bloody havoc. Thus, white slaveowners
needed to imagine their slaves as happy, contented, and harmless,
and Sambo provided a comforting psychological projection of how
they wanted their slaves to behave. In this way, the historiography
of slave resistance begins with considerations and analyses of this
literary symbol and psychological projection which, in many re-
gards, pervaded the consciousness of white Southerners into the
twentieth century.

In the nineteenth century, efforts to refute the moonlight and
magnolias plantation myth became another early beginning in the
long historiography of slave resistance in the United States. The
first revisionist historians, in this regard, were abolitionists of all
kinds—gradualists and immediatists, white and Black—who shared

a commitment to ending the American paradox of human bondage in the land of the liberty. In speeches, pamphlets, published slave narratives, book-length fictions, and plays, abolitionists and their sympathizers sought to produce stark and realistic images of slavery that countered those produced by slaveowners. By doing so, abolitionists also provided the best explanation for the existence of slave resistance. While some abolitionists espoused pacifism and sought a nonviolent end to slavery, they could not help but be mesmerized by Nat Turner's 1831 revolt in Southampton County, Virginia, which claimed the lives of fifty-six whites. Few in the antebellum era were as committed to Christian ideals of pacifism as the famed abolitionist William Lloyd Garrison, yet even he did not hesitate to publish the graphic details of Nat Turner's revolt, and later compare it to an earlier attempted slave rebellion in Virginia—Gabriel's 1800 slave conspiracy in Richmond—in the *Liberator*, the weekly abolitionist newspaper he published in Boston.[5] For Garrison, Nat Turner's slave revolt demonstrated that slavery was in and of itself an arch-crime against humanity that enslaved people justifiably resisted.

In this way, abolitionists seeking to end slavery in the United States offered the first and most perceptive reason for slave resistance. Simply put, slavery generated its own enemies in the form of aggrieved bondspeople who would, when opportunity presented itself, seek revenge and avenues to freedom.[6] The interpretations of slave resistance proffered by nineteenth-century observers—slaveowners and abolitionists—would continue to shape understandings *into the twentieth century.* In certain ways, the early professional historians and mid-twentieth-century scholars owe significant intellectual debts to their nineteenth-century predecessors.

Between the end of the Civil War and the beginning of the twentieth century, the fight between slavery's apologists and opponents continued to rage. In the ongoing debate, slavery apologists among the early professional historians had more publication outlets for their ideas and a larger, more receptive audience. As such, more of their views garnered attention, shaping broader understandings of slavery and the American past. Writing in the 1890s, James Schouler epitomized this approach when he noted—with confidence—that "nothing, however, made American slavery on the whole so tolerable a condition for both enslaver and enslaved as the innate patience, docility, and child-like simplicity of the negro race."[7] Breathing new life into the Sambo stereotype for late nineteenth-century readers, Schouler continued that "African negroes were often dull, clodpated, stupid, and indolent" while mixed-race people were "nearer to the European in intellect and sensitiveness . . . and less easily kept to brute subjection."[8] In short, native-born Africans and those close to them culturally and genetically had an innate proclivity to passivity and obedience. They were, in his estimate, Sambos by biological endowment and intellectual capacity. Schouler noted that the American-born descendants of Africans, mentally addled and cowards by birthright, were "easily intimidated, incapable of deep plots."[9] On the other hand, biracial women and men—owing to their superior if partial European heritage—were less tractable and more resistant in his view.

The era in which Schouler could publish such blatantly white supremacist polemics was what historian Rayford Logan defined as *the Black nadir*. In the aftermath of Reconstruction, race became a convulsive issue in American life; racism shaped everything from public policy to social etiquette. In the period between 1877 and 1901, African Americans collectively suffered under a new racial regime that Logan and others deemed to be on par with—or even worse than—chattel slavery. The five-headed hydra of disfranchisement, de jure segregation, sharecropping, racial violence (e.g., lynching and race riots), and anti-Black propaganda represented a stifling combination of forces that circumscribed all aspects of Black life.[10] Not only do the social dynamics of this era explain why the ideas of historians like Schouler held sway, but also contributed to the absence of effective scholarly counterbalances. In a period that witnessed the tremendous commercial success and popularity of a film celebrating white supremacy—D. W. Griffith's *The Birth of a Nation* (1915)—few publishing outlets printed works that challenged the moonlight and magnolias myth. By early 1916, Carter G. Woodson's *Journal of Negro History* became one of the first scholarly platforms for Black and white professional historians who sought to challenge the growing consensus view of the New South school. Antiracist, defiant, and strident in tone, Woodson and the authors who published works in the *Journal* were largely ignored by the mainstream historical profession.[11]

Ulrich B. Phillips best epitomizes the New South school's growing influence, particularly regarding antebellum slavery and slave resistance. Phillips's *American Negro Slavery* (1918) reads as a complete rearticulation of the moonlight and magnolias myth, perhaps owing to the fact that Phillips—a rural Georgia native—was a racist who embraced the idea that Africans and their American-born descendants were inherently and biologically inferior to whites. Though in more than five hundred pages of text he never mentions Sambo by name, Phillips clearly had this stereotype in mind when he noted that Africans were "inertly obeying minds and muscles." In his view, the enslaved, or *darkies* as he referred to them at times, had "a courteous acceptance of subordination," "a readiness for loyalty," and worked in conditions without "general prevalence of severity and strain."[12] In this idyllic setting, in which slaves were rarely punished for their misdeeds and were treated as respected members within a paternalistic order, the very notion of slave resistance would be impossible to fathom. Such was Phillips's implied argument in including all instances of slave revolts, plots, and other forms of what would be normally categorized as resistance in a chapter titled "Slave Crime."

The innate and inborn biological inferiority of Africans and their descendants explained, in Phillips's mind, the "natural amenability of the blacks." On this note, he added that enslaved African Americans "for the most part were by racial quality submissive rather than defiant, light-hearted instead of gloomy, amiable and ingratiating instead of sullen, and whose very defects invited paternalism rather than repression."[13] In Phillips's framing, plantation owners, standing at the top of a patriarchal and paternalistic order, rarely earned profit through slavery, and the system provided several tangible social benefits—particularly for the enslaved—if few economic ones for their masters. As an apologist for slavery, Phillips viewed the institution as harmless, protective, and even beneficial for African Americans, as a school of sorts that lifted savage and primitive Africans to the stage of civilized and Christian humanity. In this formulation of docile slaves and kindly masters, again, slave resistance would be a virtual impossibility. Most people understand resistance as a justifiable reaction to oppression and exploitation. Crime in this context, on the other hand, is the irrational behavior of a formerly savage and unsaved people. Thus, in the "Slave Crime" chapter, Phillips emphasized violent assaults against whites (particularly white women), murder, and other so-called *negro felonies* as a means of demonstrating the abhorrent and deviant nature of acts that should actually be seen as defiance to injustice.[14]

Although scholars like Schouler and Phillips predominated historical interpretations of slavery before the mid-twentieth century, they would not go entirely unchallenged. Joining Woodson's efforts, W. E. B. Du Bois published an epic treatment in 1935 titled *Black Reconstruction.* An unabashedly polemical work, Du Bois set his sights at William A. Dunning and the New South school. While much of the focus of *Black Reconstruction* sought to combat the notion that Reconstruction represented a tragic era in the history of the US South, Du Bois fashioned an argument about Black agency during the Civil War that offered novel insights into the historical possibilities of slave resistance. As he poignantly stated, "one fact and one alone explains the attitude of most recent writers toward Reconstruction; they cannot conceive Negroes as men."[15] More accurately, scholars like Schouler, Phillips, and Dunning could not conceive of African Americans—in any era—as historical actors and agents. In countering this notion, Du Bois proffered an interpretation called the *general strike thesis,* in which enslaved workers consciously refused to labor for Confederate planters and ran away to Union lines by the thousands during the Civil War. Among those who absconded were tens of thousands who received military training, weapons, and backing from the US government to fight against those invested in human bondage. Some ninety-eight thousand of the two hundred thousand Black soldiers who fought for the Union were enslaved men living in the South just before or during the Civil War. From their vantage, these former slaves-turned-soldiers understood the war effort as a crusade to end slavery. Thus, in Du Bois's formulation, what began as concerted labor strikes on plantations and mass acts of absconding developed into the largest and most successful slave revolt in American history.[16] Black agency—in this case, various acts of slave resistance—would profoundly shape the course of US history.

Though scholars like Woodson and Du Bois continued to challenge Phillips and his school's historical interpretations, it was not until the 1943 publication of Herbert Aptheker's *American Negro Slave Revolts* that a sustained critique of the moonlight and magnolias myth appeared in print. However, most historians and the American public ignored Aptheker's work at the time due to his political affiliations and his progressive views on race. As an antiracist Marxist, Aptheker naturally gravitated toward history's underdogs and the dispossessed. He sided with workers, peasants, and slaves in his historical analyses, and his brand of antiracist Marxism shaped and sharpened his interpretations of the roles those groups played as historical actors. In slaves, Aptheker saw a people who lived courageous lives. In slave rebels, he saw individuals who risked dismemberment and torturous public executions in their quest for liberty and justice—individuals who may have been the most heroic Americans to ever live. For his political leanings and historical interpretations, Aptheker struggled to gain his peers' acceptance. After testifying before a New York State investigating committee in 1938 and subsequently being labeled a communist, it took him more than thirty years to even find academic employment. Only a campus-wide protest called by Black students at Bryn Mawr College in Pennsylvania explains Aptheker's removal from the academic blacklist and his appointment there as a professor of Afro-American studies beginning in 1969.[17] In the wake of McCarthyism, red-baiting, and the Cold War, historians all but neglected Aptheker's monumental work; he was marginalized for decades following the publication of *American Negro Slave Revolts*.[18]

In some ways, Woodson, Du Bois, and Aptheker inaugurated what can be described as the *neoabolitionist* interpretation of slave resistance, and it was just as polemical and political as anything written by Frederick Douglass or William Lloyd Garrison. Neoabolitionist scholars like Woodson, Du Bois, and Aptheker typically espoused radical political ideologies and fully embraced antiracist historical interpretations. Indeed, they should more properly be understood as scholar-activists interested in correcting the historical record about slavery and race while seeking ways to ameliorate the effects of racism, inequality, and social injustice in the twentieth century. Aptheker's book, written in an era when Nazi atrocities during the Holocaust caused a growing number of Americans to question the continued currency of racism and white supremacy, was forward-thinking and revolutionary. By cataloging more than two hundred and fifty instances of slave revolts, conspiracies, and other acts of slave resistance in the United States, Aptheker hoped to permanently put to rest the notion that African Americans passively accepted an abusive and exploitative labor regime. He addressed Phillips's interpretation directly, noting that before he published *American Negro Slave Revolts* in 1943, "the controlling view held that the response of the slave in the United States to his bondage 'was one of passivity and docility.' . . . That opinion, so decisive a part of the chauvinism afflicting the nation, was shown to be false."[19] In countering this aspect of the moonlight and magnolias myth, Aptheker argued that enslaved people never accepted slavery and that this sentiment was frequently expressed in the form of violent discontent.

Like abolitionists a century earlier, Aptheker claimed that the root cause of slave resistance was slavery, destroying any romantic interpretations of plantation life. In his own words, Aptheker wanted to demonstrate through his work that "African-American people, in slavery, forged a record of discontent and resistance comparable to that marking the history of any other oppressed people."[20] Thus, he viewed slave resistance as a necessary and natural phenomenon: in essence, slave resistance was a normal human response to inhumane conditions. Making the claim that African Americans were indeed humans who had the full range of human emotion, behavior, and potential as any other group, Aptheker positioned the story of plantation slavery as an epic human drama with actors like Nat Turner, Denmark Vesey, and Gabriel—all leaders of major slave revolts and conspiracies—as heroic protagonists. Like Woodson and Du Bois, Aptheker's ideas about race and slavery were well ahead of their time.

If scholars like Woodson, Du Bois, and Aptheker—largely unappreciated by their scholarly contemporaries—created the neoabolitionist school among the midcentury scholars, both Kenneth Stampp and Stanley Elkins became its champions during the 1950s and 1960s. In many ways, their combined interpretations of slavery and slave personality helped to bury once and for all some of the moonlight and magnolias myth's worst dimensions. In 1956, Stampp's *The Peculiar Institution: Slavery in the Antebellum South* offered the first sustained and widely accepted challenge to Phillips and other New South school historians. In depicting the institution of slavery as a profitable yet brutal mode of labor exploitation that dehumanized its victims and created within them a spirit of resistance, Stampp laid the groundwork for a complete rethinking of the plantation South. In his work, slavery meant rape, mutilation, other forms of physical mistreatment; severe material deprivation to the degree that most enslaved people were underfed and not sufficiently clothed or housed, even in harsh winter weather; and a debilitating disease ecology that greatly shortened their life expectancies. Stampp explicitly meant his work to be antiracist when he noted: "I have assumed that the slaves were merely ordinary human beings, that innately Negroes *are,* after all, only white men with black skins, nothing more, nothing less."[21] Though in hindsight this statement is problematic, Stampp intended to contest the venom about the innate biological or cultural inferiority of African Americans by scholars like Schouler and Phillips. In understanding enslaved people as human beings, slavery must be viewed—by the objective reader—as unjust, and slave resistance as both natural and normal. In Stampp's view, slaves expressed their justifiable discontent in myriad ways, including revolts and plots as well as more subtle, everyday forms of resistance, like temporarily absconding, breaking tools, and feigning illness.[22]

The 1950s provided a facilitating social and political environment for Stampp's interpretations to take root. Two years before *The Peculiar Institution* appeared, *Brown v. Board of Education* overturned decades of school segregation across the South and became the first of many steps toward enforcing the Fourteenth Amendment, granting African Americans citizenship rights and equal protection under the law.[23] In 1955, the Montgomery bus boycott shocked the South and the nation, proving wrong the claims made in 1963 by Southern writer William Styron that slavery had reduced its victims "to the status of children . . . tranquilized, totally defenseless, ciphers and ants."[24] Racist views like this one persisted. Reflecting on his experiences at a segregated Georgia army camp during World War I, none other than Ulrich Phillips remarked that "the negroes themselves show the same easy-going, amiable, serio-comic obedience and the same personal attachments to white men, as well as the same sturdy light-heartedness and the same love of laughter and of rhythm, which distinguished their forbears [*sic*]."[25]

Amiable Sambos, seriocomic children, obedient ciphers, and light-hearted ants do not make history, initiate shifts in the laws and social policies of an entire nation, and mesmerize the world through the effective combination of direct mass action and the philosophy of nonviolent social protest. The Civil Rights movement fundamentally changed American society and politics, and it was indeed a movement led and soldiered by African Americans. What Stampp accomplished in *The Peculiar Institution* was to inject the social and political milieu of the mid- to late 1950s into historical understandings of and discussions about African Americans. Essentially, even slaves had historical agency and could shape the world around them through their actions.

If Stampp represented a step toward recognizing enslaved people as historical agents, Stanley Elkins's *Slavery: A Problem in American Institutional and Intellectual Life* (1959) took several steps backward toward Phillips's end of the historiographic spectrum. In many ways, the triad of historiographic interpretations through the 1950s form a dialectic, with Phillips representing the thesis; Woodson, Du Bois, Aptheker, and Stampp combining to generate the antithesis;

and Elkins offering a synthesis of the previous two approaches. Although he did contend that "racist bigotry" colored Phillips's work, Elkins certainly did not agree with Aptheker that slaves were consummate rebels either.[26] Like Aptheker and Stampp, Elkins viewed slavery as a profitable and brutal mode of labor exploitation. Indeed, Elkins's emphasis on slavery's brutality becomes the central point of his analysis and one of the main reasons for the criticism levied against his work by historians. As a neoabolitionist, Elkins clearly sympathized with the enslaved and was antiracist in his approach. However, his sympathy went too far in his claim that slavery was so brutal, stifling, and closed that it infantilized the enslaved, turning them into childlike Sambos. In this view, US slavery, as a closed social system similar to a prison, offered little to no latitude for the enslaved to exert their humanity and agency. The system did everything to limit or dwarf the enslaved's human potential, and in this regard, it was largely successful. Stripped of both their African cultural heritage and their human sensibilities, slaves were transformed into the docile, happy-go-lucky, submissive children of the moonlight and magnolias myth. Whereas Phillips contended that Africans' natural endowment explained the submissive nature of the enslaved, Elkins countered that it was the brutality of slavery itself that destroyed the human potential of enslaved Africans and their American-born descendants. Despite this distinction, the end result was the same: slaves collectively became docile Sambos incapable of resistance.

In part, Elkins reached his conclusion about slave docility in the US South by employing a comparative, hemispheric historical framework. This larger geographic frame of reference would be one of his numerous scholarly innovations. Having read broadly in preparation for writing his 1959 book, Elkins encountered the works of Frank Tannenbaum and Gilberto Freyre, who wrote about comparative Latin American and Brazilian slavery. Tannenbaum, in his 1946 *Slave and Citizen: The Negro in the Americas,* claimed that differences in religious institutions, customs, and laws explain why Latin American slavery was comparatively more benign and "open" than US slavery.[27] Employing Tannenbaum's thesis, Elkins mirrored his conclusions by contending that Latin American slavery was indeed an open system that granted the enslaved a greater degree of freedom and latitude than the system that took root in North America. Since the Latin American system was comparatively more open and benign, then, the human spirit of the enslaved did not suffer through infantilization—the process by which men and women are transformed, psychologically, into pliable and docile children. According to Elkins, this divergence could be tracked by the fact that no Sambo-like character ever appeared in the writings of slaveowners and their literary sympathizers in Brazil or other locales in Latin America. Sambo's appearance in antebellum US writings reflected a historical reality for Elkins, and the Sambo personality type meant that slaves had become infantilized there as a direct result of the closed, abusive, and suffocating nature of slavery in the plantation South. US slavery, then, as a closed system could in Elkins's view be best compared to prisons or concentration camps. Basing this part of his argument on research conducted by psychologist Bruno Bettelheim on Nazi concentration camp survivors following World War II, Elkins used a novel interdisciplinary approach to argue that a totalitarian and closed system of slavery destroyed the capacity of the enslaved to resist. Slaves lacked the ability to be historical agents, Elkins argued; indeed, the only thing they could be in this view was victims. This singular fact explained for Elkins the infrequency of slave revolts in the United States in comparison with Brazil. In sum, slavery defeated the enslaved in the United States, and the worst expression of this defeat came in the form of Sambo as the dominant African American personality type.[28]

The scholarly reaction to Elkins moved the historiographic discourse from questions about whether enslaved people rebelled against or acquiesced to their oppression to questions regarding how the enslaved managed to assert their historical agency. Thus, a number of historians questioned Elkins's victimization thesis, instead opting for analyses centered on varying expressions of slave agency—ranging from resistance to accommodation. Referred to in the overview essay of this volume as the slave community school,

this trend coincided with the rise of a new wave of Black professional historians who began teaching at predominantly white universities in the 1960s and 1970s. Influenced by Black Power organizations like the Black Panther Party, the Black Student Movement
of the late 1960s was in essence a concerted effort to push white
universities to include African Americans in both the curriculum
and the professoriate. Two of the principal results of this movement
were the creation of Black studies departments across the United
States by the early 1970s and more diversified curricula within existing academic departments and programs. Both of these developments led to dozens of new Black faculty members teaching African
American history and studies courses at major universities across
the United States. Unlike Woodson and Du Bois, this new wave of
Black scholars—including historians Vincent Harding, John Blassingame, Sterling Stuckey, Lerone Bennett Jr., and Albert J. Raboteau—
would find wide support and readership for their ideas.

For perhaps obvious reasons, African American professional
historians had personal interests in the debate about Black agency,
and nothing illustrates this investment more than the fight over a
piece of historical fiction—William Styron's *The Confessions of Nat
Turner* (1967).[29] Written from a first-person perspective, *Confessions*
does not call into question the agency of slaves, or the existence
of slave resistance. Styron, a white Virginia native, used his literary license to question Nat's motivations. In his Pulitzer Prize-
winning treatment, Styron depicted Nat as having masturbatory
dreams about a white woman, Margaret Whitehead, and a sexual
encounter with a male slave. Far from the committed revolutionary Aptheker depicted in 1943, Styron's Nat was a sexually re-
pressed, religious zealot full of self-loathing and doubt. Even in his
planning of the revolt, Styron's Nat appeared as little more than
an incompetent, troubled man teetering on the edge of lunacy. In
addition, Styron partly revived the moonlight and magnolias myth
in depicting slaveowners in his novel as mostly genteel, benevolent, and caring—complicating even further Nat's true motivations
for the slave revolt. Interpreting Styron's depiction of Nat as a personal affront, a number of Black scholars and writers responded

in kind.[30] In many ways, the scholarly energies of numerous historians were monopolized by the Styron debate for the half decade after the publication of *Confessions*.

Perhaps the debate over Styron's attempt to peer into the psyche of an enslaved rebel sparked renewed efforts to critique Elkins's use of psychological approaches in theorizing the Sambo personality type in the plantation South. The first and most successful challenge to Elkins came with John Blassingame's *The Slave Community: Plantation Life in the Antebellum South* (1972). Influenced by the neoabolitionist school and inaugurating the aptly named slave community school, Blassingame saw slavery as both brutal and profitable and demonstrated that the enslaved resisted their oppression whenever they had the opportunity. In sharp contrast to Phillips, Blassingame defined resistance not as crime but as justifiable and rational behavior, thus his inclusion of a chapter titled "Rebels and Runaways." Blassingame also took full aim at Elkins's analysis of Sambo as the dominant personality type of the enslaved, as well as his emphasis on Black victimization. Though he understood Sambo as a psychological projection of the desires and biases of the master class, Blassingame actually embraced the problematic icon as part of a larger range of slave personality types. He wrote:

> The inescapable conclusion which emerges from an examination of several different kinds of sources is that there were many different personality types. Sambo was one of them. But, because masters varied so much in character, the system was open at certain points, and the slave quarters, religion, and family helped to shape behavior, it was not the dominant slave personality.[31]

In this view, the compliant and obedient slave existed in the antebellum South not as a mask, behind which hid a transcript of counterhegemonic political discourse, but as a real personality type.

In what was then a sophisticated argument for Black agency, Blassingame claimed that there were in fact three broad slave personality types: there were indeed a few "lazy, inefficient, irresponsible, dishonest, childish, [and] stupid" Sambos on Southern plantations, but they were joined by several *Nats,* the consummate and ever-present rebels, and *Jacks,* the middle ground between the two extremes.[32] For Blassingame, these personalities combined literary stereotypes and historical archetypes. "The typical slave," in his view, "feigned humility . . . worked industriously only when he was treated humanely, simulated deference, was hostilely submissive and occasionally obstinate, ungovernable, and rebellious."[33] In sum, slaves were as multidimensional and as full of paradox and contradiction as any other group. Equipped with a diverse range of emotions, behaviors, and potentialities, enslaved people could disguise intense hatred toward the master class with smiles and hide murderous intent with vocal acts of submission and deference. The fact that even a rebel like Nat Turner—a trusted and loyal slave on his owner's plantation—had served as an overseer proves the point that any slave had the potential to both accommodate and resist slavery.

For Blassingame, another key element of resistance was the ability of the enslaved to maintain discreet cultural and social practices that stood in sharp contrast to white norms. Far from the *white men with black skins* imagined by Stampp, enslaved people carved out unique and even autonomous cultural spaces in the United States, and their collective Africanity can be viewed as active and conscious resistance to attempts to assimilate them. Blassingame added, "clearly one of the general means by which Africans resisted bondage was by retaining their link with the past. Rather than accept the slaveholders' view of their place in society, the African tried to hold on to African cultural determinants of his status."[34] In this regard, Blassingame followed the lead of Sterling Stuckey, who, in an influential 1968 article titled "Through the Prism of Folklore: The Black Ethos in Slavery," maintained that enslaved people cannot be "studied as if they had moved in a cultural cyclotron, continually bombarded by devastating, atomizing forces which denuded them of meaningful Africanisms while destroying any and all impulses toward creativity."[35] In countering Elkins's Sambo thesis, Stuckey claimed that slave folklore contained evidence of the ability of the enslaved to repulse the dwarfing of their human potential. Using African-centered themes in their folktales, among other mediums, the enslaved expressed feelings of moral and intellectual superiority over whites, conveyed subtle and didactic messages about resistance to their children, and continually affirmed their humanity in ways that "left a lasting imprint on American culture."[36] Both Stuckey and Blassingame contended that the very existence of an African-derived and influenced slave culture was evidence not only of slave resistance but also that certain cultural manifestations—namely, folktales, songs, and religious beliefs—could contain embedded and hidden meanings encouraging further recalcitrance.

The same year that Blassingame's *The Slave Community* appeared in print, Gerald Mullin added to the historiography of slavery with his 1972 *Flight and Rebellion: Slave Resistance in Eighteenth-Century Virginia,* which detailed the links between culture and resistance. Moving away from the false monolith of US slavery, this regional study focused on Black agency mostly in the form of resistance—highlighted by Gabriel's 1800 slave plot in Richmond, Virginia. In addition to asserting and defending Black agency, Mullin's most immediate historiographic contribution was his analysis of acculturation as a dimension of slave behavior and as a means of measuring types or modes of resistance engaged in by a range of demographic cohorts on slave plantations. For Mullin, slaves could be placed into three categories that more or less determined the types of resistance they would engage in: the unacculturated African-born or so-called *outlandish slaves;* the partially acculturated *new Negroes;* and the fully acculturated and American-born creoles. With an inability to speak *sensibly* or to have an *intelligent demeanor,* according to Mullin, the unacculturated African-born slaves engaged in modes of resistance that were inwardly focused. By Mullin's definition, inward modes of resistance were limited, self-defeating, self-destructive, and short-ranged. African-born slaves sought goals like sating hunger or thirst, easing fatigue, or seeking revenge on an overseer or owner. Owing to their alleged lack of intelligence and worldliness, their responses to enslavement were characteristically knee-jerk and impulsive. The more assimilated *new Negroes* and creoles tended to be literate, could speak good English, and were skilled and resourceful. All these attributes meant, in Mullin's estimation, that their modes of resistance were much more outwardly focused. By casting their plots and revolts broadly, the more assimilated creoles sought capacious and far-reaching goals such as freedom or the complete eradication of bondage. Mullin's analytical calculus is quite simple: the more acculturated enslaved people were, the more likely they were to have intelligent demeanors, develop a political consciousness or engage in politically inspired actions against oppressive economic and social structures, and mastermind plans of resistance that threatened the very foundations of human bondage.[37]

Mullin's thesis represents a rather intriguing dialectic. On the one hand, he agreed with Aptheker, Stampp, and Blassingame about Black agency and slave resistance. On the other, Mullin disagreed with Blassingame and Stuckey about the role of African culture in slave resistance and harkens back to Phillips's ethnocentric dismissal of African-born slaves' cultural heritage. Phillips saw nothing redeemable in African culture and viewed the African background as little more than barbaric bliss that nurtured the innate African tendency for passivity. In addition, he understood African slaves to be tabula rasae, or blank slates, upon which whites could encode their own sociocultural instructions. In other words, slaves—as merely passive objects—were nothing more or less than what their masters made or instructed them to be.[38] Taking a cue from Phillips, in part, Mullin contended African culture did not connote resourcefulness, ingenuity, or aptitude, and that African-born slaves lacked the intelligence and imagination necessary to plan and carry out large-scale rebellions. He argued that African culture served as an obstacle, effectively preventing enslaved people from articulating and acting out planned attacks against slavery as a system. Slaves had to be, in his words, *enlightened, assimilated,* and *acculturated* before assaults could be mounted against this peculiar mode of labor exploitation. For Mullin, only American-born creoles—who were socially, culturally, and intellectually more *European* than *African*—could execute such complicated and risky ventures.[39]

By the time Eugene Genovese published his 1974 *Roll, Jordan, Roll: The World the Slaves Made* and his 1979 *From Rebellion to*

Revolution: Afro-American Slave Revolts in the Making of the Modern World, the historical fact of slave resistance in the United States was no longer a contested or debatable topic among professional historians. Both of Genovese's books operated from a comparative framework similar to the one that Tannenbaum and Elkins utilized earlier, but to radically different ends. While slave rebellions in the Caribbean and Brazil threatened entire colonial regimes, Genovese sought to understand the "low intensity of revolts in the Old South relative to those elsewhere."[40] Instead of resorting to elaborate literary analyses and psychological assessments of the enslaved, Genovese relied on his own unique brand of Marxism to explain the relatively fewer and less intense resistance movements among slaves in the antebellum United States. Whereas Aptheker's Marxism led him to empathize with the enslaved and to focus on slave revolts, even when he was probably tracking more general acts of recalcitrance and white fears of slave rebellion, Genovese did not see nearly as much resistance as he expected initially given the significant social and political gulfs between masters and slaves. In his analysis, both paternalism and Christianity ameliorated the slave condition and allowed the enslaved to "hate slavery but not necessarily their individual masters."[41] Paternalism, for Genovese, was not the cozy and familial relationship between masters and enslaved imagined by Phillips and other moonlight and magnolias proponents. In his reading, the enslaved used their masters' paternalism as part of an unwritten and unspoken contract in which they compliantly consented to provide labor in exchange for improved material conditions and semiautonomous social spaces that fostered the growth of slave culture. Christianity, as a core aspect of this new slave culture, became a form of cultural resistance as it shielded the enslaved from the most degrading and dehumanizing aspects of their status and condition. Instead of *opiating* the enslaved, as many Marxists would contend it did, religion itself was a form of resistance in Genovese's eyes, and it undergirded the activities of slave rebels like Nat Turner.

Between the two works, Genovese also advanced several thoughtful arguments about the nature of slave resistance. In

Roll, Jordan, Roll, he complicated the idea of day-to-day forms of recalcitrance as resistance by casting them against the truly revolutionary acts that sought to destabilize or destroy entire systems of human bondage. Feigning illness, work slowdowns, arson, and other general acts of recalcitrance, as more localized and immediate actions to counter the abuses of masters and mistresses, were decidedly prepolitical actions or even acts of accommodation to Genovese. A slave who, for example, broke a farming implement in defiance of the labor demands of a master or an overseer did not threaten slavery as a system, and by this logic was not engaged in what most would define as resistance. The very next day, or the within the hour, the temporary, local, and personal act of breaking a plow would not change the fact that the slave was still a slave; the act itself was meant to ameliorate the condition of their labor without challenging the entire system and logic of human bondage. In other words, slave work slowdowns, outlying or temporary absconding, and the breaking of farming tools were actions that sought better work conditions and *accommodated* slavery's continued existence. Instead of understanding *resistance* and *accommodation* as actions at opposite poles in the larger spectrum of human responses to slavery, they can be understood to form a continuum of action that—at times—could be indistinct from each other. For Genovese, fits of temper, bad behavior, and momentary rage never constituted true resistance. By divorcing everyday acts of bad behavior from resistance and understanding these actions as survival techniques or accommodations to a hegemonic order, Genovese complicated the meaning of agency by demonstrating a much broader range of responses to oppression by the enslaved.

In *From Rebellion to Revolution,* Genovese employed a comparative hemispheric perspective to demonstrate real distinctions between slave revolts and slave revolutions. "Until Afro-American slave revolts and maroon movements merged with the transatlantic bourgeois-democratic revolutions of the late eighteenth century," Genovese contended, "[slave rebels] looked toward the restoration of as much of a traditional African way of life as could be remembered and copied."[42] The Haitian Revolution represented something different in comparison with the movements preceding it, and was for this reason a real historical watershed. According to Genovese, before 1791, several restorationist or *reactionary* revolts sought to erect African-based ethnic states while simultaneously withdrawing from existing social arrangements. The truly *revolutionary* movements, like the one that transformed French Saint-Domingue into Haiti between 1791 and 1804, drew inspiration from liberal-democratic ideals and movements like the French and American Revolutions and sought to implement European-derived concepts in restructuring and reconstructing former slave societies. Genovese channeled Mullin's earlier work when he noted that "[the] revolution in Saint-Domingue marked the passage from an Afro-American religious call to holy war to the universalist claims of the Rights of Man."[43] In essence, for Genovese, as slave movements moved further away from African cultural influences and closer to European intellectual and political ones, they became more effective and approached the stature of *real* revolutions.

The same year that *Roll, Jordan, Roll* appeared, Peter H. Wood's *Black Majority: Negroes in Colonial South Carolina from 1670 through the Stono Rebellion* (1974) added a new dimension to historical interpretations of slave resistance. Whereas most of the historians writing about slavery focused on the antebellum period, Wood's treatment was among the first to assess slavery and resistance during the colonial era.[44] With a primary focus on Black agency, he demonstrated that while Atlantic Africans were instrumental in the maintenance and prosperity of colonial South Carolina, they represented a destabilizing force, and their resistance to slavery profoundly shaped the region's history. Due to an Africanized disease ecology—complete with such tropical diseases as malaria and yellow fever—and the early reliance on African knowledge of cattle herding and rice cultivation, Atlantic Africans and their American-born descendants quickly became the majority population in the colony. According to Wood, fears of the Black majority convulsed the colony and led to a series of repressive legal measures meant to curtail the movement and economic activities of slaves. In turn, enslaved people reacted to the new legislation through concerted acts of resistance.[45]

In *Black Majority,* Wood depicted slaves as fully articulated human beings who did whatever they could to resist oppression, escaping rice plantations and engaging in other forms of resistance with great frequency. In some cases, enslaved people stole goods from white colonists, poisoned their food, committed arson, conspired to rebel, engaged in verbal insolence, and murdered and assaulted whites.[46] All of this resistance, which Wood described in detail, culminated in the 1739 Stono Rebellion—the largest colonial-era slave revolt in British North America. Importantly, Wood countered Mullin's work by demonstrating that across a broad range of resistance, both Atlantic Africans and American-born creoles were equally implicated and capable of long-range planning. Moreover, Wood joined Blassingame and Stuckey in exploring connections between Atlantic African culture and slave resistance. Accepting the idea that Atlantic African cultures were not simply forgotten by *acculturated* and *assimilated* slaves, Wood proffered the idea that these cultures could sustain, define, and shape the slave experience and slave consciousness. In Wood's words, the various historical connections between Atlantic African and North American slavery "must one day become the subject of separate and intensive study."[47]

By the 1980s, a new crop of historians began to reassess the emphasis on slave resistance in the previous decade's scholarship. Though the debate about whether enslaved people resisted was largely over, by overemphasizing resistance and the semiautonomous slave community in the 1970s, scholars unwittingly obscured the truly oppressive, suffocating, and malevolent elements of plantation life. Human agency does not equate to slaves' ability to be their own masters and to repulse the worst and most stifling aspects of human bondage; in some cases, slaves opted to survive— in itself a courageous act in the antebellum South. Survival could mean that many enslaved men and women learned to live within plantation society without outwardly resisting slavery or their owners. By the 1980s and 1990s, most scholars accepted that enslaved people engaged in a variety of strategies—resistance, accommodation, survival—and that they could be both victims and historical agents. Just as studies seeking to prove that slaves were human or that they resisted slavery are no longer needed, historians no longer debate whether or not the enslaved were historical actors and agents.[48]

From the 1980s to the present, two generative trends in the study of slavery have created new historiographic possibilities—studies of enslaved women and gender, and works focusing on Atlantic African and other Atlantic world influences.[49] Until 1985, historians had largely ignored enslaved women in their assessments of colonial North American and antebellum US slavery. Indeed, missing from Elkins's and Blassingame's historical discussions about slave personalities, historical archetypes, and pseudopsychological profiles—namely, Blassingame's Sambo, Nat, and Jack—were any consideration about their female counterparts. After the publication of Deborah Gray White's *Ar'n't I a Woman? Female Slaves in the Plantation South* (1985), leaving enslaved women out of historical analyses of US slavery was no longer an option. This pioneering work was one of the most important historiographic turning points over the past century.[50]

White added both *Mammy* and *Jezebel* to the conversation about slave archetypes as complex psychosexual rationales for rape developed in the minds of elite Southern white men. Understanding the female slave body as a battlefield, upon which wars were constantly fought, won, and lost, White moved well beyond understandings of enslaved women as slavery's ultimate victims in her insightful discussions of everyday resistance, the rebelliousness of enslaved women, and the networks of communication that enslaved women developed for mutual support.[51] If daily acts of recalcitrance can be defined as resistance, then those who had the greatest access to the food, living quarters, and children of white slaveowners could deliver the most devastating blows against the plantation order. Thus, as cooks, maids, and the primary caretakers of elite white children, enslaved women may in fact have been the most successful and the largest demographic of slave rebels. Stephanie Camp's *Closer to Freedom: Enslaved Women and Everyday Resistance in the Plantation South* (2004) presented just such an argument in direct opposition to Genovese's depiction of everyday resistance as simply prepolitical or accommodationist fits of temper. Even above and beyond obvious acts of resistance, Camp showed how enslaved women organized illicit parties, engaged in short-term absenteeism, and adorned their living quarters with abolitionist newsprint as part of forging a *rival geography* within which they defined and used particular kinds of spaces for their own benefit. These mechanisms of *spatial control* may not have been on par with mass slave revolts, but according to Camp, these acts can only be understood as resistance.[52]

As Katherine Chilton emphasizes in her chapter in this volume on gender and slavery, in addition to their frequent association with all sorts of day-to-day forms of resistance common among all slaves, enslaved women employed uniquely gendered modes of resistance and rebelliousness. Various forms of *gynecological resistance,* including the manufacture of abortifacients and other means of reducing fertility, all the way to more drastic measures like infanticide were conscious attempts to deny plantations new generations of slaves; at the very least, enslaved women made decisions that saved many untold thousands from living the everyday hell of chattel slavery in the United States.[53]

Another recent trend has been the increased emphasis on the role of cultural and sociopolitical influences emanating from Atlantic Africa, the Caribbean, or other regions of the Atlantic world. A growing number of studies illustrate this trend. This transnational approach, inaugurated perhaps by Peter Wood, works against the notion that Atlantic Africans suffered an immediate and determined cultural genocide or social death in North America.[54] In an influential article about the Stono slave revolt, Africanist historian John K. Thornton demonstrated how the west-central African sociopolitical and cultural backgrounds of the Angolans involved in the revolt shaped the course of events in profound ways. In combination, the work of Thornton, Mark Smith, and Jason Young reveal that Angolans in colonial South Carolina used a combination of their military training in the use of firearms, their affinity for Africanized Christianity, and their geopolitical knowledge of the Atlantic world as inducements to both rebel and to seek political asylum in Spanish Florida.[55]

Another group of scholars have demonstrated continuities of resistance beginning on the shores of Atlantic Africa and continuing amid the frightening conditions prevailing on the many slave ships traversing the Atlantic.[56] In addition, scholars have paid increasing attention in recent years to the influence of the Haitian Revolution and of unique hemispheric geopolitical forces on North American slave resistance movements.[57] Though this transnational turn is far from new, the more recent historical works that provide broader geographic frames do so as an implicit attack on notions of US exceptionalism. Many of the comparative approaches of earlier historiographic moments accepted the idea that the United States followed a unique, even exceptional historical course in comparison with other Western Hemisphere nation-states. Works by Tannenbaum, Elkins, and Genovese clearly follow this line of thinking. The more recent transnational approaches to slavery written by scholars in the 1990s and the early years of the twenty-first century, particularly the approaches of Atlantic world historians, seek to understand the many historical vectors that explain phenomena across a range of geographies. Instead of focusing energies assessing why the United States had fewer mass rebellions in comparison with Brazil or Jamaica, transnational historians are beginning to ask different kinds of historical questions—for example, how did political, intellectual, or religious movements in Atlantic Africa, France, Haiti, or Virginia affect slave resistance in other regions? And, how does the existence of slave resistance in the United States prove the limits of the European Enlightenment, classical liberalism, and liberal-democratic revolutions?[58] Edward Rugemer addressed this question directly by comparing responses to slave resistance in Barbados and the United States, with one producing emancipation by law and the other by civil war.[59] This interpretive approach, which tracked and assessed the historical interconnectedness of the Atlantic world, mirrors in some ways the growing importance of globalization in the first two decades of the twenty-first century.

The long and contentious historiography of US slave resistance has moved quite far from the interpretations of nineteenth-century observers and participants. Sambo has been dethroned and historians of slavery can describe the system as it really was—without the overly romanticized perspectives of slaveowners, apologists, or advocates of the New South school. Historians have offered nuanced interpretations of the gradations of resistance and the responses to rebellious plots. Responding to a provocative essay by Michael Johnson on the 1822 Denmark Vesey plot, scholars in a multi-edition forum in the *William and Mary Quarterly* in 2001 and 2002 debated the relationship between clandestine communication networks and insurrectionary conspiracies as well as the nature and reliability of different kinds of sources on slave resistance.[60] Reassessments of Nat Turner's revolt, Northern free Black communities (described by Steven Hahn as *maroon communities*), myriad forms of resistance to the 1850 Fugitive Slave Act, and the activism of leading African American abolitionists show how seriously modern scholars take the actions of enslaved people to challenge their own bondage.[61] At the same time, historians understand that resistance was but one of a range of possibilities in the spectrum of human agency. Indeed, if the historiography of slave resistance successfully developed just one lasting consensus, it is that enslaved people were simply humans who had a similar range of concerns, trials, travails, and reactions as any other group under similar circumstances. The gulf existing between the popularity of *The Birth of a Nation* in 1915 and the 2013 epic *12 Years a Slave*—a movie based on Solomon Northrup's capture and escape from slavery—demonstrates the societal and interpretive distance traversed on the issues of US slavery, slave resistance, and race over the past century.[62] In this particular regard, both historians and the American public have come a very long way.

NOTES

1. Sharpe, "Negro Plot of 1712"; K. Scott, "Slave Insurrection"; Sharpe, "Proposal," 352-53.

2. "Minutes of the Court of Quarter and General Sessions, begun August 7th Anno 1694," and "Minutes Book of the Court of General Sessions," (1705-14), New York City Municipal Archives; and Rucker, *River Flows On,* 27-29.

3. See Genovese, "Race and Class," 355. See also Fleming, *Gone with the Wind*.

4. *Sambo* would later be superseded by three new stereotypes of Black men in the era after emancipation—*Coon, Zip Coon,* and *the Brute*. Both Coon and Zip Coon harkened back to slavery in specific ways: Coon was simply a rearticulation of Sambo—simpleminded, happy-go-lucky, and lazy. Zip Coon represented African Americans living in Northern cities as stuttering and lazy imbeciles, ill-suited for civilized, modern, and particularly urban society. The Brute caricature literally cost thousands of African American men their lives as this fiendish murderer and rapist of white women provided a rationale for lynching and race riots in the period between 1880 and 1940. Mobilized in the popular imaginary of many whites in the late nineteenth and early twentieth centuries, these three stereotypes symbolized Black struggles in freedom and modernization. The subtle lesson behind all these images appears to be that slavery was, indeed, a societal good that controlled the impulses of savages and actively engaged the labor of a naturally lazy people. See Fredrickson, *Black Image in the White Mind;* Dormon, "Shaping the Popular Image"; and Lemons, "Black Stereotypes."

5. Garrison, "The Insurrection" and "Gabriel's Defeat."

6. See for example Coffin, *Account of Some Principal Slave Insurrections;* and Higginson, *Travellers and Outlaws,* 116-326.

7. Schouler, *History of the United States,* 2:264.

8. Schouler, *History of the United States,* 2:263-65.

9. Schouler, *History of the United States,* 2:267.

10. Logan, *Negro in American Life and Thought.*

11. The strident and antiracist tone is clear in the first article published in the *Journal of Negro History.* See Woodson, "Negroes of Cincinnati." See also Griffith, *Birth of a Nation.*

12. U. Phillips, *American Negro Slavery,* 339, 291, 307-9.

13. U. Phillips, *American Negro Slavery,* 454-58, 341-42.

14. U. Phillips, *American Negro Slavery,* 455.

15. Du Bois, *Black Reconstruction,* 726.

16. Du Bois, *Black Reconstruction,* 57-63, 120.

17. Okihiro, *In Resistance,* 21-23, 216.

18. Of Aptheker's contribution to understandings of slavery and slave resistance, noted Harvard sociologist Orlando Patterson once wrote:

The man and his work have literally been purged from the company of polite scholars. For all its faults, *American Negro Slave Revolts* cannot be dismissed as some monstrous emanation of the Communist Party line. Like the work of [Stanley] Elkins (1959), it did break new ground; and like that work it was largely wrong in its conclusions and biased in its interpretations. We therefore find it difficult to understand why it is that Elkins remains respectable and continues to be credited with the initiation of new studies in American slave studies, yet Aptheker is totally rejected, even ridiculed. Something is amiss here.

See Patterson, "Slavery"; also quoted in Okihiro, *In Resistance,* 10-11. Another work, largely ignored by historians and other scholars, that preempts Aptheker by five years is James, *History of Negro Revolt.* Like Aptheker, James was an avowed Marxist theoretician; as a native of Trinidad, he was also Black. *History of Negro Revolt*'s orientation was decidedly Pan-African and anticolonial. Some combination of these factors may explain why American historians overlooked James's scholarly contribution to the historiographic debates about slave resistance.

19. Aptheker, *American Negro Slave Revolts,* xi.

20. Aptheker, *American Negro Slave Revolts,* xi.

21. Stampp, *Peculiar Institution,* viii.

22. Raymond and Alice Bauer coined the term *day-to-day resistance* more than a decade before Stampp's book appeared. See Bauer and Bauer, "Day to Day Resistance to Slavery."

23. *Brown v. Board of Education* (1954); US Const. amend. XIV, § 1.

24. Styron, "Review: *American Negro Slave Revolts.*"

25. U. Phillips, *American Negro Slavery,* viii.

26. Elkins, *Slavery,* 17.

27. Tannenbaum, *Slave and Citizen.* For scholarly claims that predate Elkins's work supporting the view that Latin American slavery was relatively benign, see Freyre, *Masters and the Slaves;* Pierson, *Negroes in Brazil;* and L. Turner, "Negro in Brazil."

28. Elkins, *Slavery,* 81-86.

29. Styron, *Confessions of Nat Turner.*

30. Clarke, *William Styron's Nat Turner.*

31. Blassingame, *Slave Community,* xi-xii.

32. Blassingame, *Slave Community,* 223-38.

33. Blassingame, *Slave Community,* 322.

34. Blassingame, *Slave Community,* 25.

35. Stuckey, *Going through the Storm,* 16.

36. Stuckey, *Going through the Storm,* 17.

37. Mullin, *Flight and Rebellion,* 35-37, 78-83, 89-92. On several occasions throughout this work, Mullin uses phrases like *sensible demeanor* or *intelligent demeanor* to denote one of the principal characteristics of the assimilated, American-born creoles. See Mullin, *Flight and Rebellion,* 89, 91-92, 97, 162.

38. For Phillips's views on Africa and African culture in relation to slave behavior, see U. Phillips, *American Negro Slavery,* 3-5, 42-44, 291, 342. Phillips was not alone in holding ethnocentric views about African culture. Kenneth Stampp, for example, specifically noted that "[if] anything, most antebellum slaves showed a desire to forget their African past and to embrace as much of white civilization as they could." See Stampp, *Peculiar Institution,*

363. Likewise, Stanley Elkins contended that "few ethnic groups have been so thoroughly and effectively detached from their prior cultural connections as was the case in the Negro's transit from Africa to North America." See Elkins, *Slavery*, 94n.

39. Mullin, *Flight and Rebellion*, vii–ix.

40. Genovese, *Rebellion to Revolution*, xxii–xxiii.

41. Genovese, *Roll, Jordan, Roll*, 282.

42. Genovese, *Rebellion to Revolution*, 82.

43. Genovese, *Rebellion to Revolution*, 123.

44. P. Wood, *Black Majority*.

45. P. Wood, *Black Majority*, xvii–xviii, 36–37, 43, 56, 112–16, 97–100, 63–64, 70, 76–80, 88–89, 90–91.

46. P. Wood, *Black Majority*, 131–32, 143–45, 210–14, 239–68.

47. P. Wood, *Black Majority*, xv.

48. Wyatt-Brown, *Southern Honor*; Kolchin, *American Slavery*; Dusinberre, *Them Dark Days*; and W. Johnson, *Soul by Soul*.

49. For detailed discussions of these historiographic trends, see Baptist and Camp, *New Studies*, 1–18.

50. D. White, *Ar'n't I a Woman?*

51. In this regard, many historians have taken to heart scholar-activist Angela Davis's earlier assessments. See A. Davis, "Reflections on Black Women's Role"; and A. Davis, *Women, Race, and Class*, 3–29.

52. Camp, *Closer to Freedom*.

53. For studies of gynecological resistance and other gendered modes of recalcitrance, see J. Morgan, *Laboring Women*; Gaspar and Hine, *More than Chattel*; Ellison, "Resistance to Oppression"; and Hine and Wittenstein, "Female Slave Resistance."

54. For works on this topic, see G. Hall, *Africans in Colonial Louisiana*; J. K. Thornton, "Coromantees"; J. K. Thornton, "War, the State, and Religious Norms"; Foote, "'Some Hard Usage'"; D. Chambers, *Murder at Montpelier*; Desch-Obi, *Fighting for Honor*; and Diouf, *Slavery's Exiles*.

55. J. K. Thornton, "African Dimensions"; M. Smith, "Remembering Mary"; Young, *Rituals of Resistance*.

56. See Diouf, *Fighting the Slave Trade*; E. Taylor, *If We Must Die*; Rediker, *Slave Ship*; and Rediker, *Amistad Rebellion*.

57. See for example Frey, *Water from the Rock*; Landers, *Black Society in Spanish Florida*; Geggus, *Impact of the Haitian Revolution*; L. Alexander, *African or American?*; and Rasmussen, *American Uprising*.

58. For works that best epitomize the transnational approach, see D. E. Walker, *No More*; Rugemer, *Problem of Emancipation*; Landers, *Atlantic Creoles*; Scott and Hébrard, *Freedom Papers*; Rediker, *Amistad Rebellion*; and Horne, *Counter-Revolution of 1776*.

59. Rugemer, *Slave Law*.

60. M. Johnson, "Denmark Vesey." For introductions to the forum in response to Johnson's article, see Gross, "Forum: The Making of a Slave Conspiracy."
61. P. Breen, *Land Shall Be Deluged*; Hahn, *Political Worlds*; Blackett, *Captive's Quest*; Delbanco, *War before the War*; Blight, *Frederick Douglass*; Sinha, *Slave's Cause*.
62. Griffith, *Birth of a Nation*; McQueen, *12 Years a Slave*.

CHAPTER SEVEN

American Slavery and
the Atlantic Slave Trade

COLLEEN A. VASCONCELLOS

In late August of 1619, the *White Lion* and *Treasurer* sailed to England's struggling, fledgling Jamestown settlement within days of each other, carrying with them around sixty Africans in total. Bartering some thirty Africans for supplies, the captains of these two Dutch men-of-war weighed anchor and set sail for Bermuda, where they sought to sell the remainder of their cargoes. These slaves, who are now famous for being the first Africans brought to America, have an interesting story beyond that simple claim that offers insight as to who they were and where they came from. Unbeknownst to Jamestown's colonists—who would have been indifferent in any event to their plight—these now-famous Africans were actually Dutch contraband stolen from the *São João Bautista,* a Portuguese slaver captained by Manuel Mendes da Cunha that was attacked by the two Dutch ships in question only a month earlier. Mendes da Cunha was traveling his usual route from Luanda, Angola, to Mexico in fulfillment of a contract to deliver slaves to the Spanish viceroyalties of the New World. The Africans themselves were prisoners of war, most likely Kimbundu speakers from the Ndongo kingdom who were sold into slavery as a result of the wars raging between the Ndongo and their Kongo neighbors to the north. After being sold, some of them stayed in Jamestown, but most were taken to nearby tobacco plantations along the James River.[1]

Although we do know snippets of information about these first enslaved Africans, their history is one that cannot be separated from the histories of those who involuntarily followed them to the Chesapeake, New England, the Low Country, and eventually the Deep South. As Tim Hashaw has argued, their arrival signaled the birth of African American history, and had a greater impact on American history as a whole than the arrival of the Mayflower in 1620.[2] Their stories are intertwined with the histories of the enslaved men, women, and children that fill the other chapters of this volume. Quite simply, one cannot understand the history of slavery in the United States without learning the history of the transatlantic slave trade, and vice versa. This chapter provides that context by focusing on the Atlantic slave trade, with special attention to the work done on North America and the United States.

Surprisingly, the slave trade to the United States is an understudied component of a much larger historiography on the transatlantic slave trade. To date, not one single monograph has examined the overall trade from Africa to North America.[3] This could be because North America sat along the periphery of that traffic as only one small component of the infamous *triangular trade,* a complex Atlantic trade network of slaves, crops, and manufactured goods that operated between the Americas, Europe, and Africa.[4] As a latecomer to the New World colonial empires, America only imported anywhere from 5 to 7 percent of the overall transatlantic trade.[5] David Eltis has calculated that more Africans arrived in the United States since 1992 than during the entire era of the American slave trade.[6] Despite those statistics, the North American side of the trade was incredibly significant in the cultural and economic formation of the early United States.[7] In fact, as Eltis contended, the transatlantic slave trade transformed the Atlantic Ocean into a commercial highway that connected the histories of Africa, Europe, and the Americas in the process.[8] As this chapter demonstrates, the exterior investigations of the wider transatlantic slave trade and its history have given rise to more sociocultural investigations of the African diaspora and North American slavery as a whole.

From the sixteenth to the late nineteenth centuries, an estimated forty to fifty thousand ships crossed the Middle Passage to the Americas.[9] According to Eltis, the transatlantic trade was the largest coerced movement of people in history, with nearly four Africans traveling across the Atlantic for every one European as late as 1820.[10] Gary B. Nash, in his work on early American settlement, has shown that six out of seven persons who arrived in the Americas before American independence were enslaved Africans.[11] Used on plantations throughout the United States, Latin America, and the Caribbean, enslaved men, women, and children were shipped largely from about twenty principal slave markets, as well as many smaller ones, along a 3,000-mile coastline stretching from Senegal to Angola.[12]

Warfare and territorial disputes between various African nation-states, slave raiding, kidnapping, and *pawnship* accounted for the vast majority of Africans traveling the Middle Passage.[13] Once enslaved, Africans made their way to West African coastal ports in coffles or caravans that periodically stopped to purchase or sell slaves at interior markets along the way. Once they reached the coast, agents readied them for sale by shaving their heads and oiling their skin, all in attempt to hide the scars, disease, and starvation from the ordeal. European ships lined the horizon, waiting to transport their cargo as quickly as possible to the plantations, mines, and urban centers of the Americas. With an average life span of five to seven years in some areas upon arrival, particularly sugar estates, demand for enslaved Africans progressively grew in the eighteenth century, leading traders to draw their supply from increasingly deep within the continent's interior. Despite the gradual abolition of the trade beginning in 1807, this traffic would continue until the last Africans were imported into Brazil in 1888.[14]

Although there is a debate as to how many Africans were imported into American ports, most historians agree that America imported an average of one thousand per year from 1701 to 1808.[15] Although New England and New York imported some slaves before the American Revolution, 93 percent of the enslaved imported into North America went to destinations in and below Maryland; 54 percent arrived in Low Country Carolina and Georgia ports, 32 percent disembarked in the Chesapeake, and the remainder found themselves sold in New England, Florida, and Louisiana ports. Of the Africans who survived the Middle Passage and arrived in the United States, nearly half embarked in Senegambia and west-central Africa.[16] The rest came from the Gold Coast of Ghana and the Bight of Biafra, or eastern Nigeria and Cameroon. Although W. E. B. Du Bois argued that nearly 10 percent of the four million enslaved persons living in the United States on the eve of the Civil War were born in Africa, the majority of America's enslaved were descended from Africans who had arrived generations earlier.[17]

Interestingly, the first studies of the transatlantic slave trade actually began in the antebellum period as part of a wider platform of abolitionist and sectionalist literature. This early period is indicative of a history that was recorded largely by its observers and participants, who shared certain assumptions about slavery, race, and class. As abolitionist critiques of the slave trade reached their peak in the 1790s, staunch reformers like Thomas Clarkson, William Wilberforce, Anthony Benezet, and Sir Thomas Fowell Buxton described horrific scenes wherein enslaved people were herded like livestock in slave coffles and coastal castle pens, only to be forced to endure the vile, subhuman conditions of the Middle Passage while crammed into vastly overcrowded slave ships. These abolitionist observers gathered firsthand accounts, ship diagrams, and trader testimony as evidence in their mission to abolish the transatlantic slave trade. Although some of these accounts did attempt to characterize the dimensions of the trade, the abolitionists were more interested in painting as graphic an image as possible to sway public and government support for their cause.

The American journalist Edward E. Dunbar's *The History of the Rise and Decline of American Slavery* (1861), a thoughtful abolitionist piece written as part of a larger serial on Mexican-American relations, was the first of a series of efforts to move past the movement's more traditional social agenda by offering a historical analysis of the trade.[18] Each of these accounts, including Dunbar's, discussed the transatlantic slave trade and its horrors as part of a larger attack on America's reliance on slave labor. Dunbar's discussion examined the American trade in an effort to fuel the sectionalist powder keg that was about to explode in 1861. He characterized a system on the brink of decline. Although he estimated that fourteen million Africans had been brought to the Americas as slaves—which he thought was probably a low estimate—Dunbar argued that America's enslaved comprised no more than one-tenth of the entire population as proof.[19] Yet, he contended, America's reliance and dependency on this system gave the South control over the North, the American people, and even the American government. His article was a call to abolish what he believed was a dying system, and it was the first study to even attempt to estimate the total number of Africans brought to the Americas.

George Moore's *Notes on the History of Slavery in Massachusetts* (1866) and William B. Weeden's "The Early African Slave-Trade in New England" (1887) continued Dunbar's analysis, though in less political terms.[20] Strong Christian undertones reminiscent of past abolitionist writings suggest that Moore and Weeden were partisans. Both definitely had their own agendas, which are evidenced in their brief but critical postwar histories of how America began importing slaves from Africa alongside their strong condemnations of the sinfulness of America's past actions. Moore especially criticized America's slaveowners and traders, going so far as to compare them to the likes of the savage, hedonistic pirates of northern Africa.[21] Weeden was more contemptuous of Europeans, whom he blamed for the serious depopulation of large portions of western Africa, while he forgave America's participation by characterizing it as pure ignorance and naiveté, considering "how little people knew of what they were doing."[22]

Although a staunch Republican and Union partisan, Moore actually stands out as more of a transitional figure during this period. John David Smith has characterized him as one of the country's "most distinguished historians of colonial and Revolutionary America."[23] Moore openly supported emancipation at the start of the Civil War, and he chastised the slow pace of Massachusetts's reform in an inflammatory pamphlet published in 1862.[24] Although Massachusetts sided with the Union, Moore thought that its residents were blind to the horrors of slavery, having had the "curtains drawn over these disagreeable features for more than a century."[25] With that in mind, Moore believed that it was his duty as a historian of slavery to "let in the light upon them" with his work.[26] As Smith argued, Moore "stood back and let his arsenal of primary sources indict Massachusetts before the world for greed and hypocrisy."[27] Despite the fact that his treatment of the slave trade did contain a good measure of abolitionist rhetoric, *Notes on the History of Slavery in Massachusetts* was based on exhaustive research conducted in the Massachusetts Archives. Unfortunately, Moore's inability to untangle his political beliefs from his work undermined his status as a professional historian, calling his objectivity into question.

Not until the publication of W. E. B. Du Bois's *The Suppression of the African Slave-Trade to the United States* (1896) did a more earnest discussion of the traffic take place, marking the dawn of the early professional period.[28] Originally written as his doctoral dissertation at Harvard University, Du Bois's refreshing departure from the partisan agendas of his predecessors provided a thorough investigation of the trade that was based on considerable archival and primary source research rather than anecdotal observation. It was not humanitarianism, he argued, but a strong reaction to the Haitian Revolution that motivated America's decision to abolish the trade. In Du Bois's analysis, the United States associated French dependence on importations from Africa with the start of the only successful slave revolt in history: the steady influx of Africans to France's Caribbean colonies created too volatile an enslaved population, and the end result was an inevitable violent revolt. Because the United States did not want to become party to another Haiti, Congress abolished the trade in 1808. Despite this legislative change, Du Bois contended that the American people were unsupportive of the ban, and that the federal government displayed a general apathy toward any enforcement of the law. Du Bois blamed America's *moral cowardice* for its failure to suppress the illegal importation of slaves into the United States—a trade that continued largely without interference until the Civil War.[29] In his mind, the persistence of that unfettered trade, coupled with the

Industrial Revolution and the spread of cotton cultivation in the South, entrenched African slavery within the American economy. Although a few histories followed Du Bois's study during the early professional period, they were largely static microstudies that focused more on narrative rather than analysis and characterized African Americans as insignificant players in American history. For example, while John Randolph Spears's *The American Slave-Trade* (1900) echoed Du Bois's arguments regarding America's failure to suppress the trade in a vivid and detailed description of an evil and immoral traffic, his tone was one of pity and sympathy for the traders and nations involved.[30] Elizabeth Donnan, most known for her impressive four-volume *Documents Illustrative of the Slave Trade* (1930), wrote impartial economic histories of the trade that focused more on the American Revolution than the trade itself.[31]

Yet Du Bois's pivotal research went on to influence several historians whose work would later pioneer the Atlantic and Pan-African approaches of decades to come. Influenced by German anthropologist Franz Boas, whose work refuted the standard arguments characterizing people of color as racially inferior and devoid of their own history and culture,[32] Du Bois and scholars like Carter G. Woodson and Melville J. Herskovits instead acknowledged a vibrant African American culture that emphasized the continuity of a West African past. Articles began to appear in the newly formed *Journal of Negro History,* founded by Woodson in 1916, examining the slave trade from an increasingly African perspective, notably Jerome Dowd's 1917 article "Slavery and the Slave Trade in Africa."[33] As the early professional period came to a close, and the outsiders were no longer categorized as such, articles by scholars like Lorenzo Turner began to argue that "students of African cultural survivals in the New World need not expect to make much progress in their investigations without first learning something about the culture of the African tribes brought here as slaves."[34]

As a result, the contributions of the midcentury scholars began to take the world focus first considered by the early professionals in new directions. Eric Williams's seminal work *Capitalism and Slavery* (1944), for example, extended Du Bois's economic arguments by focusing on the trade's economic impact on industrialization within the wider British Empire, arguing that economics, not racism, drove the transatlantic slave trade and led to its abolition.[35] According to Williams, the trade provided the British Empire with enough working capital to industrialize in the 1840s, but rendered the institution of slavery obsolete in the process. He further argued that those same capitalists who once depended on slavery for their economic gain emancipated their slaves. Other scholars considered Du Bois's arguments concerning the state's effectiveness at suppressing the trade through a political rather than an economic lens. Christopher Lloyd investigated the British Royal Navy's work in suppressing the illegal trade in the nineteenth century; both he and Bernard Nelson considered England's efforts at persuading other foreign powers to abolish the trade by placing the traffic within England's larger foreign policy agenda.[36]

By the mid-1960s, however, historical developments outside of academia produced significant changes within the field, as historians found themselves considerably influenced by the American Civil Rights movement, post-World War II European decolonization, and the rapid rise of independent African governments. African and African American history programs grew in record numbers, eventually becoming markers of intellectual prestige and inclusion, as students and historians alike were influenced by ideas of Black nationalism and Pan-Africanism. Studies during the Civil Rights era took many different trajectories as the field experienced a series of growth spurts. Generalized studies of the slave trade such as Basil Davidson's *Black Mother* (1961), Daniel P. Mannix and Malcolm Cowley's *Black Cargoes* (1962), and James Pope-Hennessey's *Sins of the Fathers* (1967) expanded on John H. Russell's earlier work to humanize the field even more with their vivid stories of violent atrocities, European manipulation, and economic greed that faintly resembled those first put forth by abolitionists over a century ago.[37] The publication of these works forced their contemporaries to reconsider past sterile characterizations of Africans as no more than a means of production within the larger plantation complex.[38] Instead, Davidson and his peers told the story of a tragically enslaved people caught in the middle of a larger historical phenomenon that would have devastating effects on the African continent as a whole, echoing Weeden and Moore's nineteenth-century sentiments. Yet these midcentury discussions of Africa were overshadowed by their more direct attacks on the Europeans who manipulated the continent for economic gain. Furthermore, these works signified an interesting shift in the historiography, as Africanists increasingly claimed the field as their own.

Meanwhile, in an effort to further humanize the trade and its suppression, the field revisited the decades-old arguments that Eric Williams made in *Capitalism and Slavery* concerning the abolition of the slave trade. Those scholars challenging what would become known as the *Williams thesis* forced historians to question the complicated relationship between Atlantic world slavery, the transatlantic trade, and the Enlightenment.[39] Although this debate began in the early Civil Rights era with the publication of critiques penned by Roger Anstey and David Brion Davis, the debate did not begin in earnest until Seymour Drescher published *Econocide* in 1977. Countering Williams's decline thesis that a capitalistic market economy coupled with self-interest led to the abolition of an obsolete trade, Drescher posited that the trade and slavery were extremely profitable, that their abolition amounted to economic suicide, and that it was the English abolitionist movement's philanthropic humanitarianism— a movement that focused on individual freedoms and the rights of man—that motivated the abolition of the transatlantic slave trade.

The larger field of historical inquiry itself also experienced a sharp shift in its methodology during the 1960s, as more and more historians began to adopt a quantitative approach to their research. Slave trade studies led this development, as the publication of Philip Curtin's *The Atlantic Slave Trade: A Census* (1969) evidences. One of the first to utilize a purely quantitative approach to the study of the transatlantic trade, Curtin's study analyzed embarkation and disembarkation figures, mortality rates, and purchase trends for each European nation participating in the trade, as well as how these patterns changed over time in order to add additional specificity to what was already known about the trade. What ensued was yet another debate within the field, as Curtin's peers and successors sought to prove or disprove his evidence. Basing his figures primarily on published sources, Curtin estimated that a total of 9,566,100 Africans were transported from Africa to the Americas through the Middle Passage.[40] Although more recent numbers center around the eleven to twelve million range, with the exception of Joseph Inikori's 1981 estimate of 15.4 million, Curtin's 1969 figure is considered to be a standard within the field and is still widely accepted as a reasonable estimate.[41]

As the quantitative debates raged on, Walter Rodney built on the work originally begun by scholars in the early 1960s like Mannix, Cowley, and Pope-Hennessey who sought to further humanize the trade. In *How Europe Underdeveloped Africa* (1972), Rodney characterized the slave trade as a historical event of catastrophic proportions, painting a severe picture of a continent stripped of its people, resources, and will to survive.[42] He described the African continent as a collection of prosperous nation-states comparable to any of those found in the West before Europe's rise in the fifteenth century. These nation-states established a series of successful trade and commercial networks that spanned the continent, each selling a variety of commodities—even slaves. Rodney's Africa was strong and prosperous, but a shift began to occur with the arrival of the Portuguese in 1441. The subsequent creation of the notorious triangular trade undermined and eventually destroyed those thriving trade networks as more and more European traders arrived with cheap alcohol and trade goods. The additional importation of advanced weaponry instigated increased warfare between Africa's nation-states through the manipulation of ethnic rivalries, and as a result, more and more enslaved Africans entered the transatlantic trade as by-products of this warfare. Rodney described a holocaust wherein Europe trapped Africa into supplying even more slaves to feed its endless hunger for commodities like sugar, tobacco, and cotton. What resulted was economic, political, and demographic stagnation that would plague Africa for centuries to come.

Although Rodney's arguments were extreme, and some in the field increasingly distanced themselves from him in the years after he published this formative work because of its tone in condemning Europe for its past actions, his interpretations of the slave trade's impact on Africa added complexity to the historiography.[43] *How Europe Underdeveloped Africa* would go on to motivate historians to look past quantitative analyses in order to consider the transatlantic slave trade's impact on the continent. While the debate over demographics continued, historians began to utilize those numbers as part of larger investigations that would take the field in several interesting directions over the next twenty years. As Africanists increasingly dominated the field of slave trade studies, many works that followed Rodney's in the 1970s and 1980s probed the overall impact of the traffic on the continent as a whole. Scholars continued to debate the validity of Curtin's estimates, but a parallel debate emerged about the degree to which those numbers negatively impacted Africa and Africans in demographic, economic, and political terms.

Although some like J. D. Fage, John Thornton, and David Eltis argued that the slave trade was insignificant in Africa and only felt marginally at best, most agreed that the modern estimates of the slave trade's volume would have had a devastating impact.[44] Historians such as Joseph Miller, along with John Thornton, analyzed how ever-changing price trends corresponded to planter purchase preferences, while David Geggus's and David Eltis's demographic models examined fluctuating age and sex ratios aboard slave ships in relation to estimates of African population trends.[45] Joseph Inikori extended Rodney's analysis regarding Africa's European-induced economic backwardness and Europe's debilitating influence, but he also sharply criticized scholars like Fage, Eltis, and Thornton who were unconcerned by the trade's negative impact on the continent and peoples of Africa.[46] Paul Lovejoy showed that increased warfare and jihad among Africa's nation-states during the four centuries of the slave trade created a cyclical domino effect that led to further economic devastation, population decline, and general vulnerability to European manipulation and invasion.[47] Although Fage, Thornton, and Eltis stood their ground and continued to argue that the repercussions were minimal, Africanists and historians of the transatlantic trade increasingly agreed with Rodney that West African merchants and traders gradually shifted their focus from most other trade commodities to slaves as a direct result of planters' increased demand for Africans.

Patrick Manning's *Slavery and African Life* (1990) continued this discussion into the next decade not only by agreeing that the devastation caused by the transatlantic slave trade stunted Africa's population growth for several centuries, but also by adding that the Atlantic traffic negatively affected the sub-Saharan and Islamic trades as well.[48] In other words, slaves were in such high demand in the Americas that the African traders who normally supplied the sub-Saharan and Islamic trades decided to redirect their supplies to transatlantic markets instead. Therefore, not only had Europe underdeveloped Africa, as Rodney had first argued nearly twenty years earlier, but Europe's economic dependency on the transatlantic slave trade affected the peripheral markets of the Middle East and even Asia in serious economic terms as well.

Manning's comparisons to other trades within Africa did more than support past claims of European dominance and manipulation in Africa; it opened the field's eyes to an entirely new idea— African participation in the trade. Scholars had previously characterized Africans as innocent pawns caught in the middle of Europe's imperial rivalries. Although Manning and Lovejoy touched on African participation, Thornton's *Africa and Africans in the Making of the Atlantic World* (1992) was the first monograph to fully address this dimension of the trade.[49] Thornton demonstrated that Africans were more active agents in the trade than was previously argued, portraying a continent comprised of powerful negotiators and businessmen. In fact, according to Thornton, Europeans not only recognized Africa's commercial achievements— they saw Africans as equals rather than subordinates. Therefore, rather than take Rodney's stance that Europeans trapped an easy mark into selling her own people to the plantations of the Americas, Thornton characterized Africans as agents of their own destiny. To Thornton, Africans exploited Africans and European slave traders were merely a third party. Thornton's arguments were difficult for some to accept and he faced serious criticism for his claims.[50] However, his work had and still has great influence on early twenty-first-century scholars.[51]

Despite these offshoot discussions on underdevelopment and African participation during the long Civil Rights period, the quantitative debates sparked by Curtin's *Census* continued into the twenty-first century. David Eltis, Stephen Behrendt, Herbert S. Klein, and David Richardson's *The Transatlantic Slave Trade: A Database on CD-ROM* (1999) estimated a total of 11,062,000 Africans embarking from Africa, with 9.6 million disembarking in the Americas.[52] These figures differ little from Curtin's original estimates made thirty years earlier, and they are based entirely on unpublished European shipping records logged from 1519 to 1867. An updated and much-expanded version of this database now appears online, offering a revised total of 12,521,336 based on new research that expands the original database's sources by 60 percent.[53] This database, its most recent update, and the subsequent companion volume *Extending the Frontiers: Essays on the New Transatlantic Slave Trade Database* (2008) have served as an invaluable resource, influencing new investigations of the slave trade and sparking repeated calls for revision of past arguments.[54]

Yet *Extending the Frontiers* was only a start. Based on new research taken from the updated database, each of the essays contained in the anthology "deal[t] with a branch of the slave trade that the new data have allowed scholars to explore systematically for the first time,"[55] demonstrating that the trade was much more complex than previously imagined. Whereas historians previously characterized the trade as a cohesive effort jointly choreographed by several European nations, *Extending the Frontiers* showed that the trade was actually a collection of separate networks located throughout the Atlantic world. Vessels originating in Liverpool or Bristol did not monopolize the trade; in fact, ships leaving Rio de Janeiro, Recife, and Bahian ports carried more enslaved Africans to the Americas.[56] Furthermore, England's place as a successful leader in enforcing the 1807 ban on the trade is also reexamined:

new assertions reminiscent of Du Bois's century-old study criticizing America's efforts at suppressing the trade suggest that England's efforts were just as ineffective.

These new findings will likely continue to improve our understanding of the transatlantic slave trade for years to come. As more twenty-first-century scholars enter the conversation, we see them attempting to steer the ships away from the quantitative interpretations of the long Civil Rights period with presentations of new evidence and fresh insight. For example, case studies by Bayo Holsey, G. Ugo Nwokeji, and Rebecca Shumway not only address African participation and the trade's effects on the continent, but they also focus on understudied ethnic groups, nation-states, and regions in Africa that participated in the trade in one form or another.[57] Emma Christopher's examination of slave ship crews and captains gave a glimpse of the mentalities of the men directly participating in this traffic, providing a more well-rounded picture of the experiences aboard ship first described by Basil Davidson and his peers in the 1960s.[58] Marcus Rediker's *The Slave Ship* (2007) similarly tried to rescue a *human history* from the quantitative approach popularized by Curtin and others.[59] These historians have added to the work that characterized the 1990s by expanding on it in greater detail and offering new ways of interpreting the sources available today.

Returning to the story of the first enslaved Africans imported into Jamestown in 1619, Tim Hashaw, in *The Birth of Black America: The First African Americans and the Pursuit of Freedom at Jamestown* (2007), chronicled their lives as well as the lives of their descendants. Informally labeling them the Bautista Africans (after the *São João Bautista*), Hashaw showed that while the majority of their days were spent planting and harvesting tobacco, they also raised cattle, traded with the Iroquois and European settlers around Jamestown and the James River region, and grew and sold produce to the various peoples that traveled in and out of the neighboring ports.[60] They married and had children, and some were eventually able to purchase their freedom. More enslaved Angolans immediately followed their arrival, probably casualties of the same wars between the Ndongo and their northern neighbors, further influencing the developing cultural landscape of the mid-Atlantic region. The grandson of one such slave, a second-generation freedman who was able to purchase a significant tract of land along Virginia's eastern shore, named his estate Angola in 1677.[61]

Until Hashaw's study of America's first Africans, most scholars largely mentioned them as a footnote within a class lecture or a larger discussion of the slave trade as a whole. Yet the transatlantic trade has taken several routes in its historiographical development, and twenty-first-century scholars are now connecting this historiography to the field of American studies, further proving the inseparability of the two fields' histories. Furthermore, as a result, a new field examining the African diaspora is beginning to develop.[62] Just as Africanists gradually co-opted the field of slave trade studies as their own in the 1960s, Americanists are following their lead through their discussions of the cultural elements and transferences of North America's slave communities. New historical trends, like those exhibited in Hashaw's examination of the Bautista Africans, are expanding on the work begun by the many scholars discussed throughout this chapter. What they reveal is a vibrant African cultural identity among America's enslaved population. Twenty-first-century scholars like Jason Young, Gwendolyn Midlo Hall, and Douglas B. Chambers have all utilized the slave trade data that Eltis and his colleagues gathered in 1999 in order to characterize what life might have been like for America's slaves.[63] Historians continue to apply Eltis's expanded data to their larger investigations of the African diaspora outside of the transatlantic slave trade. At the same time, scholars like Sowande' Mustakeem and Sharla Fett have turned their attention to the experiences of the enslaved on ships in the Middle Passage, relying on the same records cataloged in the *Slave Voyages* project but employed to tell the human story of the slave trade at sea.[64]

The blending of these two fields allows scholars to explore an intricately diverse culture among America's slaves, and, in doing so, to present a new research agenda that considers the links between Africa and America's enslaved. What this new generation of historians is discovering is a fluid, complex African cultural identity within

America's slave communities—one that is nearly as complex as the African diaspora itself.[65] As John Thornton has argued, enslaved people throughout the Americas perceived themselves as part of communities that had distinct national roots.[66] Yet at the same time, enslaved Africans and their descendants mixed and matched old and new ways in order to build on common traditions and cultures that would be distinctly African American. As this chapter illustrates, that tradition seems to have continued among historians as well. Amid these recent historiographical developments, scholars of the transatlantic slave trade and American slavery have found themselves part and parcel of a larger, more encompassing discussion examining the African diaspora as a whole. While scholars will continue to research the trade through quantitative, economic, political, and cultural lenses, their findings have and will continue to promote the understanding of the complex historical connections between Africans, African Americans, and their descendants in the wider Atlantic world. The degrees to which these groups are connected will become clearer as historians continue their research and more evidence becomes available.

NOTES

1. For more on these early experiences in Jamestown and the African diaspora, see J. K. Thornton, "African Experience"; and Hashaw, *Birth of Black America*.

2. See Hashaw, *Birth of Black America*.

3. This is not to say that there are no books on the American slave trade. Those books, however, largely discuss the domestic slave trade within the British North American colonies and later the United States, or the specific trade routes to particular states. Only Peter Duignan's concise but comprehensive history considers the overall trade to the United States. See Duignan, *United States and the African Slave Trade*. See also Wax, "Negro Imports into Pennsylvania"; Wax, "Black Immigrants"; Coughtry, *Notorious Triangle;* Minchinton, *Virginia Slave Trade Statistics;* R. Bailey, "Slave(ry) Trade"; Starks, *Freebooters and Smugglers;* and Trammell, *Richmond Slave Trade*.

4. The most notorious leg of this journey was the *Middle Passage,* a term coined by eighteenth-century traders to describe the voyage between Africa and the Americas.

5. Fogel and Engerman, *Time on the Cross,* 15, 25; Eltis et al., "Patterns in the Transatlantic Slave Trade," 26; and J. W. Sweet, "Subject of the Slave Trade," 3.

6. Eltis, "U.S. Transatlantic Slave Trade," 347.

7. Peter Duignan argued this point repeatedly in his history of the slave trade to America. See Duignan, *United States and the African Slave Trade.*

8. Eltis, "Brief Overview of the Trans-Atlantic Slave Trade."

9. H. Thomas, *Slave Trade,* 809, 862.

10. Eltis, "Brief Overview of the Trans-Atlantic Slave Trade."

11. Nash, *Red, White, and Black,* 140.

12. The majority of North America's slaves came primarily from six West African regions: Senegambia (modern-day Senegal, Gambia, Guinea-Bissau, and Mali); west-central Africa (Angola, Congo, the Democratic Republic of Congo, and Gabon); Sierra Leone; the Windward Coast (the northern corner of modern-day Liberia to the eastern border of modern Côte d'Ivoire); the Gold Coast (modern-day Ghana); and the stretch of African coast between the Niger River and Cape Lopez known as the Bight of Biafra. An extremely small percentage came from the Bight of Benin and Madagascar.

13. The African system of *pawnship* (or debt bondage) involved the assurance of people rather than goods as collateral to secure debt repayment. When these debts came due, debtors turned over their slaves and/or family members as payment when funds were not available. In many cases, the debtor was also enslaved for nonpayment of debt.

14. France was the first to abolish the slave trade in 1794, only to reinstate it in 1802 under Napoleon. Denmark abolished the trade in 1802, with England and the United States following in 1807 and 1808, respectively. The rest of Europe, Latin America, and the Caribbean gradually abolished slavery over the next fifty years, although the illegal trade continued unabated. The last ship transporting illegally enslaved Africans to America—the schooner *Clotilda*—docked in Mobile, AL, in 1860. For more on this voyage, see Diouf, *Dreams of Africa.*

15. Curtin, *Atlantic Slave Trade,* 216; Fogel and Engerman, *Time on the Cross,* 25; Deyle, "'By farr the most profitable trade,'" 108. Philip Curtin sets the number at 399,000; David Eltis comes in just a bit lower at 389,000. See Curtin, *Atlantic Slave Trade,* 72-75, 216; and Eltis, "U.S. Transatlantic Slave Trade," 349, 350, 351, 353.

16. Lovejoy, "Main Areas of Destination."

17. Du Bois, *Black Reconstruction in America,* 1 (reprint edition). Unfortunately, it is impossible to know how many African-born American slaves lived in the United States in 1860, as the 1860 census included a nativity question for free individuals only. According to that census, only 7,011 people of color in 1860 were *foreign born;* the place of their birth was not specified. See Katz, *Negro Population of the United States,* 54, 61.

18. E. E. Dunbar, *Mexican Papers.*

19. See "New Publications: The Mexican Papers." According to Philip Curtin, Dunbar's estimates were his own and were not based on any substantial research at all. Interestingly, Joseph Inikori estimated a similar total a century later. See Curtin, *Atlantic Slave Trade*, 7; and Inikori, *Forced Migration*, 20.

20. G. Moore, *Notes on the History of Slavery;* Weeden, "Early African Slave-Trade."

21. G. Moore, *Notes on the History of Slavery*, 81.

22. G. Moore, *Notes on the History of Slavery*, 81.

23. J. Smith, "George H. Moore," 212.

24. J. Smith, "George H. Moore," 214.

25. G. Moore, *Notes on the History of Slavery*, 224.

26. G. Moore, *Notes on the History of Slavery*, 224.

27. J. Smith, "George H. Moore," 214.

28. Du Bois, *Suppression of the African Slave-Trade.*

29. Du Bois, *Suppression of the African Slave-Trade*, 196.

30. Spears, *American Slave-Trade.*

31. See Donnan, "Slave Trade into South Carolina"; Donnan, "New England Slave Trade"; and Donnan, *Documents.*

32. L. Baker, "Columbia University's Franz Boas."

33. Dowd, "Slavery and the Slave Trade in Africa."

34. L. Turner, "Some Contacts of Brazilian Ex-Slaves," 55.

35. E. Williams, *Capitalism and Slavery.*

36. B. Nelson, "Slave Trade as a Factor"; Lloyd, *Navy and the Slave Trade.*

37. Davidson, *Black Mother;* Mannix and Cowley, *Black Cargoes;* Pope-Hennessey, *Sins of the Fathers;* and Russell, *Free Negro in Virginia.*

38. See H. Klein, *Atlantic Slave Trade*, 214.

39. For more on this debate, see Anstey, "Capitalism and Slavery"; D. Davis, *Problem of Slavery;* Engerman, "Slave Trade"; Drescher, *Econocide;* Carrington and Drescher, "Debate"; Drescher, "Decline Thesis"; Eltis, *Economic Growth;* Drescher, *Capitalism and Anti-Slavery;* T. Holt, "Explaining Abolition"; Bender, *Anti-Slavery Debate;* and Drescher, *Abolition.*

40. Curtin, *Atlantic Slave Trade*, 268. Interestingly, Edward E. Dunbar and Robert Dale Owen are credited with the earliest estimates of the total number of people taken from West Africa. Dunbar's 1861 figure placed the total number at nearly 14 million; Owen raised the number to just over 15.5 million just three years later. Unfortunately, neither Dunbar nor Owen considered the 15-20 percent mortality rates of the Middle Passage or the fact that Africans were still being transported to Cuba and Brazil until 1888. Although many estimates have been made since Dunbar and Owen published their miscalculated findings, Philip Curtin set the standard with the publication of *The Atlantic Slave Trade: A Census* in 1969. See Lovejoy, "Volume of the Atlantic Slave Trade," 495. Lovejoy's book also presented a historiographical discussion on mortality rates in the Middle Passage.

41. See Inikori, *Forced Migration,* 20. Edward E. Dunbar estimated that 14 million Africans were transported from Africa to the Americas in his discussion of America's dependency on the trade and the decline of American slavery in the 1860s. See E. E. Dunbar, *History of the Rise and Decline,* 269-70.

42. Rodney, *How Europe Underdeveloped Africa.*

43. See M. Klein, "Review: *How Europe Underdeveloped Africa*"; Legassick, "Perspectives on African 'Underdevelopment'"; and Wallerstein, "Walter Rodney."

44. See Fage, "Slavery and the Slave Trade"; Fage, "Effect of the Slave Trade"; J. K. Thornton, "Demographic Effect"; and Eltis, *Economic Growth,* 15, 77.

45. See J. Miller, *Way of Death;* J. K. Thornton, "Demographic Effect"; Geggus, "Sex Ratio, Age, and Ethnicity"; and Eltis, "Fluctuations."

46. See Inikori, *Forced Migration.*

47. Lovejoy, "Impact of the Atlantic Slave Trade," 389.

48. P. Manning, *Slavery and African Life.*

49. J. K. Thornton, *Africa and Africans.*

50. See for instance P. Manning, "Review: *Africa and Africans*"; Law, "Review: *Africa and Africans*"; Webster, "Review: *Africa and Africans*"; and Berlin, "Review: *Africa and Africans.*"

51. For instance, various works examine African participation through the lens of enslaved Africans rather than Thornton's focus on African middlemen. See Diouf, *Fighting the Slave Trade;* and E. Taylor, *If We Must Die.*

52. Eltis et al., *Trans-Atlantic Slave Trade: A Database on CD-ROM.*

53. Paul Lovejoy and James Rawley also posit estimates within range of Curtin's original number. Whereas Lovejoy estimates 11,863,000, Rawley places his a bit lower at 11,345,000. Robert Fogel and Stanley Engerman come closest to Curtin's original estimate with 9,735,000, proving that Curtin's estimate is no less reputable than any other. See the *Slave Voyages: The Trans-Atlantic Slave Trade Database* website, http://www.slavevoyages.org; Lovejoy, "Impact of the Atlantic Slave Trade," 373; Rawley, *Transatlantic Slave Trade,* 428; and Fogel and Engerman, *Time on the Cross,* 16.

54. Eltis and Richardson, *Extending the Frontiers.*

55. Eltis and Richardson, *Extending the Frontiers,* 4.

56. Eltis and Richardson, *Extending the Frontiers,* 39, 122.

57. See Holsey, *Routes of Remembrance;* Nwokeji, *Slave Trade and Culture;* and Shumway, *Fante and the Transatlantic Slave Trade.*

58. Christopher, *Slave Ship Sailors.*

59. Rediker, *Slave Ship.*

60. Hashaw, *Birth of Black America.*

61. J. K. Thornton, "African Experience," 434.

62. On the Black diaspora, see especially Segal, *Black Diaspora;* Gomez, *Exchanging Our Country Marks;* and M. Wright, *Becoming Black.*

63. See D. Chambers, "Ethnicity in the Diaspora"; D. Chambers, *Murder at Montpelier;* G. Hall, *Slavery and African Ethnicities;* and Young, *Rituals of Resistance.*

64. Mustakeem, *Slavery at Sea;* Fett, *Recaptured Africans; Slave Voyages: The Trans-Atlantic Slave Trade Database* website.

65. See Holloway, *Africanisms in American Culture;* Rucker, *River Flows On;* L. Levine, *Black Culture and Black Consciousness;* and Smallwood, *Saltwater Slavery.*

66. J. K. Thornton, *Africa and Africans,* 195-97.

CHAPTER EIGHT

American Slavery and
Free African Americans

KELLY BIRCH AND THOMAS C. BUCHANAN

Slavery was legal in the United States until the Civil War, but not
all African Americans were enslaved. From the earliest days of the
American colonial settlements, there were also free Black people
in America who were not born to a free mother but who managed to secure their liberty through self-purchase, by their owner's
manumission, or by running away to freedom. In the years following the American Revolution, free Black populations increased,
particularly in the North as states enacted gradual emancipation
laws. This *freedom,* however, did not engender equality with white
Americans. All free people of color, those living both in the North
and in the South, experienced various forms of discrimination that
effectively limited their possibilities for inclusion in American life.
Although class and color differences created divisions among free
African Americans, they remained part of a shared experience,
born of their common cultural background and the challenges they
faced in American society.

Historians have had a long-standing interest in this relatively
small group of Americans for two important reasons.[1] First, free
Black peoples represented the possibilities of freedom, and as
such were intimately linked to scholarly assessments of enslaved
people. Were free Black people successful when freed from bondage? The question underscores the immorality of slavery itself,

and the debate surrounding it was significant particularly through the early decades of the twentieth century. Second, the anomalous status of free people of color attracted scholars seeking to augment the historiography of the African American experience. Whereas racist thinking presumed that all African American people were fundamentally the same, free Black people suggested variety and complexity. By the 1960s, these divisions had become highly politicized, as historians debated the role of free people of color in the broader African American liberation struggle. The subject thus adds an important element to this volume.

This chapter follows the five historical periods outlined in the introduction, from the original debates over Black freedom in the antebellum years through the recent post-Civil Rights era contemporary accounts. It considers Northern and Southern free Blacks as a whole despite considerable regional differences in the origins of these communities and their historical experiences. Similarly, its historical coverage moves between the colonial, Revolutionary, and antebellum periods in its historical coverage; this breadth captures trends over time that cut across investigations of a diverse range of free Black experiences. Historians working in very different periods were often shaped by similar concerns based on the common contemporary contexts that influenced their work.

In the first period, the nineteenth century, free Black people were particularly important early contributors to the public debate. In their writings, they emphasized the advantages of freedom, the diversity of free Black people, and the unfairness of racism. Henry Bibb, for example, enthralled with the freedom of the North, commented that, "I now feel as if I had been aroused from sleep." William Wells Brown recalled that during his escape, "as we travelled toward a land of liberty, my heart would at times leap for joy." Solomon Northrup, born free in the North, wrote of his "sorrow and despair" following his capture and sale south, which precipitated years spent as a slave "shut out from the sweet light of liberty."[2] According to Julie Winch, Cyprian Clamorgan, a wealthy free African American, wrote his narrative in 1858 hoping to convince Americans "that the black community was not a monolith."[3]

While Clamorgan emphasized class distinctions, the narratives of Mary Prince and Harriet Jacobs, for instance, highlighted the vulnerability of women in slavery, implicitly recognizing that freedom afforded protection against sexual abuse and stability for families. Although most narratives romanticized the North, Frederick Douglass famously contributed a word of caution when he noted that during his attempt to get work on a dock in New Bedford, Massachusetts, "such was the strength of prejudice against color, amongst the white caulkers, that they refused to work with me."[4]

Southern supporters of slavery countered with their own stories of Black freedom. Slave criminal confessions were quite popular during the Revolutionary era and became more robust in their detail over time. William L. Andrews wrote that in criminal confessional accounts of gallows-bound African American convicts, "the narrator's first and greatest mistake is his rejection of parental advice and/or his master's supervision in favor of a bid for self-sufficiency in the world."[5] Whereas accounts by Frederick Douglass and other runaways are now classic texts, it is important to remember that Southern whites in the antebellum period were more persuaded by criminal confessions such as those by free Blacks Amos Warrick, James Seward, and Charles Brown—men hung in St. Louis in 1841 for murder during a bank robbery. Their jailhouse stories, shaped by their proslavery amanuenses, reveal escalating careers of crime, all of which stemmed ostensibly from having too much freedom.[6] For Southern white readers, allowing Blacks to be free resulted in poverty, crime, and rebellion. From the outset, there were different sectional perspectives on free Black life.

This debate continued in the postwar period, fueled first by partisan interpretations and then by reconciliation accounts of the Civil War that based sectional peace on mutual racism.[7] Serious disagreements developed between pro-Northern and pro-Southern military leaders, scholars, journalists, folklorists, and fiction writers, who sometimes included free Blacks in the debate about the cause of the Civil War. For example, writing in the 1870s, the Republican vice president Henry Wilson cited District of Columbia laws in 1827 and afterward presuming that African Americans were slaves unless they could prove otherwise as evidence of the encroaching *slave power* that eventually plunged the nation into war.[8] Most Northern white partisans, however, neglected the experiences or contributions of both enslaved and free African Americans, making only isolated references to the tenuous position of free Blacks.[9]

African American writers, in contrast, continued to address free people of color in their writings, often with renewed emphasis, balancing in various ways new evidence of antebellum racism with examples of Black achievement. For example, William Wells Brown, in an adaptation of his antebellum narrative, included a new chapter on free people of color in the South in which he noted civil and penal laws, as well as social customs, that were designed to exclude and subjugate free African American people. Their condition, he asserted, was often worse than that of bondspeople.[10] Others emphasized the success that free Black people had in overcoming racism. "An industrious, enterprising, thrifty, and intelligent free black population," Frederick Douglass asserted, in a new section added to his antebellum narrative in 1881, was "the most telling . . . refutation of slavery."[11]

Southern partisans picked up the antebellum discourse regarding the incompatibility of African Americans and freedom and extended it in significant ways. In the context of the Jim Crow South, which curtailed Black civil rights, white authors published fictional slave narratives and folklore tales offering American readers romanticized portraits of traditional Southern slave life that vindicated and ardently perpetuated racial discrimination. These accounts often contained pessimistic readings of free Black life in the Old South. In Charles Chandler's 1894 narrative, the protagonist enjoyed his life as the faithful slave on the Choteaux family plantation in Alabama, dismissing "freedom and the franchise, with their magnificent political possibilities," claiming "[they] brought no pleasures to me."[12] Joel Chandler Harris's folk character Free Joe embraced his freedom, but is described as "a black atom, drifting hither and thither without an owner, blown about by all the winds of circumstance, and given over to shiftlessness."

He died free but completely alone—a fate attributed to his tenuous position as a "man of color" lost without a master's paternal care.[13]

America's first generation of professionally trained historians brought a significant shift to the historiography in terms of research methods. This process changed white interpretations little, however, as racist readings of the past solidified around what most agreed was a *negro problem*. As segregation became legally entrenched, many white scholars—both Southerners and Northerners—saw African American freedom as a problem not only for former slaves and their descendants but also for America as a whole. For instance, Lewis Cecil Gray wrote that postbellum *Black codes* were necessary to curb African Americans' deviant behaviors.[14] Philip Alexander Bruce agreed, urging legislators to enforce further segregation by establishing separate governing bodies for African American people.[15]

The most influential scholar of slavery in these years, Ulrich B. Phillips, while not as proscriptive as scholars like Gray and Bruce, nonetheless shared his doubts about the prospects of Black freedom. Phillips included numerous insights into free Black life in the chapter "Free Negros" in his seminal work *American Negro Slavery* (1918).[16] He was not altogether unsympathetic to the plight of free Blacks, taking note of the "private rebuffs and oppressions which they met, [which] greatly complicated the problem of social adjustment that colored freedmen everywhere encountered." He argued that their status was less contested and resented by Southern whites compared with their Northern counterparts because of their more thoroughly subordinate status in the South. This subordination was ameliorated by what he called "solaces" to be found in the "lightheartedness" of Southern "negroes" who enjoyed "sincere friendships" with whites. In contrast, he noted the criminal tendencies that developed in Northern free Black communities, suggesting that Northern free Blacks were more likely to resort to criminal behavior and to end up in prison.[17]

John H. Russell's *The Free Negro in Virginia* (1913) provided the first full-scale scholarly study on the subject during the early professional years. Russell was more positive than Phillips about the history and future of free Black freedom, casting the changing contours of legal discrimination in Virginia against social customs and implicitly recognizing the need for the Fourteenth Amendment to the Constitution, which demanded equality under the law.[18] Through an examination of state laws and county court records, Russell showed that the legal status of free Black individuals in Virginia bore a complicated relationship to their social status. Citing slave conspiracies and rebellions, the state legislature gradually curtailed many of the rights and freedoms that it had previously extended to free Black residents, whom they deemed disruptive to slavery. As Russell argued, however, slaveholders' economic interests and personal ties to the free Black community meant that legal changes were not always enforced, and owing to this space between code and custom, he concluded, Virginia's free Black population steadily grew in the decades preceding the Civil War. James M. Wright agreed, asserting in *The Free Negro in Maryland* (1921) that "the progress of the negro depended on the types of whites [with whom] they came into contact."[19] These professional white scholars, while clearly sympathetic to the struggles of free people of color and not altogether pessimistic about the prospects for Black freedom, nonetheless agreed with Phillips that free people of color depended on whites to maintain their freedom from plantation slavery.

African American intellectuals, many of whom were making their way through graduate school at the time, joined the new professional class, but as outsiders often excluded from professional meetings and journals. Carter G. Woodson led the movement. Woodson, along with fellow members of the Association for the Study of Negro Life and History, which was founded 1915, all demonstrated the ways in which free African Americans embraced liberty.[20] The themes of Woodson's work are evident in a seminal article that he wrote in the first edition of the *Journal of Negro History* titled "The Negroes of Cincinnati Prior to the Civil War." In it, he argued that there was "striking evidence" that "colored people generally thrive[d]" and that they achieved so much that they were generally "the most progressive people in the world." Despite severe racism in Cincinnati, which led to their periodic expulsion

from the city, Woodson documented considerable property ownership and institution building, including "improvement in religion and morals," all of which developed in part due to benevolent
whites but also through the industry of free people of color.[21]

Woodson made numerous other contributions as well. In particular, he revealed how racism divided the labor market, depriv-
ing free African American men of skilled work, and instead forced
them to work as seamen, day laborers, and domestic workers. His
book *Free Negro Ownership of Slaves in the United States in 1830*, published in 1924, revealed the presence of free Black slaveholders,
which he explained by arguing that free Black men and women
often purchased family and kin for benevolent reasons.[22] These
purchased kin were generally immediately emancipated in the colonial era, but by the early national and antebellum periods, legislative reforms curtailed slaveholders' rights to emancipate their
slaves, and some demanded that newly manumitted slaves be ex-
pelled from the state. These laws, Woodson argued, encouraged
many African American slaveholders in these years to maintain
legal ownership of their enslaved kin. Despite their thorough archival research and growing publication base, Woodson and other
African American scholars were not quickly accepted or even acknowledged by white members of the academy.[23]

The 1930s and early 1940s saw a few notable interpretative ad-
vances made in the field. A 1930 article by Avery O. Craven, which
blended environmental and social history, suggested a variety of
points of contact between the races, a point that would further be
explored by later historians.[24] More significantly, Herbert Aptheker's *American Negro Slave Revolts* (1943) made clear the role of free
Black people in Southern rebellions.[25] Aptheker, a Marxist, demonstrated that ordinary whites feared free Black people and enacted
a variety of legal measures to control their influence. By the time
American Negro Slave Revolts was published, a midcentury shift in
the historiography was well under way. A number of African American scholars, including Luther Porter Jackson, John Hope Franklin, Benjamin Quarles, and Lorenzo Johnston Greene, were forging
new pathways. They published works on free Black history that

made their way into the mainstream professional historical community, even if their research was not always celebrated.[26] In many respects, the works that these scholars produced were similar to the works of Woodson and his collaborators: they focused on state histories and on African American achievement amid racist structures.

As mid-twentieth-century scholarship became much more critical of slavery, a broader intellectual space emerged for consideration of Southern free people of color who were not dependent on planters' patronage. In this climate, Luther Porter Jackson's research on rural Southern free Blacks, published in 1942 and previously obscured by histories of grand plantations and urban economic development, advanced the field. Using county clerks' records and deed books, *Free Negro Labor and Property Holding in Virginia* dispelled stereotypical images of free African Americans, revealing residents of rural Virginia to be independent, enterprising, and economically self-sustaining. Through hard work, Jackson demonstrated, a substantial number of farm hands earned promotions, rising through the ranks as managers and tenants, while others purchased their own tracts of land, often with little assistance from white neighbors. Although Jackson concurred with Russell, citing the significance of economic forces in the development of Virginia's free Black population, he asserted that these landowning men and women took initiative in accumulating their land and wealth.[27]

John Hope Franklin's *The Free Negro in North Carolina* (1943) similarly examined a rural community of free African Americans.[28] Racial tension, Franklin argued, was less prevalent in colonial and early national North Carolina than in Virginia and Maryland because of the state's large population of white small farmers, who cared little about the interests of large-scale slaveowners and therefore perceived no threat from free Black neighbors. The situation shifted, however, by the mid-1820s, as slaveholding planters rose in power and passed new laws regulating enslaved as well as free Black residents. Franklin demonstrated that social and economic context mattered greatly in determining free Black prospects, and that no one state study could capture the varied experiences of free Blacks.

Midcentury historians also began to contextualize the discrimination faced by free Blacks in new ways that highlighted US particularities. In his book *Slave and Citizen* (1946), Frank Tannenbaum compared Iberian America with the British and North American slave experiences, noting the particularly hostile legal climate for free Black people in the United States, which limited their possibilities for inclusion in American life.[29] In 1950, following the same theme, Oscar and Mary F. Handlin engaged the development of Southern slavery in the 1600s with a groundbreaking article that concluded that "the particularities of the American environment" created a new association of Blackness and servitude that limited the possibilities of all African-descended Americans.[30] Such ideas coalesced in Stanley Elkins's *Slavery: A Problem in American Institutional and Intellectual Life* (1959), which compared the "total" US system of slavery with the "open" system elsewhere in the Americas, a situation that led to servility for all African Americans.[31] Together, these works signaled a new comparative direction in the scholarship, but also a growing awareness among white scholars that free Blacks played an important role in American history.

The Civil Rights era that began in the late 1950s continued the growing interest in free Black people as scholars, invested in the movement, became interested in previous generations of African Americans who fought for freedom amid racial discrimination. The traditional emphasis on individual perseverance and African American achievement, long present in African American historical writing, changed in this new political climate. On the one hand, left-leaning white scholars sought to deepen the critique of racist structures faced by free people of color, following on Tannenbaum's and Elkins's insights. On the other hand, African American scholars were moved to emphasize free Black leadership in resistance to slavery. Portrayals of this resistance varied, however: some heralded the heroic leadership of the community, while others, influenced by Black nationalist thought, described free Blacks in the North as divided between integrationist and separatist strands.[32] Black leaders, for this second group of historians, came to be viewed either as accommodationists or as champions of the race.

The deeper engagement with racism was evident in Leon F. Litwack's pathbreaking *North of Slavery: The Negro in the Free States* (1961).[33] Litwack challenged previous works that had relegated the history of free Black people to a side issue in larger narratives of slavery and Southern secession. The struggles, antagonisms, and accomplishments of free Black people and their communities were not, in Litwack's view, part of a Southern story, stemming from a Southern institution, but a significant part of the national story. Litwack emphasized that the North, though free territory, had not always been a haven. White supremacist thought and action was prevalent in the North, he contended, with state legislatures denying citizenship and basic civil rights to African American residents. Their labor rights were not protected and their educational resources were vastly unequal. Furthermore, a cruel combination of social exclusion, poverty, draconian policing, and inadequate legal representation led to a disproportionate number of African American convicts in Northern prisons—a point on which he agreed with Phillips. Litwack attributed the flourishing of Black religious congregations not so much to religious conviction or freedom of expression but to racial disparagement that drove African American people out of existing denominations. For Litwack, the problems of *free negroes* were very much still present in the 1960s. Benjamin Quarles, who had spent his career writing books showing active African American participation in key events of American history, took a different approach. In the context of the Civil Rights movement, Quarles turned his attention to free Black protest in the North. His *Black Abolitionists* (1969) highlighted Northern free Black leaders who led the fight against slavery.[34] The book had a powerful impact in that it showed African Americans as politically important—a perspective that would further engage later scholars.

The Black nationalist school of interpretation portrayed a more complicated dynamic within the African American community. Comparing Black leaders in the antebellum North, Harold Cruse found in the *Crisis of the Negro Intellectual: A Historical Analysis of the Failure of Black Leadership* (1967) that the "present day conflict within the Negro ethnic group, between integrationist and separatist tendencies has its origins in the historical arguments between personalities such as Frederick Douglass and Martin R. Delany."[35] Cruse focused his study on the twentieth century, but other scholars such as Sheldon H. Harris, Victor Ullman, and Joel Schor produced studies of protonationalist free Black Northern leaders—men who wanted to return to Africa.[36] The Black nationalist strand of interpretation achieved its full flowering much later, in Sterling Stuckey's *Slave Culture: Nationalist Theory and the Foundations of Black America* (1987), which posited a class divide between bourgeois Northern free Black leaders, who were mostly assimilationist in orientation, and the folk culture of the Black masses rooted in the slave experience.[37]

Scholarship on Southern free Blacks was less drawn into the new nationalist interpretative framework, perhaps because most Southern free Blacks were not as visible in the public sphere as their Northern counterparts, but the topic became fashionable among historians nonetheless. Explaining American race relations was a key theme, and scholars took up Tannenbaum's comparative framework to explore the issue.[38] The most notable was Carl N. Degler. In *Neither Black nor White: Slavery and Race Relations in Brazil and the United States* (1971), Degler argued America was distinctive in its restrictive racial attitudes. In his interpretation, free Blacks were tied to slaves in the minds of whites through a vision of race whereby "one drop" of African blood consigned people to inferiority and a legally subordinate status.[39]

Although not a study of different nations, Ira Berlin's prodigious *Slaves without Masters: The Free Negro in the Antebellum South* (1974) similarly used a comparative method to show variations in race relations and free Black community formation.[40] Berlin drew from the fashionable field of social history, which sought to write history from the perspective of ordinary people, to reveal the texture of free Black life in the South to an unprecedented degree. Unlike previous scholars who focused on state-based studies, Berlin identified clear regional distinctions across a range of variables. In the upper South, he argued that free Blacks were likely to have been manumitted as a result of the social and political climate sparked by the American

Revolution, "when a minority of slaveholders, motivated by egalitarian ideology, freed a number of slaves who were not related to them by kinship ties."[41] In the Deep South, however, and particularly along the Gulf Coast, most free Blacks achieved their freedom as a result of interracial unions with free white residents. Nearly forty years after its publication, *Slaves without Masters* still stands as the standard reference on free Southern Black Americans.

Stephen Innes and T. H. Breen's *"Myne Owne Ground": Race and Freedom on Virginia's Eastern Shore* (1980) also engaged Civil Rights-era concerns.[42] Extending the work of Russell, the Handlins, and others, Innes and Breen argued that racism in early seventeenth-century Virginia was not an unrelenting and unchanging part of the American experience, but rather it ebbed and flowed depending on circumstances. Crucially, the authors found that race was secondary to class for several decades, and that free people of color were able to use interracial client-patron relations to achieve social mobility. Racism—and the discriminatory legislation that came with it—only became rooted at the end of the seventeenth century, when slavery became the colony's dominant labor form. The story was hopeful in the sense that, by showing how race relations could change over time, it highlighted the possibility for their improvement to create a new era of opportunity for African Americans. At the same time, Barbara Fields's 1984 study of slavery, slave hiring, and free Blacks in Maryland underscored the tenuousness of free Blacks' status along the slave/free border of the upper South.[43] Later work on slave hiring across the South revealed a continuity of possibilities and perils for free Blacks before the Civil War.[44]

Scholars remained interested in the Civil Rights historical framework—highlighting Black achievement amid racism—even as the Civil Rights movement gradually faded from view in the 1980s and 1990s. In these years, race, class, and gender analyses flourished while cultural analysis rose in importance. In some ways, the field reached the height of its significance in these years as interest in African American history surged nationwide. The cumulative effect was a greater understanding of the complexity of African American life than had ever been rendered before.

The inclusion of gender into historical analysis was a crucial advancement in these decades. Suzanne Lebsock was an early pioneer in this area, raising the profile of a field that heretofore had centered on the extent to which Black matriarchs (both slave and free) defined the antebellum African American family structure.[45] Lebsock argued, based on her analysis of free Black households in Petersburg, Virginia, that women were often heads of households, and that they owned property at higher rates than white women. But she was quick to add that these supposed *matriarchs* were also victims of persecution, excluded from most male occupations, punished by public whippings when convicted of crimes, and subject to the laws that regulated all free Black people. Racism undermined African American family life at every turn, Lebsock contended, concluding, "the tragedy was that the racism that made autonomy possible also made it contemptible."[46]

A number of scholars have followed up on Lebsock's insightful analysis with a variety of community studies and broad overviews.[47] Kimberly Hanger confirmed some of Lebsock's findings in her deeply researched 1997 study of New Orleans's free Black community.[48] Wilma King's *The Essence of Liberty: Free Black Women during the Slave Era* (2006) provided the first comprehensive survey, showing how free women of color contributed to a range of topics in African American history. Building from Berlin's analytical framework, King's work emphasized that free Black people were far from homogenous, and that free Black women even had certain advantages not enjoyed by free Black men. For example, free women of African descent faced fewer objections when they supported abolitionist movements. Ten years prior, David Barry Gaspar and Darlene Clark Hine had applied the same approach as King to an Atlantic framework.[49] Others, such as James Oliver Horton, inspired by the possibilities of gender analysis, have explored the construction of free Black masculinity as an important part of their identity.[50]

Another key development in these years was the formation of a distinctive body of literature centered on the urban experience of free African Americans, which increasingly became a focus of public discussion after the riots of the late 1960s. Although scholars had discussed free Black urban communities since the days of Carter G. Woodson, the field deepened in numerous ways in the late years of the twentieth century. Scholars brought new focus to Black leaders and their relationships to ordinary free people of color, debating the extent to which these groups cohered or were in opposition.[51] Following social history's quantitative trend, they traced the social mobility of free Blacks, comparing the experience of those who had been enslaved with those born in freedom. Resistance also came into focus, as scholars became more attuned to the various ways that urban free Blacks, both elite and working-class, struggled to end slavery.[52]

Several highlights of this literature made a lasting impression on the field. Leonard Curry's *The Free Black in Urban America* (1981) compared the nature of free Black life in fifteen of the largest cities in North America.[53] Curry's thesis was simple: free African Americans moved to cities for a better life; when their dreams were not fulfilled, it was not because they lacked aspirational values, but rather because racism hindered their advancement in both Southern and Northern cities. Curry's book compiled new data on a range of topics and remains a key source on free Black urban life.

Gary Nash drew similar conclusions in his book *Forging Freedom: The Formation of Philadelphia's Black Community* (1988), as did James Oliver Horton in *Free People of Color: Inside the African American Community* (1993).[54] Recalling Luther Porter Jackson, Nash and Horton documented the *successes* of free African American men and women—those who established community aid societies and took part in protest activities. At the same time, Horton learned from the Black nationalist literature and documented the discord and debate that prevailed among members of different socioeconomic classes. Individuals and groups expressed their freedom in debates over gender roles, skin color, national identity, leadership styles, and politics. In the end, however, he found much more evidence that free Black society could cooperate than had the Black nationalist historians.

Historians also grew interested in Black slaveholders, revisiting Woodson's classic *The Negro in Our History* (1922). Michael P. Johnson and James L. Roark's *Black Masters: A Free Family of Color in the Old South,* Larry Koger's *Slaveowners: Free Black Slave Masters in South Carolina,* and Loren Schweninger's *Black Property Owners in the South* were all published in the 1980s and 1990s. Woodson's limited access to archival materials had led him to conclude that the majority of African American slaveholders invested in their enslaved kin for benevolent purposes; these modern historians drew on a diverse range of sources to reveal how free Black slaveowners in fact profited from slaveholding. Although their specific conclusions varied, these authors all proved that free Blacks could be driven by the same modern economic impulses and ambitions as their white counterparts.[55]

While Roark, Koger, and Schweninger focused on Southern free Black property owners, Julie Winch wrote a series of books beginning in the early 1990s that focused on Northern elites. Winch's combined work agreed with Horton and Nash in insisting on viewing the African American community as dynamic and encompassing debate and contradictory impulses. Berlin, in his review of Winch's 1988 *Philadelphia's Black Elite,* commented that her approach moved "beyond the tired divisions between integrationism and nationalism, self-help and political activism."[56] This approach informed Winch's later works, such as her biography of James Forten, which was itself indicative of a trend toward biographies of free people of color in these years.[57]

Cultural historians of free Black life achieved perhaps the most acclaim in these years. This methodological shift, stemming from Lawrence W. Levine's enduring influence on the field of African American history, was evident in Shane White's *Stories of Freedom in Black New York* (2002), which illuminated the experiences of Black New Yorkers as they created a free culture. At the center of White's book, which uncovers the world of New York's ballrooms, theatres, police stations, and street corners, is a theater troupe comprised of African American actors. White documents the African Company's performances, noting their expressions of freedom, which often elicited negative responses from their white audiences.[58] James Oliver Horton and Lois E. Horton's well-reviewed *In Hope of Liberty,* which became the leading work on free Black life in the North because of its scope and attention to social and cultural complexity, further demonstrated this cultural history trend. The Hortons wrote from a Civil Rights perspective when they noted that "as free black people, African Americans were never isolated, they were never passive, and they were never a monolithic group."[59] But the book went in new directions by showing the fluid integration and contest between African, African American, and American cultural forms. Patrick Rael's *Black Identity and Black Protest in the Antebellum North* (2002) followed on from these insights. Analyzing cartoons and close readings of free Black writings, Rael built on the work of Black community scholars, but like the Hortons, he went further by integrating their ideas into the broader American story involving debates over national identity, class status, and racial meaning. *Black Identity and Black Protest* remains a central text for understanding the mentality of Black elites in the antebellum North. Like Horton and Winch, Rael sought to view relationships in the African American community in complex ways.[60] Joanne Pope Melish's *Disowning Slavery* (1998) is another key work in the cultural history vein, showing how the idea of a free white New England materialized and how free Blacks were marginalized from the region's identity.[61]

Recent years have seen the beginnings of a potential shift away from Civil Rights-era scholarship's central tenets—the focus on African Americans taking action and the emphasis on white racism's power. Whereas scholars in the 1980s and 1990s had begun the process of revising the scholarship of the early Civil Rights era, there is evidence that a deeper shift may now be under way. One of the most interesting developments in recent years has been the reassessment of the relative power of racism in American life. With the brutality and exploitation of slavery no longer in question, and the role of racism as an abhorrent and destructive belief system well revealed by numerous scholars, historians began to explore the complexities of race relations in much more nuanced ways than had been done before. While cultural historians of race increasingly focused on *whiteness* in order to reemphasize the broader importance of race in American history, revisionist social historical studies of daily life told a different story—one in which the daily necessities of work enforced a remarkable degree of interaction and familiarity among working-class peoples.

This trend was first identified by scholars of enslaved peoples, who noted that in the underground economies of the American South, slaves and poor whites often interacted with surprising ease amid plantation slavery.[62] Melvin Patrick Ely's award-winning *Israel on the Appomattox: A Southern Experiment in Black Freedom* (2005) extended such insights and argued that culture, faith, affection, and economic interest allowed close relations between free Blacks and poor whites.[63] Much of the previous literature had emphasized how whites hated free Blacks in the South due to their threat to slavery; Ely's account expanded on some of John Hope Franklin's insights and showed how virulent racism and pervasive day-to-day racial accommodation coexisted among ordinary Southerners in one Virginia county. This new approach called into question the legal categories that had long been assumed to represent reality in everyday life. By the late twentieth century, categories such as *slave* and *free* as well as *Black* and *white* were no longer seen to be self-evident; rather, scholars now attempted to show how people created these categories. While never denying the exploitation and oppression that went along with these structures, they increasingly have demonstrated that their constructed and contingent nature meant that African Americans could pass between these categories, sometimes passing as white to their advantage. Together, these changes have increasingly shown the tremendous variation in how free people of color experienced American society.[64]

Newer scholarship diverges from the Civil Rights–era emphasis on Black agency. This shift was evident in the field's first major controversy: the debate over the interpretation of the Denmark Vesey affair. Denmark Vesey, a free Black sailor in Charleston, South Carolina, was executed in 1822 for leading an alleged conspiracy that aimed to free the region's slaves. The alleged conspiracy was embraced as factual by African American scholars such as Carter G. Woodson and John Hope Franklin, as well as by Herbert Aptheker, who all saw it as an example of enslaved people's revolutionary aspirations and free Blacks' commitment to advancing the cause.[65]

Richard Wade disagreed with this view in a 1964 article arguing that inconsistencies between the original trial manuscript and later published versions suggest a conspiracy by whites to cover up their wanton violence against an imaginary plot.[66] Civil Rights-era scholars eager to uncover Black resistance (namely, David M. Roberson, Douglas R. Egerton, and Edward A. Pearson) rejected this interpretation, looking to the African American community to uncover the revolutionary context that influenced Denmark Vesey.[67]

All of this would be considered normal historical revisionism, but Michael Johnson's extended review of Robertson's, Egerton's, and Pearson's books in the *William and Mary Quarterly* set off a firestorm of controversy that reached the national media and has continued to reverberate in the two decades since.[68] Johnson researched the trial documents and argued that "almost all historians have failed to exercise due caution in reading the testimony of witnesses recorded by the conspiracy court," and that alternatively "reading and rumors transmuted white orthodoxies into black heresies."[69] Johnson accused historians of undue conjecture and signaled a return to a more restrictive reading of documents. The most immediate result of Johnson's critique was that Pearson's publisher pulled *Designs against Charleston,* which was found to be riddled with errors, but the larger debate remains unresolved and is ongoing. The most recent interpretation suggested that the conspiracy did exist but may not have involved Vesey at all.[70]

Drawing on the Atlantic world scholarship emerging in the 1990s, post-Civil Rights era scholars have pulled the lens back to reassess the role of free African Americans in helping deliver enslaved people from bondage to the North or to Africa. Manisha Sinha offered a broad synthesis of abolitionism with free Blacks at the center of narrative, while David Brion Davis connected free Black networks to transatlantic activism and reform.[71] Steven Hahn's *The Political Worlds of Slavery and Freedom* (2009) interpreted Northern free Black communities as akin to maroon societies in the Caribbean and Brazil, their status always tenuous and provisional.[72] Eric Foner's 2015 study of the Underground Railroad in New York revealed how free Blacks in that major port city forged hidden networks that helped undermine slavery even as ship-pers fueled slavery's expansion.[73] New scholarship on coloniza-tion of free Blacks to Africa from Beverly Tomek, inspired in part by Hahn's earlier, Pulitzer Prize-winning *A Nation under Our Feet* (2005), has helped recast the relationship between free Blacks and transnational missionary and colonial *civilizationist* movements.[74]

These recent developments underscore broader shifts in the way scholars understand free people of color across time and space. For much of the twentieth century, concern about racism led to increas-ing interest, first by African American historians who aimed to show the suitability and resourcefulness of the free Black commu-nity. They were then joined by white scholars sympathetic with the Black Freedom movement who sought to document African Ameri-can power and early examples of African American free communi-ties as an inspiration to contemporary movements. These lines of inquiry have matured the field, with differences between elites and masses, men and women, rural and urban now all receiving atten-tion in the literature. Recent scholarship has shown renewed inter-est in class as a variable amid the contemporary context, suggesting that in the future, free Black Americans may well be considered as part of a holistic working-class experience, one fractured by race to be sure, but one that should not be considered in isolation from poor whites. Thus, the task of integrating free Black Americans into a broader American—and indeed transnational—story shows no sign of abating.

NOTES

The authors would like to thank Julie Winch and the anonymous reviewers for their helpful comments on this chapter.

1. Scholarly assessments of this historiography include Horton, *Free People of Color,* 1-13; Holland and Greene, "Not Chattel, Not Free"; Rael, "Free Black Activism"; Rael, "New Directions"; and Parish, *Slavery,* chapter 6.

2. Osofsky, *Puttin' On Ole Massa,* 67, 205, 233.

3. Clamorgan, *Colored Aristocracy,* 2.

4. Osofsky, *Puttin' On Ole Massa,* 74.

5. W. Andrews, *To Tell a Free Story,* 41.

6. A. Chambers, *Trials and Confessions.*

7. Towers, "Partisans, New History, and Modernization," 241-42. For the shift toward reconciliation and racism, see Blight, *Race and Reunion.*

8. H. Wilson, *History of the Rise and Fall,* 300-301.

9. See for example J. Logan, *Great Conspiracy.*

10. W. Brown, *My Southern Home,* 37, 115-20, 144-51.

11. Douglass, *Life and Times,* 357.

12. Chandler, *Story of a Slave,* 1.

13. J. Harris, *Free Joe,* 1.

14. L. Gray, "Southern Agriculture."

15. Bruce, "Evolution of the Negro Problem."

16. U. Philips, *American Negro Slavery,* 425-53.

17. U. Philips, *American Negro Slavery,* 448-50.

18. Russell, *Free Negro in Virginia,* vii.

19. J. Wright, *Free Negro in Maryland,* 328.

20. See Woodson, *Free Negro Heads of Families;* Greene and Woodson, *Negro Wage Earner;* and Woodson, *Free Negro Owners of Slaves.*

21. Woodson, "Negroes of Cincinnati," 1, 9, 11.

22. Woodson, *Free Negro Owners of Slaves.*

23. Charles W. Ramsdell, for instance, criticized Woodson for a lack of eloquence and scientific objectivity. See Ramsdell, "Review: *The Education of the Negro.*" For a broader perspective on Woodson and the racism within the historical profession at the time, see Goggin, "Countering White Racist Scholarship."

24. Craven, "Poor Whites and Negroes."

25. Aptheker, *American Negro Slave Revolts.*

26. Key books written by these historians include L. Jackson, *Free Negro Labor;* Quarles, *Negro in the Civil War;* Quarles, *Negro in the American Revolution;* J. Franklin, *Free Negro in North Carolina;* and L. Greene, *Negro in Colonial New England.* For an example of the reception of these works, see Schoen, "Review: *The Free Negro in North Carolina.*" Schoen complained that Franklin was "simply ploughing an infertile field." See also Goggin, "Countering White Racist Scholarship," 359-60.

27. L. Jackson, "Virginia Free Negro Farmer," 420. See also Jackson's book-length work, L. Jackson, *Free Negro Labor.*

28. Franklin, *Free Negro in North Carolina.*

29. Tannenbaum, *Slave and Citizen.*

30. Handlin and Handlin, "Origins of the Southern Labor System," 221.

31. Elkins, *Slavery.*

32. For a historiographical discussion of Black nationalism, see Rael, "Free Black Activism," 216-21.

33. Litwack, *North of Slavery.* Much later, in the 1970s, A. Leon Higginbotham applied the renewed interest in racism to an important study of law and African American colonial history, revealing the landscape of early free Black jurisprudence to an unprecedented degree. See A. Higginbotham, *In the Matter of Color.*

34. Quarles, *Black Abolitionists.*

35. Cruse, *Crisis of the Negro Intellectual,* 4-5 (2005 edition).

36. S. Harris, *Paul Cuffe;* Ullman, *Martin R. Delany;* Schor, *Henry Highland Garnet.*

37. Stuckey, *Slave Culture.*

38. L. Foner, "Free People of Color"; Cohen and Greene, *Neither Slave nor Free.*

39. Degler, *Neither Black nor White.*

40. Berlin, *Slaves without Masters.* Berlin broadened his comparative analysis of African American communities to include the Mississippi River valley and the North in later works. See Berlin, *Many Thousands Gone.*

41. Berlin, *Slaves without Masters,* 60.

42. Breen and Innes, *"Myne Owne Ground."* Breen and Innes followed the broad contours of Edmund S. Morgan's argument in *American Slavery, American Freedom* but provided much greater depth on what the shift in race relations meant for free Black people. See also Morgan, *American Slavery, American Freedom.*

43. Fields, *Slavery and Freedom.*

44. J. Martin, *Divided Mastery.*

45. Frazier, *Negro Family;* Moynihan, *Negro Family.* This thesis was challenged in the 1970s. See Gutman, *Black Family;* and Furstenberg, Hershberg, and Modell, "Origins of the Female-Headed Black Family."

46. Lebsock, *Free Women of Petersburg,* 90.

47. For an example of an early study devoted to free women of color, see A. Alexander, *Ambiguous Lives;* and Gaspar and Hine, *Beyond Bondage.*

48. Hanger, "Coping in a Complex World"; and Hanger, *Bounded Lives.*

49. Gaspar and Hine, *More than Chattel.*

50. Horton, *Free People of Color,* chapter 4.

51. Horton, *Free People of Color,* 7-9. The introduction to Horton's volume contained a wonderful analysis of how the approaches to free Black people matured in the 1960s, 1970s, and 1980s.

52. Quarles, *Black Abolitionists;* Cheek, *Black Resistance.*

53. Curry, *Free Black in Urban America.* For an important article on how free Black sailors were jailed in the South due to their presumed threat to slavery, see Tansey, "Out-of-State Free Blacks."

54. Nash, *Forging Freedom;* Horton, *Free People of Color.*

55. Johnson and Roark, *Black Masters;* Koger, *Slaveowners;* Schweninger, *Black Property Owners.*

56. Berlin, "Review: *Philadelphia's Black Elite,*" 91.

57. Winch, *Gentlemen of Color.* See also Winch, *Clamorgans.* For other examples of biographies, both of elites and non-elites, that emerged in the late twentieth and early twenty-first centuries, see Armstead, *Freedom's Gardener;* Biddle and Dubin, *Tasting Freedom;* R. Newman, *Freedom's Prophet;* C. Long, *New Orleans Voudou Priestess;* Cheek and Cheek, *John Mercer Langston;* Painter, *Sojourner Truth;* and J. Walker, *Free Frank.*

58. S. White, *Stories of Freedom.* For an expansion of White's analysis, see L. Harris, *Shadow of Slavery;* and Peterson, *Black Gotham.*

59. Horton and Horton, *Hope of Liberty,* xi.

60. Rael, *Black Identity and Black Protest.*

61. Melish, *Disowning Slavery.*

62. For examples of interactions between slaves and poor whites, see B. Wood, *Women's Work, Men's Work;* Shelton, "On Empire's Shore"; and Forret, *Race Relations.*

63. Ely, *Israel on the Appomattox.*

64. For examples of free Blacks constructing a free identity, see Rael, *Black Identity and Black Protest.* For examples of slaves passing as both free whites and free Blacks during escape attempts, see Buchanan, *Black Life on the Mississippi.*

65. Woodson, *Negro in Our History;* J. Franklin, *Slavery to Freedom,* 210 (1957 edition); and Aptheker, *American Negro Slave Revolts,* 270.

66. Wade, "Vesey Plot." Wade's interpretation was rejected by William W. Freehling, who asserted the Civil Rights-era critique. See Freehling, *Reintegration of American History,* 34-58.

67. Egerton, *He Shall Go Out Free;* Robertson, *Denmark Vesey;* Pearson, *Designs against Charleston.*

68. M. Johnson, "Denmark Vesey."

69. M. Johnson, "Denmark Vesey," 915-16.

70. Spady, "Power and Confession."

71. Sinha, *Slave's Cause;* D. Davis, *Problem of Slavery in the Age of Emancipation.*

72. Hahn, *Political Worlds.*

73. E. Foner, *Gateway to Freedom.*

74. Tomek, *Colonization;* Tomek and Hetrick, *New Directions.*

CHAPTER NINE

American Slavery and Emancipation

AARON ASTOR

In the hundred days between President Abraham Lincoln's preliminary Emancipation Proclamation of September 1862 and full Emancipation Proclamation of January 1, 1863, Frederick Douglass tolled a bell of celebration, though tinged as ever with prophetic caution. "Verily, the work does not end with the abolition of slavery, but only begins." The creation of "elevating and civilizing institutions," schools for the "education of dusky millions," and the "family relation" still waiting "to be established" would mark the tasks of freedom in Douglass's mind. But for the longtime abolitionist, the momentous joy of emancipation could not and should not be tempered by the great responsibilities following the end of slavery. "This old and grim obstacle removed, . . . jets of heavenly light will speedily illumine the land long covered with darkness, cruelty and crime."[1]

It would take much more than a presidential decree to remove the "old and grim obstacle" of slavery, as Douglass and millions of other African Americans understood. It would require the successful prosecution of a *great Civil War* to full Union victory, a commitment by the Union army and the federal government to an emancipationist war aim, and the passage and ratification of the Thirteenth Amendment to the US Constitution. The final act would occur eight more months after the Confederate armies surrendered.

President Andrew Johnson insisted that the former Confederate states could not return to the Union unless they legally acknowledged slavery's end, preferably by ratifying the amendment. When Secretary of State William Seward proclaimed the amendment in effect on December 18, 1865, just two Union slave states—Delaware and Kentucky—still clung to the peculiar institution. At long last, slavery was dead in the largest and wealthiest slaveholding nation in modern history.

How exactly did it happen? And how have historians and commentators, both in and outside the academy, characterized this seemingly impossible task coming to pass in so short a time? As with other chapters in this volume, this essay begins with an appraisal of the reflections of those who witnessed emancipation in the nineteenth century, then goes on to discuss the early professional historiography of wartime emancipation in the early twentieth century. It then addresses some of the mid-twentieth-century developments, notably the contributions of African American scholars in the 1910s to the 1930s, Marxist historians in the 1930s and 1940s, and post-World War II historians who began to challenge the presuppositions of the early professional era. It goes on to discuss the massive outpouring of scholarship during the Civil Rights era that drew explicit links between twentieth- and nineteenth-century freedom struggles. And finally, it examines the field's twists and turns in the early twenty-first century, including transnational studies and a new emphasis on emancipation in Civil War scholarship. Although emancipation events did occur during and after the American Revolution, this essay focuses on the period during and after the Civil War.

At every phase, observers and historians have understood that emancipation could be assessed from several chronological lenses—as a long emancipation beginning in the North or a quick burst of freedom during the Civil War—and from different geographic perspectives, including both comparative and international histories as well as local studies. Also crucial to the discussion of emancipation are agency and structure questions: how much did individual actors play in destroying slavery, which ones were most important, and which institutions did the most to facilitate slavery's demise? Or, as James McPherson put it more bluntly in a 1995 review of Civil Rights-era scholarship on emancipation: "who freed the slaves?"[2]

Douglass's numerous writings both before and after emancipation provide the clearest contemporary vision of the promises and process of emancipation from the perspective of a Black, male abolitionist. His writings offer modern readers a longitudinal perspective on emancipation as it unfolded, from his early charges of white hypocrisy—most famously in his "What to the Slave Is the Fourth of July?" speech in 1852—to his calls for Black military action during the Civil War.[3] In the years to follow, he supplemented his words of warning and calls to action with reflections on the long course of emancipation.

Quickly following the Civil War, however, politicians and scholars—both Black and white—began to write more dispassionate histories of the process of emancipation. Many of these writers, like Henry Wilson, the Massachusetts senator, had played a central role in bringing an end to the institution, while others had grown up during the Civil War era and wrote primarily of their own experiences or those of their own fathers and mothers leaving the house of bondage.

Less than two years after the Civil War ended, William Wells Brown, a former fugitive slave, abolitionist orator, and Douglass contemporary, penned *The Negro in the American Rebellion: His Heroism and His Fidelity* (1867).[4] Collecting dozens of battle reports and anecdotes, Brown offered a remarkably thorough set of stories detailing the roles of enslaved men in running for Union lines, in working as spies for the Union army, and eventually in fighting as Union soldiers. Brown emphasized Black soldiers' heroism and the revolutionary implications of enslaved men whipping their masters, both literally and metaphorically, and he framed Black service as part of a long tradition going back to the Revolutionary War. The book had limited impact compared with his earlier antislavery writings and incorporated very little analysis to contextualize the Black military experience. But it stood as the first sizable publication on both Black enlistment and on the role of enslaved people in emancipating themselves.

Henry Wilson's three-volume study, *The Rise and Fall of the Slave Power in America* (1872-77), appeared a few years later and was one of the first to look broadly at emancipation from its eighteenth-century roots through the recent Civil War.[5] Celebrating the work of his fellow white Northern abolitionists, Wilson spent much of his first two volumes tracing abolitionist writings and activities from the times of the Quaker Anthony Benezet in the 1750s through the American Revolution and slavery's abolition in the North. He continued with extensive coverage of the political debate over slavery's expansion into the West and with the emergence of militant antislavery organizations led by William Lloyd Garrison, Elijah Lovejoy, and others, and he concluded his second volume with the 1860 presidential election. Throughout the first two volumes, Wilson paid special attention to the actions of abolitionist societies, most of them led by whites. However, he also wrote extensively of the actions of African Americans, including fugitive slaves, free Blacks, and the African Americans on the Underground Railroad.

As the title of Wilson's book suggests, its Radical Republican author viewed slavery's perpetuation in the nineteenth century as the product of a *slave power conspiracy* that was finally checked and defeated in the Civil War. The third volume, published in 1877 after Wilson's death, emphasized the multiple forces leading to emancipation, including the work of the Union army, the pressure from white and Black abolitionists, the leadership of congressional Radical Republicans, the slow but steady acceptance of emancipation as an official war aim by President Lincoln, and the actions of enslaved men themselves who ran to Union lines and eventually enlisted as soldiers. Though the third volume continued into the early 1870s with commentary on Reconstruction, it curiously ignored the lengthy political debate over the Thirteenth Amendment's passage and ratification. Regardless, Wilson's series must be considered the first full-length scholarly treatment of emancipation.

The most important African American historian of emancipation to appear in the nineteenth century was George Washington

Williams. Volume two of Williams's *History of the Negro Race in America, 1619-1880* was published in 1882 with the purpose of showing the active role that African Americans played in their own resistance to slavery and in overthrowing the institution during the Civil War. Continuing on his first volume, with its assessment of Black resistance to slavery during the Revolutionary War, the second volume detailed the myriad attempts by free and enslaved African Americans to raise awareness of the horrors of slavery, and to escape the institution via the Underground Railroad. Perhaps most important, however, was Williams's insistence that Black participation in the Union army dealt slavery its death blow. "And when his soul was quickened to the sublime idea of liberty for himself and kindred—that his home and country were to be rid of the triple curse of slavery—his enthusiasm was boundless."[6] In a later book devoted entirely to the role of Black soldiers, Williams offered the most comprehensive account of Black soldiers in the Civil War ever written, one not surpassed in detail and interpretative sophistication until the middle of the twentieth century. In the preface of that 1888 work, *A History of the Negro Troops in the War of the Rebellion,* Williams emphasized that his evidence came from the recently published official records of the US War Department, among other respected sources.[7] The purpose of this disclaimer was to highlight the dispassionate and scholarly nature of his research, which was still largely ignored or belittled by most historians of the day. Along with Henry Wilson's three-volume series, Brown's collection of emancipation vignettes, a smaller annotated chronology by Joseph T. Wilson called *Emancipation: Its Course and Progress from 1102 to 1875* (1881), and Wilson's memoir of service titled *The Black Phalanx: A History of Negro Soldiers of the United States in the Wars of 1775-1812, 1861-1865* (1888), Williams's *History of the Negro Race* and *History of the Negro Troops* would lay the groundwork for scholars in the mid-twentieth century to reassess African Americans' role in attaining their freedom.[8]

Unfortunately, the first large-scale scholarly books on the political and social changes of the Civil War era appearing at the beginning of the twentieth century tended to ignore this scholarship on Black actions during the Civil War. When emancipation was discussed at all, it was treated mostly through the document of the Emancipation Proclamation, which was interpreted as a simple and benevolent act of President Lincoln, though one without much thought given to its aftermath. Though few of the early scholarly histories blasted emancipation itself, they tended to view enslaved people's participation in it as minimal at best, thus marking them as incapable of taking on the more contentious task of Reconstruction. The famous New South historians at Columbia University led by William A. Dunning, including the proto-Dunningite John W. Burgess, established the precedent: they accepted slavery's centrality to the Civil War and the necessity of destroying it in order to put down the rebellion,[9] but they viewed efforts to provide African Americans with equal rights and political power as a dangerous mistake that led to corruption, anarchy, and bloodshed. As for emancipation itself, it was just a wartime measure carried to completion by the Union army, the Republican Congress, and President Lincoln; enslaved men and women played no role.

James Ford Rhodes, a Cleveland, Ohio-based industrial magnate, reinforced the Dunning view with his Pulitzer Prize-winning *History of the Civil War, 1861-1865* (1917).[10] Rhodes, too, placed slavery and the agitation over it at the center of the war, and he celebrated the Emancipation Proclamation as a singular achievement of Lincoln. But as for the enslaved themselves, Rhodes claimed that "instead of rising they remained patiently submissive and faithful to their owners." This supposed passivity was "one of the strange things in this eventful history" to Rhodes, as "the peaceful labor of three and one-half million negro slaves whose presence in the South was the cause of the war and whose freedom was fought for after September 1862 by the Northern soldiers."[11] Rhodes's *History of the Civil War* set the standard for emancipation historiography in the first half of the twentieth century, with other scholars echoing his befuddlement at the enslaved's ostensible lack of agency in their own emancipation.

Few white historians challenged Burgess's and Rhodes's assessments that emancipation was a policy delivered from on high by a

mix of abolitionist activists, radical generals, and a Lincoln administration looking to win the war by denying the Confederacy both the
labor of the enslaved and the moral advantage in Europe's courts.
Those who did, including especially the Progressive historians,
viewed emancipation as a largely amoral ploy by industrial elites to
undermine their political rivals.[12] One typical Civil War book, published in 1928, aptly summarized the prevailing view, while George
Washington Williams's work continued to gather dust:

> The American Negroes are the only people in the history of the
> world, so far as I know, that ever became free without any ef-
> fort of their own. . . . It [the Civil War] was not their business.
> They had not started the war nor ended it. They twanged banjos
> around the railroad stations, sang melodious spirituals, and be-
> lieved that some Yankee would soon come along and give each of
> them forty acres and a mule.[13]

One challenge to the *passive Negro* view came with the emergence of Carter G. Woodson's *Journal of Negro History* in 1916. The
new journal offered a countervailing interpretation that drew from
the work of Williams and Wilson and built a bridge to the Civil
Rights-era scholars to come. Foreshadowing some of the controversial assessments of Lincoln later in the century, scholars began
to challenge both the Dunning school and the prevailing Lincolnian
scholarship. One piece by Charles H. Wesley, published in the journal in 1919, reminded readers of Lincoln's plan for colonizing freed
Blacks as late as 1862.[14] Similarly, Fred Shannon wrote in 1926 of
the deep reluctance among white Northerners to convert a war for
union into a war for emancipation. Regarding antislavery sentiment
in the old Northwest, Shannon noted that "the Westerner not only
wished to keep the Western territories free, but he wanted them
Negroless."[15] Remarkably, the *Journal of Negro History* still had little
to say about Black soldiers and self-emancipation until the 1930s,
when Rayford Logan heralded the publication of W. E. B. Du Bois's
Black Reconstruction in America (1935) as a "brilliant attack upon the
sacred institutions and beliefs of the South both Old and New."[16]

Marxist scholars were among those who broke this historio-graphic silence. Du Bois and Herbert Aptheker, along with others, began to identify Black resistance and rebellion as part of a larger class struggle for emancipation. Du Bois's *Black Reconstruction in America* offered a sustained interpretation of emancipation as a "general strike," with slavery falling apart as a result.[17] Aptheker's work on slave rebellions and on the Civil War similarly cast African American enlistment in the Union army in Marxian terms.[18] Early non-Marxist social historians like Bell Irvin Wiley also challenged the dominant view of the passive and submissive slave. Wiley's dis-sertation, *Southern Negroes: 1861-1865,* completed in 1933 and pub-lished in 1938, described enslaved people running from their mas-ters whenever possible, and fighting against discrimination once in the Union army.[19] As research, Wiley's work began to fill an ex-traordinary gap. Interpretively, however, it was just beginning to break free of the early professional views of Wiley's dissertation adviser, Ulrich B. Phillips.

Following World War II, three important works began to shift the debate over emancipation and place the enslaved back in the center of their own story. John Hope Franklin's seminal 1949 *From Slavery to Freedom* on the whole course of African American history framed Black agency in the context of thousands of years of African (and later African American) history. Benjamin Quarles's *The Negro in the Civil War* (1953) synthesized much of the work on African Americans as fugitives, contrabands, spies, and heroic soldiers and sailors. Quarles's book also explicitly credited African Americans serving in the recently desegregated US military in Korea. Though released before the pivotal *Brown v. Board of Education* decision, Quarles's work celebrated African American heroism as the "key factor to the Civil War" and the African American as "an active member of the cast. . . . To him, freedom was a two-way street; indeed he gave prior to receiving."[20] Perhaps the most thorough account since 1888 of African Americans as self-emancipators and as soldiers came with the 1956 publication of Dudley Taylor Cor-nish's *The Sable Arm: Negro Troops in the Union Army, 1861-1865.*[21] A scholarly monograph, *The Sable Arm* addressed the development of Union emancipation and Black enlistment policy, the service of Black Union soldiers and their white officers in both Western and Eastern theaters, and the experiences of African Americans as they forged their own paths to freedom. It is telling that even as main-stream post–World War II white historians like Allan Nevins were beginning to bring the emancipation story back within the Civil War narrative, African Americans themselves still appeared largely absent in popular narratives of the war.[22] Cornish took notice.

Not surprisingly, the Civil Rights movement would provoke the greatest reassessment of emancipation yet, just as was true in other areas of African American history. However, it was the coinciden-tal centennial of the Civil War and of emancipation that provided the moment for large-scale scholarly reassessment. The second edition of Cornish's *The Sable Arm,* published in 1966, included a striking comment in the foreword on the changes apparent in the emancipation historiography. "All Americans ought to realize or at least have an opportunity to learn that the American Negro has been more than a cotton-chopping, banjo-strumming, irrespon-sible, shadowy figure on the outskirts of American life, prominent only in athletics and entertainment. Fortunately there are more and more books which today tell this neglected story; the combination of the Civil War Centennial and the Civil Rights Revolution is hav-ing a healthful effect on American historiography. . . . As American society becomes less Jim Crow, so will American history expand to include all Americans who have played parts in its drama."[23]

As Cornish pointed out, several historians had begun to reas-sess the active role that enslaved people played in their own libera-tion in works published in the early 1960s. James McPherson's *The Negro's Civil War* (1965) offered a kaleidoscope of sketches from Af-rican Americans facing emancipation, including their aspirations, fears, and expectations at the moment of liberation.[24] Joel William-son's *After Slavery: The Negro in South Carolina during Reconstruction,* published the same year, connected the Black struggle for freedom with the ongoing process of reconstructing the South.[25] A year earlier, Willie Lee Rose's *Rehearsal for Reconstruction* assessed the interplay between white abolitionists and newly freed men and women in Port Royal, South Carolina.[26] These three books would transform the emancipation historiography by placing the actions of enslaved people at the center of any and all accounts.

Still, the Civil War centennial also invited scholars to reassess the importance of the Emancipation Proclamation. Franklin and Quarles wrote complimentary accounts of Lincoln's view of emancipation generally, and his attitude toward the highly legalistic Proclamation. Whereas Quarles presented Lincoln generally as a man of changing and complex views on race, Franklin focused on the drafting of the Proclamation and the immediate moral and military pressures behind it.[27] Both scholars understood that Lincoln's views on race were evolving, and that he had long been opposed to slavery in principle. But while each scholar's focus—one on the man and one on the document—produced a different kind of book, both left readers to debate the significance of the *Great Emancipator* for decades to come.

From the mid-1960s onward, the historiographic field lay wide open for scholars interested in reassessing the roles of enslaved men and women, masters and mistresses, nonslaveholding whites, politicians, Union and Confederate officers and soldiers, pro- and antislavery activists, and diplomats and observers from other nations. The social history revolution of the 1970s, coupled with the proliferation of newly filmed documents from deep in the National Archives, allowed historians to delve much more deeply into the process of emancipation in specific places and into the peculiarities of emancipation's chronology.

Animating the post-1960s historiography of emancipation were questions of agency, structure, contingency, and perspective. Of all the people and forces that contributed to slavery's demise, which were most influential? How important were the leadership decisions made by individual politicians and commanders? How vital were the roles of specific enslaved people in attaining their own freedom? Was emancipation a mostly structural phenomenon, brought on by an ideological war that dismantled the mechanisms of slave control and unleashed the powers of liberation and the destruction of slavery? And then there was the question of timing—when exactly did slavery collapse, and how did the complex interplay of military and political events manifest themselves in different parts of the country at different times? Finally, how did people make sense of this process? What did slaves and slaveholders, Northern and Southern whites, freeborn Blacks, politicians and soldiers, women and men think and say about slavery's collapse? How did emancipation square with their expectations, and what did it reveal about the different meanings of freedom? And how did enslaved people and their descendants remember this struggle?

Since these analytical questions have animated so much of the scholarship since the 1970s, the remainder of this chapter focuses on particular targets of study, with the historiography presented less chronologically than thematically. First to be discussed are grassroots social histories of emancipation, which had the most far-reaching effect on the scholarship. Next are reviews of the literature on regional distinctions, gender and the destruction of slavery, the Union army's role, the influence of abolitionists during the Civil War, Lincoln's leadership, the Republican Party's political and legal work during and after the Civil War, transnational and comparative approaches, and finally, the memory of emancipation. Though the slavery, emancipation, and Reconstruction historiographies often blend together, the chapter focuses only on those studies that reach significantly into wartime emancipation itself.

None of these themes and subfields have run their course, so to speak, to be replaced by newer kinds of questions and approaches. Rather, they have each continued in conversation with one another. In many cases, these new approaches have employed the newer methods used throughout the post-1970 historical profession, including data-based social history, discourse-centric cultural history, and transnational turns in the literature. In other ways, however, recent approaches to the study of emancipation have been directly influenced by—or developed in reaction to—contemporary political and cultural events, including new cinematic depictions of Black soldiers, assertions of US military power as a *liberating* force in Iraq and Afghanistan, and revisionist claims of *black Confederates* by neo-Confederate heritage groups.[28] If there is any dynamic at work, it is a dialectical one; scholars emphasizing the self-emancipation narrative have encountered more sophisticated institutional histories, which in turn have helped contextualize the grassroots story. The result has been a richer and more complex field than ever.

The most comprehensive reassessment of the social history of emancipation came with the work of the Freedmen and Southern Society Project (FSSP) at the University of Maryland. Combing through millions of previously ignored documents in the US Army Continental Command records, the Provost Marshal General records, the Bureau of Refugees, Freedmen and Abandoned Lands (Freedmen's Bureau) records, and myriad other nooks and crannies of the National Archives, the FSSP offered an unprecedented view of emancipation from the bottom up. Founded in the 1970s by Ira Berlin and Leslie Rowland, the project has resulted in the publication of numerous edited volumes, essay collections, and monographs. More than fifty thousand of these documents have been presented and annotated in a multivolume collection called *Freedom: A Documentary History of Emancipation, 1861-1867.* The first series began with *The Destruction of Slavery* (1986), which addressed the ground-level process of emancipation directly with reports from slaves, slaveholders, and military officials across the South.[29] It continued with *The Wartime Genesis of Free Labor* (1990, 1993), which captured over two volumes the diverse process through which freed people and former slaveholders negotiated new terms of labor across both the upper and lower South.[30] One of the signal strengths of the entire project was the attention paid to geographic distinctions between emancipation in border states like Kentucky and Missouri and in Deep South states like Louisiana and Mississippi. The second series, *The Black Military Experience* (1982), examined the process and meaning of military service for Black men and their families in more detail than any previous publication.[31] A third series, *Land and Labor* (2008, 2013), drew heavily from Freedmen's Bureau records and planter accounts and explored the early stages of grassroots Reconstruction.[32] In addition to these volumes, the FSSP released four general-use books—*Free at Last* (1993), *Slaves No More* (1992), *Families and Freedom* (1997), *and Freedom's Soldiers* (1998)—that include both primary documents and interpretative essays.[33]

With such a rich array of sources at its disposal, and a methodological commitment to telling the story of emancipation from the ground up, the FSSP set the standard for modern studies that emphasize slave agency in the emancipation process. Dozens of newer studies followed on the heels of the project, including many books written by former scholars of the project. In addition to Berlin and Rowland, these include Julie Saville, Barbara Fields, Joseph Reidy, Susan O'Donovan, Thavolia Glymph, Stephen Miller, Steven Hahn, John Rodrigue, Anthony Kaye, Kate Masur, René Hayden, and Stephen A. West. Work by FSSP scholars and their graduate students across the country has redefined the historiography of emancipation by combining the deep social history found in the National Archives documents with sophisticated analyses of slave culture, slave communities, and slave households. For example, Saville's *Work of Reconstruction* (1995) and O'Donovan's *Becoming Free in the Cotton South* (2007) each traced how work and household traditions in slavery shaped the ambitions and adjustments to freedom, though in contrasting labor regimes—South Carolina's task system-based rice fields and southwest Georgia's cotton belt.[34] Steven Hahn's *A Nation under our Feet* (2005) revealed the deeply political nature of slave resistance and the ways in which socially meaningful networks among enslaved people facilitated the press for freedom during the Civil War.[35]

Myriad other scholars have likewise enhanced the historiography. Justin Behrend's *Reconstructing Democracy* (2015) similarly examined the grassroots politics of emancipation by focusing on the Natchez district of Mississippi and Louisiana.[36] Armstead Robinson's dissertation, completed under the tutelage of Eugene Genovese in 1977 and published after Robinson's death as *Bitter Fruits of Bondage* (2004), demonstrated how enslaved people's innumerable steps toward self-emancipation materially damaged the Confederate war effort and helped bring about the slave system's final destruction.[37] In each of these cases, scholars demonstrated how the actions of individual enslaved people and small, kin-based networks of slaves (and often free Blacks) systematically destroyed the institution of slavery in the midst of a civil war. Bruce Levine's *Fall of the House of Dixie* (2013) synthesized much of this scholarship to show how the enslaved ultimately destroyed the system from within.[38]

Essential to these grassroots studies of emancipation is the role of enslaved men as soldiers in the Union army and navy. Broad histories of the recruitment, training, and service of the US Colored Troops that expanded on the work of Dudley Cornish and the FSSP include William Dobak's *Freedom by the Sword* (2013), Noah Trudeau's *Like Men of War* (1998), and an edited collection of essays by John David Smith called *Black Soldiers in Blue* (2004).[39] Some of the best scholarship has come from studies of single Black regiments,[40] which offer perspectives sometimes shared across regiments, and other times unique to specific emancipation and military experiences. Works on specific military engagements, such as Linda Barnickel's *Milliken's Bend* (2013) and Melvin Claxton and Mark Puls's *Uncommon Valor* (2005) on New Market Heights underscored the meaning of fighting and bravery in combat in the Black struggle for emancipation.[41] For documentary work that gives voice to the Black soldiers themselves, the best collection beyond the FSSP is Edwin Redkey's *A Grand Army of Black Men* (1992).[42] An edited and annotated collection of photographs of Black Union soldiers by Ronald Coddington presented the emancipation experience more powerfully than could a word of text.[43] The popular 1990 movie *Glory*, featuring the 54th Massachusetts Infantry, reflected this newer scholarship on Black Union soldiers and helped stimulate popular interest in the Black military experience.[44]

The navy was also a key site of emancipation, though not on the scale of the army. Barbara Brooks Tomblin's *Bluejackets and Contrabands* (2009) and Steven Ramold's *Slaves, Sailors, Citizens* (2001) both told the story of Black Union sailors.[45] However, as W. Jeffrey Bolster described in *Black Jacks: African American Seamen in the Age of Sail* (1997), the long tradition of Blacks at sea faced new challenges in the age of emancipation, especially as white sailors began to view Black shipmates as competitors.[46]

Whereas most of the collections and monographs on Black Union soldiers and sailors emphasized the heroic struggle for self-emancipation, other historians have stressed the profound challenges that enslaved men, women, and children faced as they emerged from bondage. Leon Litwack's *Been in the Storm So Long* (1980) gathered hundreds of tales of despair, damage, and quickly dashed dreams as enslaved people emerged from slavery.[47] Jim Downs's *Sick from Freedom* (2012) highlighted the physical ailments that the formerly enslaved encountered as they first tasted freedom.[48] In both cases, the experience of being uprooted largely defined the process and feeling of emancipation. Thomas Buchanan made a similar case for the experience of emancipation and movement on the Mississippi River, while Yael Sternhell traced the geographic movement of freedom-seeking slaves in the context of larger movements of humanity in the Civil War South.[49] Together, these works revealed the unstable geography of emancipation as families torn apart in slavery reconstituted themselves in freedom. As Nicole Etcheson argued in a review essay on the *microhistory* of emancipation and movement, emancipation's diaspora has helped bridge the gap between grand synthetic histories of emancipation and local studies that "reveal the patterns of life in a particular place and time."[50]

Scholarship on the grassroots emancipation experience has revealed intriguing regional patterns that outline the contingent nature of emancipation across four chaotic years of war. Paul Escott's "The Context of Freedom" (1974) and Clarence Mohr's *On the Threshold of Freedom* (2001) each assessed emancipation in Georgia, while Peter Ripley's *Slaves and Freedmen* (1976) explored the demise of freedom in Louisiana.[51] Lynda Morgan's excellent *Emancipation in Virginia's Tobacco Belt* (1992) examined the destruction of a particularly fluid form of slavery that had relied heavily on slave hiring.[52] In fact, many of the intriguing regional studies have focused on the upper and border South, especially as scholars have tended to view the region as somewhat atypical compared with the cotton belt of the Deep South.[53] In addition to these border/upper South studies, Barbara Krauthammer explored the peculiarity of emancipation in the Indian Territory, where Choctaw and

Chickasaw slaveholders were forced to renegotiate triracial relations in the context of emancipation.[54] Perhaps most intriguing is Kate Masur's *An Example for All the Land* (2010), which focused on Washington, DC, and the powerful symbolic and practical effect of destroying slavery in the nation's capital.[55]

The use of gender as a category of analysis has opened new avenues for research into emancipation, both at the grassroots and the legal and institutional levels. Since the publication of Elizabeth Fox-Genovese's *Within the Plantation Household* in 1988, scholars have assessed the gendered implications of the breakdown of the slaveholding household during and after the Civil War.[56] Thavolia Glymph outlined in *Out of the House of Bondage* (2008) the struggle between enslaved women and mistresses as the slave system collapsed.[57] LeeAnn Whites's *Civil War as a Crisis in Gender* (1995) explored emancipation's implications for slaveholding women and men in the households of Augusta, Georgia.[58] Stephanie Camp's study of women's resistance in slavery, *Closer to Freedom* (2004), joined other scholars in stressing the power of movement during the Civil War.[59] One example of the movement necessitated by emancipation was the search for families broken by the slave trade, a subject explored in depth in Noralee Frankel's *Freedom's Women* (1999).[60] Focusing on the labor performed by enslaved women in the South Carolina rice fields, Leslie Schwalm highlighted the ways in which slavery itself shaped the struggle over emancipation.[61] Similarly, Nancy Bercaw's *Gendered Freedoms* (2003) captured the subjective meaning of relationships within Mississippi plantation households at the moment of emancipation.[62] Like Steven Hahn, Susan O'Donovan, Diane Mutti Burke, Julie Saville, and Lynda Morgan, Schwalm and Bercaw emphasized the importance of local contexts of power and work in specific plantation settings.

Some of the most promising work in recent years has examined the changing relationships between women and the state, including enslaved women at the moment of emancipation. Mary Farmer-Kaiser's *Freedwomen and the Freedmen's Bureau* (2010) provided the first detailed look at how newly freed women negotiated labor demands and calls for justice with a federal bureaucracy designed to transition the South away from a slave economy.[63] More far-reaching was Stephanie McCurry's *Confederate Reckoning* (2010), which highlighted the contradictory impulse at the heart of the Confederate project, and the ways that women—free and enslaved—worked to undermine the Confederate state from within.[64]

One of the most significant points of contention in the historiography of emancipation is the relative power of the federal government, including the federal army, in ending slavery. While some of the most impressive scholarship has focused on the grassroots efforts of enslaved people to undermine the slave system during the Civil War, an equally impressive outpouring of work has explored how white-led institutions made emancipation even possible. Nowhere is this greater than in studies of the Union army, where scholars have reassessed the changing (or unchanging) ideological value of the war, the attitudes of soldiers and officers, and the effect of the Union army's presence at particular places on the course of emancipation. Though they largely disagreed on the relative value of *union* and *emancipation* as soldierly war aims, Gary Gallagher's *The Union War* (2011) and Chandra Manning's *What This Cruel War Was Over* (2008) each found that soldiers understood how revolutionary their presence was in the slaveholding heartland.[65] Sometimes attitudes changed as a result of direct experience with haughty planters, as Stephen Ash discussed in *When the Yankees Came* (1999), or as a result of widely disseminated stories of Black valor, as was the experience of white officers of black regiments recounted in Joseph Glatthaar's *Forged in Battle* (2000).[66] But the contingencies of campaign struggle may have mattered the most in shaping Union soldiers' approaches to emancipation: as Glenn Brasher revealed in *The Peninsula Campaign and the Necessity of Emancipation* (2012), the failures of General McClellan's mighty *Army of the Potomac* in the spring of 1862 had a crucial impact on the debate in Washington over emancipation, and the desire among Union soldiers to make a more concerted attack on slavery.[67] In fact, as Jonathan W. White argued in *Emancipation, the Union Army, and the Reelection of Abraham Lincoln* (2014), it may have been hatred of slaveholders rather than sympathy for the enslaved that pushed so many Union soldiers to

embrace emancipation.[68] All the while, enslaved people made their
own case for freedom when appearing at Union lines, drawing
mixed responses from soldiers and officers who tried to navigate
the changing Union emancipation policy.[69] And in the first significant study of African Americans in contraband camps created by the
Union army, *Embattled Freedom* (2018), Amy Murrell Taylor outlined
just how contingent and precarious emancipation was for enslaved
men and women in the indeterminant worlds between military bureaucracy, local economies, and slave kinship networks.[70]

As becomes apparent in these studies of the Union army and
its shift toward a more deliberate campaign against slavery, the
power of abolitionists, the power of the Republican and Democratic Parties, and the leadership of President Lincoln mattered
enormously. With some exceptions, books on abolitionists have
typically focused on the work of slavery's opponents before the
war. As Allen Carden stressed in *Freedom's Delay* (2014), slavery's
opponents continually wrestled with slavery's expansion in the
South and its apologists within the North.[71] The competing ideological strains in the North over free soil and popular sovereignty
placed Black and white abolitionists in a curious quandary: should
they engage with the political process at all? And what were they
to do once the nation descended into civil war? The titles of Caleb
McDaniel's *The Problem of Democracy in the Age of Slavery* (2013) and
David Brion Davis's *The Problem of Slavery in the Age of Emancipation* (2014) made a common literary gesture toward the power of
reform in the coming of the Civil War.[72] James Oakes's *The Scorpion's Sting* (2014) demonstrated abolitionists' success in driving
Republican Party policy before the war, confronting proslavery
Democrats, and maintaining Republican commitment to ending slavery during the war.[73] And as David Blight and William S.
McFeely have shown, Frederick Douglass positioned himself to
maintain his influence in Republican Party circles once the war
began.[74] But work on lesser-known abolitionists, like David Cecelski's 2001 study of Abraham Galloway, has shown the extent
to which Black abolitionists committed their energy to the practical destruction of slavery. In fact, some of the most pathbreaking

work on abolitionists has focused not on elite white Northerners who moved south during the war, but on African Americans in the North who committed themselves to both freeing and teaching the enslaved. Russell Duncan discussed the work of Tunis Campbell, who arrived in McIntosh County, Georgia, in 1864 and helped lead the freed people to develop a political agenda in Reconstruction.[75] Ronald Butchart's *Schooling the Freed People* (2013), based on a comprehensive reassessment of teachers in the postwar South, may have the most far-reaching implications as it suggests how much the struggles over freedom's meaning occurred in intraracial as opposed to interracial conversation.[76]

So what, then, have historians had to say about Abraham Lincoln, the Great Emancipator? Those casting doubt on Lincoln's emancipation bona fides have always garnered more attention than their numbers or interpretive power deserve. Usually stressing Lincoln's racial attitudes and continued support for colonization as late as 1862, many of the "loathers of Lincoln" have suggested that he was a reluctant emancipator who had to be "forced into glory."[77] On the contrary, biographers from David Donald and LaWanda Cox to Michael Burlingame and Ronald White have all placed Lincoln's racial views in context of the nineteenth-century American West, and have largely rescued his emancipationist value system.[78] Eric Foner's *The Fiery Trial* (2011), by focusing specifically on Lincoln's attitudes toward slavery, helped consolidate the view of a man who was consistently antislavery, even if not consistently antiracist.[79] Lincoln's defenders have emphasized his fundamental pragmatism and, more importantly, his penchant for framing the war in ideological and revolutionary terms.[80]

In reassessing Lincoln's commitment to emancipation, scholars in recent years have reconsidered the document at the heart of the Civil War, the *Emancipation Proclamation*. Why, many scholars have wondered, was a document so central to the war and to Lincoln's legacy delivered in such legalistic prose? And did the Emancipation Proclamation really free many slaves at all? The Proclamation's sesquicentennial has encouraged many scholars to reemphasize its centrality in the emancipation process. This is especially true of Allen Guelzo's *Lincoln's Emancipation Proclamation* (2006) and Louis Masur's *Lincoln's Hundred Days* (2012), both of which stressed the counterpressures against Lincoln that could have driven him to limit or even rescind the Proclamation during the militarily difficult days of late 1862.[81] In *Emancipating Lincoln* (2012), Harold Holzer defended the document's text and application, including its staid language and frustrating limitations,[82] arguing that the law required as much, and that Lincoln understood the greatest risk of all—that the Proclamation would not stand the test of peace and time. Still, the scholars contributing to the edited collection, *Lincoln's Proclamation* (2012), rightfully pointed out the myriad other forces that were necessary to make the Proclamation anything other than a dead letter.[83]

The study of emancipation and the Constitution has produced some dramatic reinterpretations in recent years, a point dramatized by the 2012 Steven Spielberg movie, *Lincoln,* which focused almost entirely on the Thirteenth Amendment's passage.[84] Considering the deeply embedded nature of slavery in the national constitutional framework, it makes sense that the disentanglement of America from slavery would require a thoroughgoing legal revolution. Recent scholars of the laws of war, including Burrus Carnahan and John Fabian Witt, have outlined the difficult legal maneuverings necessary to declare slavery dead, especially insofar as it was recognized as a legal form of property for so many years prior.[85] As for the Thirteenth Amendment, Michael Vorenberg's *Final Freedom* (2001) offered the most comprehensive analysis of the process through which the amendment became law.[86] As for its ideological roots in the Declaration of Independence and its significance for American legal history, Alexander Tsesis's *The Thirteenth Amendment and American Freedom* (2004) is essential reading.[87]

Beyond the Thirteenth Amendment, scholars have also examined the legal implications of eliminating a form of property. Silvana Siddali's *From Property to Person* (2005) traced the Northern debate on the implications of the Confiscation Acts, while Amy Dru Stanley's *From Bondage to Contract* (1998) assessed the legal significance of removing household slaves from the status of property.[88] As for the legal and constitutional implications of the federal government's expanded role in managing the process of emancipation, Herman Belz's *Emancipation and Equal Rights* (1978), *Abraham Lincoln, Constitutionalism, and Equal Rights in the Civil War Era* (1997), and *A New Birth of Freedom: The Republican Party and Freedmen's Rights* (2000) highlighted the significant—if incremental—structural changes that cemented emancipation in American law.[89] Steven Hahn's 2013 essay "Slave Emancipation, Indian Peoples, and the Projects of the New American Nation-State" showed how a consolidated national government empowered to eliminate slavery in the South was used in similar fashion to subjugate Native Americans in the West.[90] As each of these studies showed, actions of the state dismantled slavery, while at the same time the unraveling of slavery substantially altered the shape, size, and ideological contours of the state.

As Belz's work on emancipation illuminated, much of the legal challenge to slavery was embedded in the Republican Party's distinct approach to slavery's legality generally. James Oakes's *Freedom National* (2012) has already had far-reaching implications in its recentering of antislavery thought in the Republican Party and its leaders.[91] Republicans had long sought to eliminate slavery by establishing a cordon of freedom that would prevent slavery from expanding. This became central to party policy, even though, as Eric Foner wrote both in *Free Soil, Free Labor, Free Men* (1970) and in his larger work *Reconstruction* (2002), opposition to slavery often had little to do with egalitarian racial views.[92] As Oakes argued, for Republicans, freedom was national and slavery was local. When the *Dred Scott* decision briefly upended that arrangement, it electrified Northern public opinion and set the Republican Party on a course of uncompromising opposition to the extension of slavery. But Oakes went much farther, showing that Republican politicians applied the *freedom national* doctrine whenever possible in the war, using the *laws of nations* to justify slavery's destruction. Not all scholars agree with Oakes on the centrality of Republican emancipationist policy in politics at the war's outset. Michael Holt's 2017 study of the 1860 presidential election directly refuted Oakes, highlighting other factors like corruption that motivated

Republicans, while Daniel Crofts emphasized Republican support for the Union-saving Corwin Amendment, which would have protected slavery in perpetuity.[93] In the end, as Gregory Downs perceptively noted in *After Appomattox* (2015), it was Andrew Johnson who finished the job of emancipation by insisting that his conservative plan of *restoration* would only work if the former Confederate states accepted the reality of emancipation.[94]

The political implications of emancipation, especially during the 1862 congressional elections and the 1864 presidential election, are the subject of fine studies by Michael Green and David Long.[95] The extent to which Northern Democrats accepted emancipation has been a source of study since Frank Klement's pioneering 1964 article "Midwestern Opposition to Lincoln's Emancipation Policy" and Joel Silbey's 1977 study of the Democratic Party *A Respectable Minority*.[96] Of Democrats who outright opposed Lincoln's war policies in full, including especially emancipation, Jennifer Weber's *Copperheads* (2008) and Thomas Mach's study, *Gentleman George Hunt Pendleton,* provided the rhetorical, partisan, and ideological context for anti-emancipation sentiment.[97]

Yet, as Armstead Robinson pointed out, the primary achievement of the Confederate States of America was the destruction of slavery.[98] This was not, of course, its intention. But Stephanie McCurry showed just how unlikely it was that the new Confederacy could continue drawing on the resources of those other than white men, all the while demanding that white men maintain a monopoly on state power.[99] In fact, as Bruce Levine revealed in his exhaustive study of Confederate emancipation, the Confederate army realized all too late that it would have to surrender its core organizing principle in order to survive.[100]

Another of the more promising directions in the study of emancipation is the use of comparative and transnational methods. Much of this scholarship began with the work of anthropologists like Sidney Mintz and Richard Price, who explored Afro-diasporic culture in Caribbean societies emerging from slavery.[101] This literature also drew comparisons with emancipation from serfdom in Europe. Rebecca Scott, Thomas Holt, Peter Kolchin, Steven Hahn, and

Carl Degler have offered specifically comparative studies of emancipation in America with Cuba, Jamaica, Russia, Prussia, and Brazil.[102] Other scholars have taken transnational approaches that transcend national boundaries and frameworks and focus on the Atlantic world generally. Eric Foner and Steven Hahn's *Nothing but Freedom* (2007) and Seymour Drescher's *From Slavery to Freedom* (1999) offered broader analyses of emancipation in the Western Hemisphere.[103] In keeping with the historiographic theme of emancipation as a global movement—of peoples and ideas—Rebecca Scott and Jean Hébrard's *Freedom Papers* (2014), Edward Rugemer's *Problem of Emancipation* (2008), and Matthew Clavin's *Toussaint Louverture and the American Civil War* (2011) each addressed transnational currents surrounding emancipation.[104] Focusing on the work of abolitionists in two societies, Enrico Del Lago's *William Lloyd Garrison and Giuseppe Mazzini* (2013) examined transatlantic antislavery currents.[105] Returning back to the politics of emancipation, Stephen Sawyer and William J. Novak's essay on emancipation and the liberal state in France and in the United States provided a helpful model for examining nation-building in the nineteenth century.[106] Jeffrey Kerr-Ritchie's *Freedom's Seekers: Essays on Comparative Emancipation* (2014) synthesized much of this comparative and transnational scholarship.[107]

Finally, memory of emancipation has become a powerful subject of scholarship, with David Blight's *Race and Reunion* (2001) placing memory of emancipation at the center of the battle over the Civil War's larger memory.[108] Mitch Kachun's *Festivals of Freedom* (2003) explored the ways in which Black communities have celebrated emancipation.[109] Sharon Romeo's 2016 study of postemancipation celebrations in Missouri emphasized the role of women in crafting a biracial vision of citizenship.[110] Donald R. Shaffer's *After the Glory* (2004) recounted the unique challenges that Black veterans faced in securing pensions, health care, and financial security; a helpful companion work, Elizabeth A. Regosin and Donald R. Shaffer's *Voices of Emancipation: Understanding Slavery, the Civil War and Emancipation through the U.S. Pension Bureau Files*, offers methodological suggestions for scholars looking to work with this large data set.[111]

Celebrating their military achievements in gaining emancipation and saving the Union, many Black veterans participated in biracial Grand Army of the Republic (GAR) posts across the North, as Barbara Gannon has shown; on the other hand, Anne Marshall revealed the profound discomfort that these Black Union veterans caused for white Kentucky Unionists.[112] Complicating the role of Black veterans, Carole Emberton's provocative 2012 essay "Only Murder Makes Men" challenged the contention that for all African Americans, serving in the Union army and committing violence in war were necessary components of either emancipation or claims to citizenship. Nevertheless, while Black communities celebrated the active role their forebears played in securing emancipation, many white-dominated commemorative works depicted enslaved people as passive, helpless, and invisible. Kirk Savage's *Standing Soldiers, Kneeling Slaves* (1999) took aim at the Lincoln emancipation statue in Washington, DC, while Kate Masur and Michael Vorenberg have critiqued Steven Spielberg's portrayal of Civil War-era Washington, DC, as nearly all-white.[113] Alas, Black veterans often toiled in painful obscurity as their status earned during war and Reconstruction was undermined by the end of the nineteenth century.

Scholarship on emancipation during the American Civil War has accelerated at a dizzying pace in recent decades as historians have applied newer approaches to answer old questions. In some ways, this is a continuation of the long Civil Rights movement in the historiography of emancipation. As is evident in Civil War syntheses by Allan Nevins, James McPherson, and Elizabeth Varon, each generation of Civil War scholarship incorporates the emancipation experience more centrally than the last.[114] The debates today continue to center around matters of timing, perspective, and long-term implications in light of global economic and political change. Rarely does one hear any longer the trope—common in the pre-Civil Rights era—of passive slaves being freed without their assistance. However, the developments in the literature since 1970 have certainly reflected contemporary assessments of the African American experience in the post-Civil Rights era. Works on emancipation are thus deeply informed by popular awareness of the promises and limits of the Black Freedom movement of the 1960s, as scholars seek linkages and ideological connections between promises betrayed in the nineteenth century and promises abandoned in the twentieth. Continued effects of institutional racism, police brutality, the military's role as an *instrument of freedom* in the twenty-first century, capitalism, and persistent poverty have all influenced new approaches to the study of emancipation. Contemporary events have accelerated this reappraisal. Confederate statues have started to come down, public history sites emphasize the Black experience more than ever before, public school curricula have been revised, and mass Black Lives Matter protests have emerged in response to the police murder of George Floyd. Coupled with the lingering devastation of the Great Recession and disproportionate impact of the novel coronavirus pandemic of 2020 on communities of color, historians are more attuned than ever to the legacies of slavery long after emancipation. Without a doubt, scholarship in the study of emancipation will continue to grow in breadth and sophistication in the coming years.

NOTES

1. Douglass, "Work of the Future."
2. McPherson, "Who Freed the Slaves?"
3. P. Foner, *Frederick Douglass,* 188-206. See also Blight, *Frederick Douglass.*
4. W. Brown, *Negro in the American Rebellion.*
5. H. Wilson, *History of the Rise and Fall.*
6. G. Williams, *History of the Negro Race,* 2:312.
7. G. Williams, *History of the Negro Troops*; United States War Department, *War of the Rebellion.*
8. J. Wilson, *Emancipation;* J. Wilson, *Black Phalanx.*
9. Smith and Lowery, *Dunning School;* Burgess, *Civil War and the Constitution.*
10. Rhodes, *History of the Civil War.*
11. Rhodes, *History of the Civil War,* 380-81.
12. Beard and Beard, *Rise of American Civilization;* Beale, *Critical Year;* Randall, "Blundering Generation."
13. W. Woodward, *Meet General Grant,* 372.
14. Wesley, "Lincoln's Plan."

15. Shannon, "Federal Government and the Negro Soldier," 563.

16. R. Logan, "Review: *Black Reconstruction in America,*" 63.

17. Du Bois, *Black Reconstruction in America.*

18. Aptheker, *Negro in the Civil War.*

19. Wiley, *Southern Negroes.*

20. Quarles, *Negro in the Civil War,* xiii; *Brown v. Board of Education* (1954).

21. Cornish, *Sable Arm.*

22. Nevins, *War for the Union,* vol. 2.

23. Cornish, *Sable Arm,* vii–ix.

24. McPherson, *Negro's Civil War.*

25. Williamson, *After Slavery.*

26. Rose, *Rehearsal for Reconstruction.*

27. J. Franklin, *Emancipation Proclamation;* Quarles, *Lincoln and the Negro.*

28. Levin, *Searching for Black Confederates.*

29. Berlin et al., *Freedom: A Documentary History of Emancipation,* series 1, vol. 1, *Destruction of Slavery.*

30. Berlin et al., *Freedom,* series 1, vol. 2, *Wartime Genesis of Free Labor: Upper South;* Berlin et al., *Freedom,* series 1, vol. 3, *Wartime Genesis of Free Labor: Lower South.*

31. Berlin et al., *Freedom,* series 2, *Black Military Experience.*

32. Hahn et al., *Freedom,* series 3, vol. 1, *Land and Labor;* Hayden et al., *Freedom,* series 3, vol. 2, *Land and Labor.*

33. Berlin et al., *Free at Last;* Berlin et al., *Slaves No More;* Berlin and Rowland, *Families and Freedom;* Berlin, Reidy, and Rowland, *Freedom's Soldiers.*

34. O'Donovan, *Becoming Free;* Saville, *Work of Reconstruction.*

35. Hahn, *Nation under Our Feet.*

36. Behrend, *Reconstructing Democracy.*

37. Robinson, Reidy, and Fields, *Bitter Fruits of Bondage.*

38. Levine, *Fall of the House of Dixie.*

39. Dobak, *Freedom by the Sword;* Trudeau, *Like Men of War;* J. Smith, *Black Soldiers in Blue.*

40. Spurgeon, *Soldiers in the Army of Freedom;* Ash, *Firebrand of Liberty;* Reid, *Freedom for Themselves;* Longacre, *Regiment of Slaves;* E. Miller, *Black Civil War Soldiers of Illinois;* Bryant, *36th Infantry United States;* Mezurek, *For Their Own Cause;* Duncan, *Where Death and Glory Meet.*

41. Barnickel, *Milliken's Bend;* Claxton and Puls, *Uncommon Valor.*

42. Redkey, *Grand Army of Black Men.*

43. Coddington, *African American Faces of the Civil War.*

44. Zwick, *Glory.*

45. Tomblin, *Bluejackets and Contrabands;* Ramold, *Slaves, Sailors, Citizens.*

46. Bolster, *Black Jacks.*

47. Litwack, *Been in the Storm So Long.*

48. J. Downs, *Sick from Freedom.*

49. Buchanan, *Black Life on the Mississippi;* Sternhell, *Routes of War.*

50. Etcheson, "Microhistory and Movement," 393.

51. Escott, "Context of Freedom"; Mohr, *On the Threshold of Freedom;* Ripley, *Slaves and Freedmen.*

52. L. Morgan, *Emancipation.*

53. Essah, *A House Divided;* Fields, *Slavery and Freedom;* Wagandt, *Mighty Revolution;* Victor B. Howard, *Black Liberation in Kentucky;* Cimprich, *Slavery's End in Tennessee;* Mutti Burke, *On Slavery's Border;* Astor, *Rebels on the Border.*

54. Krauthamer, *Black Slaves, Indian Masters.*

55. Masur, *Example for All the Land.*

56. Fox-Genovese, *Within the Plantation Household.*

57. Glymph, *Out of the House of Bondage.*

58. Whites, *Civil War as a Crisis in Gender;* Whites, *Gender Matters.*

59. Camp, *Closer to Freedom.*

60. Frankel, *Freedom's Women.*

61. Schwalm, *Hard Fight for We.*

62. Bercaw, *Gendered Freedoms.*

63. Farmer-Kaiser, *Freedwomen.*

64. McCurry, *Confederate Reckoning.* See also McCurry, *Women's War.*

65. Gallagher, *Union War;* C. Manning, *What This Cruel War Was Over.*

66. Ash, *When the Yankees Came;* Glatthaar, *Forged in Battle.*

67. Brasher, *Peninsula Campaign.*

68. J. White, *Emancipation.*

69. Teters, *Practical Liberators.*

70. A. Taylor, *Embattled Freedom.*

71. Carden, *Freedom's Delay.*

72. D. Davis, *Problem of Slavery in the Age of Emancipation;* and McDaniel, *Problem of Democracy.*

73. Oakes, *Scorpion's Sting.*

74. McFeely, *Frederick Douglass;* Oakes, *Radical and the Republican;* Blight, *Frederick Douglass.*

75. Duncan, *Freedom's Shore.*

76. Butchart, *Schooling the Freed People.*

77. Barr, *Loathing Lincoln;* Bennett, *Forced into Glory.*

78. L. Cox, *Lincoln and Black Freedom;* Burlingame, *Abraham Lincoln;* D. H. Donald, *Lincoln;* R. White, *A. Lincoln.*

79. E. Foner, *Fiery Trial.*

80. Fredrickson, *Big Enough;* McPherson, *Abraham Lincoln;* Oates, *With Malice toward None.*

81. Guelzo, *Lincoln's Emancipation Proclamation;* L. Masur, *Lincoln's Hundred Days.*

82. Holzer, *Emancipating Lincoln.*

83. Blair and Younger, *Lincoln's Proclamation.*

84. Kushner and Goodwin, *Lincoln*.

85. Carnahan, *Act of Justice;* Witt, *Lincoln's Code*.

86. Vorenberg, *Final Freedom*.

87. Tsesis, *Thirteenth Amendment*.

88. Siddali, *Property to Person;* Stanley, *Bondage to Contract*.

89. Belz, *Emancipation and Equal Rights;* Belz, *Abraham Lincoln;* Belz, *New Birth of Freedom*.

90. Hahn, "Slave Emancipation."

91. Oakes, *Freedom National*.

92. E. Foner, *Free Soil, Free Labor;* E. Foner, *Reconstruction*.

93. M. Holt, *Election of 1860;* Crofts, *Lincoln*.

94. G. Downs, *After Appomattox*.

95. Green, *Freedom, Union, and Power;* Long, *Jewel of Liberty*.

96. Klement, "Midwestern Opposition"; Silbey, *Respectable Minority*.

97. Mach, *Gentleman George Hunt Pendleton;* Weber, *Copperheads*.

98. Robinson, Reidy, and Fields, *Bitter Fruits of Bondage,* 1-10.

99. McCurry, *Confederate Reckoning*.

100. B. Levine, *Confederate Emancipation*.

101. Mintz and Price, *Birth of African-American Culture*.

102. Cooper, Holt, and Scott, *Beyond Slavery;* Degler, *Neither Black nor White;* Hahn, "Class and State"; Kolchin, *Sphinx;* Kolchin, *Unfree Labor;* R. Scott, *Degrees of Freedom*.

103. Foner and Hahn, *Nothing but Freedom;* Drescher, *Slavery to Freedom*.

104. Scott and Hébrard, *Freedom Papers;* Rugemer, *Problem of Emancipation;* Clavin, *Toussaint Louverture*.

105. Dal Lago, *William Lloyd Garrison*.

106. Sawyer and Novak, "Emancipation."

107. Kerr-Ritchie, *Freedom's Seekers*.

108. Blight, *Race and Reunion*.

109. Kachun, *Festivals of Freedom*.

110. Romeo, *Gender and the Jubilee*.

111. Shaffer, *After the Glory;* Regosin and Shaffer, *Voices of Emancipation*.

112. Gannon, *Won Cause;* Marshall, *Creating a Confederate Kentucky*.

113. Emberton, "Only Murder Makes Men"; Savage, *Standing Soldiers, Kneeling Slaves;* K. Masur, "In Spielberg's 'Lincoln'"; Vorenberg, "Spielberg's Lincoln"; M. Jones, "History and Commemoration."

114. Nevins, *War for the Union;* McPherson, *Battle Cry of Freedom;* Varon, *Armies of Deliverance*.

Bibliography

Acemoglu, Daron, and Alexander Wolitzky. "The Economics of Labor Coercion." *Econometrica* 79, no. 2 (Mar. 2011): 555-600.

Adams, Catherine, and Elizabeth H. Pleck. *Love of Freedom: Black Women and Colonial and Revolutionary New England.* New York: Oxford Univ. Press, 2010.

Aitken, Hugh G. L., ed. *Did Slavery Pay? Readings in the Economics of Black Slavery in the United States.* Boston: Houghton Mifflin, 1971.

Alexander, Adele Logan. *Ambiguous Lives: Free Women of Color in Rural Georgia, 1789-1879.* Fayetteville: Univ. of Arkansas Press, 1991.

Alexander, Leslie. *African or American? Black Identity and Political Activism in New York City, 1784-1861.* Urbana: Univ. of Illinois Press, 2008.

"An Act for the Gradual Abolition of Slavery." Mar. 1, 1780. Record group 26, Pennsylvania State Archives, Harrisburg, PA. http://www.phmc.state.pa.us/portal/communities/documents/1776-1865/abolition-slavery.html (accessed Nov. 22, 2020).

Anderson, Kristen Layne. *Abolitionizing Missouri: German Immigrants and Racial Ideology in Nineteenth-Century America.* Baton Rouge: Louisiana State Univ. Press, 2016.

Anderson, Ralph V., and Robert E. Gallman. "Slaves as Fixed Capital: Slave Labor and Southern Economic Development." *Journal of American History* 64, no. 1 (June 1977): 24-46.

Andrews, Donald R., and Ralph D. Christy. "The Profitability of Slavery: A Review of the Classical Economic Position." In *Plantation Society and Race Relations: The Origins of Inequality,* edited by Thomas J. Durant Jr. and J. David Knottnerus, 89-99. New York: Praeger, 1999.

Andrews, William L. *To Tell a Free Story: The First Century of Afro-American Autobiography, 1760-1865.* Urbana: Univ. of Illinois Press, 1986.

Anstey, Roger. *The Atlantic Slave Trade and British Abolition, 1760-1810.* Atlantic Highlands, NJ: Humanities Press, 1975.

———. "Capitalism and Slavery: A Critique." *Economic History Review* 21, no. 2 (Aug. 1968): 307-20.

Aptheker, Herbert. *American Negro Slave Revolts.* New York: Columbia Univ. Press, 1943. Reprint, New York: International Publishers Co., Inc., 1983.

———. "Negro Casualties in the Civil War." *Journal of Negro History* 32, no. 1 (Jan. 1947): 10-80.

———. *The Negro in the Civil War.* New York: International Publishers, 1938.

Armstead, Myra B. Young. *Freedom's Gardener: James F. Brown, Horticulture, and the Hudson Valley in Antebellum America.* New York: New York Univ. Press, 2012.

Ash, Stephen V. *Firebrand of Liberty: The Story of Two Black Regiments that Changed the Course of the Civil War.* New York: W. W. Norton & Co., 2008.

———. *Middle Tennessee Society Transformed: War and Peace in the Upper South.* Knoxville: Univ. of Tennessee Press, 1988.

———. *When the Yankees Came: Conflict and Chaos in the Occupied South, 1861-1865.* Chapel Hill: Univ. of North Carolina Press, 1999.

Ashworth, John. *Slavery, Capitalism, and Politics in the Antebellum Republic.* Vol. 1, *Commerce and Compromise.* New York: Cambridge Univ. Press, 1995.

———. *Slavery, Capitalism, and Politics in the Antebellum Republic.* Vol. 2, *The Coming of the Civil War.* New York: Cambridge Univ. Press, 2008.

Astor, Aaron. *Rebels on the Border: Civil War, Emancipation, and the Reconstruction of Kentucky and Missouri.* Baton Rouge: Louisiana State Univ. Press, 2012.

Ayers, Edward L. *In the Presence of Mine Enemies: The Civil War in the Heart of America, 1859-1864.* New York: W. W. Norton & Co., 2004.

Bailey, Anne. *The Weeping Time: Memory and the Largest Slave Auction in American History.* New York: Cambridge Univ. Press, 2017.

Bailey, Ronald. "The Slave(ry) Trade and the Development of Capitalism in the United States: The Textile Industry in New England." *Social Science History* 14, no. 3 (Autumn 1990): 373-414.

———. "'Those Valuable People, the Africans': The Economic Impact of the Slav(ry) Trade on Textile Industrialization in New England." In *The Meaning of Slavery in the North,* edited by David Roediger and Martin H. Blatt, 3-31. New York: Garland, 1997.

Bailyn, Bernard. *The Ideological Origins of the American Revolution.* Cambridge, MA: Harvard Univ. Press, 1967.

———. "Slavery and Population Growth in Colonial New England." In *Engines of Enterprise: An Economic History of New England,* edited by Peter Temin, 253-59. Cambridge, MA: Harvard Univ. Press, 2000.

Baker, Bruce, and Brian Kelly, eds. *After Slavery: Race, Labor and Citizenship in the Reconstruction South.* Gainesville: Univ. Press of Florida, 2014.

Baker, Lee D. "Columbia University's Franz Boas: He Led the Undoing of Scientific Racism." *Journal of Blacks in Higher Education* 22 (Winter 1998-99): 89-96.

Bales, Kevin. *Disposable People: New Slavery in the Global Economy.* Berkeley: Univ. of California Press, 2000.

Bancroft, Frederic. *Slave Trading in the Old South.* Baltimore: J. H. Furst, 1931.

Bancroft, George. *History of the United States, from the Discovery of the American Continent.* 10 vols. Boston: Little, Brown & Co., 1834-74.

Baptist, Edward E. "'Cuffy,' 'Fancy Maids,' and 'One-Eyed Men': Rape, Commodification, and the Domestic Slave Trade in the United States." *American Historical Review* 106, no. 5 (Dec. 2001): 1619-50.

———. *The Half Has Never Been Told: Slavery and the Making of American Capitalism.* New York: Basic Books, 2014.

———. "Toxic Debt, Liar Loans, Collateralized and Securitized Human Beings, and the Panic of 1837." In *Capitalism Takes Command: The Social Transformation of Nineteenth-Century America,* edited by Michael Zakim and Gary J. Kornblith, 69-92. Chicago: Univ. of Chicago Press, 2012.

Baptist, Edward, and Stephanie Camp, eds. *New Studies in the History of American Slavery.* Athens: Univ. of Georgia Press, 2006.

Barber, William J., ed. *Economists and Higher Learning in the Nineteenth Century.* New Brunswick, NJ: Transaction Publishers, 1993.

Barnes, L. Diane, Brian Schoen, and Frank Towers, eds. *The Old South's Modern Worlds: Slavery, Region, and the Nation in the Age of Progress.* New York: Oxford Univ. Press, 2011.

Barney, William L. *Road to Secession: A New Perspective on the Old South.* New York: Praeger, 1972.

———. *Secessionist Impulse: Alabama and Mississippi in 1860.* Princeton, NJ: Princeton Univ. Press, 1974.

Barnickel, Linda. *Milliken's Bend: A Civil War Battle in History and Memory.* Baton Rouge: Louisiana State Univ. Press, 2013.

Barr, John McKee. *Loathing Lincoln: An American Tradition from the Civil War to the Present.* Baton Rouge: Louisiana State Univ. Press, 2014.

Barrus, Jeff. "Nikole Hannah-Jones Wins Pulitzer Prize for 1619 Project." Pulitzer Center on Crisis Reporting, Washington, DC, May 4, 2020. https://pulitzercenter.org/blog/nikole-hannah-jones-wins-pulitzer-prize-1619-project (accessed Oct. 29, 2020).

Bateman, Fred, and Thomas Weiss. *A Deplorable Scarcity: The Failure of Industrialization in the Slave Economy.* Chapel Hill: Univ. of North Carolina Press, 1981.

Baucom, Ian. *Specters of the Atlantic: Finance Capital, Slavery, and the Philosophy of History.* Durham, NC: Duke Univ. Press, 2005.

Bauer, Raymond A., and Alice H. Bauer. "Day to Day Resistance to Slavery." *Journal of Negro History* 27, no. 4 (Oct. 1942): 388-419.

Beale, Howard K. *The Critical Year: A Study of Andrew Johnson and Reconstruction.* New York: Harcourt, Brace & Co., 1930.

Beard, Charles A. *An Economic Interpretation of the Constitution of the United States.* New York: Macmillan, 1913.

Beard, Charles A., and Mary R. Beard. *The Rise of American Civilization.* New York: Macmillan, 1930.

Beckert, Sven. *Empire of Cotton: A Global History.* New York: Alfred A. Knopf, 2014.

Beckert, Sven, and Seth Rockman, eds. *Slavery's Capitalism: A New History of American Economic Development.* Philadelphia: Univ. of Pennsylvania Press, 2016.

Behrend, Justin. *Reconstructing Democracy: Grassroots Black Politics in the Deep South after the Civil War.* Athens: Univ. of Georgia Press, 2015.

Belz, Herman. *Abraham Lincoln, Constitutionalism, and Equal Rights in the Civil War Era.* New York: Fordham Univ. Press, 1997.

————. *Emancipation and Equal Rights: Politics and Constitutionalism in the Civil War Era.* New York: W. W. Norton & Co., 1978.

————. *A New Birth of Freedom: The Republican Party and Freedmen's Rights.* New York: Fordham Univ. Press, 2000.

Bender, Thomas, ed. *The Anti-Slavery Debate: Capitalism and Abolition as a Problem in Historical Interpretation.* Berkeley: Univ. of California Press, 1992.

Bennett, Lerone, Jr. *Forced into Glory: Abraham Lincoln's White Dream.* Chicago: Johnson Publishing Co., 2000.

Benson, Lee. *The Concept of Jacksonian Democracy: New York as a Test Case.* Princeton, NJ: Princeton Univ. Press, 1961.

Bercaw, Nancy. *Gendered Freedoms: Race, Rights, and the Politics of Household in the Delta, 1861-1875.* Gainesville: Univ. Press of Florida, 2003.

Bergad, Laird W. "American Slave Markets during the 1850s: Slave Price Rises in the United States, Cuba, and Brazil in Comparative Perspective." In *Slavery in the Development of the Americas,* edited by David Eltis, Frank D. Lewis, and Kenneth L. Sokoloff, 219-35. New York: Cambridge Univ. Press, 2004.

Berlin, Ira. *Generations of Captivity: A History of African American Slaves.* Cambridge, MA: Harvard Univ. Press, 2003.

————. *The Long Emancipation: The Demise of Slavery in the United States.* Cambridge, MA: Harvard Univ. Press, 2015.

————. *Many Thousands Gone: The First Two Centuries of Slavery in North America.* Cambridge, MA: Harvard Univ. Press, 1998.

————. "Review: Africa and Africans in the Making of the Atlantic World, 1400-1680 by John Thornton." *William and Mary Quarterly* 51, no. 3 (July 1994): 544-47.

————. "Review: Philadelphia's Black Elite: Activism, Accommodation, and the Struggle for Autonomy, 1787-1848 by Julie Winch." *Journal of American Ethnic History* 10, no. 3 (Spring 1991): 91-95.

————. *Slaves without Masters: The Free Negro in the Antebellum South.* New York: New Press, 1974.

————. "Time, Space, and the Evolution of Afro-American Society on British Mainland North America." *American Historical Review* 85, no. 1 (Feb. 1980): 44-78.

Berlin, Ira, Barbara J. Fields, Thavolia Glymph, Joseph P. Reidy, and Leslie S. Rowland, eds. *Freedom: A Documentary History of Emancipation, 1861-1867.* Series 1, vol. 1, *The Destruction of Slavery.* New York: Cambridge Univ. Press, 1986.

Berlin, Ira, Barbara J. Fields, Steven F. Miller, Joseph P. Reidy, and Leslie S. Rowland, eds. *Free at Last: A Documentary History of Slavery, Freedom, and the Civil War.* New York: New Press, 1993.

Berlin, Ira, Barbara J. Fields, Steven F. Miller, Joseph P. Reidy, and Leslie S. Rowland, eds. *Slaves No More: Three Essays on Emancipation and the Civil War.* New York: Cambridge Univ. Press, 1992.

Berlin, Ira, Thavolia Glymph, Steven F. Miller, Joseph P. Reidy, Leslie S. Rowland, and Julie Saville, eds. *Freedom: A Documentary History of Emancipation, 1861-1867.* Series 1, vol. 3, *The Wartime Genesis of Free Labor: The Lower South.* New York: Cambridge Univ. Press, 1990.

Berlin, Ira, and Leslie M. Harris, eds. *Slavery in New York.* New York: New Press, 2005.

Berlin, Ira, Steven F. Miller, Joseph P. Reidy, and Leslie S. Rowland, eds. *Free-dom: A Documentary History of Emancipation, 1861-1867.* Series 1, vol. 2, *The Wartime Genesis of Free Labor: The Upper South.* New York: Cambridge Univ. Press, 1993.

Berlin, Ira, and Phillip D. Morgan, eds. *Cultivation and Culture: Labor and the Shaping of Slave Life in the Americas.* Charlottesville: Univ. Press of Virginia, 1993.

Berlin, Ira, Joseph P. Reidy, and Leslie S. Rowland, eds. *Freedom: A Documentary History of Emancipation, 1861-1867.* Series 2, *The Black Military Experience.* New York: Cambridge Univ. Press, 1982.

Berlin, Ira, Joseph P. Reidy, and Leslie S. Rowland, eds. *Freedom's Soldiers: The Black Military Experience in the Civil War.* New York: Cambridge Univ. Press, 1998.

Berlin, Ira, and Leslie S. Rowland, eds. *Families and Freedom: A Documentary History of African-American Kinship in the Civil War Era.* New York: New Press, 1997.

Bernath, Michael T. *Confederate Minds: The Struggle for Intellectual Independence in the Civil War South.* Chapel Hill: Univ. of North Carolina Press, 2010.

Berry, Daina Ramey. "'In Pressing Need of Cash': Gender, Skill, and Family Persistence in the Domestic Slave Trade." *Journal of African American History* 92, no. 1 (Winter 2007): 22-36.

———. *The Price for Their Pound of Flesh: The Value of the Enslaved, from Womb to Grave, in the Building of a Nation.* Boston: Beacon Press, 2017.

———. *Swing the Sickle for the Harvest Is Ripe: Gender and Slavery in Antebellum Georgia.* Urbana: Univ. of Illinois Press, 2007.

———. "Teaching *Ar'n't I a Woman?*" *Journal of Women's History* 19, no. 2 (Summer 2007): 139-45.

Berry, Daina Ramey, and Leslie Harris, eds. *Sexuality and Slavery: Reclaiming Intimate Histories in the Americas.* Athens: Univ. of Georgia Press, 2018.

Biddle, Daniel R., and Murray Dubin. *Tasting Freedom: Octavius Catto and the Battle for Equality in Civil War America.* Philadelphia: Temple Univ. Press, 2010.

Blackett, R. J. M. *The Captive's Quest for Freedom: Fugitive Slaves, the 1850 Fugitive Slave Law, and the Politics of Slavery.* New York: Cambridge Univ. Press, 2018.

———. *Making Freedom: The Underground Railroad and the Politics of Freedom.* Chapel Hill: Univ. of North Carolina Press, 2013.

Blackburn, Robin. *The Making of New World Slavery: From the Baroque to the Modern, 1492-1800.* London: Verso, 1997.

———. *The Overthrow of Colonial Slavery, 1776-1848.* London: Verso, 1988.

Blackmon, Douglas A. *Slavery by Another Name: The Re-Enslavement of Black Americans from the Civil War to World War II.* New York: Anchor Books, 2008.

Blair, William A., and Karen Fisher Younger, eds. *Lincoln's Proclamation: Emancipation Reconsidered.* Chapel Hill: Univ. of North Carolina Press, 2012.

Blanck, Emily. *Tyrannicide: Forging an American Law of Slavery in Revolutionary South Carolina and Massachusetts.* Athens: Univ. of Georgia Press, 2014.

Blassingame, John W. *The Slave Community: Plantation Life in the Antebellum South.* New York: Oxford Univ. Press, 1972. Revised ed., 1979.

Blight, David W. *Frederick Douglass: Prophet of Freedom.* New York: Simon & Schuster, 2018.

———, ed. *Passages to Freedom: The Underground Railroad in History and Memory.* Washington, DC: Smithsonian Institution Press, 2001.

————. *Race and Reunion: The Civil War in American Memory.* Cambridge, MA: Harvard Univ. Press, 2001.

————. *A Slave No More: Two Men Who Escaped to Freedom, Including Their Own Narratives of Emancipation.* New York: Houghton Mifflin, 2007.

Bogue, Allan G. "United States: The 'New' Political History." *Journal of Contemporary History* 3, no. 1 (Jan. 1968): 5-27.

Bolster, W. Jeffery. *Black Jacks: African American Seamen in the Age of Sail.* Cambridge, MA: Harvard Univ. Press, 1997.

Bonner, Thomas N. "Civil War Historians and the 'Needless War' Doctrine." *Journal of the History of Ideas* 17, no. 2 (Apr. 1956): 193-216.

Boodry, Kathryn. "August Belmont and the World the Slaves Made." In *Slavery's Capitalism: A New History of American Economic Development,* edited by Sven Beckert and Seth Rockman, 163-78. Philadelphia: Univ. of Pennsylvania Press, 2016.

Bordewich, Fergus. *Bound for Canaan: The Underground Railroad and the War for the Soul of America.* New York: Amistad, 2005.

Bowman, Shearer Davis. *Masters and Lords: Mid-Nineteenth-Century U.S. Planters and Prussian Junkers.* New York: Oxford Univ. Press, 1993.

Brasher, Glenn David. *The Peninsula Campaign and the Necessity of Emancipation: African Americans and the Fight for Freedom.* Chapel Hill: Univ. of North Carolina Press, 2012.

Braudel, Fernand. *Capitalism and Material Life, 1400-1800.* Translated by Miriam Kochan. New York: Harper and Row, 1973.

Breen, Patrick. *The Land Shall Be Deluged in Blood: A New History of the Nat Turner Revolt.* New York: Oxford Univ. Press, 2015.

Breen, T. H. *Tobacco Culture: The Mentality of the Great Tidewater Planters on the Eve of Revolution.* Princeton, NJ: Princeton Univ. Press, 1985.

Breen, T. H., and Stephen Innes. *"Myne Owne Ground": Race and Freedom on Virginia's Eastern Shore, 1640-1676.* New York: Oxford Univ. Press, 1980.

Brom and Bett v. J. Ashley Esq. Supreme Judicial Court of Massachusetts (1781).

Brooks, James. *Captives and Cousins: Slavery, Kinship, and Community in the Southwest Borderlands.* Chapel Hill: Univ. of North Carolina Press, 2002.

Brown v. Board of Education of Topeka. 347 U.S. 483 (1954).

Brown, Bertram Wyatt. *Southern Honor: Ethics and Behavior in the Old South.* New York: Oxford Univ. Press, 1982.

Brown, Kathleen M. *Good Wives, Nasty Wenches, and Anxious Patriarchs: Gender, Race, and Power in Colonial Virginia.* Chapel Hill: Univ. of North Carolina Press, 1996.

Brown, William Wells. *My Southern Home: The South and Its People.* Boston: A. G. Brown & Co., 1880. Reprint, Chapel Hill: Univ. of North Carolina Press, 2011.

————. *The Negro in the American Rebellion: His Heroism and His Fidelity.* Boston: Lee and Shepard, 1867.

Bruce, Philip Alexander. "Evolution of the Negro Problem." *Sewanee Review* 19, no. 4 (Oct. 1911): 385-99.

Bryant, James K., II. *The 36th Infantry United States Colored Troops in the Civil War: A History and Roster.* Jefferson, NC: McFarland & Co., 2012.

Buchanan, Thomas C. *Black Life on the Mississippi: Slaves, Free Blacks, and the Western Steamboat World.* Chapel Hill: Univ. of North Carolina Press, 2004.

Burgess, John William. *The Civil War and the Constitution, 1859-1865.* 2 vols. New York: Charles Scribner's Sons, 1901.

———. *The Middle Period, 1817-1858.* New York: Charles Scribner's Sons, 1897.

Burke, Peter. *What Is Cultural History?* Malden, MA: Polity, 2008.

Burlingame, Michael. *Abraham Lincoln: A Life.* Baltimore: Johns Hopkins Univ. Press, 2013.

Bush, M. L., ed. *Serfdom and Slavery: Studies in Legal Bondage.* New York: Longman, 1996.

Butchart, Ronald E. *Schooling the Freed People: Teaching, Learning, and the Struggle for Black Freedom, 1861-1876.* Chapel Hill: Univ. of North Carolina Press, 2013.

Camp, Stephanie M. H. *"Ar'n't I a Woman?* In the Vanguard of the History of Race and Sex in the United States." *Journal of Women's History* 19, no. 2 (Summer 2007): 146-50.

———. *Closer to Freedom: Enslaved Women and Everyday Resistance in the Plantation South.* Chapel Hill: Univ. of North Carolina Press, 2004.

Campbell, Gwyn, Suzanne Miers, and Joseph C. Miller. "Women in Western Systems of Slavery: Introduction." *Slavery and Abolition* 26, no. 2 (2005): 161-79.

———, eds. *Women and Slavery.* Vol. 1, *Africa, the Indian Ocean World, and the Medieval North Atlantic.* Athens: Ohio Univ. Press, 2007.

———, eds. *Women and Slavery.* Vol. 2, *The Modern Atlantic.* Athens: Ohio Univ. Press, 2008.

Carden, Allen. *Freedom's Delay: America's Struggle for Emancipation, 1776-1865.* Knoxville: Univ. of Tennessee Press, 2014.

Carlton, David L., and Peter A. Coclanis. *The South, the Nation, and the World: Perspectives on Southern Economic Development.* Charlottesville: Univ. of Virginia Press, 2003.

Carnahan, Burrus M. *Act of Justice: Lincoln's Emancipation Proclamation and the Law of War.* Lexington: Univ. Press of Kentucky, 2007.

Carney, Judith Ann. *Black Rice: The African Origins of Rice Cultivation in the Americas.* Cambridge, MA: Harvard Univ. Press, 2001.

Carr, Lois Green, Philip D. Morgan, and Jean B. Russo, eds. *Colonial Chesapeake Society.* Chapel Hill: Univ. of North Carolina Press, 1989.

Carrington, Selwyn H. H., and Seymour Drescher. "Debate: *Econocide* and West Indian Decline, 1783-1806." *Boletin de Estudios Latinoamericanos y del Caribe* 36 (June 1984): 13-67.

Cartwright, Samuel A. "Diseases and Peculiarities of the Negro Race." *DeBow's Review* (New Orleans) 11, no. 3 (Sept. 1851): 331-36.

Cecelski, David S. *The Waterman's Song: Slavery and Freedom in Maritime North Carolina.* Chapel Hill: Univ. of North Carolina Press, 2001.

Chambers, A. B., ed. *Trials and Confessions of Madison Henderson, alias Blanchard, Alfred Amos Warrick, James W. Seward, and Charles Brown, Murderers of Jesse Baker and Jacob Weaver, as Given by Themselves.* St. Louis, MO: Chambers and Knapp, 1841.

Chambers, Douglas B. "Ethnicity in the Diaspora: The Slave Trade and the Creation of African 'Nations' in the Americas." *Slavery and Abolition* 22, no. 3 (2001): 25-39.

———. *Murder at Montpelier: Igbo Slaves in Virginia.* Jackson: Univ. of Mississippi Press, 2005.

Chandler, Charles. *The Story of a Slave. A Realistic Revelation of a Social Relation of Slave Times Hitherto Unwritten.* Chicago: Wesley, Elmore & Benson, 1894.

Cheek, William F. *Black Resistance before the Civil War.* Beverly Hills, CA: Glencoe Press, 1970.

Cheek, William, and Aimee L. Cheek. *John Mercer Langston and the Fight for Black Freedom, 1829-65.* Chicago: Univ. of Illinois Press, 1996.

Childers, Christopher. *The Failure of Popular Sovereignty: Slavery, Manifest Destiny, and the Radicalization of Southern Politics.* Lawrence: Univ. Press of Kansas, 2012.

Christopher, Emma. *Slave Ship Sailors and Their Captive Cargoes, 1730-1807.* New York: Cambridge Univ. Press, 2006.

Cimprich, John. *Slavery's End in Tennessee, 1861-1865.* Tuscaloosa: Univ. of Alabama Press, 2002.

Clark-Pujara, Christy. *Dark Work: The Business of Slavery in Rhode Island.* New York: New York Univ. Press, 2016.

Clarke, John Henrik, ed. *William Styron's Nat Turner: Ten Black Writers Respond.* Boston: Beacon Press, 1968.

Clavin, Matthew J. *The Battle of Negro Fort: The Rise and Fall of a Fugitive Slave Community.* New York: New York Univ. Press, 2019.

———. *Toussaint Louverture and the American Civil War: The Promise and Peril of a Second Haitian Revolution.* Philadelphia: Univ. of Pennsylvania Press, 2011.

Claxton, Melvin, and Mark Puls. *Uncommon Valor: A Story of Race, Patriotism, and Glory in the Final Battles of the Civil War.* Hoboken, NJ: Wiley, 2005.

Clamorgan, Cyprian. *The Colored Aristocracy of St. Louis.* Edited by Julie Winch. Columbia: Univ. of Missouri Press, 1999.

Clinton, Catherine. *Harriet Tubman: The Road to Freedom.* New York: Little, Brown & Co., 2004.

———. *The Plantation Mistress: Woman's World in the Old South.* New York: Pantheon Books, 1982.

———. *Southern Families at War: Loyalty and Conflict in the Civil War South.* New York: Oxford Univ. Press, 2000.

Clinton, Catherine, and Michele Gillespie, eds. *The Devil's Lane: Sex and Race in the Early South.* New York: Oxford Univ. Press, 1997.

Clinton, Catherine, and Nina Silber. *Divided Houses: Gender and the Civil War.* Oxford: Oxford Univ. Press, 1992.

Coclanis, Peter A. "How the Low Country Was Taken to Task: Slave-Labor Organization in Coastal South Carolina and Georgia." In *The South, the Nation, and the World: Perspectives on Southern Economic Development,* edited by David L. Carlton and Peter A. Coclanis, 24-34. Charlottesville: Univ. of Virginia Press, 2003.

———. "Tracking the Economic Divergence of the North and the South." *Southern Cultures* 6, no. 4 (Winter 2000): 82-103.

Coddington, Ronald S. *African American Faces of the Civil War: An Album.* Baltimore: Johns Hopkins Univ. Press, 2012.

Cody, Cheryll Ann. "Naming, Kinship, and Estate Dispersal: Notes on Slave Family Life on a South Carolina Plantation, 1786 to 1833." *William and Mary Quarterly* 32, no. 1 (Jan. 1982): 192-211.

———. "There Was No 'Absalom' on the Ball Plantations: Slave-Naming Practices in the South Carolina Low Country, 1720-1865." *American Historical Review* 92, no. 3 (June 1987): 563-96.

Coelho, Philip R., and Robert A. McGuire. "Diets Versus Diseases: The Anthropometrics of Slave Children." *Journal of Economic History* 60, no. 1 (Mar. 2000): 232-46.

Coffin, Joshua. *An Account of Some Principal Slave Insurrections.* New York: American Anti-Slavery Society, 1860.

Cohen, D. W., and J. P. Greene. *Neither Slave nor Free: The Freedman of African Descent in the Slave Societies of the New World.* Baltimore: Johns Hopkins Univ. Press, 1972.

Cohen Max. "Slavery in America: Some Historical Sites Try to Show the Horrors. Others Are Far Behind." *USA Today,* Oct. 17, 2019.

Cole, Arthur C. *The Irrepressible Conflict, 1850-1865.* New York: Macmillan, 1934.

———. "Lincoln's Election an Immediate Menace to Slavery in the States?" *American Historical Review* 36, no. 4 (July 1931): 740-67.

Cole, Shawn. "Capitalism and Freedom: Manumissions and the Slave Market in Louisiana, 1725-1820." *Journal of Economic History* 65, no. 4 (Dec. 2005): 1008-27.

Commonwealth of Massachusetts v. Nathaniel Jennison. Supreme Judicial Court of Massachusetts (1783).

Congressional Globe. 46 vols. Washington, DC: Blair & Rives, 1833-73.

Conrad, Alfred H., and John R. Meyer. "The Economics of Slavery in the Ante Bellum South." *Journal of Political Economy* 66, no. 2 (Apr. 1958): 95-130.

———. *The Economics of Slavery and Other Studies in Econometric History.* Chicago: Aldine Publishing, 1964.

Coontz, Stephanie. *The Way We Never Were: American Families and the Nostalgia Trap.* New York: Basic Books, 1992. Reprint, 2000.

Cooper, Anna Julia. "The Attitude of France on the Question of Slavery between 1789 and 1848." PhD diss., Sorbonne Université, 1925.

Cooper, Frederick, Thomas C. Holt, and Rebecca J. Scott. *Beyond Slavery: Explorations of Race, Labor, and Citizenship in Postemancipation Societies.* Chapel Hill: Univ. of North Carolina Press, 2000.

Cooper, Thomas. *Lectures on the Elements of Political Economy.* Columbia, SC: Doyle E. Sweeny, 1826.

Cornish, Dudley Taylor. *The Sable Arm: Negro Troops in the Union Army, 1861-1865.* New York: W. W. Norton & Co., 1966.

Coughtry, Jay. *The Notorious Triangle: Rhode Island and the African Slave Trade, 1700-1807.* Philadelphia: Temple Univ. Press, 1981.

Cox, Anna-Lisa. *The Bone and Sinew of the Land: America's Forgotten Black Pioneers and the Struggle for Equality.* New York: Hachette Book Group, 2018.

Cox, LaWanda. *Lincoln and Black Freedom: A Study in Presidential Leadership.* Columbia: Univ. of South Carolina Press, 1981.

Craven, Avery O. *The Coming of the Civil War.* New York: Charles Scribner's Sons, 1942.

———. "Poor Whites and Negroes in the Antebellum South." *Journal of Negro History* 15, no. 1 (Jan. 1930): 14-25.

———. *The Repressible Conflict, 1830-1961.* Baton Rouge: Louisiana State Univ. Press, 1939.

Creel, Margaret Washington. *"A Peculiar People": Slave Religion and Community-Culture Among the Gullah.* New York: New York Univ. Press, 1991.

Crofts, Daniel. *Lincoln and the Politics of Slavery: The Other Thirteenth Amendment and the Struggle to Save the Union.* Chapel Hill: Univ. of North Carolina Press, 2016.

Cruse, Harold. *The Crisis of the Negro Intellectual: A Historical Analysis of the Failure of Black Leadership.* New York: Morrow, 1967.

Curry, Leonard P. *The Free Black in Urban America, 1800-1850: The Shadow of the Dream.* Chicago: Univ. of Chicago Press, 1981.

Curtin, Philip D. *The Atlantic Slave Trade: A Census.* Madison: Univ. of Wisconsin Press, 1969.

Dagbovie, Pero Gaglo. "Black Women Historians from the Late Nineteenth Century to the Dawning of the Civil Rights Movement." *Journal of African American History* 89, no. 3 (Summer 2004): 241-61.

Dal Lago, Enrico. *William Lloyd Garrison and Giuseppe Mazzini: Abolition, Democracy, and Radical Reform.* Baton Rouge: Louisiana State Univ. Press, 2013.

Dari-Mattiacci, Giuseppe. "Slavery and Information." *Journal of Economic History* 73, no. 1 (Mar. 2013): 79-116.

Darity, William, Jr. "The Numbers Game and the Profitability of the British Trade in Slaves." *Journal of Economic History* 45, no. 3 (Sept. 1985): 693-703.

Dattel, Eugene R. *Cotton and Race in the Making of America: The Human Costs of Economic Power.* Chicago: Ivan R. Dee, 2009.

David, Paul A., Herbert G. Gutman, Richard Sutch, Peter Temin, and Gavin Wright. *Reckoning with Slavery: A Critical Study in the Quantitative History of American Negro Slavery.* New York: Oxford Univ. Press, 1976.

Davis, Angela. "Reflections on Black Women's Role in the Community of Slaves." *Black Scholar* 3, no. 4 (Dec. 1971): 2-15.

———, ed. *Women, Race, and Class.* New York: Vintage Books, 1983.

Davis, Charles S. *The Cotton Kingdom in Alabama.* Montgomery: Alabama Department of Archives and History, 1943.

Davis, David Brion. *Inhuman Bondage: The Rise and Fall of Slavery in the New World.* New York: Oxford Univ. Press, 2006.

———. *The Problem of Slavery in the Age of Emancipation.* New York: Alfred A. Knopf, 2014.

———. *The Problem of Slavery in the Age of Revolution, 1770-1823.* Ithaca, NY: Cornell Univ. Press, 1975.

———. *The Problem of Slavery in Western Culture.* Ithaca, NY: Cornell Univ. Press, 1966.

———. "A Review of the Conflicting Theories on the Slave Family." *Journal of Blacks in Higher Education* 16 (Summer 1997): 100-103.

———. *Slavery in the Colonial Chesapeake.* Williamsburg, VA: Colonial Williamsburg Foundation, 1986.

Davis, Edwin Adams. *Plantation Life in the Florida Parishes of Louisiana, 1836-1846, as Reflected in the Diary of Bennet H. Barrow.* New York: Columbia Univ. Press, 1943.

Davis, Jefferson. *The Rise and Fall of the Confederate Government.* 2 vols. New York: D. Appleton & Co., 1881.

Davidson, Basil. *Black Mother: The Years of the African Slave Trade.* Boston: Little, Brown & Co., 1961.

DeBow, J. D. B. "General Walker's Policy in Central America." *DeBow's Review* 28, no. 2 (Aug. 1860): 154-73.

Degler, Carl N. *Neither Black nor White: Slavery and Race Relations in Brazil and the United States.* New York: Macmillan, 1971.

Delbanco, Andrew. *The Abolitionist Imagination.* Cambridge, MA: Harvard Univ. Press, 2012.

———. *The War before the War: Fugitive Slaves and the Struggle for America's Soul from the Revolution to the Civil War.* New York: Penguin Press, 2018.

Desch-Obi, T. J. *Fighting for Honor: The History of African Martial Arts in the Atlantic World.* Columbia: Univ. of South Carolina Press, 2008.

Deverell, William. *Whitewashed Adobe: The Rise of Los Angeles and the Remaking of its Mexican Past.* Berkeley: Univ. of California Press, 2004.

DeVoto, Bernard. "The Easy Chair." *Harper's* 192, Apr. 1946, 126.

Dew, Charles B. *Apostles of Disunion: Southern Secession Commissioners and the Causes of the Civil War.* Charlottesville: Univ. of Virginia Press, 2001.

———. *Bond of Iron: Master and Slave at Buffalo Forge.* New York: W. W. Norton & Co., 1994.

———. *Ironmaker to the Confederacy: Joseph R. Anderson and the Tredegar Iron Works.* New Haven, CT: Yale Univ. Press, 1966.

Dew, Thomas R. *Lectures on the Restrictive System.* Richmond, VA: Samuel Shepherd & Co., 1829.

———. *Review of the Debate in the Virginia Legislature of 1831 and 1832.* Richmond, VA: T. W. White, 1832.

Deyle, Steven. "'By farr the most profitable trade': Slave Trading in British Colonial North America." *Slavery and Abolition* 10, no. 2 (1989): 107-25.

———. *Carry Me Back: The Domestic Slave Trade in American Life.* New York: Oxford Univ. Press, 2005.

———. "Rethinking the Slave Trade: Slave Traders and the Market Revolution in the South." In *The Old South's Modern Worlds: Slavery, Region, and Nation in the Age of Progress,* edited by L. Diane Barnes, Brian Schoen, and Frank Towers, 104-19. New York: Oxford Univ. Press, 2011.

Diemer, Andrew. *The Politics of Black Citizenship: Free African Americans in the Mid-Atlantic Borderland.* Athens: Univ. of Georgia Press, 2016.

Diouf, Sylviane A. *Dreams of Africa in Alabama: The Slave Ship Clotilda and the Story of the Last Africans Brought to America.* New York: Oxford Univ. Press, 2007.

———, ed. *Fighting the Slave Trade: West African Strategies.* Athens: Ohio Univ. Press, 2003.

———. *Slavery's Exiles: The Story of the American Maroons.* New York: New York Univ. Press, 2014.

Dobak, William A. *Freedom by the Sword: The U.S. Colored Troops, 1862-1867.* New York: Skyhorse Publishing, 2013.

Dodd, William E. *The Cotton Kingdom: A Chronicle of the Old South.* New Haven, CT: Yale Univ. Press, 1919.

Domosh, Mona. "A 'Civilized' Commerce: Gender, 'Race,' and Empire at the 1893 Chicago Exposition." *Cultural Geographies* 9, no. 2 (Apr. 2002): 181-201.

Donald, David. "American Historians and the Causes of the Civil War." *South Atlantic Quarterly* 59, no. 3 (Summer 1960): 351-55.

————. "An Excess of Democracy: The American Civil War and the Social Process." *Centennial Review* 5, no. 1 (Winter 1961): 21-39.

————. *Lincoln*. New York: Simon & Schuster, 1996.

Donnan, Elizabeth. *Documents Illustrative of the Slave Trade to America*. Washington, DC: Carnegie Institution of Washington, 1930.

————. "The New England Slave Trade after the Revolution." *New England Quarterly* 3, no. 2 (Apr. 1930): 251-78.

————. "The Slave Trade into South Carolina before the Revolution." *American Historical Review* 33, no. 4 (July 1928): 804-28.

Dormon, James H. "Shaping the Popular Image of Post-Reconstruction American Blacks: The 'Coon Song' Phenomenon of the Gilded Age." *American Quarterly* 40, no. 4 (Dec. 1988): 450-71.

Douglass, Frederick. *The Heroic Slave: Autographs for Freedom*. Boston: John P. Jewett & Co., 1853.

————. *Life and Times of Frederick Douglass, Written by Himself*. Hartford, CT: Park Publishing, 1881. Originally published as *Narrative of the Life of Frederick Douglass, an American Slave*. Boston: Anti-Slavery Office, 1845.

————. *My Bondage and My Freedom*. New York: Miller, Orton and Mulligan, 1855.

————. *Narrative of the Life of Frederick Douglass, an American Slave, Written by Himself*. Boston: Anti-Slavery Office, 1845.

————. "The Work of the Future." *Douglass' Monthly*, Nov. 1862.

Dowd, Jerome. "Slavery and the Slave Trade in Africa." *Journal of Negro History* 2, no. 1 (Jan. 1917): 1-20.

Downs, Gregory. *After Appomattox: Military Occupation and the Ends of War*. Cambridge, MA: Harvard Univ. Press, 2015.

Downs, Jim. *Sick from Freedom: African-American Illness and Suffering during the Civil War and Reconstruction*. New York: Oxford Univ. Press, 2012.

Dred Scott v. Sandford, 60 U.S. (19 How.) 393 (1857).

Drescher, Seymour. *Abolition: A History of Slavery and Anti-Slavery*. Cambridge, MA: Cambridge Univ. Press, 2009.

————. *Capitalism and Anti-Slavery: British Mobilization in Comparative Context*. Oxford: Oxford Univ. Press, 1987.

————. "The Decline Thesis of British Slavery since *Econocide*." *Slavery and Abolition* 7, no. 1 (1986): 3-24.

————. *Econocide: British Slavery in the Era of Abolition*. Pittsburgh, PA: Univ. of Pittsburgh Press, 1977.

————. *From Slavery to Freedom: Comparative Studies in the Rise and Fall of Atlantic Slavery*. New York: New York Univ. Press, 1999.

Duara, Prasenjit. *Rescuing History from the Nation: Questioning Narratives of Modern China*. Chicago: Univ. of Chicago Press, 1995.

Du Bois, W. E. B. *Black Reconstruction in America: Toward a History of the Part which Black Folk Played in the Attempt to Reconstruct Democracy in America, 1860-1880*. New York: Harcourt, Brace & Co., 1935. Reprint, London: Transaction Publishers, 2013.

————, ed. *The Negro American Family*. Atlanta, GA: Atlanta Univ. Press, 1909.

————. "Reconstruction and Its Benefits." *American Historical Review* 15, no. 4 (July 1910): 781-99.

————. *The Suppression of the African Slave-Trade to the United States of America, 1638-1870.* New York: Longmans, Green & Co., 1896. Reprint, New York: Oxford Univ. Press, 2007.

Duberman, Martin B., ed. *The Antislavery Vanguard.* Princeton, NJ: Princeton Univ. Press, 1965.

Duignan, Peter. *The United States and the African Slave Trade, 1619-1862.* Stanford, CA: Hoover Institution on War, Revolution, and Peace, 1963.

Dumond, Dwight. *Antislavery: The Crusade for Freedom in America.* New York: W. W. Norton & Co., 1961.

Dunaway, Wilma A. *The African American Family in Slavery and Emancipation.* New York: Cambridge Univ. Press, 2003.

————. *The First American Frontier: Transition to Capitalism in Southern Appalachia, 1700-1860.* Chapel Hill: Univ. of North Carolina Press, 1996.

————. *Slavery in the American Mountain South.* New York: Cambridge Univ. Press, 2003.

Dunbar, Edward E. *The History of the Rise and Decline of Commercial Slavery in America.* New York: Carlton, 1863.

————. *The Mexican Papers: The History of the Rise and Decline of Commercial Slavery in America, with Reference to the Future of Mexico.* New York: J. A. H. Hasbrouck & Co., 1861.

Dunbar, Erica Armstrong. *A Fragile Freedom: African American Women and Emancipation in the Antebellum City.* New Haven, CT: Yale Univ. Press, 2008.

Duncan, Russell. *Freedom's Shore: Tunis Campbell and the Georgia Freedmen.* Athens: Univ. of Georgia Press, 1986.

————. *Where Death and Glory Meet: Colonel Robert Gould Shaw and the 54th Massachusetts Infantry.* Athens: Univ. of Georgia Press, 1999.

Dunning, William Archibald. *Reconstruction, Political and Economic, 1865-1877.* New York: Harper & Brothers, 1907.

Dusinberre, William. *Them Dark Days: Slavery in the American Rice Swamps.* New York: Oxford Univ. Press, 1996.

Earle, Jonathan H. *Jacksonian Antislavery and the Politics of Free Soil, 1824-1854.* Chapel Hill: Univ. of North Carolina Press, 2004.

Earle, Jonathan H., and Diane Mutti Burke, eds. *Bleeding Kansas, Bleeding Missouri: The Long Civil War on the Border.* Lawrence: Univ. Press of Kansas, 2013.

Eaton, Clement. *A History of the Old South.* New York: Macmillan, 1949. Reprint, 1966.

Edwards, Justene Hill. *Unfree Markets: The Slaves' Economy and the Rise of Capitalism in South Carolina.* New York: Columbia Univ. Press, 2021.

Edwards, Laura. *Scarlett Doesn't Live Here Anymore: Southern Women in the Civil War Era.* Urbana: Univ. of Illinois Press, 2004.

Efford, Alison Clark. *German Immigrants, Race, and Citizenship in the Civil War Era.* New York: Cambridge Univ. Press, 2013.

Egerton, Douglas R. *He Shall Go Out Free: The Lives of Denmark Vesey.* Madison, WI: Madison House Publishers, 1999.

————. "Markets without a Market Revolution: Southern Planters and Capitalism." *Journal of the Early Republic* 16, no. 2 (Summer 1996): 207-21.

————. "Slaves to the Marketplace: Economic Liberty and Black Rebelliousness in the Atlantic World." *Journal of the Early Republic* 26, no. 4 (Winter 2006): 617-39.

————. *Year of Meteors: Stephen Douglas, Abraham Lincoln, and the Election that Brought on the Civil War.* New York: Bloomsbury, 2010.

Eichhorn, Niels. *Liberty and Slavery: European Separatists, Southern Secession, and the American Civil War.* Baton Rouge: Louisiana State Univ. Press, 2019.

Eichstedt, Jennifer L., and Stephen Small. *Representations of Slavery: Race and Ideology in Southern Plantation Museums.* Washington, DC: Smithsonian Institution Press, 2002.

Elkins, Stanley M. *Slavery: A Problem in American Institutional and Intellectual Life.* Chicago: Univ. of Chicago Press, 1959. Reprint, New York: Grosset & Dunlap, 1963.

Ellison, Mary. "Resistance to Oppression: Black Women's Response to Slavery in the United States." *Slavery and Abolition* 4, no. 1 (1983): 56-63.

Eltis, David. "A Brief Overview of the Trans-Atlantic Slave Trade." *Slave Voyages: The Trans-Atlantic Slave Trade Database* (website), Emory Univ., Atlanta, GA, 2007. https://www.slavevoyages.org/voyage/essays#interpretation/a-brief-overview-of-the-trans-atlantic-slave-trade/introduction/0/en (accessed Oct. 29, 2020).

————. *Economic Growth and the Ending of the Transatlantic Slave Trade.* New York: Oxford Univ. Press 1987.

————. "Fluctuations in the Age and Sex Ratios of Slaves in the Nineteenth-Century Transatlantic Slave Traffic." *Slavery and Abolition* 7, no. 3 (1986): 257-72.

————. "The U.S. Transatlantic Slave Trade, 1644-1867: An Assessment." *Civil War History* 54, no. 4 (Dec. 2008): 347-78.

————. "The Volume and Structure of the Transatlantic Slave Trade: A Reassessment." *William and Mary Quarterly* 58, no. 1 (Jan. 2001): 17-46.

Eltis, David, and David Richardson, eds. *Extending the Frontiers: Essays on the New Transatlantic Slave Trade Database.* New Haven, CT: Yale Univ. Press, 2008.

Eltis, David, Stephen D. Behrendt, David Richardson, and Herbert S. Klein. *The Trans-Atlantic Slave Trade: A Database on CD-ROM.* Cambridge: Cambridge Univ. Press, 1999.

Eltis, David, David Richardson, and Stephen Behrendt. "Patterns in the Transatlantic Slave Trade, 1662-1867: New Indications of African Origins of Slaves in the Americas." In *Black Imagination and the Middle Passage,* edited by Maria Diedrich, Henry Louis Gates Jr., and Carl Pedersen, 21-32. Oxford: Oxford Univ. Press, 1999.

Ely, Melvin Patrick. *Israel on the Appomattox: A Southern Experiment in Black Freedom from the 1790s through the Civil War.* New York: Alfred A. Knopf, 2005.

Emberton, Carole. "Only Murder Makes Men." *Journal of the Civil War Era* 2, no. 3 (Sept. 2012): 369-93.

Engerman, Stanley L. "Quantitative and Economic Analyses of West Indian Slave Societies: Research Problems." In *Comparative Perspectives on Slavery in New World Plantation Societies: Annals of the New York Academy of Sciences,* edited by Vera Rubin and Arthur Tuden, 597-609. New York: New York Academy of Sciences, 1977.

————. "The Slave Trade and British Capital Formation in the Eighteenth Century: A Comment on the Williams Thesis." *Business History Review* 46, no. 4 (Winter 1972): 430-43.

An Epistle of Caution and Advice concerning the Buying and Keeping of Slaves. Philadelphia Yearly Meeting of the Religious Society of Friends. Church-Alley, PA: James Chattin, 1754.

Epps, Kristen. *Slavery on the Periphery: The Kansas-Missouri Border in the Antebellum and Civil War Eras.* Athens: Univ. of Georgia Press, 2016.

Equiano, Olaudah. *The Interesting Narrative of the Life of Olaudah Equiano, or Gustavus Vassa, the African. Written by Himself.* London, 1789.

Escott, Paul D. "The Context of Freedom: Georgia's Slaves during the Civil War." *Georgia Historical Quarterly* 58, no. 1 (Apr. 1974): 79-104.

Essah, Patience. *A House Divided: Slavery and Emancipation in Delaware, 1638-1865.* Charlottesville: Univ. Press of Virginia, 1996.

Etcheson, Nicole. *Bleeding Kansas: Contested Liberty in the Civil War Era.* Lawrence: Univ. Press of Kansas, 2004.

———. *The Emerging Midwest: Upland Southerners and the Political Culture of the Old Northwest, 1787-1861.* Bloomington: Indiana Univ. Press, 1996.

———. *A Generation at War: The Civil War in a Northern Community.* Lawrence: Univ. Press of Kansas, 2011.

———. "Microhistory and Movement: African American Mobility in the Nineteenth Century." *Journal of the Civil War Era* 3, no. 3 (Sept. 2013): 392-404.

Evans, Sara. *Personal Politics: The Roots of Women's Liberation in the Civil Rights Movement and the New Left.* New York: Vintage Books, 1980.

Fage, J. D. "The Effect of the Slave Trade on African Population." In *The Population Factor in African Studies,* edited by R. P. Moss and R. J. A. R. Rathbone, 15-23. London: Univ. of London Press, 1975.

———. "Slavery and the Slave Trade in the Context of West African History." *Journal of African History* 10, no. 3 (July 1969): 393-404.

Farmer-Kaiser, Mary J. *Freedwomen and the Freedmen's Bureau: Race, Gender, and Public Policy in the Age of Emancipation.* New York: Fordham Univ. Press, 2010.

Faust, Drew Gilpin, ed. *The Ideology of Slavery: Proslavery Thought in the Antebellum South, 1830-1860.* Baton Rouge: Louisiana State Univ. Press, 1981.

———. *James Henry Hammond and the Old South: A Design for Mastery.* Baton Rouge: Louisiana State Univ. Press, 1982.

———. *Mothers of Invention: Women of the Slaveholding South in the American Civil War.* Chapel Hill: Univ. of North Carolina Press, 2006.

———. *A Sacred Circle: The Dilemma of the Intellectual in the Old South, 1840-1860.* Baltimore: John Hopkins Univ. Press, 1977.

Federal Writers' Project. *Slave Narratives: A Folk History of Slavery in the United States from Interviews with Former Slaves.* 17 vols. Washington, DC: Library of Congress, 1941. Also available in digital form as part of the Library of Congress digital collection *Born in Slavery: Slave Narratives from the Federal Writers' Project, 1936-1938.* https://www.loc.gov/collections/slave-narratives from-the-federal-writers-project-1936-to-1938/about-this-collection (accessed Nov. 22, 2020).

Fehrenbacher, Don E. "The New Political History and the Coming of the Civil War." *Pacific Historical Review* 54, no. 2 (May 1985): 117-42.

———. *The Slaveholding Republic: An Account of the United States Government's Relations to Slavery.* New York: Oxford Univ. Press, 2001.

Fett, Sharla M. *Recaptured Africans: Surviving Slave Ships, Detention, and Dislocation in the Final Years of the Slave Trade.* Chapel Hill: Univ. of North Carolina Press, 2017.

————. *Working Cures: Healing, Health and Power on Southern Slave Plantations.* Chapel Hill: Univ. of North Carolina Press, 2002.

Fields, Barbara Jeanne. *Slavery and Freedom on the Middle Ground: Maryland during the Nineteenth Century.* New Haven, CT: Yale Univ. Press, 1984.

Filler, Louis. *The Crusade against Slavery, 1830-1860.* New York: Harper, 1960.

Finkelman, Paul. *Slavery and the Founders: Race and Liberty in the Age of Jefferson.* New York: Taylor and Francis, 2014.

————. *Supreme Injustice: Slavery in the Nation's Highest Court.* Cambridge, MA: Harvard Univ. Press, 2018.

Finley, Alexandra J. *An Intimate Economy: Enslaved Women, Work, and America's Domestic Slave Trade.* Chapel Hill: Univ. of North Carolina Press, 2020.

Fitzhugh, George. *Cannibals All! or, Slaves without Masters.* Richmond, VA: A. Morris, 1857.

————. *Sociology for the South, or, The Failure of Free Society.* Richmond, VA: A. Morris, 1854.

Flanders, Ralph B. *Plantation Slavery in Georgia.* Chapel Hill: Univ. of North Carolina Press, 1933.

Fleisig, Heywood. "Slavery, the Supply of Agricultural Labor, and the Industrialization of the South." *Journal of Economic History* 36, no. 3 (Sept. 1976): 572-97.

Fleming, Victor, dir. *Gone with the Wind.* Culver City, CA: Selznick International Pictures, 1939.

Fogel, Robert William. *The Slavery Debate, 1952-1990: A Retrospective.* Baton Rouge: Louisiana State Univ. Press, 2003.

————. *Without Consent or Contract: The Rise and Fall of American Slavery.* New York: W. W. Norton & Co., 1989.

Fogel, Robert W., and Stanley L. Engerman. *Time on the Cross: The Economics of American Negro Slavery.* Boston: Little, Brown & Co., 1974.

Follett, Richard. "'Lives of Living Death': The Reproductive Lives of Slave Women in the Cane World of Louisiana." *Slavery and Abolition* 26, no. 2 (2005): 289-304.

————. *The Sugar Masters: Planters and Slaves in Louisiana's Cane World, 1820-1860.* Baton Rouge: Louisiana State Univ. Press, 2005.

Follett, Richard, Sven Beckert, Peter Coclanis, and Barbara Hahn. *Plantation Kingdom: The American South and Its Global Commodities.* Baltimore: Johns Hopkins Univ. Press, 2016.

Foner, Eric. *The Fiery Trial: Abraham Lincoln and American Slavery.* New York: W. W. Norton & Co., 2011.

————. *Forever Free: The Story of Emancipation and Reconstruction.* New York: Alfred A. Knopf, 2005.

————. *Free Soil, Free Labor, Free Men: The Ideology of the Republican Party before the Civil War.* New York: Oxford Univ. Press, 1970.

————. *Gateway to Freedom: The Hidden History of the Underground Railroad.* New York: W. W. Norton, 2015.

————. *Politics and Ideology in the Age of the Civil War.* New York: Oxford Univ. Press, 1980.

————. *Reconstruction: America's Unfinished Revolution, 1863-1877.* New York: Harper Perennial Modern Classics, 2002.

————. *The Second Founding: How the Civil War and Reconstruction Remade the Constitution.* New York: W. W. Norton & Co., 2019.

Foner, Eric, and Steven Hahn. *Nothing but Freedom: Emancipation and Its Legacy.* Baton Rouge: Louisiana State Univ. Press, 2007.

Foner, Laura. "The Free People of Color in Louisiana and Saint Domingue." *Journal of Social History* 3, no. 4 (Summer 1970): 406-30.

Foner, Philip, ed. *Frederick Douglass: Selections from His Writings.* New York: International Publishers, 1945.

Foote, Thelma. "'Some Hard Usage': The New York City Slave Revolt." *New York Folklore* 28 (2001): 147-59.

Ford, Lacy K. *Origins of Southern Radicalism: The South Carolina Upcountry, 1800-1860.* New York: Oxford Univ. Press, 1991.

Formisano, Ronald P. *The Birth of Mass Political Parties: Michigan, 1827-1861.* Princeton, NJ: Princeton Univ. Press, 1971.

Forret, Jeff. *Race Relations at the Margins: Slaves and Poor Whites in the Antebellum Southern Countryside.* Baton Rouge: Louisiana State Univ. Press, 2006.

————. *Slave against Slave: Plantation Violence in the Old South.* Baton Rouge: Louisiana State Univ. Press, 2015.

Forret, Jeff, and Christine E. Sears, eds. *New Directions in Slavery Studies: Commodification, Community, and Comparison.* Baton Rouge: Louisiana State Univ. Press, 2015.

Foster, Thomas A. "The Sexual Abuse of Black Men under American Slavery." *Journal of the History of Sexuality* 20, no. 3 (Sept. 2011): 445-64.

Fox-Genovese, Elizabeth. *Within the Plantation Household: Black and White Women of the Old South.* Chapel Hill: Univ. of North Carolina Press, 1988.

Frankel, Noralee. *Freedom's Women: Black Women and Families in Civil War Era Mississippi.* Bloomington: Indiana Univ. Press, 1999.

Franklin, Benjamin. "Petition from the Pennsylvania Society for Promoting the Abolition of Slavery to Vice President John Adams." Feb. 3, 1790. Record group 46, Benjamin Franklin's Anti-Slavery Petitions to Congress, Records of the United States Senate, Center for Legislative Archives, Washington, DC. https://www.archives.gov/legislative/features/franklin (accessed Oct. 29, 2020).

Franklin, John Hope. *The Emancipation Proclamation.* New York: Doubleday, 1963.

————. *The Free Negro in North Carolina, 1790-1860.* Chapel Hill: Univ. of North Carolina Press, 1943.

————. *From Slavery to Freedom: A History of American Negroes.* New York: Alfred A. Knopf, 1947.

————. *The Militant South, 1800-1861.* Cambridge, MA: Harvard Univ. Press, 1956.

Frazier, E. Franklin. *The Negro Family in the United States.* Chicago: Univ. of Chicago Press, 1939.

Fredrickson, George M. *Big Enough to Be Inconsistent: Abraham Lincoln Confronts Slavery and Race.* Cambridge, MA: Harvard Univ. Press, 2009.

————. *The Black Image in the White Mind: The Debate on Afro-American Character and Destiny, 1817-1914.* New York: Harper & Row, 1971.

Fredrickson, George M. and Christopher Lasch. "Resistance to Slavery." *Civil War History* 13, no. 4 (Dec. 1967): 315-29.

Freehling, William W. "The Founding Fathers and Slavery." *American Historical Review* 7, no. 1 (Feb. 1972): 81-93.

———. *Prelude to Civil War: The Nullification Controversy in South Carolina, 1816-1836.* New York: Harper & Row, 1966.

———. *The Reintegration of American History: Slavery and the Civil War.* New York: Oxford Univ. Press, 1994.

———. *The Road to Disunion.* Vol. 1, *Secessionists at Bay, 1776-1854.* New York: Oxford Univ. Press, 1990.

———. *The Road to Disunion.* Vol. 2, *Secessionists Triumphant, 1854-1861.* New York: Oxford Univ. Press, 2007.

———. *The South vs. The South: How Anti-Confederate Southerners Shaped the Course of the Civil War.* New York: Oxford Univ. Press, 2001.

Freeman, Joanne. *The Field of Blood: Violence in Congress and the Road to Civil War.* New York: Farrar, Straus and Giroux, 2018.

Freudenberger, Herman, and Jonathan B. Pritchett. "The Domestic United States Slave Trade: New Evidence." *Journal of Interdisciplinary History* 21, no. 3 (Winter 1991): 447-77.

Frey, Sylvia R. *Water from the Rock: Black Resistance in a Revolutionary Age.* Princeton, NJ: Princeton Univ. Press, 1991.

Frey, Sylvia R., and Betty Wood. *Come Shouting to Zion: African American Protestantism in the American South and British Caribbean to 1830.* Chapel Hill: Univ. of North Carolina Press, 1998.

Freyre, Gilberto. *The Masters and the Slaves: A Study in the Development of Brazilian Civilization.* Translated by Samuel Putnam. New York: Alfred A. Knopf, 1946. Reprint, 1956.

Frost, Karolyn Smardz, and Veta Smith Tucker. *A Fluid Frontier: Slavery, Resistance, and the Underground Railroad in the Detroit River Borderland.* Detroit: Wayne State Univ. Press, 2016.

Furstenberg, François. *In the Name of the Father: Washington's Legacy, Slavery, and the Making of a Nation.* New York: Penguin Press, 2006.

Furstenberg, François, Theodore Hershberg, and John Modell. "The Origins of the Female-Headed Black Family: The Impact of the Urban Environment." In *Philadelphia: Work, Space, Family and Group Experience in the Nineteenth Century,* edited by Theodore Hershberg, 435-55. New York: Oxford Univ. Press, 1981.

Gabrial, Brian. *The Press and Slavery in America, 1791-1859: The Melancholy Effect of Popular Excitement.* Columbia: Univ. of South Carolina Press, 2016.

Galenson, David W. "Labor Market Behavior in Colonial America: Servitude, Slavery, and Free Labor." In *Markets in History: Economic Studies of the Past,* edited by David Galenson, 52-96. New York: Cambridge Univ. Press, 1989.

Gallagher, Gary W. *The Union War.* Cambridge, MA: Harvard Univ. Press, 2011.

Gallay, Alan. *The Indian Slave Trade: The Rise of the English Empire in the American South, 1670-1717.* New Haven, CT: Yale Univ. Press, 2002.

Gallman, Robert E. "Slavery and Southern Economic Growth." *Southern Economic Journal* 45, no. 4 (Apr. 1979): 1007-22.

Gannon, Barbara A. *The Won Cause: Black and White Comradeship in the Grand Army of the Republic.* Chapel Hill: Univ. of North Carolina Press, 2014.

Garrison, William Lloyd. "The Insurrection." *The Liberator* (Boston), Sept. 3, 1831.

———. "Gabriel's Defeat." *The Liberator,* Sept. 17, 1831.

Garrison, Zachary Stuart. *German Americans on the Middle Border: From Antislavery to Reconciliation, 1830-1877.* Carbondale: Southern Illinois Univ. Press, 2019.

Gaspar, David Barry, and Darlene Clark Hine, eds. *Beyond Bondage: Free Women of Color in the Americas.* Urbana: Univ. of Illinois Press, 2004.

———, eds. *More than Chattel: Black Women and Slavery in the Americas.* Bloomington: Indiana Univ. Press, 1996.

Geggus, David, ed. *The Impact of the Haitian Revolution in the Atlantic World.* Columbia: Univ. of South Carolina Press, 2001.

———. "Sex Ratio, Age, and Ethnicity in the Atlantic Slave Trade: Data from French Shipping and Plantation Records." *Journal of African History* 30, no. 1 (Mar. 1989): 23-44.

Genovese, Eugene D. *From Rebellion to Revolution: Afro-American Slave Revolts in the Making of the Modern World.* Baton Rouge: Louisiana State Univ. Press, 1979.

———. *The Political Economy of Slavery: Studies in the Economy and Society of the Slave South.* New York: Pantheon, 1965.

———. "Race and Class in Southern History: An Appraisal of the Work of Ulrich Bonnell Phillips." *Agricultural History* 41, no. 4 (Oct. 1967): 345-58.

———. *Roll, Jordan, Roll: The World the Slaves Made.* New York: Pantheon, 1974. Reprint, New York: Vintage, 1976.

Genovese, Eugene D., and Elizabeth Fox-Genovese. *Fruits of Merchant Capital: Slavery and Bourgeois Property in the Rise and Expansion of Capitalism.* New York: Oxford Univ. Press, 1983.

———. "Slavery, Economic Development, and the Law: The Dilemma of the Southern Political Economists, 1800-1860." *Washington and Lee Law Review* 41, no. 1 (Winter 1984): 1-29.

Gienapp, William. *The Origins of the Republican Party, 1852-1856.* New York: Oxford Univ. Press, 1987.

Glatthaar, Joseph T. *Forged in Battle: The Civil War Alliance of Black Soldiers and White Officers.* Baton Rouge: Louisiana State Univ. Press, 2000.

Glymph, Thavolia. *Out of the House of Bondage: The Transformation of the Plantation Household.* New York: Cambridge Univ. Press, 2008.

Goggin, Jacqueline. "Countering White Racist Scholarship: Carter G. Woodson and *The Journal of Negro History.*" *Journal of Negro History* 68, no. 4 (Autumn 1983): 355-56.

Goldin, Claudia. "Cliometrics and the Nobel." *Journal of Economic Perspectives* 9, no. 2 (Spring 1995): 191-208.

———. *Urban Slavery in the American South, 1820-1860.* Chicago: Univ. of Chicago Press, 1976.

Gomez, Michael A. *Exchanging Our Country Marks: The Transformation of African Identities in the Colonial and Antebellum South.* Chapel Hill: Univ. of North Carolina Press, 1998.

Goodheart, Lawrence B., Richard D. Brown, and Stephen G. Rabe, eds. *Slavery in American Society.* Lexington, MA: D. C. Heath, 1969.

Gordon-Reed, Annette. *Thomas Jefferson and Sally Hemings: An American Controversy.* Charlottesville: Univ. Press of Virginia, 1997.

Govan, Thomas P. "Was Plantation Slavery Profitable?" *Journal of Southern History* 8, no. 4 (Nov. 1942): 513-35.

Gramsci, Antonio. *Selections from the Prison Notebooks.* New York: International Publishers, 1971.

Gray, Elizabeth Kelly. "'Whisper to him the word 'India'": Trans-Atlantic Critics and American Slavery, 1830-1860." *Journal of the Early American Republic* 28, no. 3 (Fall 2008): 379-406.

Gray, Lewis Cecil. *History of Agriculture in the Southern United States to 1860.* Washington, DC: Carnegie Institution of Washington, 1933.

———. "Southern Agriculture, Plantation System, and the Negro Problem." *Annals of the American Academy of Political and Social Science* 40, no. 1 (Mar. 1912): 90-99.

Grayson, William J. *The Hireling and the Slave.* Charleston, SC: John Russell, 1855.

Greenberg, Kenneth S. *Masters and Statesmen: The Political Culture of American Slavery.* Baltimore: John Hopkins Univ. Press, 1985.

Green, Michael. *Freedom, Union, and Power: Lincoln and His Party in the Civil War.* New York: Fordham Univ. Press, 2004.

Greene, Jack P. *Pursuits of Happiness: The Social Development of Early Modern British Colonies and the Formation of American Culture.* Chapel Hill: Univ. of North Carolina Press, 1988.

Greene, Lorenzo Johnston. *The Negro in Colonial New England, 1620-1776.* New York: Columbia Univ. Press, 1942.

Greene, Lorenzo J., and Carter G. Woodson. *The Negro Wage Earner.* Washington, DC: Association for the Study of Negro Life and History, 1930.

Griffith, D. W., dir. *The Birth of a Nation.* (Original title: *The Clansman.*) Hollywood, CA: David W. Griffith Corp., 1915.

Grimshaw, William. *History of the United States, from Their First Settlement as Colonies, to the Period of the Fifth Census, in 1830: Comprising Every Important Political Event.* Philadelphia: Grigg & Elliot, 1840.

Grivno, Max. *Gleanings of Freedom: Free and Slave Labor along the Mason-Dixon Line, 1790-1860.* Urbana: Univ. of Illinois Press, 2014.

Gross, Robert A. "Forum: The Making of a Slave Conspiracy, part 1—Introduction." *William and Mary Quarterly* 58, no. 4 (Oct. 2001): 913-14.

———. "Forum: The Making of a Slave Conspiracy, part 2." *William and Mary Quarterly* 59, no. 1 (Jan. 2002): 135-36.

Gudmestad, Robert H. *A Troublesome Commerce: The Transformation of the Interstate Slave Trade.* Baton Rouge: Louisiana State Univ. Press, 2003.

Guelzo, Allen C. *Lincoln's Emancipation Proclamation: The End of Slavery in America.* New York: Simon & Schuster, 2006.

Guterl, Matthew Pratt. *American Mediterranean: Southern Slaveholders in the Age of Emancipation.* Cambridge, MA: Harvard Univ. Press, 2008.

Gutman, Herbert G. *The Black Family in Slavery and Freedom, 1750-1925.* New York: Pantheon Books, 1976.

———. *Slavery and the Numbers Game: A Critique of Time on the Cross.* Urbana: Univ. of Illinois Press, 1975. Reprint, 2003.

———. "Work, Culture, and Society in Industrializing America, 1815-1919." *American Historical Review* 78, no. 3 (June 1973): 531-88.

Hahn, Steven. "Class and State in Postemancipation Societies: Southern Planters in Comparative Perspective." *American Historical Review* 95, no. 1 (Feb. 1990): 75-98.

———. *A Nation under Our Feet: Black Political Struggles in the Rural South from Slavery to the Great Migration.* Cambridge, MA: Harvard Univ. Press, 2005.

———. *The Political. Worlds of Slavery and Freedom.* Cambridge, MA: Harvard Univ. Press, 2009.

———. "Slave Emancipation, Indian Peoples, and the Projects of a New American Nation-State." *Journal of the Civil War Era* 3, no. 3 (Sept. 2013): 307-30.

Hahn, Steven, Steven F. Miller, Susan E. O'Donovan, John C. Rodrigue, and Leslie S. Rowland, eds. *Freedom: A Documentary History of Emancipation, 1861-1867.* Series 3, vol. 1, *Land and Labor, 1865.* Chapel Hill: Univ. of North Carolina Press, 2008.

Hall, Gwendolyn Midlo. *Africans in Colonial Louisiana: The Development of Afro-Creole Culture in the Eighteenth Century.* Baton Rouge: Louisiana State Univ. Press, 1992.

———. *Slavery and African Ethnicities in the Americas: Restoring the Links.* Chapel Hill: Univ. of North Carolina Press, 2005.

Hall, Jacquelyn Dowd. "The Long Civil Rights Movement and the Political Uses of the Past." *Journal of American History* 91, no. 4 (Mar. 2005): 1233-63.

Hammond, James Henry. *Selections from the Letters and Speeches of the Hon. James H. Hammond of South Carolina.* New York: J. F. Trow & Co., 1866.

Hammond, John Craig. *Slavery, Freedom, and Expansion in the Early American West.* Charlottesville: Univ. of Virginia Press, 2007.

Hammond, John Craig, and Matthew Mason, eds. *Contesting Slavery: The Politics of Bondage and Freedom in the New American Nation.* Charlottesville: Univ. of Virginia Press, 2011.

Handlin, Oscar, and Mary F. Handlin. "Origins of the Southern Labor System." *William and Mary Quarterly* 7, no. 2 (Apr. 1950): 199-222.

Hanes, Christopher. "Turnover Cost and the Distribution of Slave Labor in Anglo-America." *Journal of Economic History* 56, no. 2 (June 1996): 307-29.

Hanger, Kimberly S. *Bounded Lives, Bounded Places: Free Black Society in Colonial New Orleans, 1769-1803.* Durham, NC: Duke Univ. Press, 1997.

———. "Coping in a Complex World: Free Black Women in Colonial New Orleans." In *The Devil's Lane: Sex and Race in the Early South,* edited by Catherine Clinton and Michele Gillespie, 218-31. New York: Oxford Univ. Press, 1997.

Hannah-Jones, Nikole, ed. "The 1619 Project" (website). *New York Times Magazine,* 2019-ongoing. https://www.nytimes.com/interactive/2019/08/14/maga zine/1619-america-slavery.html (accessed Oct. 29, 2020).

Harlow, Luke. *Religion, Race, and the Making of Confederate Kentucky, 1830-1880.* New York: Cambridge Univ. Press, 2014.

Harris, Joel Chandler. *Free Joe and Other Georgian Sketches.* New York: Charles Scribner's Sons, 1887.

Harris, Leslie M. *"Ar'n't I a Woman?,* Gender, and Slavery Studies." *Journal of Women's History* 19, no. 2 (Summer 2007): 151-55.

———. "Enchained Masculinity: African American Men of the Slave South." (Manuscript in progress.)

———. *In the Shadow of Slavery: African Americans in New York City, 1626-1863.* Chicago: Univ. of Chicago Press, 2003.

Harris, Leslie, and Daina Ramey Berry, eds. *Slavery and Freedom in Savannah.* Athens: Univ. of Georgia Press, 2013.

Harris, Sheldon H. *Paul Cuffe: Black America and the African Return.* New York: Simon & Schuster, 1972.

Harrold, Stanley. *Border War: Fighting over Slavery before the Civil War.* Chapel Hill: Univ. of North Carolina Press, 2010.

Hartman, Saidiya V. *Scenes of Subjection: Terror, Slavery, and Self-Making in Nineteenth-Century America.* New York: Oxford Univ. Press, 1997.

Hashaw, Tim. *The Birth of Black America: The First African Americans and the Pursuit of Freedom at Jamestown.* New York: Basic Books, 2007.

Hayden, René, Anthony E. Kaye, Kate Masur, Steven F. Miller, Susan E. O'Donovan, Leslie S. Rowland, and Stephen A. West, eds. *Freedom: A Documentary History of Emancipation, 1861-1867.* Series 3, vol. 2, *Land and Labor, 1866-1867.* Chapel Hill: Univ. of North Carolina Press, 2013.

Haywood, Linda M., and John K. Thornton. *Central Africans, Atlantic Creoles, and the Foundation of the Americas, 1585-1660.* New York: Cambridge Univ. Press, 2007.

Helg, Aline. *Slave No More: Self-Liberation before Abolitionism in the Americas.* Chapel Hill: Univ. of North Carolina Press, 2019.

Helper, Hinton Rowan. *The Impending Crisis of the South: How to Meet It.* New York: Burdick Brothers, 1857.

Hershberg, Theodore, ed. *Philadelphia: Work, Space, Family and Group Experience in the Nineteenth Century.* New York: Oxford Univ. Press, 1981.

Herskovits, Melville J. *The Myth of the Negro Past.* New York: Harper & Brothers, 1941. Reprint, Boston: Beacon Press, 1990.

Heywood, Linda M., and John K. Thornton. *Central Africans, Atlantic Creoles, and the Foundation of the Americas, 1585-1660.* New York: Cambridge Univ. Press, 2007.

Higginbotham, A. Leon, Jr., *In the Matter of Color: Race and the American Legal Process—The Colonial Period.* New York: Oxford Univ. Press, 1978.

Higginbotham, Evelyn Brooks. "African-American Women's History and the Metalanguage of Race." *Signs* 17, no. 2 (Winter 1992): 251-74.

Higginson, Thomas Wentworth. *Travellers and Outlaws: Episodes in American History.* Boston: Lee and Shepard, 1889.

Higman, B. W. *Slave Population and Economy in Jamaica, 1807-1834.* New York: Cambridge Univ. Press, 1977.

Hilde, Libra R. *Slavery, Fatherhood, and Paternal Duty in African American Communities over the Long Nineteenth Century.* Chapel Hill: Univ. of North Carolina Press, 2020.

Hine, Darlene Clark. *"Ar'n't I a Woman? Female Slaves in the Plantation South: Twenty Years After."* *Journal of African American History* 92, no. 1 (Winter 2007): 13-21.

Hine, Darlene Clark, and Kate Wittenstein. "Female Slave Resistance: The Economics of Sex." In *The Black Woman Cross-Culturally,* edited by Filomena Chioma Steady, 289-99. Cambridge, MA: Schenkman, 1981.

Hine, Darlene Clark, William C. Hine, and Stanley Harrold. *The African-American Odyssey.* Vol. 1, *To 1877.* Upper Saddle River, NJ: Pearson, 2000.

Hinks, Peter P. *To Awaken My Afflicted Brethren: David Walker and the Problem of Antebellum Slave Resistance.* University Park: Pennsylvania State Univ. Press, 1996.

Hodes, Martha. *White Women, Black Men: Illicit Sex in the Nineteenth-Century South.* New Haven, CT: Yale Univ. Press, 1999.

Hofstadter, Richard. *The Progressive Historians: Turner, Beard, Parrington.* New York: Alfred A. Knopf, 1968.

Holland, Antonio F., and Debra Foster Greene. "Not Chattel, Not Free: Quasi-Free Blacks in the Colonial Era." In *A Companion to African American History*, edited by Alton Hornsby Jr., 105-20. Boston: Blackwell Publishing, 2005.

Holloway, Joseph E., ed. *Africanisms in American Culture*. Bloomington: Indiana Univ. Press, 1990.

Holsey, Bayo. *Routes of Remembrance: Refashioning the Slave Trade in Ghana*. Chicago: Univ. of Chicago Press, 2008.

Holt, Michael F. *The Election of 1860: A Campaign Fraught with Consequences*. Lawrence: Univ. Press of Kansas, 2017.

———. *Forging a Majority: The Formation of the Republican Party in Pittsburgh, 1848-1860*. New Haven, CT: Yale Univ. Press, 1969.

———. *The Political Crisis of the 1850s*. New York: Wiley, 1978.

Holt, Thomas C. "Explaining Abolition." *Journal of Social History* 24, no. 2 (Winter 1990): 371-78.

Holzer, Harold. *Emancipating Lincoln: The Proclamation in Text, Context, and Memory*. Cambridge, MA: Harvard Univ. Press, 2012.

Honeck, Mischa. *We Are the Revolutionists: German-Speaking Immigrants and American Abolitionists after 1848*. Athens: Univ. of Georgia Press, 2011.

Horne, Gerald. *The Counter-Revolution of 1776: Slave Resistance and the Origins of the United States of America*. New York: New York Univ. Press, 2014.

Horton, James Oliver. *Free People of Color: Inside the African American Community*. Washington, DC: Smithsonian Institution Press, 1993.

Horton, James Oliver, and Lois E. Horton. *In Hope of Liberty: Culture, Community and Protest among Northern Free Blacks, 1700-1860*. New York: Oxford Univ. Press, 1997.

———, eds. *Slavery and Public History: The Tough Stuff of American Memory*. Chapel Hill: Univ. of North Carolina Press, 2006.

Howard, Victor B. *Black Liberation in Kentucky: Emancipation and Freedom, 1862-1884*. Lexington: Univ. Press of Kentucky, 1983.

Hudson, Larry E. *To Have and to Hold: Slave Work and Family Life in Antebellum South Carolina*. Athens: Univ. of Georgia Press, 1997.

Hull, Gloria T., Patricia Bell Scott, and Barbara Smith, eds. *All the Women Are White, All the Blacks Are Men, But Some of Us Are Brave: Black Women's Studies*. Old Westbury, NY: Feminist Press, 1982.

Hunter, Tera W. *Bound in Wedlock: Slave and Free Marriage in the Nineteenth Century*. Cambridge, MA: Harvard Univ. Press, 2019.

———. *To 'Joy My Freedom: Southern Black Women's Lives and Labors after the Civil War*. Cambridge, MA: Harvard Univ. Press, 1997.

Hurston, Zora Neale. *Barracoon: The Story of the Last "Black Cargo."* Edited by Deborah G. Plant. New York: Amistad, 2018.

Huston, James L. *The American and British Debate over Equality, 1776-1920*. Baton Rouge: Louisiana State Univ. Press, 2017.

———. *Calculating the Value of the Union: Slavery, Property Rights, and the Economic Origins of the Civil War*. Chapel Hill: Univ. of North Carolina Press, 2003.

Inikori, Joseph E. *Africans and the Industrial Revolution in England: A Study in International Trade and Economic Development*. New York: Cambridge Univ. Press, 2002.

————, ed. *Forced Migration: The Impact of the Export Slave Trade on African Societies*. London: Hutchinson, 1982.

————. "Measuring the Atlantic Slave Trade: An Assessment of Curtin and Anstey." *Journal of African History* 17, no. 2 (Apr. 1976): 197-223.

Inscoe, John C., ed. *Appalachians and Race: The Mountain South from Slavery to Segregation*. Lexington: Univ. Press of Kentucky, 2001.

————. "Generation and Gender as Reflected in Carolina Slave Naming Practices: A Challenge to the Gutman Thesis." *South Carolina Historical Magazine* 94, no. 4 (Oct. 1993): 252-63.

————. *Mountain Masters: Slavery and the Sectional Conflict in Western North Carolina*. Knoxville: Univ. of Tennessee Press, 1989.

Jabour, Anya. *Marriage in the Early Republic: Elizabeth and William Wirt and the Companionate Ideal*. Baltimore: Johns Hopkins Univ. Press, 2002.

————. "Perspectives on the Historiography of the Slave Family." *Southern Historian* 13 (Apr. 1992): 48-65.

Jackson, Kellie Carter. *Force and Freedom: Black Abolitionists and the Politics of Violence*. Philadelphia: Univ. of Pennsylvania Press, 2019.

Jackson, Luther Porter. *Free Negro Labor and Property Holding in Virginia, 1830-1860*. New York: D. Appleton-Century Co., 1942.

————. "The Virginia Free Negro Farmer and Property Owner, 1830-1860." *Journal of Negro History* 24, no. 4 (Oct. 1939): 390-439.

Jacobs, Harriet. *Incidents in the Life of a Slave Girl. Written by Herself.* Edited by L. Maria Child. Boston, 1861. Reprint, edited by Jean Fagan Yellin, Cambridge, MA: Harvard Univ. Press, 1987.

James, C. L. R. *The Black Jacobins: Toussaint L'Ouverture and the San Domingo Revolution*. London: Secker and Warburg, 1938.

————. *A History of Negro Revolt*. London: Independent Labour Party, 1938.

Jefferson, Thomas. *Notes on the State of Virginia*. Boston: Lilly and Wait, 1832.

Jenkins, William Sumner. *Pro-Slavery Thought in the Old South*. Chapel Hill: Univ. of North Carolina Press, 1935.

Johnson, Michael P. "Denmark Vesey and His Co-Conspirators." *William and Mary Quarterly* 58, no. 4 (Oct. 2001): 915-76.

Johnson, Michael P., and James L. Roark. *Black Masters: A Free Family of Color in the Old South*. New York: W. W. Norton & Co., 1986.

Johnson, Walter, ed. *The Chattel Principle: Internal Slave Trades in the Americas*. New Haven, CT: Yale Univ. Press, 2005.

————. "On Agency." *Journal of Social History* 37, no. 1 (Fall 2003): 113-25.

————. *River of Dark Dreams: Slavery and Empire in the Cotton Kingdom*. Cambridge, MA: Harvard Univ. Press, 2013.

————. "Slavery, Reparations, and the Mythic March of Freedom." *Raritan* 27, no. 2 (Fall 2007): 41-67.

————. *Soul by Soul: Life inside the Antebellum Slave Market*. Cambridge, MA: Harvard Univ. Press, 1999.

Jones, Charles Colcock. *The Religious Instruction of the Negroes in the United States*. Savannah, GA: Thomas Purse, 1842.

Jones, Jacqueline. *Labor of Love, Labor of Sorrow: Black Women, Work, and the Family from Slavery to the Present*. New York: Basic Books, 1985. Reprint, 2010.

Jones, Martha S. *Birthright Citizens: A History of Race and Rights in Antebellum America*. New York: Cambridge Univ. Press, 2018.

———. "History and Commemoration: The Emancipation Proclamation at 150." *Journal of the Civil War Era* 3, no. 4 (Dec. 2013): 452-57.

Jones, Norrece T. *Born a Child of Freedom, Yet a Slave: Mechanisms of Control and Strategies of Resistance in Antebellum South Carolina*. Middletown, CT: Wesleyan Univ. Press, 1990.

Jones-Rogers, Stephanie. *They Were Her Property: White Women as Slave Owners in the American South*. New Haven, CT: Yale Univ. Press, 2019.

Jordan, Weymouth T. *Hugh Davis and His Alabama Plantation*. Tuscaloosa: Univ. of Alabama Press, 1948.

Jordan, Winthrop D., ed. *Slavery and the American South*. Jackson: Univ. Press of Mississippi, 2003.

———. *The White Man's Burden: Historical Origins of Racism in the United States*. New York: Oxford Univ. Press, 1974.

———. *White over Black: American Attitudes toward the Negro, 1550-1812*. Chapel Hill: Univ. of North Carolina Press, 1968.

Kachun, Mitch. *Festivals of Freedom: Memory and Meaning in African American Emancipation Celebrations, 1808-1915*. Amherst: Univ. of Massachusetts Press, 2003.

Kendi, Ibram. *Stamped from the Beginning: The Definitive History of Racist Ideas in America*. New York: Nation Books, 2016.

Kantrowitz, Stephen. *More than Freedom: Fighting for Black Citizenship in a White Republic, 1829-1889*. New York: Penguin, 2012.

Kaplan, Amy. *The Anarchy of Empire in the Making of U.S. Culture*. Cambridge, MA: Harvard Univ. Press, 2002.

Karp, Matthew. *This Vast Southern Empire: Slaveholders at the Helm of American Foreign Policy*. Cambridge, MA: Harvard Univ. Press, 2016.

Katz, William Loren, ed. *Negro Population of the United States, 1790-1915*. New York: Arno Press and the *New York Times*, 1968.

Kaye, Anthony E. "The Second Slavery: Modernity in the Nineteenth-Century South and the Atlantic World." *Journal of Southern History* 75, no. 3 (Aug. 2009): 627-50.

Kennedy, Michael V. "The Hidden Economy of Slavery: Commercial and Industrial Hiring in Pennsylvania, New Jersey and Delaware, 1728-1800." *Essays in Economic and Business History* 21, no. 1 (2003): 115-25.

Kennington, Kelly. *In the Shadow of Dred Scott: St. Louis Freedom Suits and the Legal Culture of Slavery in Antebellum America*. Athens: Univ. of Georgia Press, 2017.

Kerr-Ritchie, Jeffrey R. *Freedom's Seekers: Essays on Comparative Emancipation*. Baton Rouge: Louisiana State Univ. Press, 2014.

———. *Rebellious Passage: The Creole Revolt and America's Coastal Slave Trade*. New York: Cambridge Univ. Press, 2019.

King, Wilma. *The Essence of Liberty: Free Black Women during the Slave Era*. Columbia: Univ. of Missouri Press, 2006.

———. "'Mad' Enough to Kill: Enslaved Women, Murder, and Southern Courts." *Journal of African American History* 92, no. 1 (Winter 2007): 37-56.

———. *Stolen Childhood: Slave Youth in Nineteenth-Century America*. Bloomington: Indiana Univ. Press, 1995.

Kiser, William. *Borderlands of Slavery: The Struggle over Captivity and Peonage in the American Southwest*. Philadelphia: Univ. of Pennsylvania Press, 2017.

Klein, Herbert S. *The Atlantic Slave Trade.* Cambridge: Cambridge Univ. Press, 1999.
Klein, Martin A. "Review: How Europe Underdeveloped Africa by Walter Rodney." *International Journal of African Historical Studies* 7, no. 2 (1974): 323-28.
Klement, Frank L. "Midwestern Opposition to Lincoln's Emancipation Policy." *Journal of Negro History* 49, no. 3 (July 1964): 169-83.
Koger, Larry. *Slaveowners: Free Black Slave Masters in South Carolina, 1790-1860.* Columbia: Univ. of South Carolina Press, 1995.
Kolchin, Peter. *American Slavery, 1619-1877.* New York: Hill and Wang, 1993. Reprint, 2003.
———. "The Big Picture: A Comment on David Brion Davis's 'Looking at Slavery from Broader Perspectives.'" *American Historical Review* 105, no. 2 (Apr. 2000): 467-71.
———. "Reevaluating the Antebellum Slave Community: A Comparative Perspective." *Journal of American History* 70, no. 3 (Dec. 1983): 579-601.
———. *A Sphinx on the American Land: The Nineteenth-Century South in Comparative Perspective.* Baton Rouge: Louisiana State Univ. Press, 2003.
———. *Unfree Labor: American Slavery and Russian Serfdom.* Cambridge, MA: Harvard Univ. Press, 1987.
Komlos, John, and Bjorn Alecke. "The Economics of Antebellum Slave Heights Reconsidered." *Journal of Interdisciplinary History* 26, no. 3 (Winter 1996): 437-57.
Kopytoff, Igor. "The Cultural Biography of Things: Commoditization as Process." In *The Social Life of Things: Commodities in Cultural Perspective,* edited by Arjun Appadurai, 64-94. New York: Cambridge Univ. Press, 1986.
Kornblith, Gary J. *Slavery and Sectional Strife in the Early American Republic, 1776-1821.* Lanham, MD: Rowman & Littlefield, 2010.
Kotlikoff, Laurence J. "The Structure of Slave Prices in New Orleans, 1804-1862." *Economic Inquiry* 17, no. 4 (Oct. 1979): 496-518.
Kotlikoff, Laurence J., and Sebastian Pinera. "The Old South's Stake in the Inter-Regional Movement of Slaves, 1850-1860." *Journal of Economic History* 37, no. 2 (June 1977): 434-50.
Krauthamer, Barbara. *"Ar'n't I a Woman?*: Native Americans, Gender, and Slavery." *Journal of Women's History* 19, no. 2 (Summer 2007): 156-60.
———. *Black Slaves, Indian Masters: Slavery, Emancipation, and Citizenship in the Native American South.* Chapel Hill: Univ. of North Carolina Press, 2013.
Kulikoff, Allan. *The Agrarian Origins of American Capitalism.* Charlottesville: Univ. Press of Virginia, 1992.
———. "The Origins of Afro-American Society in Tidewater Maryland and Virginia, 1700-1790." *William and Mary Quarterly* 35, no. 2 (Apr. 1978): 226-59.
———. *Tobacco and Slaves: The Development of Southern Cultures in the Chesapeake, 1680-1800.* Chapel Hill: Univ. of North Carolina Press, 1986.
Kushner, Tony, and Doris Kearns Goodwin. *Lincoln: The Screenplay.* New York: Theatre Communications Group, 2013.
Kvach, John F. *De Bow's Review: The Antebellum Vision of a New South.* Lexington: Univ. Press of Kentucky, 2013.
Kytle, Ethan J., and Blain Roberts. *Denmark Vesey's Garden: Slavery and Memory in the Cradle of the Confederacy.* New York: New Press, 2018.
Landers, Jane. *Atlantic Creoles in the Age of Revolutions.* Cambridge, MA: Harvard Univ. Press, 2010.

————. *Black Society in Spanish Florida.* Urbana: Univ. of Illinois Press, 1999.

Landis, Michael. *Northern Men with Southern Loyalties: The Democratic Party and the Sectional Crisis.* Ithaca, NY: Cornell Univ. Press, 2014.

Larson, Kate Clifford. *Harriet Tubman, Portrait of an American Hero: Bound for the Promised Land.* New York: One World, 2004.

Lassuna, Sergio. *My Brother Slaves: Friendship, Masculinity, and Resistance in the Antebellum South.* Lexington: Univ. Press of Kentucky, 2016.

Laurie, Bruce. *Beyond Garrison: Antislavery and Social Reform.* New York: Cambridge Univ. Press, 2005.

Law, Robin. "Review: Africa and Africans in the Making of the Atlantic World, 1400-1680 by John Thornton." *International Journal of African Historical Studies* 26, no. 1 (1993): 190-92.

Lears, T. J. Jackson. "The Concept of Cultural Hegemony: Problems and Possibilities." *American Historical Review* 90, no. 3 (June 1985): 567-93.

Lebsock, Suzanne. *The Free Women of Petersburg: Status and Culture in a Southern Town, 1784-1860.* New York: W. W. Norton & Co., 1984.

Lee, Jean Butenhoff. "The Problem of Slave Community in the Eighteenth-Century Chesapeake." *William and Mary Quarterly* 43, no. 3 (July 1986): 333-61.

Legassick, Martin. "Perspectives on African 'Underdevelopment.'" *Journal of African History* 17, no. 3 (July 1976): 435-40.

Lemons, Stanley. "Black Stereotypes as Reflected in Popular Culture, 1880-1920." *American Quarterly* 29, no. 1 (Spring 1977): 102-16.

Lerner, Gerda. *Black Women in White America: A Documentary History.* New York: Vintage Books, 1973.

————. *The Grimké Sisters from South Carolina: Pioneers for Women's Rights and Abolition.* New York: Houghton Mifflin, 1967.

Levin, Kevin. *Searching for Black Confederates: The Civil War's Most Persistent Myth.* Chapel Hill: Univ. of North Carolina Press, 2019.

Levine, Bruce. *Confederate Emancipation: Southern Plans to Free and Arm Slaves during the Civil War.* New York: Oxford Univ. Press, 2007.

————. *The Fall of the House of Dixie: The Civil War and the Social Revolution that Transformed the South.* New York: Random House, 2013.

————. *Half Slave and Half Free: The Roots of the Civil War.* New York: Hill and Wang, 1992.

Levine, Lawrence W. *Black Culture and Black Consciousness: Afro-American Folk Thought from Slavery to Freedom.* Oxford: Oxford Univ. Press, 2007.

Lewis, Earl. "To Turn as on a Pivot: Writing African-Americans into a History of Overlapping Diasporas." *American Historical Review* 100, no. 3 (June 1995): 765-87.

Lewis, Patrick. *For Slavery and Union: Benjamin Buckner and Kentucky Loyalties in the Civil War.* Lexington: Univ. Press of Kentucky, 2015.

Lichtenstein, Nelson. "The Return of Merchant Capitalism." *International Labor and Working-Class History* 81 (Spring 2012): 8-27.

Lightner, David L. *Slavery and the Commerce Power: How the Struggle against the Interstate Slave Trade Led to the Civil War.* New Haven, CT: Yale Univ. Press, 2006.

Lincoln, Abraham. *Proceedings of the Republican State Convention, June 16, 1858.* Springfield, IL: Bailhache & Baker, 1858.

———. "Speech in Chicago on July 10, 1858." In *Collected Works of Abraham Lincoln,* vol. 2, edited by Roy P. Basler, 484-502. New Brunswick: Rutgers Univ. Press, 1953.

Link, William A. *Roots of Secession: Slavery and Politics in Antebellum Virginia.* Chapel Hill: Univ. of North Carolina Press, 2003.

Littlefield, Daniel C. *Rice and Slaves: Ethnicity and the Slave Trade in Colonial South Carolina.* Urbana: Univ. of Illinois Press, 1991.

Litwack, Leon F. *Been in the Storm So Long: The Aftermath of Slavery.* New York: Vintage, 1980.

———. *North of Slavery: The Negro in the Free States.* Chicago: Univ. of Chicago Press, 1961.

Lloyd, Christopher. *The Navy and the Slave Trade: The Suppression of the African Slave Trade in the Nineteenth Century.* New York: Routledge, 1949.

Logan, John Alexander. *The Great Conspiracy: Its Origin and History.* New York: A. R. Hart & Co., 1886.

Logan, Rayford W. *The Negro in American Life and Thought: The Nadir, 1877-1901.* New York: Dial Press, 1954.

———. "Review: *Black Reconstruction in America, 1860-1880* by W. E. B. Du Bois." *Journal of Negro History* 21, no. 1 (Jan. 1936): 61-63.

Long, Carolyn Morrow. *A New Orleans Voudou Priestess: The Legend and Reality of Marie Laveau.* Gainesville: Univ. Press of Florida, 2006.

Long, David E. *The Jewel of Liberty: Abraham Lincoln's Re-election and the End of Slavery.* Mechanicsburg, PA: Stackpole Books, 2008.

Long, Gretchen. *Doctoring Freedom: The Politics of African American Medical Care in Slavery and Emancipation.* Chapel Hill: Univ. of North Carolina Press, 2012.

Longacre, Edward G. *Regiment of Slaves: The 4th United States Colored Infantry, 1863-1866.* Mechanicsburg, PA: Stackpole Books, 2003.

Lovejoy, Paul E. "The Impact of the Atlantic Slave Trade on Africa: A Review of the Literature." *Journal of African History* 30, no. 3 (Nov. 1989): 365-94.

———. "The Main Areas of Destination: The U.S. Slave Trade." The Abolition of the Slave Trade (website). Schomberg Center for Research in Black Culture, New York Public Library. https://wayback.archive-it.org/13235/20200727213652/http://abolition.nypl.org/essays/us_slave_trade/3 (accessed Nov. 22, 2020).

———. "The Volume of the Atlantic Slave Trade: A Synthesis." *Journal of African History* 23, no. 4 (Oct. 1982): 473-501.

Lussana, Sergio. *My Brother Slaves: Friendship, Masculinity, and Resistance in the Antebellum South.* Lexington: Univ. Press of Kentucky, 2016.

Lynch, John R. "Some Historical Errors of James Ford Rhodes." *Journal of Negro History* 2, no. 4 (Oct. 1917): 345-68.

Lynd, Staughton. *Class Conflict, Slavery, and the United States Constitution: Ten Essays.* Westport, CT: Greenwood Press, 1980.

Lynd, Staughton, and David Waldstreicher. "Free Trade, Sovereignty, and Slavery: Toward an Economic Interpretation of American Independence." *William and Mary Quarterly* 68, no. 4 (Oct. 2011): 597-630.

Mach, Thomas S. *Gentleman George Hunt Pendleton: Party Politics and Ideological Identity in Nineteenth-Century America.* Kent, OH: Kent State Univ. Press, 2007.

MacLean, Nancy. *Freedom Is Not Enough: The Opening of the American Workplace.* Cambridge, MA: Harvard Univ. Press, 2008.

MacLeod, Duncan J. *Slavery, Race, and the American Revolution.* New York: Cambridge Univ. Press, 1974.

Majewski, John. *A House Dividing: Economic Development in Pennsylvania and Virginia before the Civil War.* New York: Cambridge Univ. Press, 2000.

———. *Modernizing a Slave Economy: The Economic Vision of the Confederate Nation.* Chapel Hill: Univ. of North Carolina Press, 2009.

———. "Who Financed the Transportation Revolution? Regional Divergence and Internal Improvements in Antebellum Pennsylvania and Virginia." *Journal of Economic History* 56, no. 4 (Dec. 1996): 763-88.

Malone, Ann Patton. *Sweet Chariot: Slave Family and Household Structure in Nineteenth-Century Louisiana.* Chapel Hill: Univ. of North Carolina Press, 1992.

Manning, Chandra. *What This Cruel War Was Over: Soldiers, Slavery, and the Civil War.* New York: Vintage, 2008.

Manning, Patrick. "Review: *Africa and Africans in the Making of the Atlantic World, 1400-1680* by John Thornton." *American Historical Review* 98, no. 2 (Apr. 1993): 469-70.

———. *Slavery and African Life: Occidental, Oriental, and African Slave Trades.* Cambridge, MA: Cambridge Univ. Press, 1990.

Mannix, Daniel P., and Malcolm Cowley. *Black Cargoes: A History of the Atlantic Slave Trade, 1518-1865.* New York: Viking Press, 1962.

Margo, Robert A., and Richard H. Steckel. "The Heights of American Slaves: New Evidence on Slave Nutrition and Health." *Social Science History* 6, no. 4 (Fall 1982): 516-38.

Margolies, Daniel S. *Henry Watterson and the New South: The Politics of Empire, Free Trade, and Globalization.* Lexington: Univ. Press of Kentucky, 2006.

Marshall, Anne E. *Creating a Confederate Kentucky: The Lost Cause and Civil War Memory in a Border State.* Chapel Hill: Univ. of North Carolina Press, 2013.

Martin, Bonnie M. "Slavery's Invisible Engine: Mortgaging Human Property." *Journal of Southern History* 76, no. 4 (Nov. 2010): 817-66.

Martin, Bonnie, and James F. Brooks, eds. *Linking the Histories of Slavery: North America and its Borderlands.* Santa Fe, NM: School for Advanced Research Press, 2015.

Martin, Jonathan D. *Divided Mastery: Slave Hiring in the American South.* Cambridge, MA: Harvard Univ. Press, 2004.

Martyn, Benjamin. *Account, Shewing the Progress of the Colony of Georgia in America from its First Establishment.* London: Order of the Honourable Trustees, 1741.

Marx, Karl. *Capital: A Critique of Political Economy.* Vol. 3, *The Process of Capitalist Production as a Whole.* Edited by Frederick Engels. 1894. Reprint, Chicago: Charles H. Kerry & Co., 1909.

Mason, Matthew. *Slavery and Politics in the Early American Republic.* Chapel Hill: Univ. of North Carolina Press, 2006.

Masur, Kate. *An Example for All the Land: Emancipation and the Struggle over Equality in Washington, D. C.* Chapel Hill: Univ. of North Carolina Press, 2010.

———. "In Spielberg's 'Lincoln,' Passive Black Characters." *New York Times,* Nov. 12, 2012. http://www.nytimes.com/2012/11/13/opinion/in-spielbergs-lincoln-passive-black-characters.html (accessed Nov. 22, 2020).

Masur, Louis P. *Lincoln's Hundred Days: The Emancipation Proclamation and the War for the Union*. Cambridge, MA: Harvard Univ. Press, 2012.

Mathisen, Erik. *The Loyal Republic: Traitors, Slaves, and the Remaking of Citizenship in Civil War America*. Chapel Hill: Univ. of North Carolina Press, 2018.

———. "The Second Slavery, Capitalism, and Emancipation in Civil War America." *Journal of the Civil War Era* 8, no. 4 (Dec. 2018): 677-99.

Matthews, Gary R. *More American than Southern: Kentucky, Slavery, and the War for an American Ideology, 1828-1861*. Knoxville: Univ. of Tennessee Press, 2014.

McCardell, John. *The Idea of a Southern Nation: Southern Nationalists and Southern Nationalism, 1830-1860*. New York: W. W. Norton & Co., 1979.

McColley, Robert. *Slavery and Jeffersonian Virginia*. Urbana: Univ. of Illinois Press, 1964.

McCurry, Stephanie. *Confederate Reckoning: Power and Politics in the Civil War South*. Cambridge, MA: Harvard Univ. Press, 2010.

———. *Masters of Small Worlds: Yeoman Households, Gender Relations, and the Political Culture of the Antebellum South Carolina Low Country*. New York: Oxford Univ. Press, 1995.

———. *Women's War: Fighting and Surviving the American Civil War*. Cambridge, MA: Harvard Univ. Press, 2019.

McCusker, John J., and Russell R. Menard. *The Economy of British America, 1607-1789*. Chapel Hill: Univ. of North Carolina Press, 1985.

McDaniel, W. Caleb. *The Problem of Democracy in the Age of Slavery: Garrisonian Abolitionists and Transatlantic Reform*. Baton Rouge: Louisiana State Univ. Press, 2013.

———. *Sweet Taste of Liberty: A True Story of Slavery and Restitution in America*. New York: Oxford Univ. Press, 2019.

McElya, Micki. *Clinging to Mammy: The Faithful Slave in Twentieth Century America*. Cambridge, MA: Harvard Univ. Press, 2007.

McFeely, William S. *Frederick Douglass*. New York: W. W. Norton & Co., 1991.

McInnis, Maurice D. *Slaves Waiting for Sale: Abolitionist Art and the American Slave Trade*. Chicago: Univ. of Chicago Press, 2011.

McMaster, John Bach. *A History of the People of the United States: From the Revolution to the Civil War*. 8 vols. New York: D. Appleton & Co., 1883-1913.

McPherson, James M. *Abraham Lincoln and the Second American Revolution*. New York: Oxford Univ. Press, 1992.

———. *Battle Cry of Freedom: The Civil War Era, 1848-1865*. New York: Oxford Univ. Press, 1988.

———. *The Negro's Civil War: How American Blacks Felt and Acted during the War for the Union*. New York: Random House, 1965.

———. "Who Freed the Slaves?" *Proceedings of the American Philosophical Society* 139, no. 1 (Mar. 1995): 1-10.

McQueen, Steve. *12 Years a Slave*. Los Angeles, CA: Regency Enterprises, River Road Entertainment, Plan B Entertainment, and New Regency Productions; and London: Film4 Productions, 2013.

Meier, August, and Elliott Rudwick. *Black History and the Historical Profession, 1915-1980*. Urbana: Univ. of Illinois Press, 1986.

Melish, Joanne Pope. *Disowning Slavery: Gradual Emancipation and 'Race' in New England, 1780-1860*. Ithaca, NY: Cornell Univ. Press, 1998.

Menard, Russell R. "The Maryland Slave Population, 1658 to 1730: A Demographic Profile of Blacks in Four Counties." *William and Mary Quarterly* 32, no 1 (Jan. 1975): 29-54.

Menard, Russell R., Lois Green Carr, and Lorena S. Walsh. "A Small Planter's Profits: The Cole Estate and the Growth of the Early Chesapeake Economy." *William and Mary Quarterly* 40, no. 2 (Apr. 1983): 171-96.

Merritt, Keri Leigh. *Masterless Men: Poor Whites and Slavery in the Antebellum South.* New York: Cambridge Univ. Press, 2017.

Mezurek, Kelly. *For Their Own Cause: The 27th United States Colored Troops.* Kent, OH: Kent State Univ. Press, 2016.

Miles, Tiya. *The Dawn of Detroit: A Chronicle of Slavery and Freedom in the City of the Straits.* New York: New Press, 2017.

———. *Tales from the Haunted South: Dark Tourism and Memories of Slavery from the Civil War Era.* Chapel Hill: Univ. of North Carolina Press, 2015.

———. *Ties that Bind: The Story of an Afro-Cherokee Family in Slavery and Freedom.* Berkeley: Univ. of California Press, 2006. Reprint, 2015.

Miller, Edward A., Jr. *The Black Civil War Soldiers of Illinois: The Story of the Twenty-ninth U.S. Colored Infantry.* Columbia: Univ. of South Carolina Press, 1998.

Miller, Joseph C. "The Numbers, Origins, and Destinations of Slaves in the Eighteenth-Century Angolan Slave Trade." *Social Science History* 13, no. 4 (Winter 1989): 381-419.

———. *The Problem of Slavery as History: A Global Approach.* New Haven, CT: Yale Univ. Press, 2012.

———, ed. *Slavery and Slaving in World History: A Bibliography.* 2 vols. New York: Routledge, 1999.

———. *Way of Death: Merchant Capitalism and the Angolan Slave Trade, 1730-1830.* Madison: Univ. of Wisconsin Press, 1988.

Millward, Jessica. "More History than Myth: African American Women's History since the Publication of *Ar'n't I a Woman?*" *Journal of Women's History* 19, no. 2 (Summer 2007): 161-67.

Minchinton, Walter. *Virginia Slave Trade Statistics, 1698-1775.* Richmond: Virginia State Library, 1984.

Mintz, Sidney W. *Sweetness and Power: The Place of Sugar in Modern History.* New York: Viking, 1985.

Mintz, Sidney W., and Richard Price. *The Birth of African-American Culture: An Anthropological Perspective.* Boston: Beacon Press, 1992. Originally published as *An Anthropological Approach to the Afro-American Past,* Institute for the Study of Human Issues, Philadelphia, PA, 1976.

Mintz, Steven, and Susan Kellogg. *Domestic Revolutions: A Social History of American Family Life.* New York: Free Press, 1989.

Moes, John E. "The Absorption of Capital in Slave Labor in the Ante-Bellum South and Economic Growth." *American Journal of Economics and Sociology* 20, no. 5 (Oct. 1961): 535-41.

Mohr, Clarence L. *On the Threshold of Freedom: Masters and Slaves in Civil War Georgia.* Baton Rouge: Louisiana State Univ. Press, 2001.

Moore, Barrington. *Social Origins of Dictatorship and Democracy: Lord and Peasant in the Making of the Modern World.* Boston: Beacon Press, 1966.

Moore, George. *Notes on the History of Slavery in Massachusetts.* New York: D. Appleton & Co., 1866.

Moore, John Hebron. "A Review of Lewis C. Gray's *History of Agriculture in the Southern United States to 1860.*" *Agricultural History* 46, no. 1 (Jan. 1972): 19-28.

Morgan, Edmund S. *American Slavery, American Freedom: The Ordeal of Colonial Virginia.* New York: W. W. Norton & Co., 1975.

Morgan, Jennifer L. *Laboring Women: Reproduction and Gender in New World Slavery.* Philadelphia: Univ. of Pennsylvania Press, 2004.

Morgan, Lynda J. *Emancipation in Virginia's Tobacco Belt, 1850-1870.* Athens: Univ. of Georgia Press, 1992.

Morgan, Philip D. *Slave Counterpoint: Black Culture in the Eighteenth-Century Chesapeake and Low Country.* Chapel Hill: Univ. of North Carolina Press, 1998.

Morrison, Michael A. *Slavery and the American West: The Eclipse of Manifest Destiny.* Chapel Hill: Univ. of North Carolina Press, 1999.

Morton, Patricia, ed. *Discovering the Women in Slavery: Emancipating Perspectives on the American Past.* Athens: Univ. of Georgia Press, 1996.

———. "Review: *Scenes of Subjection: Terror, Slavery, and Self-Making in Nineteenth-Century America* by Saidiya V. Hartman." *Journal of Southern History* 67, no. 1 (Feb. 2001): 173-75.

Moynihan, Daniel Patrick. *The Negro Family: The Case for National Action.* Washington, DC: Office of Policy Planning and Research, United States Department of Labor, 1965.

Mullin, Gerald W. *Flight and Rebellion: Slave Resistance in Eighteenth-Century Virginia.* New York: Oxford Univ. Press, 1972.

Mustakeem, Sowande' M. *Slavery at Sea: Terror, Sex, and Sickness in the Middle Passage.* Urbana: Univ. of Illinois Press, 2016.

Mutti Burke, Diane. *On Slavery's Border: Missouri's Small Slaveholding Households, 1815-1865.* Athens: Univ. of Georgia Press, 2010.

Myers, Amrita Chakrabarti. *Forging Freedom: Black Women and the Pursuit of Liberty in Antebellum Charleston.* Chapel Hill: Univ. of North Carolina Press, 2011.

Myrdal, Gunnar. *An American Dilemma: The Negro Problem and Modern Democracy.* New York: Harper & Row, 1944. Reprint, 1962.

Nash, Gary B. *Forging Freedom: The Formation of Philadelphia's Black Community, 1720-1840.* Cambridge, MA: Harvard Univ. Press, 1988.

———. *Red, White, and Black: The Peoples of Early North America.* Upper Saddle River, NJ: Prentice-Hall, 1974. Reprint, 2000.

"A Negro Acting as Pastor for White People." *African Repository* (American Colonization Society, Washington, DC) 35, Aug. 1859, 255-56.

Nelson, Bernard H. "The Slave Trade as a Factor in British Foreign Policy, 1815-1862." *Journal of Negro History* 27, no. 2 (Apr. 1942): 192-209.

Nevins, Allan. *The Emergence of Lincoln.* 2 vols. New York: Charles Scribner's Sons, 1950.

———. *The War for the Union.* 4 vols. New York: Charles Scribner's Sons, 1959-71.

"New Publications: The Mexican Papers. Number Five [...] by Edward E. Dunbar." *New York Times,* May 12, 1861.

Newman, Philip. "Ulrich Bonnell Phillips—The South's Foremost Historian." *Georgia Historical Quarterly* 25, no. 3 (Sept. 1941): 244-61.

Newman, Richard S. *Freedom's Prophet: Bishop Richard Allen, the AME Church, and the Black Founding Fathers*. New York: New York Univ. Press, 2008.

North, Douglas C. *The Economic Growth of the United States, 1790-1860*. Englewood Cliffs, NJ: Prentice Hall, 1961.

Northup, Solomon. *Twelve Years a Slave: Narrative of Solomon Northup*. London: Sampson Low, Son & Co., 1853.

Nott, Josiah C., and George R. Gliddon. *Types of Mankind, or Ethnological Researches, Based on Ancient Monuments, Paintings, Sculptures, and Crania of Races*. Philadelphia: Lippincott, Grambo & Co., 1854.

Novick, Peter. *That Noble Dream: The "Objectivity Question" and the American Historical Profession*. New York: Cambridge Univ. Press, 1988.

Nwokeji, G. Ugo. *The Slave Trade and Culture in the Bight of Biafra*. Cambridge: Cambridge Univ. Press, 2010.

Oakes, James. *Freedom National: The Destruction of Slavery in the United States, 1861-1865*. New York: W. W. Norton & Co., 2012.

———. *The Radical and the Republican: Frederick Douglass, Abraham Lincoln, and the Triumph of Antislavery Politics*. New York: W. W. Norton & Co., 2008.

———. *The Ruling Race: A History of American Slaveholders*. New York: Alfred A. Knopf, 1982.

———. *The Scorpion's Sting: Antislavery and the Coming of the Civil War*. New York: W. W. Norton & Co., 2014.

———. *Slavery and Freedom: An Interpretation of the Old South*. New York: Alfred A. Knopf, 1990.

Oates, Stephen B. *With Malice toward None: A Life of Abraham Lincoln*. New York: Harper Perennial, 2011.

O'Brien, Michael. *Conjectures of Order: Intellectual Life and the American South, 1810-1860*. 2 vols. Chapel Hill: Univ. of North Carolina Press, 2004.

O'Connor, Michael J. L. *The Origins of Academic Economics in the United States*. New York: Columbia Univ. Press, 1944.

O'Donovan, Susan Eva. *Becoming Free in the Cotton South*. Cambridge, MA: Harvard Univ. Press, 2010.

Oertel, Kristen Tegtmeier. *Bleeding Borders: Race, Gender, and Violence in Pre-Civil War Kansas*. Baton Rouge: Louisiana State Univ. Press, 2009.

Okihiro, Gary, ed. *In Resistance: Studies in African, Caribbean, and Afro-American History*. Amherst: Univ. of Massachusetts Press, 1986.

Opie, John. "The Melancholy Career of 'Father' David Rice." *Journal of Presbyterian History* 47, no. 4 (Dec. 1969): 295-319.

Osofsky, Gilbert, ed. *Puttin' On Ole Massa: The Slave Narratives of Henry Bibb, William Wells Brown, and Solomon Northrup*. New York: Harper and Row, 1969.

Owsley, Frank L. "The Fundamental Cause of the Civil War: Egocentric Sectionalism." *Journal of Southern History* 7, no. 1 (Feb. 1941): 3-18.

———. "The Irrepressible Conflict." In *I'll Take My Stand: The South and the Agrarian Tradition*, 61-91. New York: Harper & Brothers, 1930.

———. *Plain Folk of the Old South*. Baton Rouge: Louisiana State Univ. Press, 1949.

Painter, Nell Irvin. *Sojourner Truth: A Life, A Symbol*. New York: W. W. Norton & Co., 1996.

———. *Southern History across the Color Line*. Chapel Hill: Univ. of North Carolina Press, 2002.

Pargas, Damian Alan. "Boundaries and Opportunities: Comparing Slave Family Formation in the Antebellum South." *Journal of Family History* 33, no. 3 (July 2008): 316-45.

Parish, Peter J. *Slavery: History and Historians.* New York: Harper and Row, 1989.

Patterson, James T. *Freedom Is Not Enough: The Moynihan Report and America's Struggle over Black Family Life from LBJ to Obama.* New York: Basic Books, 2010.

Patterson, Orlando. "Slavery." *Annual Review of Sociology* 3 (1977): 407-47.

———. *Slavery and Social Death.* Cambridge, MA: Harvard Univ. Press, 1982.

Paulus, Carl. *The Slaveholding Crisis: Fear of Insurrection and the Coming of the Civil War.* Baton Rouge: Louisiana State Univ. Press, 2017.

Pearson, Edward A. *Designs against Charleston: The Trail Record of the Denmark Vesey Slave Conspiracy of 1822.* Chapel Hill: Univ. of North Carolina Press, 1999.

Peck, Graham. *Making an Antislavery Nation: Lincoln, Douglas, and the Battle over Freedom.* Urbana: Univ. of Illinois Press, 2017.

Penningroth, Dylan C. *The Claims of Kinfolk: African American Property and Community in the Nineteenth-Century South.* Chapel Hill: Univ. of North Carolina Press, 2003.

———. "My People, My People: The Dynamics of Community in Southern Slavery." In *New Studies in the History of American Slavery,* edited by Edward E. Baptist and Stephanie M. H. Camp, 166-76. Athens: Univ. of Georgia Press, 2006.

Peterson, Carla L. *Black Gotham: A Family History of African Americans in Nineteenth-Century New York City.* New Haven, CT: Yale Univ. Press, 2012.

Phillips, Christopher. *The Rivers Ran Backward: The Civil War and the Remaking of the American Middle Border.* New York: Oxford Univ. Press, 2016.

Phillips, Ulrich B. *American Negro Slavery: A Survey of the Supply, Employment, and Control of the Negro Labor as Determined by the Plantation Regime.* New York: D. Appleton & Co., 1918. Reprint, Baton Rouge: Louisiana State Univ. Press, 1966.

———. "The Decadence of the Plantation System." *Annals of the American Academy of Political and Social Science* 35, no. 1 (Jan. 1910): 37-41.

———. *Life and Labor in the Old South.* Boston: Little, Brown & Co., 1929.

Phillips, Ulrich B. *The Slave Economy of the Old South: Selected Essays in Economic and Social History.* Edited by Eugene D. Genovese. Baton Rouge: Louisiana State Univ. Press, 1968.

Phillips, Wendell. *The Constitution, a Proslavery Compact, or, Extracts from the Madison Papers, etc.* New York: American Anti-Slavery Society, 1844. Reprint, 1856.

———. *Speech of Wendell Phillips, Esq., in the Vindication of the Course Pursued by the American Abolitionists.* London: William Tweedie, 1853.

Pierson, Donald. *Negroes in Brazil: A Study of Race Contact at Bahia.* Chicago: Univ. of Chicago Press, 1942.

Plath, Lydia, and Sergio Lassuna. *Black and White Masculinity in the American South, 1800-2000.* Newcastle upon Tyne, UK: Cambridge Scholars Publishing, 2009.

Plessy v. Ferguson. 163 U.S. 537 (1896)

Pollard, Edward A. *The Lost Cause: A New Southern History of the War of the Confederates.* New York: E. B. Treat & Co., 1866.

Pope-Hennessey, James. *Sins of the Fathers: A Study of the Atlantic Slave Traders, 1441-1807.* New York: Alfred A. Knopf, 1967.

Potter, David M. *The Impending Crisis, 1848-1861.* New York: Harper & Row, 1976.

Pritchett, J. B., and H. Freudenberger. "A Peculiar Sample: The Selection of

Slaves for the New Orleans Market." *Journal of Economic History* 52, no. 1 (Mar. 1992): 109-28.

Quarles, Benjamin. *Black Abolitionists*. New York: Oxford Univ. Press, 1969.

———. *Lincoln and the Negro*. New York: Oxford Univ. Press, 1962.

———. *The Negro in the Civil War*. Boston: Little, Brown & Co., 1953.

———. *The Negro in the American Revolution*. Chapel Hill: Univ. of North Carolina Univ. Press, 1961.

Rael, Patrick. *Black Identity and Black Protest in the Antebellum North*. Chapel Hill: Univ. of North Carolina Press, 2002.

———. *Eighty-Eight Years: The Long Death of Slavery in the United States, 1777-1865*. Athens: Univ. of Georgia Press, 2015.

———. "Free Black Activism in the Antebellum North." *History Teacher* 39, no. 2 (Feb. 2006): 215-53.

———. "New Directions in the History of Free Black Activism in the Antebellum North." *History Compass* 2, no. 1 (Jan. 2004): 1-4.

Rahman, Aliyah Abdul. "The Strangest Freaks of Despotism: Queer Sexuality in African American Slave Narratives." *African American Review* 40, no. 2 (Summer 2006): 223-37.

Raibmon, Paige. *Authentic Indians: Episodes of Encounter from the Late-Nineteenth-Century Northwest Coast*. Durham, NC: Duke Univ. Press, 2006.

Ramage, James A., and Andrea S. Watkins. *Kentucky Rising: Democracy, Slavery, and Culture from the Early Republic to the Civil War*. Lexington: Univ. Press of Kentucky, 2011.

Ramold, Steven J. *Slaves, Sailors, Citizens: African Americans in the Union Navy*. DeKalb: Northern Illinois Univ. Press, 2001.

Ramsdell, Charles W. "The Changing Interpretation of the Civil War." *Journal of Southern History* 3, no. 1 (Feb. 1937): 3-27.

———. "Review: *The Education of the Negro Prior to 1861: A History of the Education of the Colored People of the United States from the Beginning of Slavery to the Civil War* by Carter G. Woodson." *Southwestern Historical Quarterly* 19, no. 4 (Apr. 1916): 441.

Randall, James G. "The Blundering Generation." *Mississippi Valley Historical Review* 27, no. 1 (June 1940): 3-28.

———. *Lincoln the President: Springfield to Gettysburg*. 4 vols. New York: Dodd, Mead & Co., 1944-55.

Ransom, Roger L., and Richard Sutch. *One Kind of Freedom: The Economic Consequences of Emancipation*. Cambridge: Cambridge Univ. Press, 1978.

Rasmussen, Daniel. *American Uprising: The Untold Story of America's Largest Slave Revolt*. New York: Harper, 2011.

Rawick, George P., ed. *The American Slave: A Composite Autobiography*. 41 vols. Westport, CT: Greenwood Press, 1972-79.

———. *From Sundown to Sunup: The Making of a Black Community*. Westport, CT: Greenwood Press, 1972.

Rawley, James A. *The Transatlantic Slave Trade: A History*. New York: W. W. Norton & Co., 1981.

Rediker, Marcus. *The Amistad Rebellion: An Atlantic Odyssey of Slavery and Freedom*. New York: Viking, 2012.

———. *The Slave Ship: A Human History*. New York: Viking, 2007.

Redkey, Edwin S. *A Grand Army of Black Men: Letters from African-American Soldiers in the Union Army, 1861-1865.* New York: Cambridge Univ. Press, 1992.

Register of Debates in Congress. Washington, DC: Gales and Seaton, 1824-37.

Reid, Richard M. *Freedom for Themselves: North Carolina's Black Soldiers in the Civil War Era.* Chapel Hill: Univ. of North Carolina Press, 2008.

Regosin, Elizabeth A., and Donald R. Shaffer, eds. *Voices of Emancipation: Understanding Slavery, the Civil War, and Reconstruction through the U.S. Pension Bureau Files.* New York: New York Univ. Press, 2008.

Rhodes, James Ford. *History of the Civil War, 1861-1865.* New York: Macmillan, 1917.

———. *History of the United States from the Compromise of 1850.* 8 vols. New York: Macmillan, 1902-19.

Richard, Leonard L. *The Slave Power: The Free North and Southern Domination, 1780-1860.* Baton Rouge: Louisiana State Univ. Press, 2000.

Ripley, C. Peter. *Slaves and Freedmen in Civil War Louisiana.* Baton Rouge: Louisiana State Univ. Press, 1976.

Robert, Joseph C. *Tobacco Kingdom: Plantation, Market, and Factory in Virginia and North Carolina, 1800-1860.* Durham, NC: Duke Univ. Press, 1938.

Robertson, David M. *Denmark Vesey: The Buried History of America's Largest Slave Rebellion and the Man Who Led It.* New York: Alfred Knopf, 1999.

Robinson, Armstead L., Joseph P. Reidy, and Barbara J. Fields. *Bitter Fruits of Bondage: The Demise of Slavery and the Collapse of the Confederacy, 1861-1865.* Charlottesville: Univ. of Virginia Press, 2004.

Robinson, Michael. *A Union Indivisible: Secession and the Politics of Slavery in the Border South.* Chapel Hill: Univ. of North Carolina Press, 2017.

Rockman, Seth. *Scraping By: Wage Labor, Slavery, and Survival in Early Baltimore.* Baltimore: Johns Hopkins Univ. Press, 2009.

———. "Slavery and Abolition along the Blackstone." In *A Landscape of Industry: An Industrial History of the Blackstone Valley. A Project of the Worcester Historical Museum and the John H. Chaffee Blackstone River Valley National Heritage Corridor,* 110-31. Lebanon, NH: Univ. Press of New England, 2009.

———. "The Unfree Origins of American Capitalism." In *The Economy of Early America,* edited by Cathy Matson, 335-61. University Park: Pennsylvania State Univ. Press, 2006.

———. "What Makes the History of Capitalism Newsworthy?" *Journal of the Early Republic* 34, no. 3 (Fall 2014): 439-66.

Rodney, Walter. *How Europe Underdeveloped Africa.* Washington, DC: Howard Univ. Press, 1972.

Rodrigue, John. *Reconstruction in the Cane Fields: From Slavery to Free Labor in Louisiana's Sugar Parishes, 1862-1880.* Baton Rouge: Louisiana State Univ. Press, 2001.

Roediger, David. *The Wages of Whiteness: Race and the Making of the American Working Class.* London: Verso, 1991.

Roediger, David, and Martin H. Blatt, eds. *The Meaning of Slavery in the North.* New York: Garland, 1997.

Romeo, Sharon. *Gender and the Jubilee: Black Freedom and the Reconstruction of Citizenship in Civil War Missouri.* Athens: Univ. of Georgia Press, 2016.

Rose, Willie Lee. *Rehearsal for Reconstruction: The Port Royal Experiment.* New York: Bobbs-Merrill, 1964.

Rosenthal, Caitlin. *Accounting for Slavery: Masters and Management.* Cambridge, MA: Harvard Univ. Press, 2018.

Rothman, Adam. *Slave Country: American Expansion and the Origins of the Deep South.* Cambridge, MA: Harvard Univ. Press, 2005.

Rothman, Joshua D. *Flush Times and Fever Dreams: A Story of Capitalism and Slavery in the Age of Jackson.* Athens: Univ. of Georgia Press, 2012.

Rothstein, Morton. "The Cotton Frontier of the Antebellum United States: A Methodological Battleground." *Agricultural History* 44, no. 1 (Jan. 1970): 149-65.

Rucker, Walter C. *The River Flows On: Black Resistance, Culture, and Identity Formation in Early America.* Baton Rouge: Louisiana State Univ. Press, 2006.

Rugemer, Edward B. *The Problem of Emancipation: The Caribbean Roots of the American Civil War.* Baton Rouge: Louisiana State Univ. Press, 2008.

———. *Slave Law and the Politics of Resistance in the Early Atlantic World.* Cambridge, MA: Harvard Univ. Press, 2018.

Rushforth, Brett. *Bonds of Alliance: Indigenous and Atlantic Slaveries in New France.* Chapel Hill: Univ. of North Carolina Press, 2012.

Russel, Robert R. "The Effects of Slavery upon Nonslaveholders in the Ante Bellum South." *Agriculture History* 15, no. 2 (Apr. 1941): 112-26.

———. "The General Effects of Slavery upon Southern Economic Progress." *Journal of Southern History* 4, no. 1 (Feb. 1938): 34-54.

Russell, John H. *The Free Negro in Virginia, 1619-1865.* Baltimore: Johns Hopkins Press, 1913.

Rydell, Robert W. *All the World's a Fair: Visions of Empire at American International Expositions, 1876-1916.* Chicago: Univ. of Chicago Press, 1984.

Salafia, Matthew. *Slavery's Borderland: Freedom and Bondage along the Ohio River.* Philadelphia: Univ. of Pennsylvania Press, 2013.

Savage, Kirk. *Standing Soldiers, Kneeling Slaves: Race, War, and Monument in Nineteenth-Century America.* Princeton, NJ: Princeton Univ. Press, 1999.

Saville, Julie. *The Work of Reconstruction: From Slave to Wage Laborer in South Carolina, 1860-1870.* New York: Cambridge Univ. Press, 1996.

Savitt, Todd L. *Medicine and Slavery: The Health Care of Blacks in Antebellum Virginia.* Urbana: Univ. of Illinois Press, 1978.

Sawyer, Stephen, and William J. Novak. "Emancipation and the Creation of Modern Liberal States in America and France." *Journal of the Civil War Era* 3, no. 4 (Dec. 2013): 467-500.

Scarborough, William Kauffman. *The Allstons of Chicora Wood: Wealth, Honor, and Gentility in the South Carolina Lowcountry.* Baton Rouge: Louisiana State Univ. Press, 2011.

Schaefer, Donald F., and Mark D. Schmitz. "The Relative Efficiency of Slave Agriculture: A Comment." *American Economic Review* 69, no. 1 (Mar. 1979): 208-12.

Schermerhorn, Calvin. *The Business of Slavery and the Rise of American Capitalism, 1815-1860.* New Haven, CT: Yale Univ. Press, 2015.

———. "Capitalism's Captives: The Maritime United States Slave Trade, 1807-1850." *Journal of Social History* 47, no. 4 (Summer 2014): 897-921.

———. *Unrequited Toil: A History of United States Slavery.* New York: Cambridge Univ. Press, 2018.

Schlesinger, Arthur, Jr. "The Causes of the Civil War, a Note on Historical Sentimentalism." *Partisan Review* 16, no. 10 (Oct. 1949): 968-81.

Schmitz, Mark, and Donald Schaefer. "Paradox Lost: Westward Expansion and Slave Prices before the Civil War." *Journal of Economic History* 41, no. 2 (June 1981): 402-7.

Schoen, Brian. *The Fragile Fabric of the Union: Cotton, Federal Politics, and the Global Origins of the Civil War.* Baltimore: Johns Hopkins Univ. Press, 2009.

Schoen, H. R. "Review: *The Free Negro in North Carolina* by John Hope Franklin." *Texas State Historical Quarterly* 147, no. 2 (Oct. 1943): 200.

Schor, Joel. *Henry Highland Garnet, A Voice of Black Radicalism in the Nineteenth Century.* Westport, CT: Greenwood Press, 1977.

Schouler, James. *History of the United States of America under the Constitution.* 7 vols. New York: Dodd, Mead & Co., 1880-1913.

Schwalm, Leslie A. *A Hard Fight for We: Women's Transition from Slavery to Freedom in South Carolina.* Urbana: Univ. of Illinois Press, 1997.

Schwartz, Marie Jenkins. *Birthing a Slave: Medicine and Motherhood in the Antebellum South.* Cambridge, MA: Harvard Univ. Press, 2006.

———. *Born in Bondage: Growing up Enslaved in the Antebellum South.* Cambridge, MA: Harvard Univ. Press, 2000.

Schweninger, Loren. *Black Property Owners in the South, 1790-1915.* Chicago: Univ. of Illinois Press, 1997.

Scott, James C. *Domination and the Arts of Resistance: Hidden Transcripts.* New Haven, CT: Yale Univ. Press, 1990.

———. *Weapons of the Weak: Everyday Forms of Peasant Resistance.* New Haven, CT: Yale Univ. Press, 1985.

Scott, Joan Wallach. *Gender and the Politics of History.* New York: Columbia Univ. Press, 1988.

Scott, Kenneth. "The Slave Insurrection in New York in 1712." *New-York Historical Society Quarterly* 45 (1961): 43-74.

Scott, Rebecca J. *Degrees of Freedom: Louisiana and Cuba after Slavery.* Cambridge, MA: Belknap Press, 2008.

Scott, Rebecca J., and Jean M. Hébrard. *Freedom Papers: An Atlantic Odyssey in the Age of Emancipation.* Cambridge, MA: Harvard Univ. Press, 2014.

Scully, Pamela, and Diana Paton. *Gender and Slave Emancipation in the Atlantic World.* Durham, NC: Duke Univ. Press, 2005.

Segal, Ronald. *The Black Diaspora: Five Centuries of the Black Experience outside Africa.* New York: Farrar, Straus and Giroux, 1995.

Serwer, Adam. "The Fight Over the 1619 Project Is Not About the Facts." *Atlantic,* Dec. 23, 2019. https://www.theatlantic.com/ideas/archive/2019/12/historians -clash-1619-project/604093 (accessed Nov. 5, 2020).

Seward, William Henry. *The Irrepressible Conflict: A Speech by William H. Seward, Delivered at Rochester, Monday, Oct. 25, 1858.* New York: New York Tribune, 1860.

Shaffer, Donald R. *After the Glory: The Struggles of Black Civil War Veterans.* Lawrence: Univ. Press of Kansas, 2004.

Sharpe, Rev. John. "The Negro Plot of 1712." *New York Genealogical and Biographical Record* 21 (1890): 162-63.

———. "Proposals for Erecting a School, Library, and Chapel at New York," 1712-13. In *Collections of the New-York Historical Society for the Year 1880,* 341-63. New York: New-York Historical Society, 1881.

Shannon, Fred A. "The Federal Government and the Negro Soldier, 1861-1865." *Journal of Negro History* 11, no. 4 (Oct. 1926): 563-83.

Shelden, Rachel A. *Washington Brotherhood: Politics, Social Life, and the Coming of the Civil War.* Chapel Hill: Univ. of North Carolina Press, 2015.

Shelton, Robert S. "On Empire's Shore: Free and Unfree Workers in Galveston, Texas, 1840-1860." *Journal of Social History* 40, no. 3 (Spring 2007): 717-30.

Shumway, Rebecca. *The Fante and the Transatlantic Slave Trade.* Rochester, NY: Univ. of Rochester Press, 2011.

Siddali, Silvana R. *From Property to Person: Slavery and the Confiscation Acts, 1861-1862.* Baton Rouge: Louisiana State Univ. Press, 2005.

Silbey, Joel H. "The Civil War Synthesis in American Political History." *Civil War History* 10, no. 2 (June 1964): 130-40.

———. *Party over Section: The Rough and Ready Presidential Election of 1848.* Lawrence: Univ. Press of Kansas, 2009.

———. *A Respectable Minority: The Democratic Party in the Civil War Era, 1860-1868.* New York: W. W. Norton & Co., 1977.

———. *The Shrine of Party: Congressional Voting Behavior, 1841-1852.* Pittsburgh, PA: Univ. of Pittsburgh Press, 1967.

Singal, Daniel Joseph. "Ulrich B. Phillips: The Old South as the New." *Journal of American History* 63, no. 4 (Mar. 1977): 871-79.

Sinha, Manisha. *The Slave's Cause: A History of Abolition.* New Haven, CT: Yale Univ. Press, 2016.

Slave Voyages: The Trans-Atlantic Slave Trade Database (website), Emory Univ., Atlanta, GA. https://www.slavevoyages.org (accessed Oct. 29, 2020).

Smallwood, Stephanie E. *Saltwater Slavery: A Middle Passage from Africa to American Diaspora.* Cambridge, MA: Harvard Univ. Press, 2007.

Smith, Adam I. P. *The Stormy Present: Conservatism and the Problem of Slavery in Northern Politics.* Chapel Hill: Univ. of North Carolina Press, 2017.

Smith, David G. *On the Edge of Freedom: The Fugitive Slave Issue in South Central Pennsylvania, 1820-1870.* New York: Fordham Univ. Press, 2013.

Smith, John David, ed. *Black Soldiers in Blue: African American Troops in the Civil War Era.* Chapel Hill: Univ. of North Carolina Press, 2004.

———. "George H. Moore—'Tormentor of Massachusetts.'" In *The Moment of Decision: Biographical Essays on American Character and Regional Identity,* edited by Randall M. Miller and John R. McKivigan, 211-30. Westport, CT: Greenwood Press, 1994.

———. "The Historiographic Rise, Fall, and Resurrection of Ulrich Bonnell Phillips." *Georgia Historical Quarterly* 65, no. 2 (Summer 1981): 138-53.

Smith, John David, and J. Vincent Lowery, eds. *The Dunning School: Historians, Race, and the Meaning of Reconstruction.* Lexington: Univ. Press of Kentucky, 2013.

Smith, John David, and John Inscoe. *Ulrich Bonnell Phillips: A Southern Historian and His Critics.* New York: Greenwood Press, 1990.

Smith, Mark M. *Debating Slavery: Economy and Society in the Antebellum American South.* Cambridge: Cambridge Univ. Press, 1998.

———. *Mastered by the Clock: Time, Slavery, and Freedom in the American South.* Chapel Hill: Univ. of North Carolina Press, 1997.

———. "Remembering Mary, Shaping Revolt: Reconsidering the Stono Rebellion." *Journal of Southern History* 67, no. 3 (Aug. 2001): 513-34.

Smith, Robert Worthington. "Was Slavery Unprofitable in the Ante-Bellum South?" *Agricultural History* 20, no. 1 (Jan. 1946): 62-64.

Smithers, Gregory D. *Slave Breeding: Sex Violence, and Memory in African American History.* Gainesville: Univ. Press of Florida, 2012.

Snyder, Christina. *Slavery in Indian Country: The Changing Face of Captivity in Early America.* Cambridge, MA: Harvard Univ. Press, 2010.

Solow, Barbara L., and Stanley Engerman, eds. *British Capitalism and Caribbean Slavery: The Legacy of Eric Williams.* New York: Cambridge Univ. Press, 1987.

Somerset v. Stewart. Court of King's Bench 98 ER 499 (1772).

Spady, James O'Neil. "Power and Confession: On the Credibility of the Earliest Reports of the Denmark Vesey Slave Conspiracy." *William and Mary Quarterly* 68, no. 2 (Apr. 2011): 287-304.

Sparks, Randy J. *The Two Princes of Calabar: An Eighteenth-Century Atlantic Odyssey.* Cambridge, MA: Harvard Univ. Press, 2009.

Spurgeon, Ian Michael. *Soldiers in the Army of Freedom: The 1st Kansas Colored, the Civil War's First African American Combat Unit.* Norman: Univ. of Oklahoma Press, 2014.

Soulsby, Hugh Graham. *The Right of Search and the Slave Trade in Anglo-American Relations: South in the Era of Slavery, 1814-1862.* Baltimore: Johns Hopkins Press, 1933.

Spears, John Randolph. *The American Slave-Trade: An Account of Its Origin, Growth and Suppression.* New York: Charles Scribner's Sons, 1900.

Stampp, Kenneth M. *The Peculiar Institution: Slavery in the Antebellum South.* New York: Alfred A. Knopf, 1956. Reprint, New York: Vintage Books, 1989.

Stanley, Amy Dru. *From Bondage to Contract: Wage Labor, Marriage, and the Market in the Age of Slave Emancipation.* New York: Cambridge Univ. Press, 1998.

———. "Wages, Sin, and Slavery: Some Thoughts on Free Will and Commodity Relations." *Journal of the Early Republic* 24, no. 2 (Summer 2004): 279-88.

Starks, Ernest Obadele. *Freebooters and Smugglers: The Foreign Slave Trade in the United States after 1808.* Little Rock: Univ. of Arkansas Press, 2007.

Starobin, Robert S. *Industrial Slavery in the Old South.* New York: Oxford Univ. Press, 1970.

Stauffer, John. *The Black Hearts of Men: Radical Abolitionists and the Transformation of Race.* Cambridge, MA: Harvard Univ. Press, 2004.

Sternhell, Yael A. "Emancipation." In *A Companion to the U.S. Civil War,* edited by Aaron Sheehan-Dean, 965-86. Malden, MA: Wiley-Blackwell, 2014.

———. *Routes of War: The World of Movement in the Confederate South.* Cambridge, MA: Harvard Univ. Press, 2012.

Stevenson, Brenda. "Distress and Discord in Virginia Slave Families, 1830-1860." In *In Joy and Sorrow: Women, Family and Marriage in the Antebellum South,* edited by Carol Bleser, 103-24. New York: Oxford Univ. Press, 1992.

———. "Introduction: Women, Slavery, and Historical Research." *Journal of African American History* 92, no. 1 (Winter 2007): 1-4.

———. *Life in Black and White: Family and Community in the Slave South.* New York: Oxford Univ. Press, 1996.

———. "The Question of Female Slave Community and Culture in the American South: Methodological and Ideological Approaches." *Journal of African American History* 92, no. 1 (Winter 2007): 74-95.

Stewart, James Brewer. *Holy Warriors: The Abolitionists and American Slavery.* New York: Hill and Wang, 1976; rev. ed., 1997.

Stowe, Harriet Beecher. *Uncle Tom's Cabin or Life Among the Lowly.* Boston: John P. Jewett & Co., 1852.

Stuckey, Sterling, ed. *Going through the Storm: The Influence of African American Art in History.* New York: Oxford Univ. Press, 1994.

———. *Slave Culture: Nationalist Theory and the Foundations of Black America.* New York: Oxford Univ. Press, 1987.

Styron, William. *The Confessions of Nat Turner.* New York: Random House, 1967.

———. "Review: *American Negro Slave Revolts* by Herbert Aptheker." *New York Times Review of Books,* Sept. 26, 1963.

Sumner, Sen. Charles. *Freedom National; Slavery Sectional: Speech of Hon. Charles Sumner, of Massachusetts, on His Motion to Repeal the Fugitive Slave Bill, in the Senate of the United States, August 26, 1852.* Boston: Ticknor, Reed, and Fields, 1852.

Surkis, Judith. "When Was the Linguistic Turn? A Genealogy." *American Historical Review* 117, no. 3 (June 2012): 700-722.

Sutch, Richard. "The Profitability of Ante Bellum Slavery—Revisited." *Southern Economic Journal* 31, no. 4 (Apr. 1965): 365-77.

Sweet, James H. "Defying Social Death: The Multiple Configurations of African Slave Family in the Atlantic World." *William and Mary Quarterly* 70, no. 2 (Apr. 2013): 251-72.

———. "The Iberian Roots of American Racist Thought." *William and Mary Quarterly* 54, no. 1 (Jan. 1997): 143-66.

Sweet, John Wood. "The Subject of the Slave Trade: Recent Currents in the Histories of the Atlantic, Great Britain, and Western Africa." *Early American Studies* 7, no. 1 (Spring 2009): 1-45.

Sweig, Donald M. "The Importation of African Slaves to the Potomac River, 1732-1772." *William and Mary Quarterly* 42, no. 4 (Oct. 1985): 507-24.

Sydnor, Charles S. *Slavery in Mississippi.* New York: D. Appleton & Co., 1933.

Tadman, Michael. *Speculators and Slaves: Masters, Traders, and Slaves in the Old South.* Madison: Univ. of Wisconsin Press, 1989.

Tannenbaum, Frank. *Slave and Citizen: The Negro in the Americas.* New York: Alfred A. Knopf, 1946.

Tansey, Richard. "Out-of-State Free Blacks in Late Antebellum New Orleans." *Louisiana History* 22, no. 4 (Autumn 1981): 369-86.

Taylor, Amy Murrell. *Embattled Freedom: Journeys through the Civil War's Slave Refugee Camps.* Chapel Hill: Univ. of North Carolina Press, 2018.

Taylor, Eric Robert. *If We Must Die: Shipboard Insurrections in the Era of the Slave Trade.* Baton Rouge: Louisiana State Univ. Press, 2006.

Temperley, Howard. "Capitalism, Slavery, and Ideology." *Past and Present* 75, no. 1 (May 1977): 94-118.

Teters, Kristopher A. *Practical Liberators: Union Officers in the Western Theater during the Civil War.* Chapel Hill: Univ. of North Carolina Press, 2018.

Thomas, Hugh. *The Slave Trade: The Story of the Atlantic Slave Trade, 1440-1870.* New York: Simon & Schuster, 1997.

Thomas, Robert Paul, and Richard Nelson Bean. "The Fishers of Men: The Profits of the Slave Trade." *Journal of Economic History* 34, no. 4 (Dec. 1974): 885-914.

Thornton, J. Mills. *Politics and Power in a Slave Society: Alabama, 1800-1860.* Baton Rouge: Louisiana State Univ. Press, 1978.

Thornton, John K. *Africa and Africans in the Making of the Atlantic World, 1400-1800.* New York: Cambridge Univ. Press, 1992.

———. "African Dimensions of the Stono Rebellion." *American Historical Review* 96, no. 4 (Oct. 1991): 1101-13.

———. "The African Experience of the '20 and Odd Negroes' Arriving in Virginia in 1619." *William and Mary Quarterly* 55, no. 3 (July 1998): 421-34.

———. "The Coromantees: An African Cultural Group in Colonial North America." *Journal of Caribbean History* 32, no. 1-2 (1998): 161-78.

———. *A Cultural History of the Atlantic World, 1250-1820.* New York: Cambridge Univ. Press, 2012.

———. "The Demographic Effect of the Slave Trade on Western Africa, 1500-1850." In *African Historical Demography,* vol. 2, edited by C. Fyfe and D. McMaster, 691-720. Edinburgh, UK: Centre of African Studies, 1981.

———. "War, the State, and Religious Norms in 'Coromantee' Thought: The Ideology of an African American Nation." In *Possible Pasts: Becoming Colonial in Early America,* edited by Robert Blair St. George, 181-200. Ithaca, NY: Cornell Univ. Press, 2000.

Tise, Larry E. *Proslavery: A History of the Defense of Slavery in America, 1701-1840.* Athens: Univ. of Georgia Press, 1987.

Tomblin, Barbara Brooks. *Bluejackets and Contrabands: African Americans and the Union Navy.* Lexington: Univ. Press of Kentucky, 2009.

Tomek, Beverly. *Colonization and Its Discontents: Emancipation, Emigration, and Antislavery in Antebellum Pennsylvania.* New York: New York Univ. Press, 2011.

Tomek, Beverly, and Matthew Hetrick, eds. *New Directions in the Study of African American Colonization.* Gainesville: Univ. Press of Florida, 2017.

Tomich, Dale. "The 'Second Slavery': Bonded Labor and the Transformation of the Nineteenth Century World Economy." In *Rethinking the Nineteenth Century: Contradictions and Movements,* edited by Francisco O. Ramirez, 103-17. Westport, CT: Greenwood Press, 1988.

———. "The Wealth of Empire: Francisco Arango y Parreño, Political Economy, and the Second Slavery in Cuba." *Comparative Studies in Society and History* 45, no. 1 (Jan. 2003): 4-28.

Torget, Andrew J. *Seeds of Empire: Cotton, Slavery, and the Transformation of the Texas Borderlands, 1800-1850.* Chapel Hill: Univ. of North Carolina Press, 2015.

Towers, Frank. "Partisans, New History, and Modernization: The Historiography of the Civil War's Causes, 1861-2011." *Journal of the Civil War Era* 1, no. 2 (June 2011): 237-64.

———. *The Urban South and the Coming of the Civil War.* Charlottesville: Univ. of Virginia Press, 2004.

Trammell, Jack. *The Richmond Slave Trade: The Economic Backbone of the Old Dominion.* Charleston, SC: History Press, 2012.

Trent, Hank. *The Secret Life of Bacon Tait, a White Slave Trader Married to a Free Woman of Color.* Baton Rouge: Louisiana State Univ. Press, 2017.

Troutman, Phillip. "Correspondences in Black and White: Sentiment and the Slave Market Revolution." In *New Studies in the History of American Slavery,* edited by Edward E. Baptist and Stephanie M. H. Camp, 211-42. Athens: Univ. of Georgia Press, 2006.

Trudeau, Noah Andre. *Like Men of War: Black Troops in the Civil War, 1862-1865.* Boston: Little, Brown & Co., 1998.

Truth, Sojourner. *Narrative of Sojourner Truth, A Bondswomen of Olden Time.* Originally dictated to Olive Gilbert. Edited by Margaret Washington. New York: Vintage, 1993.

———. *Narrative of Sojourner Truth, A Northern Slave.* Boston: J. B. Yerrinton & Son, 1850.

Tsesis, Alexander. *The Thirteenth Amendment and American Freedom: A Legal History.* New York: New York Univ. Press, 2004.

Tucker, George. *The History of the United States, from Their Colonization to the End of the Twenty-Sixth Congress, in 1841.* 4 vols. Philadelphia: J. B. Lippincott & Co., 1856-58.

———. *Political Economy for the People.* Philadelphia: C. Sherman & Son, 1859.

———. *Progress of the United States in Population and Wealth, as Exhibited by the Decennial Census.* Boston: Little and Brown, 1843.

Turner, Frederick Jackson. *The Frontier in American History.* New York: H. Holt & Co., 1920.

———. "Problems in American History." *Ægis* (Univ. of Wisconsin-Madison) 7, Nov. 4, 1892.

———. "The Significance of the Section in American History." *Wisconsin Magazine of History* 8, no. 3 (Mar. 1925): 255-80.

Turner, Lorenzo D. "The Negro in Brazil." *Chicago Jewish Forum* 15, no. 4 (Summer 1957): 232-36.

———. "Some Contacts of Brazilian Ex-Slaves with Nigeria, West Africa." *Journal of Negro History* 27, no. 1 (Jan. 1942): 55-67.

Twitty, Anne. *Before Dred Scott: Slavery and Legal Culture in the American Confluence, 1787-1857.* New York: Cambridge Univ. Press, 2016.

Tyson, George F., ed. *Toussaint L'Ouverture.* Englewood Cliffs, NJ: Prentice Hall, 1973.

Ullman, Victor. *Martin R. Delany: The Beginnings of Black Nationalism.* Boston: Beacon Press, 1971.

United States War Department. *The War of the Rebellion: A Compilation of the Official Records of the Union and Confederate Armies.* 128 vols. Washington, DC: Government Printing Office, 1880-1901.

Van Deburg, William. *Slavery and Race in American Popular Culture.* Madison: Univ. of Wisconsin Press, 1984.

VanderVelde, Lea. *Redemption Songs: Suing for Freedom before Dred Scott.* New York: Oxford Univ. Press, 2014.

Varon, Elizabeth. *Armies of Deliverance: A New History of the Civil War.* New York: Oxford Univ. Press, 2019.

———. *Disunion! The Coming of the American Civil War, 1789-1859.* Chapel Hill: Univ. of North Carolina Press, 2008.

Von Holst, Hermann. *The Constitution and Political History of the United States.* 8 vols. Translated by John J. Lalor and Alfred B. Mason. Chicago: Callaghan, 1881-92.

Vidal, Cecile. *Caribbean New Orleans: Empire, Race, and the Making of a Slave Society.* Chapel Hill: Univ. of North Carolina Press, 2019.

———, ed. *Louisiana: Crossroads of the Atlantic World.* Philadelphia: Univ. of Pennsylvania Press, 2014.

Vorenberg, Michael. *Final Freedom: The Civil War, the Abolition of Slavery, and the Thirteenth Amendment.* New York: Cambridge Univ. Press, 2001.

———. "Spielberg's Lincoln: The Great Emancipator Returns." *Journal of the Civil War Era* 3, no. 4 (Dec. 2013): 549-72.

Wade, Richard C. "The Vesey Plot: A Reconsideration." *Journal of Southern History* 30, no. 2 (May 1964): 143-61.

Wagandt, Charles Lewis. *The Mighty Revolution: Negro Emancipation in Maryland, 1862-1864.* Baltimore: Maryland Historical Society, 2004.

Waldstreicher, David. *Slavery's Constitution: From Revolution to Ratification.* New York: Hill and Wang, 2009.

Walker, Daniel E. *No More, No More: Slavery and Cultural Resistance in Havana and New Orleans.* Minneapolis: Univ. of Minnesota Press, 2004.

Walker, David. *Appeal to the Coloured Citizens of the World, but in particular, and very expressly, to those of the United States of America.* Boston: David Walker, 1830.

Walker, Juliet E. K. *Free Frank: A Black Pioneer on the Antebellum Frontier.* Lexington: Univ. Press of Kentucky, 1983.

Wall, Bennett H. *Writing Southern History: Essays in Historiography in Honor of Fletcher M. Green.* Baton Rouge: Louisiana State Univ. Press, 1965.

Wallerstein, Immanuel. *Capitalist Agriculture and the Origins of the European World-Economy in the Sixteenth Century.* New York: Academic Press, 1974.

———. *The Modern World-System IV: Centrist Liberalism Triumphant, 1789-1914.* Berkeley: Univ. of California Press, 2011.

———. "Walter Rodney: The Historian as Spokesman for Historical Forces." *American Ethnologist* 13, no. 2 (May 1986): 330-37.

Walsh, Lorena S. "Plantation Management in the Chesapeake, 1620-1820." *Journal of Economic History* 49, no. 2 (June 1989): 393-406.

Walther, Eric H. *The Fire-Eaters.* Baton Rouge: Louisiana State Univ. Press, 1992.

Ward, Andrew. *The Slaves' War: The Civil War in the Words of Former Slaves.* New York: Houghton Mifflin, 2008.

Warren, Wendy. *New England Bound: Slavery and Colonization in Early America.* New York: Liveright Publishing, 2017.

Washington, Margaret. "'From Motives of Delicacy': Sexuality and Morality in the Narratives of Sojourner Truth and Harriet Jacobs." *Journal of African American History* 92, no. 1 (Winter 2007): 57-73.

Washington, Margaret, ed. *Narrative of Sojourner Truth, A Bondswomen of Olden Time.* Originally dictated to Olive Gilbert. New York: Vintage, 1993.

———. *Sojourner Truth's America.* Urbana: Univ. of Illinois Press, 2011.

Wax, Darrold. "Black Immigrants: The Slave Trade in Colonial Maryland." *Maryland Historical Magazine* 73, no. 1 (Spring 1978): 30-45.

———. "Negro Imports into Pennsylvania, 1720-1766." *Pennsylvania History* 32, no. 3 (July 1965): 254-87.

Weber, Jennifer L. *Copperheads: The Rise and Fall of Lincoln's Opponents in the North.* New York: Oxford Univ. Press, 2008.

Webster, J. B. "Review: *Africa and Africans in the Making of the Atlantic World, 1400-1680* by John Thornton." *Canadian Journal of African Studies/Revue Canadienne des Études Africaines* 28, no. 1 (1994): 180-81.

Weeden, William B. "The Early African Slave-Trade in New England." *Proceedings of the American Antiquarian Society* (Oct. 1887): 107-28.

Weiner, Dana. *Race and Rights: Fighting Slavery and Prejudice in the Old Northwest, 1830-1870.* DeKalb: Northern Illinois Univ. Press, 2013.

Weiner, Marli F. *Mistresses and Slaves: Plantation Women in South Carolina, 1830-80.* Urbana: Univ. of Illinois Press, 1998.

Welch, Kimberly. *Black Litigants in the Antebellum American South.* Chapel Hill: Univ. of North Carolina Press, 2018.

Wesley, Charles H. "Lincoln's Plan for Colonizing the Emancipated Negroes." *Journal of Negro History* 4, no. 1 (Jan. 1919): 7-21.

West, Emily. *Chains of Love: Slave Couples in Antebellum South Carolina.* Urbana: Univ. of Illinois Press, 2004.

———. "The Debate on the Strength of Slave Families: South Carolina and the Importance of Cross-Plantation Marriages." *Journal of American Studies* 33, no. 2 (Aug. 1999): 221-41.

———. *Family or Freedom: People of Color in the Antebellum South.* Lexington: Univ. Press of Kentucky, 2012.

———. "Surviving Separation: Cross-Plantation Marriages and the Slave Trade in Antebellum South Carolina." *Journal of Family History* 24, no. 2 (Apr. 1999): 212-31.

Wheatley, Phillis. *Poems on Various Subects, Religious and Moral.* London: A. Bell, 1773.

White, Deborah Gray. "Afterward: A Response." *Journal of Women's History* 19, no. 2 (Summer 2007): 168-69.

———. *Ar'n't I a Woman? Female Slaves in the Plantation South.* New York: W. W. Norton & Co., 1985.

———. "'Matter out of place': *Ar'n't I a Woman?* Black Female Scholars and the Academy." *Journal of African American History* 92, no. 1 (Winter 2007): 5-12.

White, Jonathan W. *Emancipation, the Union Army, and the Reelection of Abraham Lincoln.* Baton Rouge: Louisiana State Univ. Press, 2014.

White, Ronald C. *A. Lincoln: A Biography.* New York: Random House Trade Paperbacks, 2010.

White, Shane. *Stories of Freedom in Black New York.* Cambridge, MA: Harvard Univ. Press, 2002.

White, Shane, and Graham White. *Sounds of Slavery: Discovering African-American History through Song, Sermons and Speech.* Boston: Beacon Press, 2005.

———. *Stylin': Afro-American Expressive Culture from Its Beginnings to the Zoot Suit.* Ithaca, NY: Cornell Univ. Press, 1998.

Whites, LeeAnn. *The Civil War as a Crisis in Gender: Augusta, Georgia, 1860-1890.* Athens: Univ. of Georgia Press, 1995.

———. *Gender Matters: Civil War, Reconstruction, and the Making of the New South.* New York: Palgrave Macmillan, 2005.

———. *Mistresses and Slaves: Plantation Women in South Carolina, 1830-80.* Urbana: Univ. of Illinois Press, 1998.

Wiencek, Henry. *Master of the Mountain: Thomas Jefferson and His Slaves.* New York: Farrar, Straus and Giroux, 2012.

Wilentz, Sean. *No Property in Man: Slavery and Antislavery at the Nation's Founding.* Cambridge, MA: Harvard Univ. Press, 2018.

Wiley, Bell Irvin. *Southern Negroes, 1861-1865.* New Haven, CT: Yale Univ. Press, 1938.

Williams, Eric. *Capitalism and Slavery.* Chapel Hill: Univ. of North Carolina Press, 1944.

Williams, George Washington. *History of the Negro Race in America from 1619 to 1880.* Vol. 2. New York: Putnam & Sons, 1882.

———. *A History of the Negro Troops in the War of the Rebellion, 1861-1865.* New York: Putnam & Sons, 1888.

Williams, Heather. *Help Me to Find My People: The African American Search for Family Lost in Slavery.* Chapel Hill: Univ. of North Carolina Press, 2012.

Williamson, Joel. *After Slavery: The Negro in South Carolina during Reconstruction, 1861-1877.* Chapel Hill: Univ. of North Carolina Press, 1965.

Wilson, Henry. *History of the Rise and Fall of the Slave Power in America.* 3 vols. Boston: James R. Osgood, 1872-77.

Wilson, Joseph T. *The Black Phalanx: A History of the Negro Soldiers of the United States in the Wars of 1775-1812, 1861-1865.* Hartford, CT: American Publishing Co., 1888.

———. *Emancipation: Its Course and Progress from 1102 to 1875.* Norfolk, VA: Normal School Steam Press, 1881.

Winch, Julie. *The Clamorgans: One Family's History of Race in America.* New York: Hill and Wang, 2011.

———. *A Gentlemen of Color: The Life of James Forten.* Oxford: Oxford Univ. Press, 2002.

Witt, John Fabian. *Lincoln's Code: The Laws of War in American History.* New York: Free Press, 2013.

Wood, Betty. *Women's Work, Men's Work: The Informal Slave Economies of Lowcountry Georgia.* Athens: Univ. of Georgia Press, 1995.

Wood, Peter H. *Black Majority: Negroes in Colonial South Carolina from 1670 through the Stono Rebellion.* New York: W. W. Norton & Co., 1974.

Woodson, Carter G. *Free Negro Heads of Families in the United States in 1830, Together with a Brief Treatment of the Free Negro.* Washington, DC: Association for the Study of Negro Life and History, 1925.

———, ed. *Free Negro Owners of Slaves in the United States in 1830, Together with Absentee Ownership of Slaves in the United States in 1830.* Washington, DC: Association for the Study of Negro Life and History, 1924.

———. *The Negro in Our History.* Washington, DC: Associated Publishers, 1922.

———. "The Negroes of Cincinnati Prior to the Civil War." *Journal of Negro History* 1, no. 1 (Jan. 1916): 1-22.

Woodward, C. Vann. *The Burden of Southern History.* Baton Rouge: Louisiana State Univ. Press, 1960.

———. *Origins of the New South, 1877-1913.* Baton Rouge: Louisiana State Univ. Press, 1951.

Woodward, W. E. *Meet General Grant.* New York: Horace Liveright, 1928.

BIBLIOGRAPHY

Woolman, John. *Some Considerations on the Keeping of Negroes.* Philadelphia: James Chattin, 1754.

Wright, Gavin. *Old South, New South: Revolutions in the Southern Economy since the Civil War.* Baton Rouge: Louisiana State Univ. Press, 1996.

———. *The Political Economy of the Cotton South: Households, Markets, and Wealth in the Nineteenth Century.* New York: W. W. Norton & Co., 1978.

———. *Slavery and American Economic Development.* Baton Rouge: Louisiana State Univ. Press, 2006.

Wright, James M. *The Free Negro in Maryland, 1634-1860.* New York: Columbia Univ. Press, 1921.

Wright, Michelle M. *Becoming Black: Creating Identity in the African Diaspora.* Durham, NC: Duke Univ. Press, 2004.

Wyatt-Brown, Bertram. *Southern Honor: Ethics and Behavior in the Old South.* New York: Oxford Univ. Press, 1982.

Yanochik, Mark A., Mark Thornton, and Bradley T. Ewing. "Railroad Construction and Antebellum Slave Prices." *Social Science Quarterly* 84, no. 3 (Sept. 2003): 723-37.

Yellin, Jean Fagan. *Harriet Jacobs: A Life.* New York: Basic Civitas, 2004.

Young, Jason R. *Rituals of Resistance: African Atlantic Religion in Kongo and the Lowcountry South in the Era of Slavery.* Baton Rouge: Louisiana State Univ. Press, 2007.

Zwick, Edward, dir. *Glory.* Culver City, CA: TriStar Pictures and Freddie Fields Productions, 1990.

Contributors

AARON ASTOR is associate professor of history at Maryville College in Maryville, Tennessee. He is the author of *Rebels on the Border: Civil War, Emancipation, and the Reconstruction of Kentucky and Missouri* and *The Civil War along Tennessee's Cumberland Plateau,* as well as eleven articles for the award-winning *New York Times* Disunion series.

THOMAS C. BUCHANAN is senior lecturer in history at the University of Adelaide, South Australia. His research focuses on the history of capitalism in several contexts. He has published one book, *Black Life on the Mississippi: Slaves, Free Blacks, and the Western Steamboat World.*

KELLY BIRCH is an independent scholar and PhD graduate from the University of Adelaide. She published an article in the journal *Slavery and Abolition* on jailing in the antebellum South.

COLLEEN A. VASCONCELLOS is a Fulbright Scholar and professor of history at the University of West Georgia. She wrote *Slavery, Abolition, and Childhood in Jamaica, 1788-1838* and coedited with Jennifer Hillman Helgren *Girlhood: A Global History.*

KATHERINE CHILTON is a lecturer at San Jose State University in San Jose, California. Her publications include "'The Proceeds of My Own Labor': Black Working Women in the District of Columbia during the Civil War" and "Beyond Big Data: Teaching Introductory U.S. History in the Age of Student Success," an article coauthored with Bridget Jones, Christopher Endy, and Brad Jones.

SEAN CONDON is interim provost and professor of history at Merrimack College in North Andover, Massachusetts. He is the author of several articles on slavery and manumission, including "The Significance of Group Manumission in Post-Revolutionary Maryland," and of the book *Shays's Rebellion: Authority and Distress in Post-Revolutionary America.*

CALVIN SCHERMERHORN is professor of history in Arizona State University's School of Historical, Philosophical, and Religious Studies. He is the author of *Unrequited Toil: A History of United States Slavery; The Business of Slavery and the Rise of American Capitalism, 1815-1860;* and *Money over Mastery, Family over Freedom: Slavery in the Antebellum Upper South.*

RYAN A. QUINTANA is associate professor of history at Wellesley College. He is the author of *Making a Slave State: Political Development in Early South Carolina.*

WALTER C. RUCKER is professor of African American studies and history at Emory University and has published more than 100 journal articles, book chapters, book reviews, essays, and encyclopedia entries in a range of venues. His books include *Gold Coast Diasporas: Identity, Culture, and Power* and *The River Flows On: Black Resistance, Culture, and Identity Formation in Early America.*

Index

abolitionists: and economy, 37, 42, 49, 52; on enslaved families, 106, 109-10; on gender and slavery, 82; and historiography of slavery, 2-4, 26-27; and neoabolitionists, 135-37, 139, 142; politics and slavery, 58-59

Abraham Lincoln, Constitutionalism, and Equal Rights in the Civil War Era (Belz), 220

Accounting for Slavery (Rosenthal), 25, 52

Africa and Africans in the Making of the Atlantic World (Thornton), 169-70

African American agency: of free African Americans, 194-95; resistance and slavery, 134-35, 138-42, 144-45, 147-50, 153

The African American Family in Slavery and Emancipation (Dunaway), 121

After Appomattox (Downs), 221

After Slavery: The Negro in South Carolina during Reconstruction (Williamson), 208-9

After the Glory (Shaffer), 222

Alabama, politics of slavery in, 73

Allen, Richard, 5

American Anti-Slavery Society, 6

American Negro Slave Revolts (Aptheker), 13-14, 135-37, 184

American Negro Slavery (Phillips), 10, 40, 107, 133-34, 182

The American Slave: A Composite Autobiography (Rawick), 17

American Slavery (Kolchin), 88-89

American Slavery, American Freedom (Morgan), 15, 25

The American Slave-Trade (Spears), 164

Anderson, Ralph V., 46

Andrews, William L., 180

Anstey, Roger, 47, 166

Appeal to the Coloured Citizens of the World (Walker), 6

Aptheker, Herbert: *American Negro Slave Revolts*, 13-14, 135-37, 184; Marxist views of, 146, 194, 207; Mullin on, 145; on Phillips school, 138-39; slave community school of thought, 16

Ar'n't I a Woman? Female Slaves in the Plantation South (White), 19-20, 87-88, 89, 150

Ash, Stephen, 216

Ashworth, John, 48

Astor, Aaron, 115, 121

Atlantic slave trade, 158-77; *The Atlantic Slave Trade: A Census* (Curtin), 17-18, 47, 166-68, 170; and Bautista Africans, 158-59, 171-72; cultural

277

Atlantic slave trade (*cont.*)
study and study of African diaspora, 172-73; *Documents Illustrative of the Slave Trade* (Donnan), 164; and early professional study of slavery and economic impact, 163-66; and emancipation, 162-63; and England's ban on trade, 170-71; family separation by, 104-5, 116; and life expectancy, 116; population statistics, 159-62, 167, 170; quantitative study of, 166-71; and Revolutionary War (American), 164; scholarship of 1990s on free African Americans, 195-96; "Slavery and the Slave Trade in Africa" (Dowd), 164; *Slave Voyages: The Trans-Atlantic Slave Trade* (database), 48, 170; transnational study of slavery, 14, 22-23, 76, 151-53, 196, 221-22; *Way of Death: Merchant Capitalism and the Angolan Slave Trade* (Miller), 48. *See also individual titles on Atlantic slave trade*
Ayers, Edward, 76

Bailey, Anne, 27
Bailey, Ronald, 50
Bailyn, Bernard, 73
Bancroft, Frederic, 41-42, 107-8, 109, 116
Bancroft, George, 36, 38
Baptist, Edward E., 25, 49-50, 51-52, 76
Barnickel, Linda, 213
Bateman, Fred, 46
Baucom, Ian, 50
Bautista Africans, 158-59, 171-72
Beard, Charles, 66-67, 71
Beckert, Sven, 25, 26, 52, 76
Becoming Free in the Cotton South (O'Donovan), 212
Been in the Storm So Long (Litwack), 214
Behrend, Justin, 23, 212
Belz, Herman, 220
Benezet, Anthony, 2, 161, 203
Bennett, Lerone, Jr., 141
Benson, Lee, 72
Bercaw, Nancy, 215

Berlin, Ira: *The Black Military Experience*, 211; on defining "slave families," 115; *The Destruction of Slavery*, 211; *Families and Freedom*, 212; *Free at Last*, 211; *Freedom: A Documentary History of Emancipation, 1861-1867*, 211; *Freedom's Soldiers*, 212; influence of, 22, 88, 92, 117, 121, 190; *Many Thousands Gone: The First Two Centuries of Slavery in North America*, 50; research of, 17; *Slaves No More*, 211; *Slaves without Masters: The Free Negro in the Antebellum South*, 188-89; *The Wartime Genesis of Free Labor*, 211
Berry, Daina Ramey, 24, 50, 93
Bettelheim, Bruno, 140
Bibb, Henry, 179
The Birth of a Nation (film), 132, 153
The Birth of Black America: The First African Americans and the Pursuit of Freedom at Jamestown (Hashaw), 171-72
Bitter Fruits of Bondage (Robinson), 212
Black Abolitionists (Quarles), 187
Blackburn, Robin, 48, 49
Black Cargoes (Cowley & Mannix), 165, 167
Blackett, R. J. M., 26, 75
The Black Family in Slavery and Freedom (Gutman), 84-85, 112
Black Freedom movement, 194, 196, 224
Black Identity and Black Protest in the Antebellum North (Rael), 193
The Black Image in the White Mind (Fredrickson), 15-16
Black Jacks: African American Seamen in the Age of Sail (Bolster), 213
The Black Jacobins: Toussaint L'Ouverture and the San Domingo Revolution (James), 39
Black Majority: Negroes in Colonial South Carolina from 1670 to the Stono Rebellion (Wood), 22, 148-49
Black Masters: A Free Family of Color in the Old South (Johnson & Roark), 191-92

The Black Military Experience (Berlin), 211
Blackmon, Douglas, 24
Black Mother (Davidson), 165-66
Black nadir, 132
Black nationalist school of interpretation, 14, 85, 141, 165, 187-88, 191
The Black Phalanx: A History of Negro Soldiers of the United States in the Wars of 1775-1812, 1861-1865 (Wilson), 204
Black Property Owners in the South (Schweninger), 192
Black Reconstruction in America (Du Bois), 11, 134-35, 206-7
Black Soldiers in Blue (Smith), 213
"Black Women in White America" (Lerner), 86
Blair, William A., 219
Blassingame, John W., 16, 83, 85, 112-13, 141-44, 145, 149, 150
Blight, David, 27, 217, 222
Bluejackets and Contrabands (Tomblin), 213
Boas, Franz, 164
Bolster, W. Jeffrey, 213
Bound in Wedlock (Hunter), 24, 124
Bowman, Shearer Davis, 49
Brasher, Glenn, 216
Braudel, Fernand, 50
Brazil, end of slave trade in, 160
Breen, T. H., 15-16, 49, 149, 189
Brown, Charles, 180
Brown, Kathleen M., 20, 90-91, 97
Brown, William Wells, 38-39, 179, 181, 202-3, 204
Brown v. Board of Education (1954), 138, 155, 207
Bruce, Philip A., 10, 182
Bryn Mawr College, 135
Buchanan, Thomas, 214
Burgess, John William, 62-63, 205
Burke, Diane Mutti, 215
Burlingame, Michael, 218
The Business of Slavery and the Rise of American Capitalism (Schermerhorn), 25-26

Butchart, Ronald, 218
Buxton, Thomas Fowell, 161

Calhoun, John C., 7
Camp, Stephanie M. H., 21, 82, 94, 150-51, 215
Campbell, Tunis, 218
Capital (Marx), 39
Capitalism and Slavery (Williams), 42, 45, 164-65, 166
Carden, Allen, 217
Carey, Henry Charles, 36
Carlyle, Thomas, 38
Carnahan, Burrus, 219
Carney, Judith A., 22
Carr, Lois Green, 49
Cartwright, Samuel A., 7
Cecelski, David, 217
census and public records analysis, 36, 111-12, 114, 116, 174. *See also* historiography of slavery
Chakrabarti, Amrita, 96
Chambers, Douglas B., 172
Chandler, Charles, 181
chattel principle, 37
The Chattel Principle (Johnson), 25
Child, Lydia Maria, 82
Childers, Christopher, 26
Chilton, Katherine, 118, 151
Christopher, Emma, 171
Civil Rights era: Black Freedom movement, 194, 196, 224; Black nationalist school of interpretation, 14, 85, 141, 165, 187-88, 191; economy and slavery, 44-47, 50-51; emancipation scholarship during, 208-10; on politics and slavery, 70-74; scholarship on free African Americans, 179, 181, 186-89, 193-95; slave community school of thought, 14-16, 19, 25, 84-85, 88, 140-42; social history interest during, 110-11, 115
Civil War: antebellum enslavement and interpretation, 1-2; emancipation and Union army's/navy's role, 213-14; 54th Massachusetts Infantry,

Douglass, Frederick: Blight's biography of, 27; on emancipation, 200, 217; on enslaved families, 58; on free African Americans, 180, 181, 188; as radical abolitionist, 58, 106; slave narratives by, 1, 6; "What to the Slave Is the Fourth of July?" speech, 202
Dowd, Douglas F., 44
Dowd, Jerome, 164
Downs, Gregory, 221
Downs, Jim, 24, 214
Dred Scott decision (1857), 8
Drescher, Seymour, 27, 47, 166, 222
Du Bois, W. E. B.: on Atlantic slave trade, 161, 171; *Black Reconstruction in America,* 11, 134-35, 206-7; on enslaved families, 107-9, 117; on enslaved men's roles, 82; as neoabolitionist, 136, 137, 138-39; on rewriting American history, 41; *The Suppression of the African Slave-Trade to the United States of America,* 39-40, 65-66, 163-65
Dumond, Dwight, 70
Dunaway, Wilma, 121
Dunbar, Edward E., 161-62
Duncan, Russell, 218
Dunmore, Lord, 5
Dunning, William A., 10, 41, 65, 66, 134, 205

Earle, Jonathan, 26
"The Early African Slave-Trade in New England" (Weeden), 162
Eaton, Clement, 41
Econocide (Drescher), 166
The Economics of Slavery and Other Studies in Econometric History (Conrad & Meyer), 43
economy and slavery, 34-56; capitalism expansion vs. paternalism, 122; centrality of slavery to capitalism, 34-35; and cliometrics, 43-44; cotton and role in, 32, 35, 37-43, 46, 52-53; early-nineteenth-century views of, 36-38; econometric stud-

ies of, 18, 35, 43-46, 48-50; economic self-interest theories, 107-8; Eugene Genovese on capitalism and slavery, 17-19, 25; labor and cultural identity, 80-81, 92-93, 111-12; post-Civil War views of, 38-40; twentieth-century views of, 35, 40-51; twenty-first-century views of, 35, 51-53. *See also* cotton; labor; *and individual titles on economics*
Edwards, Justene Hill, 52
Edwards, Laura, 98
Efford, Alison, 76
Egerton, Douglas R., 195
Eichhorn, Niels, 76
Eichstedt, Jennifer, 27
Elkins, Stanley M.: on "closed system" of domination, 19; on enslaved families, 16, 110, 111, 117; and neoabolitionist school, 137; and "Sambo" stereotype, 85, 150; on slave revolts, 14, 146, 152; *Slavery: A Problem in American Institutional and Intellectual Life,* 13, 83, 138-40, 142, 143, 186
Eltis, David, 48, 159-60, 168, 170, 172
Ely, Melvin Patrick, 194
Emancipating Lincoln (Holzer), 219
emancipation, 200-224; abolitionists' power in, 217-18, 222; and African American Northerners, 218; Civil Rights-era views of, 208-10; Democratic Party's role in, 217, 221; early-twentieth-century views of, 204-7; and effect on families, 124; and Emancipation Proclamation importance, 200, 205, 209, 218-19; gender analysis of, 215-16; historiographical assessment and perspectives of, 201-2, 210-11; and Lincoln's leadership, 200, 203, 205-6, 209-10, 216-21; memory studies on, 222; Moore on, 162-63; nineteenth-century views of, 202-4; post-World War II views of, 207-8; and Reconstruction, 203, 205-12, 218, 220, 223; regional distinctions of, 23, 211-15;

American Nation-State," 220; on
slaves and freedmen as political ac-
tors, 75, 215
Haitian Revolution, 5, 11, 40, 76, 147-
48, 152
*The Half Has Never Been Told: Slavery
and the Making of American Capital-
ism* (Baptist), 51-52
Hall, Gwendolyn Midlo, 22, 172
Hammond, James Henry, 7-8, 61-62,
107
Hammond, John Craig, 26, 75
Handlin, Mary F., 186, 189
Handlin, Oscar, 186, 189
Hanger, Kimberly, 190
Harding, Vincent, 16, 141
Harris, Joel Chandler, 181
Harris, Leslie, 89
Harris, Sheldon H., 188
Harrold, Stanley, 26
Hartman, Saidiya V., 24, 66
Hashaw, Tim, 159, 171-72
Hayden, René, 212
Hébrard, Jean, 222
Helper, Hinton Rowan, 8-9
Help Me to Find My People (Williams),
124
Herskovits, Melville, 14, 16, 109, 164
Higman, Barry W., 47
Hine, Darlene Clark, 190
Hispaniola, revolt in, 4
historiography of slavery, 1-33; abolitionists on, 2-4, 26-27; antebellum
enslavement and interpretation,
1-2; antebellum study of Atlantic
slave trade, 161; census and public records analysis, 36, 111-12, 114,
116, 174; Civil Rights era and social
history interest, 110-11, 115; and
cliometrics, 17, 43-46, 49, 114; early
computer analysis, 111; early professional historiography of twentieth century, 10-14; in early-twenty-
first century, 21-23; and effect of
slavery on white Northerners, 8-9;
emancipation assessment and perspectives of, 201-2, 210-11; on en-

slaved families, 16-17; and Eugene
Genovese on capitalism and slavery, 17-19, 25; gender studies and
women's roles in slavery, 19-21, 26;
and memory studies field, 27-28;
and narratives and protests of enslaved people, 4-5; passive African
Americans theory, 13-14, 145, 193,
206-7; and political continuities between slavery and freedom, 23-25,
27; and proslavery arguments, 5-8,
26; and quantitative (cliometric)
histories of slavery in 1960s/1970s,
17-18; about resistance and slavery,
2, 140-41, 148-51; scientific racism
of nineteenth century, 106-7; and
slave community school of thought
of Civil Rights era, 14-16; slave
trade, cultural study, and study of
African diaspora, 172-73; transnational approach as area of study, 14,
22-23, 76, 151-53, 196, 221-22; and
view of "benign" slavery, 9-10. *See
also* Civil Rights era; Civil War; cultural identity; quantitative histories
(cliometrics); *and individual titles
about historiography*
*History of Agriculture in the Southern
United States to 1860* (Gray), 41
History of the Civil War, 1861-1865
(Rhodes), 205
*History of the Negro Race in America,
1619-1880* (Williams), 203-4
*A History of the Negro Troops in the War
of the Rebellion* (Williams), 204
A History of the Old South (Eaton), 41
*The History of the Rise and Decline of
American Slavery* (Dunbar), 161-62
The History of the United States
(Tucker), 36-37
Hodes, Martha, 123
Hofstadter, Richard, 13
Holsey, Bayo, 171
Holt, Michael, 220
Holt, Thomas, 221
Holzer, Harold, 219
Honeck, Mischa, 76

Passell, Peter, 49

passive African Americans theory, 13-14, 145, 193, 206-7

paternalism and patriarchy: capitalism expansion vs. paternalism, 122; Civil War and paternalism, 98-99; families and paternalistic master/slave relationship, 113; and gender issues of slavery, 96, 113; *Good Wives, Nasty Wenches, and Anxious Patriarchs* (Brown), 20, 97; and resistance, 146

Paulus, Carl, 26, 76

Pearson, Edward A., 195

Peck, Graham, 26

The Peculiar Institution: Slavery in the Antebellum South (Stampp), 13, 42-43, 70, 137, 138

The Peninsula Campaign and the Necessity of Emancipation (Brasher), 216

Penningroth, Dylan C., 23, 75, 122-23

Pennsylvania, slavery abolished by, 3, 4

Philadelphia's Black Elite (Winch), 192

Phillips, Christopher, 76

Phillips, Ulrich B.: *American Negro Slavery*, 10, 40, 107, 133-34, 182; *Life and Labor in the Old South*, 10, 40; New South school, influence, and refutation of, 10-14, 17, 19, 41-45, 65-66, 82, 106-9, 136-39, 142, 145-46, 187, 207

Phillips, Wendell, 37-38, 58-59, 62

Plain Folk of the Old South (Owsley), 68

Planck, Max, 52

The Plantation Mistress (Clinton), 86-87

Plath, Lydia, 100

Plessy v. Ferguson (1896), 66

Political Economy for the People (Tucker), 37

The Political Economy of Slavery (Genovese), 18-19

The Political Economy of the Cotton South: Households, Markets, and Wealth in the Nineteenth Century (Wright), 46

The Political Worlds of Slavery and Freedom (Hahn), 195

politics and slavery, 57-79; centrality of slavery within America's political history, 63-64; Civil Rights era and theories on, 70-74; Civil War causation debate about, 57-63, 75-76; Civil War causation and revisionist theories, 67-70; historiography of slavery on, 23-25, 27; Progressive school, 64-67; social historians on class, race, and gender, 74-75; transatlantic context of, 76. *See also individual titles about politics*

Pollard, Edward A., 38

Pope-Hennessey, James, 165, 167

Price, Richard, 221

The Price for Their Pound of Flesh (Berry), 24

Prince, Mary, 180

Pritchett, Jonathan, 49

The Problem of Democracy in the Age of Slavery (McDaniel), 217

Problem of Emancipation (Rugemer), 222

The Problem of Slavery in the Age of Emancipation (Davis), 217

property ownership: and Confiscation Acts, 219-20; by enslaved families, 122-23

proslavery arguments: and effect on enslaved families, 106-7, 117; and free African Americans, 180; and historiography of slavery, 5-8, 26; historiography of slavery and view of "benign" slavery, 9-10; "Mammy" and "Jezebel" stereotypes, 150; "moonlight and magnolias" interpretation of plantation life, 129-33, 135-37, 139, 141, 146; "Nat" and "Jack" stereotypes, 85, 143, 150; "Sambo" stereotype, 13, 16, 85, 129-33, 138-40, 142-43

Puls, Mark, 213

Quaker abolitionists, 2-3

quantitative histories (cliometrics): for analysis of historical records, 114, 117-18; of Atlantic slave trade, 166-68, 170-71; on cultural identity

slavery (*cont.*)

family separation, 108, 114, 116-21; Kansas-Nebraska Act (1854), 7, 60-61; Missouri Compromise, 6, 60; "second slavery," 24, 48; Slave Power conspiracy, 8, 62-63, 181, 203; Thirteenth Amendment, 76, 200-201, 203, 219. *See also* Atlantic slave trade; Civil War; economy and slavery; emancipation; families, enslaved; free African Americans; gender and slavery; historiography of slavery; politics and slavery; resistance and slavery; *and individual states*

Slavery: A Problem in American Institutional and Intellectual Life (Elkins), 13, 83, 138-40, 142, 143, 186

Slavery: History and Historians (Parish), 88

Slavery and African Life (Manning), 169

"Slavery and the Slave Trade in Africa" (Dowd), 164

Slavery by Another Name (Blackmon), 24

Slavery's Capitalism: A New History of American Economic Development (Beckert & Rockman), 26, 52

Slaves, Sailors, Citizens (Ramold), 213

Slaves and Freedmen (Ripley), 214

The Slave Ship (Rediker), 171

Slaves No More (Berlin), 211

Slaves without Masters: The Free Negro in the Antebellum South (Berlin), 188-89

slave trade. *See* Atlantic slave trade

Slave-Trading in the Old South (Bancroft), 41-42

Slave Voyages: The Trans-Atlantic Slave Trade database (Eltis & Richardson), 48, 170

Small, Stephen, 27

Smallwood, Stephanie, 51

Smith, Adam I. P., 76

Smith, John David, 42, 162, 163, 213

Smith, Mark, 151

Snyder, Christina, 23

Some Considerations on the Keeping of Negroes (Woolman), 2

Soul by Soul: Life Inside the Antebellum Slave Market (Johnson), 49, 121-22

Sounds of Slavery (White & White), 21

South Carolina: gender and slavery in, 97; Nullification Crisis of 1832, 6; politics and slavery in, 73-74; secession of, 9

Southern History across the Color Line (Painter), 24

Southern Negroes: 1861-1865 (Wiley), 207

Spears, John Randolph, 164

Speculators and Slaves: Masters, Traders, and Slaves in the Old South (Tadman), 49

Spielberg, Steven, 219, 223

Stamped from the Beginning (Kendi), 24

Stampp, Kenneth M.: *The Peculiar Institution: Slavery in the Antebellum South*, 13, 42-43, 70, 137, 138; portrayal of enslaved people by, 14, 18, 73, 138-39, 143, 145; on slave marriages, 109-10

Standing Soldiers, Kneeling Slaves (Savage), 223

Stanley, Amy Dru, 51, 219

Stanton, Henry, 37

Starobin, Robert, 44

Steckel, Richard H., 46

Stephens, Alexander, 9-10

Sternhell, Yael, 214

Stevenson, Brenda, 119-20

Stories of Freedom in Black New York (White), 192

Stowe, Harriet Beecher, 1, 106

Stuckey, Sterling, 16, 141, 143-44, 145, 149, 188

Stylin': Afro-American Expressive Culture from Its Beginnings to the Zoot Suit (White & White), 21

Styron, William, 138, 141-42

Sumner, Charles, 4, 71

The Suppression of the African Slave-Trade to the United States of America (Du Bois), 39-40, 65-66, 163-65

Surkis, Judith, 20
Sutch, Richard, 44, 45, 46
Sweet, James H., 123-24
*Sweet Chariot: Slave Family and House-
hold Structure in Nineteenth-Century
Louisiana* (Malone), 118-21
*Sweetness and Power: The Place of
Sugar in Modern History* (Mintz), 48

Tadman, Michael, 49, 116-17, 121
Tallmadge, James, 6
Tannenbaum, Frank, 42, 139, 146, 152,
186, 188
Taylor, Amy Murrell, 217
Temin, Peter, 45
Texas, annexation of, 7
They Were Her Property (Jones-Rogers),
26, 98
Thirteenth Amendment, 76, 200-201,
203, 219. See also emancipation
*The Thirteenth Amendment and Ameri-
can Freedom* (Tsesis), 219
Thompson, E. P., 44
Thompson, George, 37
Thompson, Holland, 10
Thornton, J. Mills, 73
Thornton, John K., 23, 151, 168-70, 173
Thornton, Mark, 51
"Through the Prism of Folklore: The
Black Ethos in Slavery" (Stuckey),
143-44
Time on the Cross (Fogel & Engerman),
18, 19, 45, 49, 114-15, 117
*Tobacco and Slaves: The Development of
Southern Cultures in the Chesapeake*
(Kulikoff), 48-49
Tomblin, Barbara Brooks, 213
Tomek, Beverly, 196
Tomich, Dale, 24, 48
Toussaint L'Ouverture (Haitian gen-
eral), 5
*Toussaint Louverture and the American
Civil War* (Clavin), 222
*The Transatlantic Slave Trade: A Data-
base* on CD-ROM, 48, 170
transnational study of slavery, 14, 22-
23, 76, 151-53, 196, 221-22

Treasurer (Dutch ship), 157
Troutman, Phillip, 123
Trudeau, Noah, 213
Trump, Donald, 28
Truth, Sojourner, 6, 82, 87
Tsesis, Alexander, 219
Tucker, George, 36-37
Turner, Frederick Jackson, 65, 66
Turner, Lorenzo, 164
Turner, Nat, 6-7, 131, 137, 141-43, 146,
147, 153, 155
12 Years a Slave (film), 153
Twelve Years a Slave (Northup), 1
Twitty, Anne, 26

Ullman, Victor, 188
Uncle Tom's Cabin (Stowe), 1
Uncommon Valor (Claxton & Puls), 213
*Unfree Labor: American Slavery and
Russian Serfdom* (Kolchin), 49
*Unfree Markets: The Slaves' Economy
and the Rise of Capitalism in South
Carolina* (Edwards), 52
The Union War (Gallagher), 216
University of Maryland, Freed-
men and Southern Society Project
(FSSP), 211-13
*Urban Slavery in the American South,
1820-1860: A Quantitative History*
(Goldin), 46

VanderVelde, Lea, 26
Varon, Elizabeth, 223
Vermont, slavery abolished by, 3
Vesey, Denmark, 137, 153, 194-95
Virginia, slavery debate in, 7
*Voices of Emancipation: Understanding
Slavery, the Civil War and Emancipa-
tion through the U.S. Pension Bureau
Files* (Regosin & Shaffer), 222
Von Holst, Herman Edward, 63, 65
Vorenberg, Michael, 219, 223

Wade, Richard, 195
Wagner, Adolph, 39
Waldstreicher, David, 26, 75
Walker, David, 6